LEARNING TO TEACH PHYSICAL EDUCATION IN THE SECONDARY SCHOOL

Praise for previous editions:

'A wealth of advice on generic aspects of teaching and learning in physical education . . . The accessibility of the text, and constant reference to ways of adapting suggestions to different situations, make this book particularly "user-friendly" and suitable for student-teachers in diverse settings.' – *European Physical Education Review*

'Essential reading for teachers who pride themselves on being "critically reflective".' – *Times Educational Supplement*

The fourth edition of *Learning to Teach Physical Education in the Secondary School* has been revised and updated in light of the latest research evidence and practice in relation to teaching and learning and changes in policy and practice within initial teacher education. Key topics covered include:

- Starting out as a teacher
- Planning and evaluation for effective learning and teaching
- Communication in PE
- Lesson organisation and management
- Motivating pupils for learning in PE[NEW]
- Assessment for and of learning
- Inclusive approaches to teaching PE
- Learner-centred teaching and physical literacy[NEW]
- Teaching safely and safety in PE
- Accredited qualifications in PE
- Teacher beliefs[NEW]
- Developing your own knowledge, skills and understanding[NEW]

This core text guides you to becoming competent in basic teaching skills, enabling you to cope in a wide range of teaching situations. It emphasises the development of your own professional judgement, your ability to reflect critically on what you are doing and on your beliefs about teaching PE.

Written with university and school-based initial teacher education in mind, *Learning to Teach Physical Education in the Secondary School* is an essential source of support and guidance for all student teachers of PE embarking on the challenging journey to becoming an effective, successful teacher.

Susan Capel is Professor of Physical Education at Brunel University, UK.

Margaret Whitehead is a physical education consultant, Visiting Professor at the University of Bedfordshire, UK, Adjunct Professor at the University of Canberra, Australia, and an Honorary Research  University of Wales Trinity Saint David, UK.

LEARNING TO TEACH SUBJECTS IN THE SECONDARY SCHOOL SERIES

Series Editors: Susan Capel and Marilyn Leask

Designed for all students learning to teach in secondary schools, and particularly those on school-based initial teacher training courses, the books in this series complement *Learning to Teach in the Secondary School* and its companion, *Starting to Teach in the Secondary School*. Each book in the series applies underpinning theory and addresses practical issues to support student teachers in school and in the training institution in learning how to teach a particular subject.

Learning to Teach in the Secondary School, 6th edition
Edited by Susan Capel, Marilyn Leask and Tony Turner

Learning to Teach Art and Design in the Secondary School, 3rd edition
Edited by Nicholas Addison and Lesley Burgess

Learning to Teach Citizenship in the Secondary School, 3rd edition
Edited by Liam Gearon

Learning to Teach Design and Technology in the Secondary School, 2nd edition
Edited by Gwyneth Owen-Jackson

Learning to Teach English in the Secondary School, 3rd edition
Edited by Jon Davison and Jane Dowson

Learning to Teach Geography in the Secondary School, 2nd edition
David Lambert and David Balderstone

Learning to Teach History in the Secondary School, 4th edition
Edited by Terry Haydn, James Arthur, Martin Hunt and Alison Stephen

Learning to Teach ICT in the Secondary School
Edited by Steve Kennewell, John Parkinson and Howard Tanner

Learning to Teach Design and Technology in the Secondary School, 3rd edition
Edited by Gwyneth Owen-Jackson

Learning to Teach Mathematics in the Secondary School, 3rd edition
Edited by Sue Johnston-Wilder, Peter Johnston-Wilder, David Pimm and Clare Lee

Learning to Teach Modern Foreign Languages in the Secondary School, 3rd edition
Norbert Pachler, Ann Barnes and Kit Field

Learning to Teach Music in the Secondary School, 2nd edition
Edited by Chris Philpott and Gary Spruce

Learning to Teach Physical Education in the Secondary School, 4th edition
Edited by Susan Capel

Learning to Teach Religious Education in the Secondary School, 2nd edition
Edited by L. Philip Barnes, Andrew Wright and Ann-Marie Brandom

Learning to Teach Science in the Secondary School, 4th edition
Edited by Rob Toplis

Learning to Teach Using ICT in the Secondary School, 3rd edition
Edited by Marilyn Leask and Norbert Pachler

Starting to Teach in the Secondary School, 2nd edition
Edited by Susan Capel, Ruth Heilbronn, Marilyn Leask and Tony Turner

LEARNING TO TEACH PHYSICAL EDUCATION IN THE SECONDARY SCHOOL

A companion to school experience

Fourth edition

Edited by Susan Capel and Margaret Whitehead

Routledge
Taylor & Francis Group

LONDON AND NEW YORK

Fourth edition published 2015
by Routledge
2 Park Square, Milton Park, Abingdon, Oxon OX14 4RN

and by Routledge
711 Third Avenue, New York, NY 10017

Routledge is an imprint of the Taylor & Francis Group, an informa business

British Library Cataloguing in Publication Data
A catalogue record for this book is available from the British Library

Library of Congress Cataloging-in-Publication Data
Learning to teach physical education in the secondary school : a companion to school experience / edited by Susan Capel, Margaret Whitehead. – Fourth edition.
pages cm. – (Learning to teach subjects in the secondary school series) Includes bibliographical references and index.
1. Physical education and training - Study and teaching (Secondary) - Great Britain.
2. Physical education teachers - Training of - Great Britain. I. Capel, Susan Anne, 1953- II. Whitehead, Margaret, 1940-
GV365.5.G7L43 2015
613.7′071′241–dc23
2014043126

ISBN: 978-1-138-78598-4 (hbk)
ISBN: 978-1-138-78599-1 (pbk)
ISBN: 978-1-315-76748-2 (ebk)

Typeset in Interstate
by Swales & Willis Ltd, Exeter, Devon, UK

Printed and bound in Great Britain by
TJ International Ltd, Padstow, Cornwall

CONTENTS

ILLUSTRATIONS

Figures

Tables

TASKS

CONTRIBUTORS

Jackie Arthur is a senior lecturer in physical and coach education in the Faculty of Sport and Health Sciences at the University of St Mark and St John, Plymouth. For further details, please visit: http://www.marjon.ac.uk/about-marjon/staff-list-and-profiles/arthur-jackie.html.

Lerverne Barber is a principal lecturer in physical education and an Associate Head with responsibility for Learning, Teaching and Student Experience within the Institute of Sport and Exercise Science at the University of Worcester. For further details, please visit: http://www.worcester.ac.uk/discover/lerverne-barber.html.

Richard Blair is the programme leader for physical education and youth sport in the Sport, Health and Exercise Sciences Division of the College of Health and Life Sciences at Brunel University, London. For further details, please visit: http://www.brunel.ac.uk/chls/life-sciences/sport-health-and-exercise-sciences/people/Dr-richard-blair.

Mark Bowler is a senior lecturer in physical education and Course Coordinator for the undergraduate Secondary Physical Education degree leading to QTS at the University of Bedfordshire. For further details, please visit: http://www.beds.ac.uk/howtoapply/departments/teacher-education/staff/mark-bowler.

Susan Capel is Professor (Physical Education) at Brunel University. For further details, please visit: http://www.brunel.ac.uk/chls/life-sciences/sport-health-and-exercise-sciences/people/professor-susan-capel.

Anne Chappell is a lecturer in education and physical education, and coordinates the PGCert Secondary Physical Education course at Brunel University, London. For further details, please visit: http://www.brunel.ac.uk/cbass/education/staff/anne-chappell.

Suzie Everley coordinates the PGCE secondary physical education at the University of Chichester. For further details, please visit: http://www.chi.ac.uk/staff/dr-suzanne-everley-0.

Michelle Flemons is a lecturer of physical education and sport at the University of Bedfordshire. For further details, please visit: http://www.beds.ac.uk/research/ispar/staff/michelle-flemons.

Gill Golder is Head of Department (Physical Education and Coaching) in the faculty of Sport and Health Sciences and Academic Lead for Secondary Education at the University College of St Mark and St John, Plymouth. For further details, please visit: http://www.marjon.ac.uk/about-marjon/staff-list-and-profiles/golder-gillian.html.

Vanessa Jones is an Associate Head of the Institute of Sport and Exercise Science at the University of Worcester. For further details, please visit: http://www.worcester.ac.uk/discover/vanessa-jones.html.

Maggie Killingbeck is a part-time lecturer at the University of Bedfordshire and Chair of the Laban Art of Movement Guild.

Julia Lawrence is Head of School Partnerships at the University of Hull. For further details, please visit: http://www2.hull.ac.uk/ifl/ces/staff/julia-lawrence.aspx.

Julia Longville is a principal lecturer in physical education and youth sport and Student Experience Coordinator in the Cardiff School of Sport at Cardiff Metropolitan University. For further details, please visit: http://www.sportwales.org.uk/about-us/about-sport-wales/our-team/sport-wales-advisory-group/julia-longville.aspx.

Dan Milton is a lecturer in physical education and sports coaching at Cardiff Metropolitan University. For further details, please visit: http://www.cardiffmet.ac.uk/schoolofsport/staff/Pages/Daniel-Milton.aspx.

Julie Money is the Programme Leader for the Sport Development with Physical Education course at Liverpool John Moores University. For further details, please visit: http://www.ljmu.ac.uk/EHC/122011.htm.

Kevin Morgan is a senior lecturer in physical education and Programme Director for the MSc Sport Coaching Course at Cardiff Metropolitan University. For further details, please visit: http://www.cardiffmet.ac.uk/schoolofsport/staff/Pages/Dr-Kevin-Morgan.aspx.

Elizabeth Myers is a lecturer in physical education and sports coaching at Liverpool John Moores University, Managing Director at Scholary and Co-founder of PE Scholar. For further details please visit: https://www.scholary.com/about/team/liz-myers/.

Angela Newton is a principal lecturer in physical education at the University of Bedfordshire. For further details, please visit: http://www.beds.ac.uk/howtoapply/departments/teacher-education/staff/angela-newton.

Julie Stevens is a senior lecturer in physical and coach education in the Faculty of Sport and Health Sciences at the University of St Mark and St John, Plymouth. For further details, please visit: http://www.marjon.ac.uk/about-marjon/staff-list-and-profiles/stevens-julie.html.

Stuart Taylor is Senior Lecturer and Programme Leader of the BEd Secondary Physical Education route in the Faculty of Sport and Health Sciences at the University of St Mark and St John, Plymouth. For further details, please visit: http://www.marjon.ac.uk/about-marjon/staff-list-and-profiles/taylor-stuart.html.

Philip Vickerman is Professor of Inclusive Education and Learning at Liverpool John Moores University. He is a National Teaching Fellow awarded by the Higher Education Academy. Philip is also Executive Director to the Vice Chancellor for Strategic Initiatives and Enhancement. For further details, please visit: http://ljmu.ac.uk/EHC/122549.htm.

Barbara Walsh is a National Teaching Fellow and Subject Head for Sport, Dance, Coaching and Outdoor Education at Liverpool John Moores University. For further details, please visit: http://www.ljmu.ac.uk/EHC/22011.htm.

Margaret Whitehead is a physical education consultant, a visiting professor at the University of Bedfordshire, UK, an adjunct professor at the University of Cranberra, Australia, and an Hon. Research Fellow at the University of Wales Trinity St David. For further details, please visit: http://www.physical-literacy.org.uk.

Kerry Whitehouse is a senior lecturer and Secondary Subject leader in PGCE physical education in the Institute of Sport and Exercise Science at the University of Worcester. For further details, please visit: http://www.worcester.ac.uk/discover/kerry-whitehouse.html.

Paula Nadine Zwozdiak-Myers is a lecturer in education and Programme Leader for both the MA in Teaching at Brunel University. For further details, please visit: http://www.brunel.ac.uk/cbass/education/staff/dr-paula-myers.

Introduction

Learning to teach

All top sports people and dancers spend hours learning and practising basic skills in order to be able to perform these effectively. Once learned, skills can be refined, adapted and combined in various ways appropriate for a performer's personality and a specific situation, in order to create a unique performance. Developing excellence in performance is informed by scientific understanding, including biomechanical, kinesiological, physiological, psychological and sociological. There is therefore art and science underpinning excellence in performance.

Likewise, there is an art and a science to teaching. There are basic teaching skills in which teachers require competence. Effective teaching also requires the development of professional judgement in order to be able to adapt the teaching skills to meet the demands of the specific situation, to take account of, for example, the needs and abilities of pupils, the space and the environment in which the lesson is being delivered. Teachers also require broader knowledge and understanding; for example, it is important that the aims of PE inform planning of schemes of work, units of work and lessons. It is also important to have knowledge and understanding of the wider world of education. However, there is no one right way to teach. Different teaching strategies are appropriate for different learning situations. Further, as we know, teachers have different personalities and characteristics. They therefore refine and adapt basic teaching skills and combine them in different ways to create their own unique teaching style. The process of development as a teacher is exciting and the ability to blend art and science should lead to a rewarding experience as a teacher.

In PE, physical skills are sometimes described on a continuum from open skills (those performed under variable conditions) to closed skills (those performed under consistent conditions). For open skills – for example, a dribble in hockey or basketball – it is important to have competence in the basic skill, but just as important to be able to use the skill appropriately in a game situation. For closed skills – for example, performing a forward roll or throwing a discus – it is most important to refine the technique and the ability to perform the skill under the pressure of competition. Some skills – for example, a putt in golf – fall along the continuum.

Different methods of practice are needed in order to learn and perform effectively skills at different points on the continuum. For an open skill practise is needed in the basic techniques of the skill, but practise is also needed in how to adapt the skill to respond to different situations which arise. On the other hand, for a closed skill it is most appropriate to practise to perfect the techniques of the skill.

Using the analogy of open and closed physical skills, teaching skills can be considered open skills. You need to practise and become competent in basic teaching skills, but you also need to be able to use the right skill in the right way at the right time. In your initial teacher education (ITE) you are likely to have a variety of opportunities and experiences to develop competence in basic teaching skills, starting in very controlled practise situations and moving on to teaching full classes. You are unlikely to become a fully effective teacher during your ITE. Refinement and the ability to adapt teaching skills as appropriate to the situation are continued into your work as a newly qualified teacher and beyond, as part of your continuing professional development (CPD) as you continue to develop your ability to reflect and your professional judgement.

There is a lot to learn to develop into an effective teacher. There are bound to be ups and downs. We cannot prepare you for a specific teaching situation, but we can help you to understand the complexities of teaching. We aim to help you to develop:

- competence in basic teaching skills (the craft of teaching), to enable you to cope in most teaching situations;
- the ability to apply these basic teaching skills to meet the needs of specific situations;
- your professional judgement;
- your ability to reflect critically on what you are doing and on your values, attitudes and beliefs about teaching PE.

In so doing, you should be able to develop, adapt and refine your teaching skills to meet the needs of specific situations, respond to the changing environment of education and inform your CPD as a teacher. You should also be able to look more critically and reflectively at aspects of teaching and to begin to articulate your own beliefs about teaching PE. This helps you to meet the requirements of working at Masters level - in your ITE, where appropriate, and/or in CPD.

About this book

This book contains 18 chapters which cover the following topics:

- Chapters 1 and 2 provide an introduction and background information about teaching and the aims of PE.
- Chapters 3-10 introduce some of the basic teaching skills in which you need to develop competence during your ITE.
- Chapter 11 looks back at the material in the chapters so far, from the perspective of the learner.
- Chapters 12-14 discuss particular areas of challenge in which you will be expected to apply basic skills.
- Chapters 15-18 look ahead to your continued development as a teacher.

In this book we look at general principles which can be applied to areas of activity/activities included in a PE curriculum. We do not consider content knowledge in detail although, throughout the book, there are references to activities included in PE curricula. You need to refer to other sources for content knowledge. There are many books which focus on specific activities included in PE curricula. In addition, you need to draw on material you covered in your first degree course, including the disciplines of biomechanics, kinesiology, physiology, psychology and sociology. Your understanding of these disciplines should underpin your work as a PE teacher; for example, the use of biomechanical principles in identifying learning/teaching points for a skill, of aspects of physiology in encouraging pupils to adopt healthy, active lifestyles, or areas of psychology in understanding the effects of competition or reasons for attrition from sport in considering an extracurricular programme.

In this book, each chapter is laid out as follows:

- *introduction* to the content of the chapter;
- *objectives*, presented as what you should know, understand or be able to do having read the chapter and carried out the tasks in the chapter;
- the *content*, based on research and evidence to emphasise that teaching is best developed by being based on evidence and critical reflection. The content is interwoven with *tasks* to aid your knowledge, understanding and skills;
- *summary and key points* of the main points of the chapter;
- *further reading*, selected to enable you to find out more about the content of each chapter.

We try to emphasise links between theory and practice by including examples from relevant practical situations throughout each chapter and interweaving theory with tasks designed to help you identify key features of the behaviour or issue. A number of different inquiry methods are used to generate information, for example, reflecting on the reading, an observation, an activity you are asked to carry out, asking questions, gathering information, observing lessons, discussing with your tutor or another student teacher. Some of the tasks involve you in activities that impinge on other people, for example, observing a PE teacher teach or asking for information. If a task requires you to do this, *you must first of all seek permission of the person concerned*. Remember that you are a guest in school(s); you cannot walk into any teacher's lesson to observe. In addition, some information may be personal or sensitive and you need to consider issues of confidentiality and professional behaviour in your inquiries and reporting. In order to support you in your Masters level work, some of the tasks are at Masters level (these are marked by a symbol in the margin). These challenge you both to look more critically and reflectively at aspects of teaching and to begin to articulate your own beliefs about teaching PE.

The main text is supported by a companion website (www.routledge.com/cw/capel) containing additional documents associated with particular chapters and web links to other important sites.

The text is also supported by other books in the series, to which we refer in a number of chapters, including:

- Capel, S. and Breckon, P. (2014) *A Practical Guide to Teaching Physical Education in the Secondary School*, 2nd edn, Abingdon, Oxon: Routledge (we particularly ask that you complete tasks in that book as they support the content of many of the chapters in this text), and two generic texts:

- Capel, S., Leask, M. and Turner, T. (eds) (2013) *Learning to Teach in the Secondary School: A Companion to School Experience*, 6th edn, London: Routledge. You can also access material on the companion website for the generic *Learning to Teach text* (www.routledge.com/cw/capel);
- Capel, S., Heilbronn, R., Leask, M. and Turner, T. (2004) *Starting to Teach in the Secondary School: A Companion to the Newly Qualified Teacher*, 2nd edn, Abingdon, Oxon: Routledge. This text is written for teachers in their early years of teaching.

About you

We recognise that you, as a student PE teacher, have a wide range of needs in your development as a teacher. We therefore do not feel that there is one best way for you to use this book. The book is designed so that you can dip in and out rather than read it from cover to cover; however, we encourage you to use the book in ways appropriate to you.

We also recognise that you are studying in different places and on different types of ITE. We have tried to address as many of your potential needs as possible, irrespective of where you are studying and what type of ITE you are undertaking. Although it is expected that most student teachers using this book are on ITE courses in which there is a partnership between a higher education institution (HEI) and schools, we recognise that for some of you your ITE may be entirely school-based or not in partnership with an HEI. The book should be equally useful to you. Where we refer to work in your HEI, you should refer to the relevant person or centre in your school.

Although ITE is generally referred to generically, where we do refer to specific requirements, we make reference to requirements in England. If you are not learning to teach in England you should refer to the specific requirements of your own ITE at this point. Where we have needed to link the theory to specific situations in schools or specific requirements of teachers in implementing the curriculum, we have linked it to the National Curriculum for Physical Education (NCPE) in England (Department for Education 2014a). We recognise that some of you are not undertaking ITE which is preparing you to teach in state schools in England, therefore we suggest that you do two things whenever information and tasks specific to the NCPE are used in the book:

1   Substitute for the information and task given the curriculum and requirements which apply to your situation.
2   Reflect on the differences between the curriculum and requirements which apply to your situation and those of the NCPE.

In doing either/both of the above, not only are the information and tasks relevant to your own situation but, also, you can attain a greater understanding by comparing your own experience with another student teacher, other requirements for ITE or another curriculum.

Your professional development portfolio

Although it is general practice for you to be required to keep a record of your development in your ITE, we strongly recommend that you keep a professional development portfolio (PDP).

As you read through the book and complete the tasks, we ask you to record information in your PDP. You can use this information for a number of purposes; for example, to refer back to when completing other tasks in this book, to help you with assignments you are required to complete as part of your ITE, to help you reflect on your development and to provide evidence of your development, your strengths and areas for further development. The material in your PDP is also useful to you as you move from ITE into your teaching career, as it can inform future decisions about your CPD. You can use your PDP in completing a Career Entry Profile (called a Career Entry and Development Profile (CEDP) in England). You should refer to the introduction to Capel *et al.* (2013) for guidance about keeping and using your PDP.

Terminology used in this book

We have tried to mix, and balance, the use of *gender terms* in order to avoid clumsy he/she terminology.

We call school children *pupils* to avoid confusion with students; the latter term refers to people in further and higher education. We use *student teachers* for people who are undertaking ITE. We refer to *ITE* as we would argue that your ITE (and this book) provides not merely training (as in initial teacher training) but also education of intending teachers. By this we mean that learning to teach is a journey of personal and professional development in which your skills of classroom management develop alongside an emerging understanding of the learning and teaching process. This process begins on the first day of your ITE and continues throughout your career.

The important staff in your life are those in your school and HEI with a responsibility for supporting your development as a teacher: we have called all these people *tutors*. Your ITE will have its own way of referring to staff.

Terminology used in this book may be different to that used in your ITE. For example, in this book we refer to a PDP, but other terminology may be used, such as a reflective journal or a portfolio of professional learning. You should check terminology used in your ITE.

We hope that you find this book useful in supporting your development as a teacher, in helping you to maximise pupils' learning. If so, tell others; if not, tell us.

We wish you well at the start of what we hope will be an enjoyable, exciting and rewarding career.

Susan Capel
Margaret Whitehead
October 2014

1　Starting out as a PE teacher

Susan Capel

Introduction

As a student PE teacher you are embarking on the long, but exciting, process of becoming an effective teacher; of translating your knowledge and love of PE into the ability to encourage pupils' learning and progress into enthusiastic and committed participants who maintain physical activity for life. You need to understand both the wider role of the teacher and your specific role as a PE teacher, as well as what you are aiming to achieve in your lessons. There are numerous teaching skills you need to develop, along with the ability to use the right teaching skill in the right way at the right time to improve pupil learning. An understanding of how teaching skills interact with each other in a lesson is also valuable. To develop into an effective teacher you also need to be aware of the range of factors that impact on your teaching, including understanding yourself, your values, attitudes and beliefs, and be able to reflect on how these influence what you are doing and therefore on how they impact on pupils' learning (see Chapter 16 for further information about teacher beliefs).

Your development into an effective teacher is challenging and not always smooth. At times you may be anxious or concerned about your development or your teaching performance, may lack confidence to try something out or may feel frustrated or despondent at not being able to cope with a situation or not knowing how to respond. Early in your development you may not have the teaching skills or experience to cope effectively with a specific situation. Part of the challenge of learning to teach is becoming able to adapt what you do to suit the unique needs of any situation. When you can adapt your teaching skills to the context and situation to achieve specific intended learning outcomes (ILOs) you are rewarded for your hard work, as you are well on the way to a satisfying career as an effective teacher. This ability enables you to change your focus from yourself to your pupils' learning.

Objectives

At the end of this chapter you should be able to:

- recognise the variety of reasons why people choose to become PE teachers;
- recognise factors which influence what, why and how you teach;

(continued)

(continued)

- have an overview of the teaching skills required to develop into an effective teacher who focuses on pupils and their learning, and begin to see how these skills interact in the teaching situation;
- have an overview of the steps you need to take to be an effective teacher.

Check the requirements of your initial teacher education (ITE) to see which relate to this chapter.

Why did you become a PE teacher?

Task 1.1 asks you to consider why people become PE teachers. Complete this task before continuing.

Task 1.1 Why do people want to become PE teachers?

List your reasons for wanting to become a PE teacher. Compare your reasons with those given by other student teachers and by experienced PE teachers you know. Are there any reasons common to all those to whom you spoke? Are there any different reasons? Why do you think this is so? Put your list in your professional development portfolio (PDP).

You have been at school for 11 years or more and in all probability wanted to become a PE teacher because you enjoyed PE, were able and successful at it, wanted to pass on your knowledge, understanding and love of PE and/or wanted to work with young people. If you found also that these were the major reasons given by other people for becoming a PE teacher, your findings support results of research (for example, Evans and Williams 1989; Mawer 1995; O'Bryant *et al.* 2000; Zounhia *et al.* 2006; McCullick *et al.* 2012). Similar reasons for becoming a PE teacher suggest some agreement/consensus/homogeneity in values, attitudes and beliefs about PE and about PE teaching (Chapter 16 looks at teacher beliefs).

Your positive experiences of PE and your ability and success in physical activities and sport give you positive perceptions of PE teachers, their role, what they do and how they teach the subject. As you are likely to spend considerable time, professionally and socially, with other PE professionals, it is easy to forget that there are many pupils in schools and, indeed, people in society at large, who do not share your values, attitudes and beliefs about PE and hence about participation in physical activity and sport. You can, no doubt, think of friends who had less positive experiences of PE at school, who have more negative perceptions about PE lessons and PE teachers. Unfortunately, these negative perceptions seem to be all too common. The sad outcome of this situation is that these individuals may well opt out of all physical activity once they leave school. An effective PE teacher is one who can help all pupils (including those who do not readily enjoy and/or who are not as able and successful at physical activities) to enjoy participation and to value their experiences and, hence, to be enthusiastic and committed to maintain physical activity for life (see Chapter 2). Your goal is to develop into such a teacher, with the benefits this brings to all young people and the satisfaction it affords to you.

An overview of teaching

First and foremost you are a teacher of pupils: a member of a profession with a responsibility to help pupils to learn by developing knowledge, practical skills and understanding to achieve broader goals of education. Second, you are a teacher of PE, with a specific responsibility for teaching the knowledge, practical skill and understanding specific to PE. You therefore have two roles – a wider role as a teacher (see Unit 8.2 (Keay) in Capel *et al.* 2013) as well as a subject-specific role as a PE teacher.

In Task 1.2 you are asked to consider the role of PE teachers.

Task 1.2 What is the role of PE teachers?

List what you believe to be the role of PE teachers. You may want to create two lists for this task: one list which identifies how the role of all teachers applies to PE teachers and one which identifies the role undertaken specifically by PE teachers. Compare your list with that of another student teacher, then discuss it with your tutor so that you understand what you are working towards, and therefore the knowledge, teaching skills and understanding required to enable you to get there. Put this information in your PDP and refer back to it at different times during your ITE.

This text concentrates on helping you to develop your skills for teaching PE. You cannot address at once all the teaching skills required to develop into an effective teacher. On your ITE, and in books such as this, teaching skills are addressed separately. If your ITE tutors, or we in this book, tried to address teaching skills in combination, we would be likely to give you too many things to think about and concentrate on at any one time, overwhelming you with information or even confusing you, rather than helping you to develop as a teacher. However, an approach in which you look at teaching skills separately, as presented in this book, only provides you with a partial picture of teaching which gradually builds up over time. You only recognise the complete picture when you suddenly realise that you see it. It is helpful, therefore, at this stage, to have an overview of teaching so that you know what you are aiming at and how the teaching skills in which you are developing competence fit together.

This overview should help you to think about what you are doing, its effectiveness in terms of pupils achieving ILOs and on which teaching skills you need to concentrate in order to develop your teaching further. This is a similar exercise to planning lessons and units of work. You know what you want to achieve by the end of a lesson (your ILOs) and by the end of a unit of work (objectives) and can plan how to achieve these (see Chapters 2 and 3).

We now look at the role of teachers, specifically focusing on part of that role, that is, teaching lessons, and the teaching skills required to promote pupil learning.

What is required for effective teaching of PE to promote pupil learning?

Teaching is a complex, multifaceted activity. First and foremost effective teaching has learning at its core and this is achieved via the appropriate blend/interaction of *what* is being taught (the content), *why* and *how* it is being taught (the process).

What is taught in PE is guided by the aims of the curriculum used in the placement school in which you are working. In England, these should be based on the government guidelines set out by the Department for Education (2014c). It is the case that in some countries there may be no government or national aims or guidelines on the content to be taught. For example, in England the aims of PE are broadly expressed and, thus, so are the activities that constitute the National Curriculum for Physical Education (NCPE); the choice of activities is so flexible that there seems to be licence to draw up a curriculum that seriously threatens the realisation of the stated aims of the curriculum. For example, despite efforts in the NCPE to focus on breadth of experience in pupils' learning, the curriculum in many schools in England is biased towards games (see, for example, Penney and Evans 1994). This and other issues in selecting content in PE are worthy of reflection. It is useful, therefore, for you to consider why games are dominant – is it due, for example, to the desire of schools to produce good school teams, the preference of the teacher, because the curriculum has always been biased towards games, or a combination of factors? Is this to the benefit of pupil learning in PE? Do *all* pupils enjoy games – in year 7, in year 9, in year 11? How many pupils choose to continue to participate in games out of school or when they leave school? Would pupils prefer to participate in other activities, e.g. non-competitive or individual activities? Would this encourage them to participate more in physical activity outside and post-school?

Task 1.3 is designed to help you familiarise yourself with the aims and content of the PE curriculum in your placement school.

Task 1.3 Activities included in the PE curriculum

Familiarise yourself with the aims and content of the PE curriculum used in your placement school. Find out what activities are included in the curriculum in your placement school. Compare these with the aims, content and activities identified by another student teacher working in another school. What are the similarities and differences and why? Are there other aims that should be addressed? Are there other activities, which are frequently taught in schools, which are not on your list? Keep these lists in your PDP for future reference.

Obviously, every teacher needs good knowledge and understanding of the subject content (Chapter 4 looks at effective observation being, at least in part, related to the depth of knowledge about the activity you are teaching). You are likely to have considerable subject content knowledge of one or more activities included in PE curricula. You need to identify which activities are your strengths and those activities in which you need to gain further experience in order to be able to use them effectively to promote pupil learning. In your ITE there is limited time available to learn about every activity you may be asked to teach.

It is therefore likely that there are a number of activities in which you have to take the initiative to improve your knowledge and understanding. This book is not designed to cover the activities included in a PE curriculum. You therefore need to consider ways in which you can gain the required knowledge and understanding of these activities. There are many ways in which you can do this, some of which are identified in Chapter 17. We advise you to start work on this aspect of your teaching as soon as you can. Alternatively, where you have good knowledge in one or some areas, you need to be clear where you gained that knowledge and how (e.g. from the PE curriculum, from sports clubs/teams) and consider whether the content and teaching methods are appropriate for the groups you are teaching.

It is also important to recognise, however, that there are other aspects of knowledge that you need to develop during and after your ITE. Together these constitute the knowledge *of* teaching. For example, Shulman (1987) identified seven knowledge bases (content knowledge; curriculum knowledge; general pedagogical knowledge; pedagogical content knowledge; knowledge of learners and their characteristics; knowledge of educational contexts; and knowledge of educational ends, purposes, values and philosophical and historical influences). These are covered in more detail in Chapter 18. If you concentrate solely on developing your subject content knowledge, that is, of the activities you are to teach, you are unlikely to develop into a fully effective teacher. Task 1.4 is designed to help you address areas for the development of subject content knowledge.

Task 1.4 Addressing areas for development in your subject content knowledge

Using the list of activities included in the curriculum in your placement school (compiled for Task 1.3), identify whether each is a strength or an area for development in terms of your knowledge and understanding. Identify ways in which you can address your areas for development (e.g. observation in schools; sharing knowledge and understanding with other student teachers on your ITE; gaining governing body awards; peer teaching; teaching PE lessons; watching matches; officiating at school activities; reading; watching video recordings). Do not try to address all areas for development at once, but consider how you can spread this over your ITE and even into your first year of teaching. Retain this information in your PDP for reference as you proceed through your ITE.

Why you are teaching PE and *why* you are teaching particular schemes of work, units of work and lessons also needs consideration. These are each of a different order and are briefly looked at one at a time.

- Why you are teaching PE has been covered in the sections above; for example, your love of physical activity and your interest in helping pupils to have similar positive experiences;
- Why you are teaching particular schemes and units of work is driven, in many countries, including England, by overall government and school policies;

- Why you are teaching specific content in a lesson, and why you are teaching it in a particular way, depends on characteristics both of the pupils and of yourself and on aspects of the teaching situation, such as the venue. What your ILOs are form the chief reason why you are teaching the way you do (see Chapter 13 on teaching strategies). Significant also are the age, ability, experience and motivation of the pupils, as well as practicalities such as the lesson length, the size of the working space and, if you are outside, the weather conditions. Why you are teaching in a particular way depends also on your teaching style (see Chapter 13). In addition, as you become more experienced, your teaching also evidences your personal values, attitudes and beliefs about the subject (see Chapter 16).

Although what you teach (the content) is often specified, *how* the content of the PE curriculum is taught is left to the professional judgement of the individual school, department and teacher (see also Unit 1.1 (Green and Leask) in Capel *et al.* 2013). How you teach relates to the aims of the school and PE curriculum, the characteristics of the pupils you are teaching, as well as your own objectives for a unit of work and ILOs for any particular lesson (see Chapters 2 and 3). In Chapter 13 aims, objectives and ILOs are considered in relation to teaching strategies. Thus, you need to think critically about how you are teaching a particular activity to ensure that you achieve your aims, objectives and ILOs.

What you see happening in a lesson is only the tip of the iceberg as far as the teacher is concerned (see Figure 1.1.1 (p. 15) in Capel *et al.* 2013). Planning and evaluating are also integral aspects of teaching. Prior to teaching a lesson, long-term aims for the scheme of work and medium-term objectives for the unit of work have been established, followed by general planning of the unit of work and detailed planning and preparation of the lesson, including short-term ILOs for the lesson. After the lesson the effectiveness or otherwise of parts of the lesson and the whole lesson should be evaluated to inform planning and preparation of the next lesson. Planning and evaluation are addressed in Chapter 3.

The tip of the iceberg, i.e. what happens while interacting with the pupils in the lesson, is of course very important. How far pupils are successful in achieving the ILOs relates to how you conduct the lesson. Included in this is how you respond to pupils in the ongoing teaching situation. You need to be flexible and to adapt the plan, if necessary; that is, if the pupils do not respond as you had expected, in relation to a particular task. How the lesson is conducted includes not only the teaching skills used but also the qualities displayed by the teacher, such as empathy, perception, sensitivity and responsiveness. All these aspects are relevant in evaluating the lesson. Task 1.5 asks you to observe what happens in a PE lesson.

Task 1.5 What happens in a PE lesson?

Observe a lesson taught by an experienced PE teacher and note the types of activities in which the teacher is involved, their sequence and the time spent on each one. You should aim to get an overview of what happens rather than great detail. You may want to organise your observation into what happens:

(continued)

Task 1.5 (continued)

- before the teaching starts (for example, the teacher takes the register whilst pupils are changing, collects, reads excuse notes and talks to any pupils not doing the lesson, collects valuables, hurries along anyone slow to change, locks the changing room after the last pupil has left);
- during the teaching part of the lesson;
- after the teaching has finished.

Chapter 6 covers organisation and management of lessons. There are some observation sheets on the companion website (see www.routledge.com/cw/capel).

Remember that the lesson starts as soon as pupils arrive at the changing rooms and finishes when they move to their next lesson or to a break in the day. Put in your PDP for future reference.

Teaching skills and teacher behaviours you may well have observed in the teaching interaction, once the pupils are in the working space, include observation, giving instructions, using PE-specific language, questioning, reminding, demonstrating, accommodating pupils of different ability, reprimanding. In addition, you may well have seen the teacher managing pupils, time and space and responding to situations in which safety needed attention. You are likely to have seen the teacher giving praise and feedback, which is intended not only to improve performance but also to promote motivation and pupil self-esteem. You may also have observed the teacher using ICT and possibly carrying out assessment procedures. You will also have seen evidence of teacher planning and teacher preparation and clearance of the working space.

Rink (2013) and Siedentop and Tannehill (2000) (see further reading) both provide an overview of teaching PE in which they categorise what a teacher does in a lesson broadly as below:

- *instructional activities* (activities associated with imparting subject content to pupils);
- *organising and managing activities* (activities associated with organising the learning environment and managing the lesson to maintain appropriate behaviour in order for learning to occur);
- *other activities* (activities to develop and maintain an effective learning environment, such as the use of praise).

It would be useful for you to examine what you identified the teacher does (from Task 1.5) and group these teacher behaviours into these three categories. All the skills listed above are drawn on in one or more of these categories and all are covered in this book. For example, Chapter 5 looks at communication, while Chapter 6 focuses on organisation and management and considers the time pupils spend actively engaged in learning (academic learning time) and how this is affected by activities that are not directly related to pupil learning. Chapter 8 discusses maintaining an effective learning environment.

Some teaching skills are specific to particular categories while others are important in all categories of teacher behaviour, for example, observation (see Chapter 4) and management of issues concerned with safety (see Chapter 12).

A starting point for identifying teaching skills in which you need to develop competence by the end of your ITE, and indeed the key reference throughout your ITE, are the skills required of newly qualified teachers (NQTs), as set out in a government publication towards which you are working or by your higher education institution (HEI). Even where skills required are centrally determined, HEIs generally also produce their own set of skills based on those in the relevant document. In Task 1.6 you are asked to consider the skills you need to pass your ITE.

Task 1.6 Teaching skills

Look at the skills identified for your ITE or other official documents that you need to develop to pass your ITE and identify those on which you should work in order to become competent. Discuss with your tutor which teaching skills you should work on immediately and which you should leave until later. As part of the regular reviews you undertake with your tutor during your ITE, consider which teaching skills you should work on at that particular time. Keep these in your PDP as they are a record of your development as a teacher.

Being competent in basic teaching skills is not enough for your lessons to be effective. In order to develop into an effective teacher you need to be able to refine and adapt these teaching skills and combine them so that they are used in a way that is appropriate to the specific situation. You need to consider how the skills interact in a lesson. Your appreciation of this interaction develops as you become more experienced. It is well to remember that *what* you teach and *how* you teach are interdependent and that ILOs will not be achieved unless you take the time to consider both of these aspects of teaching fully (see Chapter 13). Very important to your teaching is your critical reflection, after each lesson, on how far your teaching was effective in achieving the ILOs and your willingness to try different approaches should these be needed. Further, you need to move your focus from yourself and your teaching to focus on pupils and their learning.

There are a number of reasons why you do not always achieve your ILOs. Sometimes this is due to lack of appropriate planning. We have seen some student teachers plan the content of their lessons thoroughly, but leave the organisation and management of the tasks, the equipment or the pupils to chance. In contrast, we have seen some student teachers plan how they are going to control a class without considering the appropriateness, quality and progression of content. If a student teacher has not planned how to organise and manage the lesson, the pupils may not be clear about what they are to do and what is expected of them; therefore the teacher has to spend considerable time organising and managing and cannot deliver the lesson in the way intended. On the other hand, if the student teacher concentrates on organising and managing the class, pupils are likely to achieve little and what they do achieve is likely to be of low quality. The importance of your planning (see Chapter 3) directs your attention to both of these.

You must be aware that pupils 'test out' student (and new) teachers and try to negotiate an acceptable standard of performance, effort or behaviour. We have all seen situations where pupils try to negotiate a longer game if they do a practice effectively or where pupils promise to work hard if they can work with friends. Discuss with another student teacher other ways in which pupils may try to negotiate boundaries so that you are aware of them as you start to teach a new class. List these in your PDP for future reference.

Make sure that you only accept performance, effort or behaviour of an acceptable standard right from the beginning, otherwise you may find it hard to get pupils to accept this later. Pupils may make less effort to complete a task appropriately in future if you accept initially a performance, effort or behaviour below that of which they are capable. You may, for example, set a task in gymnastics which requires pupils to develop a sequence comprising five movements, with at least one each of three different types of movements - rolls, jumps and balances. Pupils are given the opportunity to develop and practise an appropriate sequence and then show this to the class. How you respond to the way pupils complete the task is important. If, for example, a pupil uses the three required movements to complete a sequence but makes no effort to link them together or to perform them in an effective way and you accept this, you send a message to the class that they can complete the task in any way they want.

There are other reasons why pupils may not perform or make an effort or behave to the standard expected. The task may be, for example, too easy or too difficult or not interesting, therefore pupils are not motivated to do the task (see Chapter 7 on motivation). You may not have presented the task clearly or you respond differently to the same performance, effort or behaviour on different occasions. Pupils may, therefore, be bored, unclear or confused about what is required of them, and therefore they may modify the task to make it easier or more difficult, try not to accomplish the task or, on occasion, refuse to do the task altogether. Can you think of any other reasons why pupils may not perform or make an effort or behave to the standard expected?

How are you going to develop into an effective PE teacher?

Many changes occur as you develop your teaching skills and teaching strategies. Changes have been identified by a number of authors as stages or phases of development (see Unit 1.2 (Allen and Toplis) in Capel *et al.* (2013) for consideration of phases of development as a teacher). Maynard and Furlong (1993) and Perrott (1982) identified stages in the development of student teachers and Siedentop and Tannehill (2000) identified these specifically for student PE teachers. Guillaume and Rudney (1993) found that, in developing as teachers, student teachers not only think about different things, but also think about the same things differently.

If there are different stages in your development as teachers, it follows that you may need different learning opportunities and experiences at different stages. Learning opportunities and experiences include observing experienced teachers teach; role play; small group micro-teaching situations with peers or groups of pupils; team teaching with your tutor, either teaching a small group for part or the whole of a lesson or the whole group for part of the lesson; teaching a full class. These are not sequential. Each can be used at any time on your

ITE in order to achieve a particular purpose. These learning opportunities and experiences allow you to practise and become competent in basic teaching skills, possibly for use for a specific purpose, and to spend time using your developing teaching skills in a variety of situations. These allow you to refine them so that you can adapt them as appropriate to the situation to enable you to use the right teaching skill in the right way at the right time to promote pupil learning. It is important also that as you become more confident in your teaching skills you reflect critically on what you want to achieve and on what you want the pupils to achieve – your aims, objectives and ILOs – therefore what teaching strategies and learning activities enable the pupils to achieve these (see Chapter 13).

Getting started

In order to make the most of the learning opportunities and experiences in school you need to understand the context in which you are working. Gathering essential background information to inform your work in school is an essential part of this. On preliminary visits prior to each school experience you need to collect information about the school and PE department. This information comes from many sources. You observe the PE environment, including the facilities, displays and equipment. You ask questions. You talk to tutors about policies and procedures of the school and PE department and observe them in practice. You read school and department documents, such as schemes and units of work, policy statements, prospectuses. A document such as the school prospectus can provide valuable information about the whole school and its pupils. Whole-school and PE policy statements covering issues such as assessment, equal opportunities and extracurricular activities are important in providing the context for your work in the department. Other documents give you essential guidance on how to conduct yourself (for example, the school dress code) and how to relate to pupils within the department. Your tutor will, no doubt, give you guidance about what information to collect and mechanisms to help you. To supplement guidance from your tutor, if needed, there are examples of questions on the companion website (www. routledge.com/cw/capel) designed to help you gather information about the school, the PE department, the PE facilities and resources, by focusing your observations and the questions you ask and identifying some key documents to look at.

The companion website (www.routledge.com/cw/capel) also includes examples of observation schedules to help you to observe different teaching skills in action. In addition to using these to observe the teaching skills identified, you can use them to help you devise your own observation schedule for a specific purpose. Chapter 4 addresses observation and other information-gathering techniques to help you make the most of your learning opportunities and experiences in schools.

Metzler (1990) indicated that tutoring should be a teaching process in itself. Your tutor should help you to make the most of the learning opportunities and experiences on your ITE in order to study, observe and practise teaching skills in situations appropriate to your stage of development. You and your tutor may undertake different roles as you have different learning opportunities and experiences in school, and therefore you need to determine how best to work with your tutor at different stages in your development, e.g. direction, guidance, negotiation, freedom.

Task 1.7 is designed to help you to work with your tutor.

Task 1.7 Working with your tutor

Discuss with your tutor your immediate development needs and what learning activities you both feel might be best to help you address those needs. Take part in the learning activity and then evaluate with your tutor how effective that activity was in addressing your development need. Keep these in your PDP and refer to them to help you to learn from them and continue to develop.

As well as undertaking a range of activities to help you develop as a teacher, it is important that you develop your ability to reflect critically. You need, for example, to think critically about what you are teaching, why and how. This is covered in Chapter 15.

Summary and key points

Your past experiences of PE have influenced your decision to become a PE teacher and have moulded your values, attitudes and beliefs about PE and about PE teaching. In order to become an effective PE teacher, you need to be aware of how your values, attitudes and beliefs influence you and to understand that not all pupils you teach, nor all parents, nor all other teachers share your values, attitudes and beliefs. You need competence in basic teaching skills before you can refine and adapt these skills to be able to use them in the right way at the right time. It is only then that you can combine them effectively to enhance pupils' learning and achieve the ILOs of a lesson and objectives of units of work and work towards achieving the aims of the schemes of work and PE curriculum in which you are working. In order to do this, you need also to understand the complex interactions between teaching skills, physical activities and pupils' learning, including how specific teaching strategies help to achieve specific ILOs. Teaching skills tend to be introduced on your ITE, and written about in books such as this, in isolation from one another. This chapter has attempted to provide a picture of how they fit together and interact so that you know at what you are aiming. One way it has done this is by approaching the whole enterprise of teaching by addressing the questions concerning the what, why and how of teaching. Chapter 2 focuses on the aims of PE. Chapters 3-10 introduce some of the basic teaching skills in which you need to develop competence during your ITE, while Chapters 12-14 focus on particular areas of challenge in which you will be expected to apply these basic teaching skills. After you have read those chapters we suggest that you return to this chapter to help you reflect on how teaching skills fit together and interact.

As you start out as a student PE teacher you are likely to find that teaching is more complex than you thought. Your previous experience, your enthusiasm and your wish to pass on your knowledge, understanding and love of PE are not enough. Your ITE is designed to give you different learning opportunities and experiences to help you develop as a PE teacher. We hope that this book helps to support your development as a teacher and that you enjoy the challenge.

Check which requirements of your ITE you have addressed through this chapter.

Further reading

Capel, S. and Whitehead, M. (eds) (2013) *Debates in Physical Education*, Abingdon, Oxon: Routledge.

This book explores and debates major issues PE teachers encounter in their everyday lives. For example, Chapter 4 debates what pupils should learn in PE; Chapter 7 debates what knowledge teachers need for teaching PE; and Chapter 8 considers why PE teachers adopt particular ways of teaching.

Green, K. and Hardman, K. (eds) (2005) *Physical Education Essential Issues*, London: Sage.

This book will give you a general overview of different aspects of teaching PE. In particular, Chapter 7 focuses on how the content is taught is as important as what is taught and looks at factors influencing how teachers teach.

Rink, J. E. (2013) *Teaching Physical Education for Learning*, 7th edn, New York: McGraw Hill Education.

Chapter 1 provides an overview of the teaching process, including content and skills of organisation and management used in a lesson.

Siedentop, D. and Tannehill, D. (2000) *Developing Teaching Skills in Physical Education*, 4th edn, New York: McGraw Hill Higher Education.

Chapter 1 addresses a number of issues concerned with learning to teach PE effectively, including stages of development of student PE teachers. Chapter 5 introduces three primary systems: the managerial task system; the instructional task system; and the pupil social system; and how they interact.

Additional resources for this chapter are available on the companion website: www.routledge.com/cw/capel.

2 Aims of PE

Margaret Whitehead

Introduction

Chapter 1 provided you with a broad overview of the role of the PE teacher and of the skills, knowledge and understanding needed to fulfil this role successfully and with confidence. Among the topics discussed were issues concerning the aims of PE and how your teaching can promote the achievement of these aspirations. This chapter looks specifically at the aims of PE and introduces you to the concept of physical literacy as the underlying aim of all PE. It is important to be clear about aims, as these are the foundation for planning schemes of work, units of work and individual lessons. Detailed guidance on planning is covered in Chapter 3. Aims influence both the content and the teaching method you select in your work with pupils. You will probably want to return to Chapters 1 and 2 regularly throughout your initial teacher education (ITE) to remind you of what you are aiming to achieve in PE.

Objectives

At the end of this chapter you should be able to:

- understand the terms aims, objectives and intended learning outcomes (ILO);
- appreciate the relationship between overall educational aims and the aims of PE;
- appreciate that the aims of PE are of two types: those unique to the subject and those that are broader educational aims shared with other curriculum subjects;
- understand that aims, objectives and ILOs influence your design and delivery of lessons;
- understand the concept of physical literacy;
- begin to formulate your own aims for PE.

Check the requirements of your ITE to see which relate to this chapter.

Aims, objectives and intended learning outcomes

You will hear the words *aims*, *objectives* and *ILOs* frequently in your ITE and beyond. These terms are different statements of intent and serve a number of purposes:

- They identify what you intend the pupils will achieve.
- They inform the content and planning of your schemes/units lessons and guide how you will teach.
- They provide a benchmark against which to assess pupil learning, thus informing you whether your planning and teaching achieved the desired ILOs.

Aims therefore give your work direction in purpose, guidance in planning and focus in assessment. These functions can be understood as essential if looked at broadly in terms of a journey you are to make. In planning and carrying out a journey you need to know where you are going, how you are going to get there and how you recognise that you have arrived. All are important in teaching.

Aims and objectives

Aims and objectives are the basis for educational planning. *Aims* provide *overall purpose and direction* and therefore relate to more general intentions. Most national governments have an educational policy spelling out the aims of education and similarly every school should have long-term aims or purposes. Aims and objectives become more focused and precise the shorter-term and closer to the point of delivery they become. Therefore, aims become more specific from education, to school, to subject. Aims of education and schools specify what should be achieved over a period of time, for example, for the time pupils are required to be at school. They offer general guidance about the purposes of, and outcomes from, education, rather than defining any specific achievements, whereas the aims of a subject such as PE, although still long-term aspirations, are more specific.

The *aims* or purposes of a subject form the starting point for devising *schemes* of work. Typically, schemes of work span a whole year or phase of education. Units of work refer to a shorter period of time, such as half a term or a term. While schemes characteristically have aims, *units have objectives*. Objectives are more specific purposes and intentions. Thus, objectives are building blocks or stepping stones which, when put together, result in the achievement of an aim or aims.

Intended learning outcomes

As indicated above, longer-term schemes of work have aims and these generate the objectives of constituent units of work. However, neither aims nor objectives can be used directly to help you plan a particular lesson. They need to be broken down into 'operational' segments, each with a more specific focus. These become ILOs for individual lessons. Aims and objectives are the intended end products of, respectively, the scheme of work or unit of work, whereas ILOs identify what pupils should achieve in a specific lesson. For example, an aim of a PE scheme of work might be to initiate pupils into playing a competitive game. An objective of a unit of work derived from this aim could be for pupils to be able to play a 5 v 5 game in, e.g. hockey. An ILO of a lesson within this unit could be that pupils understand and can demonstrate the roles of attack and defence in a 5 v 5 situation in hockey. ILOs describe what pupils should be able to do, know or understand at the end of a lesson. They are usually included at the start of a lesson plan and are introduced by a statement such as 'by the end of the lesson pupils will be able to. . . .'. They are fundamental aspects of a lesson plan and should be decided before any planning takes place. They challenge the teacher to devise specific learning activities and teaching strategies in the interests of their achievement. In addition, ILOs focus the pupils' and teacher's attention during the lesson in that they are likely to generate specific tasks for individual pupils, initiate key teaching points and be the focus of pupil assessment. Furthermore they are the ground against which you evaluate the success of a lesson.

Aims of education

Unit 7.1 (Haydon) in Capel *et al*. (2013) considers aims of education in some detail. It is suggested that you refer to that unit now for background information. It would be useful at this point to read the aims of the whole school/curriculum in your placement school. Any school aims are likely to reflect the current broad philosophy underlying a country's overall education philosophy. The 2014 National Curriculum for England (Department for Education (DfE) 2014a) opens with the broad aspiration that schools should provide:

> a curriculum which is broad and balanced and which:
>
> - promotes the spiritual, moral, cultural, mental and physical development of the pupils at the school and of society;
> - prepares pupils at school for the opportunities, responsibilities and experiences of later life.
>
> (DfE 2014a: 5)

In addition the document specifies that: 'All schools should make provision for personal, social, health and economic education (PHSE)' and that the curriculum should provide 'pupils with an introduction to the essential knowledge that they need to be educated citizens' and introduce 'pupils to the best that has been thought and said', helping them to develop 'an appreciation of human creativity and achievement' (DfE 2014a: 6).

All schools and all teachers are expected to make a contribution to the achievement of these aims. School curricula will be designed and managed to ensure that pupils experience a broad and balanced range of subject areas and that cross-curricular aims such as social development and preparing pupils for opportunities in later life are addressed by all teachers via work in their own subject area. It is suggested that teachers will accomplish the first task via initiating pupils into the material of their subject and will accomplish the second expectation via careful consideration of how they guide the pupils to learn.

Aims of PE

PE has taken a number of forms since its inclusion in the school curriculum in the United Kingdom in the late nineteenth century. Early forms of PE were called drill and physical training (Davis *et al*. 2000). The term PE was introduced in 1945 when the then Department

Table 2.1 Aims of PE to which teachers have aspired

1	Develop physical skills
2	Develop self-esteem
3	Foster physical literacy
4	Introduce every pupil to a wide range of activities
5	Ensure pupils continue with physical activity after leaving school
6	Develop creativity and inventiveness
7	Promote knowledge and understanding of cultural forms of physical activity
8	Produce world-class athletes
9	Provide activity to keep youngsters off the street and away from crime
10	Alert pupils to the role of physical activity in stress prevention
11	Promote joint flexibility and muscle strength
12	Promote respect for the environment
13	Enable pupils to handle competition
14	Promote cooperative learning
15	Develop social and moral skills
16	Prepare pupils to be knowledgeable spectators
17	Prepare pupils to adopt support roles in physical activity events
18	Develop understanding of the place of sport/dance in UK culture
19	Open up possibilities for post-school employment
20	Promote health and fitness – freedom from illness, especially cardiovascular health
21	Promote physical growth and development
22	Foster independence
23	Develop perseverance
24	Promote emotional development
25	Win inter-school matches and tournaments
26	Alert pupils to be aware of safety at all times
27	Provide an area of potential success for the less academic
28	Develop water confidence to promote personal survival
29	Develop aesthetic sensitivity
30	Enable pupils to express themselves through movement
31	Promote cognitive development

of Education took over responsibility for the subject from the Ministry of Health. Since its introduction into schools the subject has worked to achieve a variety of aims. For many years those teaching PE were free to select the specific aims towards which they worked. Early aims included promoting health, improving discipline and developing loyalty and teamwork. A list of aims gathered from surveying teachers' priorities is given in Table 2.1.

Now carry out Task 2.1, which encourages you to reflect on the list in Table 2.1.

Task 2.1 Prioritising aims of PE

Study the list in Table 2.1 and identify the four aims that you feel are most important to PE. Compare this list with that created by another student teacher, discussing and defending your different priorities. Record this debate and put the notes in your professional development portfolio (PDP).

Nowadays, however, in England, the National Curriculum spells out what each subject should work to achieve. Aims extracted from the National Curriculum for Physical Education (NCPE) (DfE 2014c) state that:

> Physical education should aim to enable pupils to:
>
> a   be competent, confident and expert in their techniques, and apply them across different sports and physical activities;
> b   succeed and excel in competitive sport and other physically demanding activities;
> c   understand what makes a performance effective and how to apply these principles to their own and others' work;
> d   build character;
> e   embed values such as fairness and respect;
> f   be physically confident in ways that support their health and fitness;
> g   understand and apply the long-term health benefits of physical activity;
> h   develop the confidence and interest to get involved in exercise, sports and activities out of school and in later life.

The two lists of aims of PE set out above include two types of aspirations. Some could be seen as tied very closely to PE, being specific to the subject area, while others are more overarching, echoing items on the list of aims of education which are not particular to PE. As indicated above, we have responsibilities to work towards both types of aim. Those unique to PE can be seen as intrinsic aims while those that emanate from broader cross-curricular aims might be called extrinsic aims.

Now complete Task 2.2.

Task 2.2 Differentiating between extrinsic and intrinsic aims of PE

Examine the two lists of aims of PE and identify those that are intrinsic to PE and those that are extrinsic. Discuss your classification with another student teacher. Record this debate and put the notes in your PDP.

Extrinsic and intrinsic aims of PE

In carrying out Task 2.2 and identifying extrinsic aims, it is likely that from Table 2.1 you have identified items such as 6, 13, 15, 22, 23, 29 and from the DfE NCPE list you have included d and e. Working to these aims, we are addressing cross-curricular issues that all subjects are expected to promote. Teachers of PE have to bear in mind both extrinsic and intrinsic aims. Extrinsic aims are essential to fulfil our role in education generally and intrinsic aims are those that make PE unique, providing a platform for the profession to argue that PE is an essential element in a broad and balanced curriculum.

While this is a challenge, PE has the capacity to work towards both types of aim. Intrinsic aims are principally realised in the context of initiating pupils into the medium of movement, across a wide range of physical activities. On the other hand, extrinsic aims are principally realised though pedagogy or how we engage pupils in their learning. For example, where the teacher devolves responsibility to the pupils to create their own targets, PE can contribute to developing independence and where the teacher plans group work PE can help to develop social skills. However, it is also the case that some activities lend themselves to achieving some of these extrinsic aims. For example, helping pupils to handle competition will best be furthered in a competitive games situation and promoting creativity will be more readily achieved in a dance setting.

It is important to realise that simply by engaging pupils in a PE activity does not guarantee that they will make progress in achieving any of these extrinsic aims. In all situations, achieving these aims depends on how you teach, not what you teach. See Table 2.2 for some suggestions of how a teacher of PE might contribute to these extrinsic PE aims or cross-curricular aims. Now complete Task 2.3.

Task 2.3 Positive and negative aspects of extrinsic aims of PE

Before reading the section below, complete the SWOT analysis grid, identifying the strengths, weaknesses, opportunities and threats to PE in adopting extrinsic aims as central to the role of PE in Education (this grid is also available on the companion website: www.routledge.com/cw/capel). Discuss your entries with another student teacher. Put these notes into your PDP.

Extrinsic aims of PE	
Strengths	**Weaknesses**
Opportunities	**Threats**

Extrinsic aims as central to the role of PE in education

There is no doubt that PE can and should contribute to the broader aims of education, so there will be strengths and opportunities for PE to address these aspirations. However, there are weaknesses and threats where any of these aims become the underpinning *raison d'être* for PE holding its place in the curriculum. A significant weakness is that it is all but impossible to prove that PE, in fact, does make a substantial contribution to, for example, social education, cognitive development or fostering independence. If asked to show evidence of our effectiveness in this regard we would be hard pressed to supply this. The threat to PE of too much focus on broader aims is twofold. Firstly, as we are not the only subject area contributing to these aims, our achievement of these aims does not depend on the contribution of PE, and secondly, working to these aims does not identify our unique

Table 2.2 Extrinsic aims of PE, teaching approaches to realise these aims and particular forms of activity in which they might best be achieved

Extrinsic aims in NCPE (DfE 2014c)	Teaching approaches to realise these aims	Forms of activity in which these aims might best be achieved
c) Build character, e.g independence, self-reliance, tolerance, initiative	Devolve responsibility to learners, set high standards regarding expectations in application, determination and initiative	All activities
d) Embed values such as fairness and respect	Sensitive teacher handling of what is right and what is wrong and development of mutual respect among learners	Involvement in any rule-governed activity, particularly in competitive situations
Extrinsic aims from Table 2.1		
6 Creativity and inventiveness	Discovery learning, problem solving	Dance; sequence work in e.g. gymnastics; game planning, challenges in the outdoors
12 Respect for the environment	Discussion, reflection	Challenges in the outdoors
13 Handle competition	Sensitive teacher debrief and development of mutual respect among learners	Any form of competitive activity
14 Cooperative learning	Delegate learning to groups of learners	All activities
15 Social and moral skills	Sensitive teacher handling of what is right and what is wrong and development of mutual respect among learners	Involvement in any rule-governed activity
22 Independence	Provide the structure, encouragement and support for learners to set their own goals, and judge their progress. Take opportunities to give the learners a voice in respect of what and how they learn	
23 Perseverance	Expectation and recognition by the teacher of hard work and application to the task in hand	All activities
26 Alert to safety	Example by the teacher and involvement of learners in creating safe environments	Most activities
29 Aesthetic sensitivity	Opportunities for aesthetic appreciation picked up by the teacher for debate and reflection	Particularly dance, gymnastics, synchronised swimming
31 Cognitive development	Introduction of areas of understanding with discussion and debate	Most activities

contribution to education. Together these issues carry the danger of PE not being seen as an area of the school curriculum to which precious time should be dedicated.

Intrinsic aims of PE as highlighting the unique contribution of PE to education

One of the intentions of this chapter is to help you begin to come to your own view concerning the aims of PE. As is clear, there is a wide range to choose from and this can make your task challenging.

In carrying out Task 2.2 and identifying intrinsic aims it is likely that from Table 2.1 you have included some or all of numbers 1, 4, 5, 11, 20, 21, 29 and from the DfE NCPE list you have included some or all of a, b, c, f, g and h. These can be seen as unique to PE.

Given the problems associated with PE focusing principally on broader educational aims, there are clear advantages of identifying and working towards the intrinsic aims of PE. These are particular to the subject and are rarely addressed by other curriculum areas. Now complete Task 2.4.

Task 2.4 Intrinsic aims of PE as particular to the subject area

Critically consider if the aims you identified in Task 2.2 as intrinsic to PE are, or could be, realised in other subject areas. Discuss your thoughts with another student teacher and put these notes into your PDP.

The dilemma for PE

The positive and negative aspects of promoting broader educational aims and the need to safeguard our unique contribution to a broad and balanced curriculum present a challenging dilemma for the profession. It is valuable to reflect on why PE has been championed as having the potential to realise so wide a range of aims. Task 2.5 challenges you to consider why this might be.

Task 2.5 Multiple aims of PE

Critically consider why there are so many aims to which PE can contribute. What benefits and problems are associated with this situation? Discuss your ideas with your tutor and keep these notes in your PDP as evidence of Masters level work.

One way to solve our problem is to stand back and ask ourselves: What is the overall purpose of our work in school? An answer could be that, in addition to fostering education-wide aims, our mission is to so inspire our pupils that they continue to participate in physical activity outside the school and beyond the years of schooling. Our aims must therefore be to ensure all pupils leave school with the motivation, confidence, physical competence, knowledge and understanding of movement and of the principles of health and fitness, to value and take responsibility for maintaining physical activity for life. This aim is in fact the definition of physical literacy, which is now seen worldwide as a viable aim of PE (Almond and Whitehead 2012a). It is to physical literacy that we now turn.

Physical literacy

Physical literacy is a concept that is relevant to everyone, whatever their physical endowment, across the whole lifespan, from birth to death. It identifies what many now believe is the underlying aim of and rationale for PE – participation in physical activity throughout life. Physical literacy is not a state that, once achieved, is maintained thereafter. Rather all individuals are on their own physical literacy journey and our role in PE is to ensure all make progress on their journey (for further information on physical literacy, see Whitehead 2010).

In its own way the concept encapsulates many of the intrinsic aims that have been identified. It is useful to study Table 2.3, which shows how promoting physical literacy can accommodate the range of intrinsic aims identified in the NCPE and many of the teachers' views in Table 2.1. In that sense it is not new. However it spells out clearly what we would hope to achieve. Significant in the wording of the concept is the priority given to motivation and confidence. There is a view that teachers of PE have been effective in promoting physical competence but less successful in motivating pupils to adopt physical activity as part of their lifestyle. The aim of the profession, unique to PE, is to provide the foundation for lifelong participation in physical activity.

Justification of PE in the curriculum

It is perhaps true that the profession has been very ready to highlight extrinsic aims to support the place of the subject in the curriculum. One cause of this is that too often physical activity, and thus PE, has been viewed as of less importance, with little value being seen in developing our physical potential per se.

Physical literacy, as a concept based on sound philosophical principles, brings to the fore the key role our embodied dimension plays in life as we know it. The concept can provide a sound justification for the inclusion of PE in the curriculum (Almond and Whitehead 2012b). The term was not coined to make a case for PE to be seen as among academic subjects in schooling but to underline the importance of the subject area in providing pupils with a broad and balanced curriculum. In other words, the concept of physical literacy has the potential to provide PE with educational validity. It goes without saying that to maintain our position in the curriculum we must be able, with confidence, to articulate our unique contribution to schooling. Task 2.6 is designed to introduce you to the underlying philosophy behind physical literacy and provide you with some arguments to support PE in the curriculum.

Task 2.6 Justification and value of physical literacy
Read Chapter 2 in Capel and Whitehead (2013), which sets out the justification and value of physical literacy. Write a 2,000-word essay critically evaluating the proposals in this chapter. Keep the essay in your PDP as evidence of Masters level work.

Table 2.3 Intrinsic aims in the NCPE and their relationship to physical literacy and teachers' views from Table 2.1

Purposes and aims of the NCPE (DfE 2014c)	Related elements of physical literacy	Related items from Table 2.1
• Develop the confidence and interest to get involved in exercise, sports and activities out of school	Motivation and confidence	Develop self-esteem and self-confidence
• Be competent, confident and expert in their techniques, and apply them across different sports and physical activities • Succeed and excel in competitive sport and other physically demanding activities	Physical competence	Develop physical skills Promote physical development and growth Introduce learners to a wide range of activities
• Understand what makes a performance effective and how to apply these principles to their own and others' work	Knowledge and understanding of movement	Promote knowledge and understanding of cultural forms of movement Enable learners to take part in competitive and cooperative physical activities
• Understand and apply the long-term health benefits of physical activity • Be physically confident in ways that support their health and fitness	Knowledge and understanding of health and fitness	Promote health and fitness - freedom from illness - especially cardiovascular health Promote joint flexibility and muscle strength Teach learners the role of physical activity in stress prevention
• Develop the confidence and interest to get involved in exercise, sports and activities out of school	Valuing and taking responsibility	Ensure learners continue with physical activity after leaving school
• Develop the confidence and interest to get involved in exercise, sports and activities out of school and in later life	Participation for life	Ensure learners continue with physical activity after leaving school

Implications of adopting physical literacy as the underlying aim of all PE

Adopting physical literacy as the underlying aim of PE has a number of implications for the way PE is conducted in school. These implications relate to sensitive teacher–learner interaction, appropriate differentiated pedagogy and carefully selected content. In addition, assessment strategies need to be individualised and learner-centred, being based on criterion-referenced rather than norm-referenced principles (for an explanation, see Chapter 9).

In respect of teacher–learner interaction and pedagogy, it is important both that teachers are enthusiastic and encourage every member of the class and that pupils leave lessons feeling that they have made progress and look forward to the next lesson. Teachers need to know each learner as an individual and adopt an optimistic and empathetic approach with each one. As far as possible teaching should be differentiated, with tasks set that are appropriate to individual pupils. As appropriate, teachers need to provide opportunities for pupils to be involved in setting their own targets. Above all, experiences in physical activity need to foster, in every learner, the motivation to participate and the development of self-confidence, irrespective of potential. See Task 2.6 for further reading on this area and also Chapter 7 on motivation and Chapter 11 on learner-centred teaching, which follow up these implications.

In respect of content it is important to develop movement skills in the context of meaningful experiences in individual, cooperative and competitive physical activities. It is important too that all pupils have rewarding experiences in a wide variety of movement forms, such as adventure, aesthetic and expressive, athletic, competitive, and fitness and health. See Task 2.7 for further reading on this topic.

Tasks 2.7 and 2.8 are designed to give you more detail of these implications and to give you the opportunity to reflect on how feasible it may be to put these into practice.

> **Task 2.7 Pedagogical implications of adopting physical literacy**
>
> Read and critically debate the following articles concerned with the pedagogical implications of adopting physical literacy as the foundation goal of PE.
>
> Almond, L. with Whitehead, M.E. (2012c) 'Translating physical literacy into practice for all teachers', *Physical Education Matters* 7, 3, Autumn: 67-70.
> Whitehead, M.E. with Almond, L. (2013) 'Creating learning experiences to foster physical literacy', *Physical Education Matters*, 8, 1, Spring: 24-27.
>
> Consider how feasible it is for teachers of PE to adopt these teaching approaches. Store your notes in your PDP as evidence of Masters level work.

> **Task 2.8 Content implications of adopting physical literacy**
>
> Read and critically debate one of the following chapters concerned with the content implications of adopting physical literacy as the foundation goal of PE.
>
> *(continued)*

> **Task 2.8** *(continued)*
>
> Capel, S. and Whitehead, M. (eds) (2013) *Debates in Physical Education*, Abingdon, Oxon: Routledge, Chapter 3, pp. 37–52.
> Whitehead, M.E. (ed.) (2010) *Physical Literacy Throughout the Lifecourse*, Abingdon, Oxon: Routledge, Chapter 15, pp. 181–188.
>
> Consider how feasible it is for teachers of PE to follow these recommendations. Store your notes in your PDP as evidence of Masters level work.

Summary and key points

The aims of education and schooling and, more specifically, the aims of curriculum subjects, including PE, used in the placement schools in which you work provide guidance about what you are aiming to achieve. In this chapter you have been introduced to the range of aims of PE and alerted to the two different types of aims: those that are unique to PE and those that are broader and are shared with other curriculum subjects.

The aims of the PE curriculum used in your placement schools should guide your decisions about objectives for units of work and ILOs for lessons, as well as the selection of appropriate content and teaching approaches. Early in your development as a PE teacher the principal ILOs for you to include in your lessons should be those that are unique to PE. At this stage, aims identifying the mastery of physical skills and the effective participation in physical activities provide the focus for your planning, teaching and assessment. As you master the challenge of planning units of work and lessons focused on achieving subject-specific ILOs and as you gain experience and confidence, you can start to address some of the broader aims of education. As explained above, achieving these broader aims depends to a considerable degree on how you teach, that is, how you engage pupils in their learning.

The chapter then considered the concept of physical literacy as the underpinning aim of PE. This concept, which embraces most of the aims of PE, as referred to earlier in the chapter, springs from the perceived importance and value of maintaining physical activity throughout life and the view that to achieve lifelong participation we need to foster motivation, confidence, physical competence and knowledge and understanding in the physical activity context. The implications of adopting physical literacy as your goal of PE were then indicated. We suggest that you return to this chapter at different points in your ITE and consider its content in detail towards the end of your ITE, when you have mastered the basic teaching skills and can reflect on the aims of PE and the implications of adopting physical literacy as the foundation aim of all our work.

Check which requirements of your ITE you have addressed through this chapter.

Further reading

Bailey, R., Armour, K., Kirk, D., Jess, M., Pickup, I. and Sandford, R. (British Educational Research Association (BERA) Physical Education and Sport Pedagogy Special Interest Group) (2008) The educational benefits claimed for physical education and school sport: an academic review, *Research Papers in Education*, 24, 1, March: 1–27.

This detailed paper looks at the research into the benefits of PE, specifically physical, affective, social and cognitive. The article below is a shorter version on the same theme.

Bailey, R. (2006) Physical education and sport in schools: a review of benefits and outcomes, *Journal of School Health*, 76, 8: 397–401.

This article explores the scientific evidence that has been gathered on the contributions and benefits of PE and sport in schools both for pupils and educational systems.

Capel, S. and Breckon, P. (2014) *A Practical Guide to Teaching Physical Education in the Secondary School*, 2nd edn, Abingdon, Oxon: Routledge.

This book contains useful chapters on 'The nature of PE' and on 'How aims and objectives influence teaching'.

Capel, S. and Whitehead, M.E. (eds) (2013) *Debates in Physical Education*, Abingdon, Oxon: Routledge.

A wide-ranging text which includes a debate on issues surrounding aims of PE. Chapters 2–4 are particularly pertinent to the aims of PE and the concept of physical literacy.

Whitehead, M.E. (ed.) (2010) *Physical Literacy Throughout the Lifecourse*, Abingdon, Oxon: Routledge.

This book sets out the background and application of the concept of physical literacy. Further information and papers can be found on the website: www.physical-literacy.org.uk.

Additional resources for this chapter are available on the companion website: www.routledge.com/cw/capel.

3 How planning and evaluation support effective learning and teaching

Jackie Arthur and Susan Capel

Introduction

Effective planning to maximise pupils' learning is at the heart of effective teaching. Indeed, Benjamin Franklin said 'If you fail to plan, you are planning to fail.' In this chapter we first consider the importance of planning for effective teaching.

We then look at the relationship between long-, medium- and short-term planning. Although lessons (short-term plans) should always be planned within a specific unit of work (medium-term plans), it is common at the beginning of your school placement to start by planning individual lessons, followed by planning series of lessons within units of work. Thus, we begin this chapter by focusing on lesson planning, after which we look at how the lessons you plan fit into units of work to promote pupil learning. Planning lessons and units of work is a skill which has to be learned and practised to ensure pupils learn. Like any skill, your confidence grows with practise, feedback, reflection and refinement; therefore it is important you maximise opportunities to plan lessons and units of work during school placement.

In order to maximise learning opportunities for pupils you need to understand that the lessons and units of work you plan are always developed in the context of longer-term plans and hence fit into existing schemes of work within the department. Although it is highly unlikely you will be expected to play an active part in planning schemes of work while on school placement, it is important that you understand the whole planning cycle, including how schemes of work are constructed. The last part of the chapter considers schemes of work to help you engage with and understand the whole planning cycle. It is therefore recommended that you read the whole chapter before you begin to plan lessons.

Objectives

At the end of this chapter you should be able to:

- understand the relationship between long-, medium- and short-term planning;
- understand the principles and components of effective lesson planning in a school context;

(continued)

(continued)

- design inclusive intended learning outcomes (ILOs);
- appreciate that planning is only as effective as the accuracy in assessing pupil needs;
- understand and experience the importance of reflection in the evaluation process and develop confidence in using evaluation to set challenging learning experiences to enable pupils to meet the lesson ILOs;
- comprehend how planning shapes learning opportunities in the short, medium and long term.

Check the requirements of your initial teacher education (ITE) to see which relate to this chapter.

The importance of planning

Planning for the long, medium and short term is important to provide direction for pupils' learning. Planning may well be based on a nationally devised programme, e.g. a National Curriculum for Physical Education (NCPE), but could equally be a school-specific programme devised to address agreed aims through a broad and balanced programme of study. Schemes of work ensure that the range of curriculum content is covered over a longer period of time, e.g. a Key Stage (KS) or a year. Units of work break the curriculum content into a manageable plan for pupils' learning. They may be an entire term to a few weeks in length. Specific learning is planned for each lesson.

Effective planning focuses on 'progression' in the planned development over time. Progression can be understood as 'the sequence built into children's learning through curriculum policies and schemes of work so that later learning builds on knowledge, skills, understanding and attitudes learned previously' (Department of Education and Science (DES) 1990: 1). Progressive planning requires you, as a teacher, to identify clearly what pupils already know as the basis on which to plan what you want them to learn. Schemes and units of work also ensure the continuity of pupil learning through building on learning that has gone before. Continuity has been defined as: 'the nature of the curriculum experienced by children as they transfer from one setting to another' (DES 1990: 13).

Planning is also important for you as the teacher. It helps you to order your thinking so that you can maximise the use of lesson time to enhance pupils' learning. Without such planning, some aspects of the curriculum could be missed and the programme of study may not provide breadth and balance of learning experiences. Such plans give direction to pupils' learning. If you are not sure where you are going, you are liable to end up somewhere else.

The relationship between long-, medium- and short-term planning

Planning for pupils' learning in schools is divided into long-term, medium-term and short-term, each with identified intentions of learning. In this chapter (and throughout this book) the following terminology is used. Check the terminology used in your ITE, as this may be different.

Long-term plans are called *schemes of work*. These are usually generic in nature and often drawn from a central programme of study (possibly a National Curriculum (NC)). They are usually planned at departmental level for a specific period of learning. Schemes of work in England are often planned for each KS in the NC, i.e. ages 5–7 years (KS1), ages 7–11 years (KS2), ages 11–14 years (KS3) and ages 14–19 years (KS4), as are particular years (e.g. year 7, 8 and 9). Schemes of work also help to ensure a broad and balanced learning experience.

Aims provide overall purpose and direction and therefore relate to more general intentions. Aims or purposes of the subject in England are specified in the NCPE. These form the starting point for devising aims for schemes of work. Aims of schemes of work form the basis for more specific purposes and intentions, as identified in unit of work objectives.

Fundamentally, the scheme of work establishes the context for planning units of work.

Medium-term plans are called *units of work*. Units of work are devised from the more generic plan in a scheme of work. They cover work over a period of time, such as a term or a half-term. They are usually planned at departmental level as a generic framework, but in discussion they may be modified to cater for a particular class. Units of work form the building blocks towards achieving the aims of a scheme of work and give teachers flexibility to design material appropriate for individual groups.

Objectives are specific purposes and intentions. Each unit of work has specific objectives which are the building blocks or stepping stones which guide the lesson ILOs and which, when put together, result in the achievement of an aim or aims in a scheme of work.

Short-term specific plans for each class you teach are called *lesson plans*. Lessons vary in length, depending on your school's curriculum design (commonly lessons are 60 or 90 minutes). A lesson plan within the same unit of work for a specific year group will differ, depending on the needs of the pupils in the class and the rate of progress the pupils are making in respect of the objectives of the unit of work.

While aims and objectives are the intended end products of, respectively, the scheme and unit of work, they cannot be used directly to help you plan a particular lesson. *Intended learning outcomes* (ILOs) identify what pupils should achieve in a specific lesson. They are the 'operational' segments, each with a specific, measurable focus, against which pupil progress is measured.

Figure 3.1 shows the relationship between a scheme of work, units of work and lesson plans. It focuses specifically on how a scheme of work for KS3 would form the basis for units of work and lessons for three educational years.

Now complete Task 3.1.

Task 3.1 Organising learning programmes

Obtain a copy of the schemes and units of work in your placement school. Analyse these and then discuss, in small groups with other student teachers, how the PE curriculum is organised in your placement schools. Record these various approaches to structuring the curriculum at each KS in your professional development portfolio (PDP) for future reference when planning a curriculum.

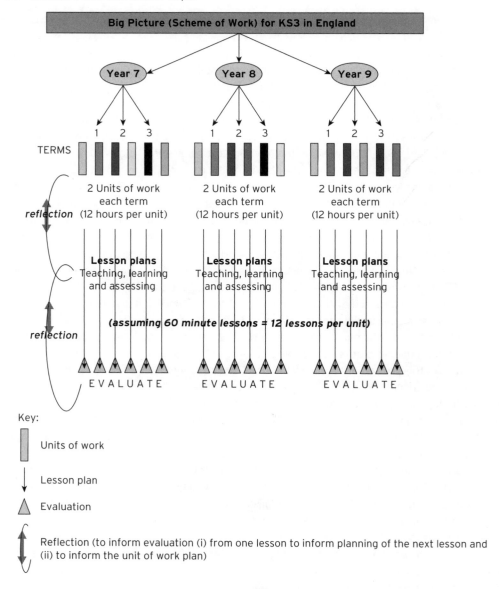

Figure 3.1 The relationship between a scheme of work, units of work and lesson plans.

The next section of the chapter looks at short-term (lesson) planning in detail. We start with lesson planning first as you are likely to plan individual lessons before you plan a series of lessons within a unit of work. However, it is important to remember that each lesson is not an isolated event; rather, it is part of a series of lessons which, together, enable pupils to work towards achieving unit of work objectives. They therefore need to be progressive.

Lesson planning

In this section we look at: the importance of lesson planning, what you need to know before you plan a lesson, planning ILOs, catering for all pupils in your planning, stages of a lesson, the principles of good lesson planning, committing your plan to paper and planning subsequent lessons.

The importance of lesson planning

Carefully thought-through lesson plans are crucial to your success in enabling pupils to learn. Bailey and Nunan (1996: 18) describe a lesson plan as 'like a road map which describes where the teacher hopes to go in the lesson'. This analogy implies that teachers should try to draw this map as clearly as possible in order to maximise opportunities for all pupils to complete the journey and learn what is intended for them to learn in the lesson (and that in a series of lessons they cover and learn the relevant material from the unit of work). There is no guarantee that pupils will learn what is intended, but a good lesson plan undoubtedly provides more opportunity for such learning. It is important to remember that the needs of the pupils you are teaching are most important in your planning and they must have first consideration; the activity or material is simply the vehicle through which learning takes place.

Although experienced teachers may appear to reduce their planning to an outline, as you are starting out it is important you plan your lessons in detail. This should help you to:

- plan appropriate/specific ILOs;
- select teaching activities, extension/intervention strategies;
- structure the content, learning experiences and progressions;
- ensure appropriate time is allocated to each stage of the lesson.

Although you plan your lessons in detail, depending on the response of pupils, you also need to be flexible and, where necessary, adapt and refocus pupils' learning as the lesson progresses. Thus, within each lesson you need to be continuously reflecting on how the pupils are responding to the tasks you set, as well as to the lesson in general. Schön (1987) calls this reflection-in-action, which enables you to keep under review the initial lesson expectations or outcomes (Vermette *et al.* 2010) and respond appropriately to the unexpected in relation to progress towards achieving ILOs.

What you need to know before you plan the lesson

Important background information needed in order to plan for a specific lesson (and series of lessons) includes information about the pupils, about the unit of work in which the lesson fits and about the facilities and equipment, i.e.:

- KS, year and specific class;
- number of pupils in the class;
- gender of pupils in the class;
- prior experiences of the class;
- attainment range of the class;
- unit of work of which the lesson is a part;

- number of lessons in the sequence;
- length of the lesson;
- facilities and equipment required/available.

This knowledge is essential if you are to devise a lesson that is appropriate for the particular pupils, accommodates the objectives of the unit of work and keeps in mind issues such as space, equipment and time.

Planning ILOs for the lesson

With this background information, the next stage is to break down the objectives of the unit of work, of which the lesson is a part, into ILOs. This will result in a list of ILOs to be covered during the series of lessons in the unit of work. You then select which ILOs you will address in the lesson in question, taking into account the nature of the pupils in the class. ILOs should be written in terms of what pupils are expected to learn. To focus your ILOs on pupils' learning, it is helpful to use a stem such as 'by the end of this lesson pupils will be able to'. The language used to write the ILOs is important to promote, but not limit, possible learning. The specificity of the lesson ILOs is crucial as they should express measurable expectations for learning and provide a focus for assessing learning.

As a general rule ILOs begin with an action word. Words can relate to, for example, performance, understanding, ability to be creative or the ability to analyse movement. Bloom's taxonomy (Bloom *et al.* 1956) identifies categories of learning objectives in the form of nouns. This is often used in specifying lesson ILOs. Examples of words you might use, based on Bloom and others who have followed up his work, are on the companion website: www.routledge.com/cw/capel.

Examples of ILOs are:

By the end of this lesson pupils will be able to:

- demonstrate the accurate placement of an overhead shot in badminton;
- analyse the accuracy of their partner when in a game situation and use this to improve understanding;

or:

- compose a short individual phrase of movement into and out of an inverted balance;
- analyse the movement of their partner and give supportive feedback.

Now complete Tasks 3.2 and 3.3.

Task 3.2 Observing lesson ILOs

Observe a PE lesson taught by an experienced PE teacher. Write down what you think the ILOs of the lesson are. Afterwards, discuss with the teacher:

(continued)

Task 3.2 *(continued)*

- the planned ILOs and those which you identified to see if you are in agreement;
- whether you think the ILOs (both yours and the teacher's, if they were different) were achieved in the lesson;
- how the lesson ILOs relate to the overall unit of work objectives.

Store this in your PDP to reflect on when you write your own ILOs.

Task 3.3 Developing effective ILOs

Write a specific ILO appropriate for the majority of pupils in a KS3 class designed to refine, develop and apply knowledge and skill within any invasion game. Discuss the ILO with your tutor and identify potential activities that could be developed to provide opportunities for the majority of your pupils to realise the ILO.

You can use the checklist below to help you with this task.

- Is the ILO pupil-centred?
- Is the ILO measurable?
- Have you used effective action verbs that specify the quality of learning you want to achieve?
- Does the activity ensure that most pupils will achieve the ILO?
- Does the ILO reflect the unit of work objectives?

Store the information in your PDP for use later.

Catering for all pupils in your planning

In your planning you need to be aware that your pupils will have different levels of success. Planning in advance how to cater for different abilities enables you to respond to pupil need. This will involve your giving some thought to how you will cater for these differences as you may well need alternative tasks for pupils who are showing different levels of success.

There are two approaches to planning to cater for all pupils: one is to be prepared for pupils to have more or less success in respect of an ILO. The other relates to the nature of the tasks you set. These can be differentiated in a variety of ways. There is a great deal of material concerning methods of differentiation (see Chapter 10).

The first way of differentiating is to be prepared for pupils to have more or less success in respect of an ILO. This is commonly recognised by differentiating ILOs into, say, three groups, using wording such as working above/beyond and working below in relation to expectations of the majority of pupils in the class. The various levels of expectation for the first ILO, given above, might look like the following example:

Learning outcome (success criteria)

Most of the class, working at the intended level of attainment, will be able to:

- demonstrate the accurate placement of an overhead shot in badminton;
- analyse the accuracy of their partner when in a game situation.

Those *working above/beyond* expected levels of attainment will be able to:

- demonstrate consistent accuracy with power when performing an overhead clear;
- analyse how accuracy of their partner's shot is used strategically in a game.

Those *working below* expected levels of attainment will be able to:

- demonstrate basic accuracy in an overhead clear;
- recognise when their partner uses the shot.

Your planning should take account of the fact that you may have to respond in the lesson to pupils having more or less success in respect of an ILO and therefore different needs. Now complete Task 3.4.

Task 3.4 Planning for differentiation

Using the ILO you developed in Task 3.3, try to visualise what the outcome will look like for the majority of pupils, those working above/beyond and those working below the expectation of most pupils. Consider the range of language you will need to describe these outcomes and then construct the outcomes. Write differentiated learning outcomes for pupils working above/beyond and those working below the expectation of most pupils. Decide how you would differentiate the activity discussed with your tutor to help pupils (collectively, in groups, individually or in pairs) working above/ beyond and below expectations to achieve the ILO you identified.

Keep these in your PDP for future reference.

As regards the second way, as can be seen in Figure 3.2, you can plan to differentiate by outcome, by stimulus and task, by task and outcome, by graded task and outcome and by resources and outcome.

You should now know what you are trying to achieve and be planning to cater for the needs of all pupils in your class, and so you can start to build up the lesson. Generally, lessons are divided into stages.

Principles of good lesson planning

There are a number of key principles to be considered in planning lessons to maximise opportunities for pupils to learn. These include planning:

- clear and specific *ILOs* for pupils' learning (one aspect of planning that many student teachers initially find difficult) (see above);

Key: P = pupil; T = Task; O = outcome; R = Resource; S = Stimulus

- Differentiating by outcome: in which all pupils undertake a common task and differentiation is sought on the basis of the quality of response or outcome.

P   T   O

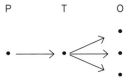

- Differentiating by stimulus and task: in which pupils are set specific stimuli/tasks matched to their ability. These may be differentiated on the basis of inherent difficulty, the amount of structure, or the amount of guidance given, or a combination of all three.

S   T   O

Working

above/beyond
Most

Working
below

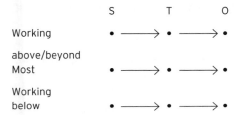

- Differentiating by task and outcome: in which pupils are given a common stimuli and provided with a choice of task which in turn results in a variety of outcomes.

P   T   O

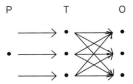

- Differentiating by graded task and outcome: in which pupils are given common stimuli and presented a series of tasks which enables them to achieve a range of outcomes.

P   T   O

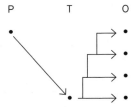

- Differentiating by resources and by outcome: in which pupils have access to a range of resources and are set a common task which results in a range of outcomes.

P   R   T   O

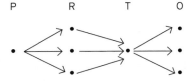

Figure 3.2 Ways of differentiating lesson material (reproduced from Davies 1990).

- *that establishes and maintains routines.* Routines provide clear signposts to expectations regarding pupil engagement and standards (see Chapter 6);
- the right *balance* of, for example, skills/techniques and application, practices and activities, in the lesson;
- lessons which have *coherence*. This enables pupils to experience smooth transitions from one activity to the next and to learn sequentially;
- *for progression* through challenging activities which build on pupils' prior experience and which stretch and motivate them and extend their knowledge, skill and understanding;
- *variety* of content, teaching activities, extension/intervention strategies and assessment which result in lessons which are interesting and motivating for pupils;
- *flexibility* to adopt varied methods of delivery within a learning episode to respond to pupils' needs in the lesson. John (2010: 68) refers to 'interactive teaching [which] requires planning that is flexible and practical from the outset';
- *that caters for all pupils* by including extension and intervention strategies that enable you to extend or reduce the challenge presented by the activity (see above and Chapter 10);
- *good use of time*. Thoughtful allocation of time in lesson planning is essential both to maximise learning time and to ensure that you cover all stages effectively. Available time will differ between the classes you teach. Time for changing and the distance of teaching venue from the changing facilities need to be factored in (see Chapter 6).

Stages of a lesson

The stages of a lesson may vary but those most commonly adopted in PE are introduction, warm-up, development and conclusion, with plenaries both during and at the end of the lesson. Although this is not a rigid structure, early in your planning these stages should help give shape to your lesson.

Introduction

Making the ILO and success criteria clear to pupils at the outset, in the introduction to a lesson, should help them focus on the intentions of the lesson and empower them to take more ownership of the activities, and hence their learning, in the lesson. Connections made with ILOs and assessment outcomes in previous lessons can help facilitate progressive learning and allow for more meaningful differentiation from the start of the lesson (Office for Standards in Education (Ofsted) 2013a). Setting levels of expectation and targeting questions appropriate to pupils' level of attainment help shape and maximise the learning time available.

Warm-up

The warm-up is a critical part of every lesson in order to prepare the pupils for the physical challenges ahead. It also helps the pupils to focus on the movement tasks and gives the teacher the opportunity to engage and enthuse the pupils. Movement tasks should anticipate the ILOs the pupils are working towards in the lesson, so laying the ground for lesson coherence.

Development

The transition between the warm-up and development phases of the lesson needs to be as seamless as possible, to maintain the progress made in activity levels and to maintain the clear focus on working towards the ILOs.

The key outcome of the development phase of the lesson is pupil progress in achieving the ILOs. You need to decide on the best approach to achieve each ILO for pupils in the specific class. For example, you could take a whole-part-whole approach in the development phase of your plan, in which pupils are exposed to a whole activity at the outset, from which a part of the activity is extracted (maybe the focus of your ILO) for greater attention and then placed back into the whole activity. Conversely, you could take a part-whole approach, where the skill or concept central to your ILO and hence, needing focus, is addressed first and then gradually built into a more complete whole activity, such as a game or sequence.

It is perfectly possible to vary your approaches within a lesson but it is important to plan the transitions within the development stage thoroughly, having considered the resources you may need and when you will need them.

Conclusion

As Webster *et al.* (2009: 85) remind us, 'expert teachers do not fade or extinguish a lesson's momentum, they maximise every last moment to reach the lesson's objectives [ILOs], secure pupil learning and prepare pupils for future success'. Thus, a meaningful conclusion, allocated an appropriate amount of time, is a valuable opportunity for pupils to consolidate new knowledge, skill and understanding acquired during the lesson. The format of the conclusion is generally dependent upon the content of the lesson but it could take the form of, for example, small-sided or full games, complete or partial sequences or routines. The opportunity for pupils to put isolated parts back into a meaningful whole is also valuable to you as the teacher, enabling you to identify any misconceptions that may have arisen and take a summative approach to assessment (see Chapter 9).

Plenaries

Plenaries should occur at strategic points within the lesson and at the end of the lesson where you want to draw together the learning of the whole class/individuals. A plenary enables the pupils to take stock, formatively consolidate and extend learning. When planning a plenary you need to consider its purpose; for example, it may be to:

- consolidate and extend learning;
- review progress against ILOs (or ILOs themselves);
- diagnose at an individual or collective level;
- recognise and value achievement;
- stimulate interest, anticipation and curiosity about the next phase of learning.

If well timed, a plenary can provide both teacher and pupils with an opportunity to reflect and determine the next steps in learning. They should be so planned that they involve all pupils in actively processing relevant information from the phase or whole lesson. Varying planned strategies for achieving this review can help crystallise what pupils have learned, enabling them to contextualise, articulate and transfer learning. All too often, the summative plenary is rushed or even omitted because of time constraints. In light of Schempp's (2003) observation that the end is what pupils remember the most, it is important to maximise the potential for learning through plenaries. Now complete Tasks 3.5 and 3.6.

Task 3.5 Compiling a plan

Using the ILOs designed and discussed with your tutor in Task 3.4, compile a lesson plan for a 20-minute lesson which shapes the learning progression in a whole-part-whole style and presents extension and intervention strategies. Try to build in opportunities for assessment *for* learning to consolidate learning. Discuss the plan with your tutor and store in your PDP until you have the opportunity to teach the lesson.

Task 3.6 Consolidating learning

Observe a range of lessons taught by experienced PE teachers in your placement school and identify when and how they consolidate learning.

- Is there evidence of a formative mini-plenary/mini-plenaries) during the development phase of the lesson and, if so, how long does it/do they take and what teaching strategies are used?
- What period of time is allocated to the summative plenary and how pupil-centred is it?

Store these ideas in your PDP to refer to in future planning.

Committing your plan to paper

As indicated above, you are well advised to write out your plan fully throughout your early months in teaching. It is likely that your higher education institution (HEI) or placement school will provide you with a lesson plan pro-forma; however, there is an exemplar on the companion website you can use or for comparison with those you are given (www.routledge.com/cw/capel).

Whatever format you use, it is advised that your plan includes space for background information, space for the activities to be carried out by the class and space for an evaluation of the lesson.

- Background information should include name of the class, date of the lesson, unit title and the ILOs for the lesson.
- The lesson activity section should include time allocation for each stage, the teaching approach you intend to use, the nature of the tasks to be carried out with key points for

observation, the learning activities and progressions, extension/intervention strategies and the organisation and equipment you will need to attend to (see further information on the companion website: www.routledge.com/cw/capel).

- Evaluation of the lesson. This can be simply addressed by answering three questions:

  1 Which ILO did the pupils achieve/not achieve? (What did they learn/not learn?)
  2 What aspects of my teaching enabled or were not helpful in promoting learning? (Why did learning take place or not?)
  3 What implications have points 1 and 2 for my plans for next week, for ILOs and my teaching? This enables you to address the question: 'So, what do I do next lesson?'

Planning subsequent lessons

As anticipated above, planning subsequent lessons will depend on how far the pupils achieved the ILOs in the previous lessons and your diagnosis of changes that you can make in your teaching that should improve pupils' learning. Working from these two perspectives, you can identify whether or not you can make the ILOs more challenging and what teaching approach/methods and learning activities you might adopt to promote learning. It might be useful to look through the section on principles of good planning above to check if attention to any of these principles would be valuable. While it is the case that all teachers can make improvements in their teaching, it is also the case that there could well be some aspects of your teaching that were particularly effective – for example, the use of pupil names – and these you should be sure to use again!

Assessing pupil learning and evaluating your own teaching are critical elements of your learning to plan lessons and promote learning. Learning through self-reflection is a fundamental professional skill for all teachers. Now complete Task 3.7.

Task 3.7 Evaluating a lesson

Deliver and evaluate the lesson you have been constructing throughout this chapter. Compile a lesson observation focusing only on the effective achievement of ILOs by the range of pupils in the class (you may want to identify one or several pupils working above/beyond; most; and below for the observer to focus on throughout the lesson). Ask your tutor to observe the lesson and complete this form.

Table 3.1 below gives examples of evaluation in relation to the differentiated ILOs that have been used as an example throughout this chapter.

Discuss your joint findings in terms of the opportunity for pupils to achieve ILOs and the effectiveness of your planning to cater for the learning of a range of pupils. Store the findings in your PDP to help inform later planning activities.

The next part of the chapter considers units of work and how your individual lessons are planned as part of a unit.

Table 3.1 Lesson evaluation: focus on pupil progress

Planned ILO from lesson plan	• Demonstrate the accurate placement of an overhead shot in badminton • Analyse the accuracy of their partner when in a game situation
Working above/ beyond	• Demonstrate consistent accuracy with power when performing an overhead clear • Analyse how accuracy of their partner's shot is used strategically in a game
	○ *Consistent shot placement by three of the four most able pupils. Responded well to sending shuttle to a specific target* ○ *Able to read the shot and specify where shot would land at point of contact*
Most pupils	• Demonstrate the accurate placement of an overhead shot in badminton • Analyse the accuracy of their partner when in a game situation
	○ *Technique evident and timing accurate for eight of ten pupils in this group* ○ *Pupils were able to recognise when the overhead shot was used and whether it was effectively executed*
Working below	• Demonstrate basic accuracy in an overhead clear • Analyse when their partner uses the shot
	○ *Consistent contact made with shuttle and many of the overhead shots demonstrated height and length* ○ *All pupils in this group (six) were able to note on a whiteboard when an overhead shot was made by their partner*

Planning units of work

A series of individual progressive lessons combine together in a unit of work. A unit is a medium-term plan which outlines expected learning for pupils within a year group over a specified period of time. Units can be one term in length (about 12 weeks), although they may be shorter (between six and ten weeks). The objectives identified for the unit should be commensurate with the length of the unit and, in turn, these should be a significant factor in considering the ILOs for the lessons you plan within the unit of work.

It is likely that your HEI or placement school will provide you with a pro-forma for a unit of work; however, there is an exemplar available on the companion website to use or compare to those you are given (www.routledge.com/cw/capel**).**

Initially, the thought of having to plan a whole unit of work may seem a little daunting. However, if you work systematically to a structure and plan step by step, you should find that it is not as difficult as it might at first seem. Before you can begin to plan a unit of work for a specific group you need to record some important background information. A simple formula for planning a unit of work might go in this order:

- From which scheme of work does the unit arise?
- Who am I teaching? (information about pupils)
- What am I teaching? (activity and material)
- What are the objectives I want the pupils to achieve in the range of curriculum requirements? (These are developed from the aims of the scheme of work into which the unit of work fits: see below.)
- How can I teach it? (learning activities, teaching strategies and organisation)

As a reminder, the needs of the pupils you are teaching are most important in your planning and they must have first consideration; the activity or material is simply the vehicle through which learning takes place. At the very heart of effective planning is taking into account the prior learning and experience of the group with whom you are working. Unless planning for the next phase of learning is based on the outcomes of previous assessments of the group/individuals, it is difficult to ensure challenge and development through continuity and progression in learning. If you are teaching the group for the first time you may need to consult a range of sources, such as assessment outcomes from previous units of work followed by the class, annual reports on the pupils or informal records kept by the teacher in their register or teacher planner. These all allow you to pitch the learning experiences appropriately and to take account of both whole-group and individual learning needs.

Once you have the information about the scheme of work and the pupils and know what the activity is, then you can begin planning by setting your objectives. Throughout each individual unit of work it is important that you plan objectives related to the total requirements of the curriculum framework and do not focus on one (often on developing motor skills). By planning the objectives of the unit of work first, you have a good idea what the outcome should be at the end of the unit and think about the ILOs you want to achieve to work towards that objective through the length of the unit of work. This forms the basis for development over the unit of work. Thus, you start by planning what you want to achieve by the end of the unit of work, first. Now complete Tasks 3.8–3.10.

Task 3.8 Analysis of a unit of work

Ask your tutor for a copy of a unit of work which has already been used in the school. How is it structured? Is the link to the scheme of work clear? Does it contain clear information about pupils; the activity and material; clear objectives which can be broken down into lesson ILOs; and how the material can be taught? Discuss the unit of work and the analysis with another student teacher who has considered another unit of work. Store your findings in your PDP for reference when you are writing units of work.

Task 3.9 Shaping learning

In many cases the first lesson in a unit of work will be the same for different classes, hence it is likely that it is only after the first lesson that differences in lesson planning and ILOs will be evident. In light of this, observe the second lesson in the same unit of work for two different classes at KS3 taught by the same experienced member of staff and identify differences in the ILOs, the content, learning progressions, teaching activities, extension/intervention strategies and assessment according to the group/individuals they are teaching. After the lessons, discuss with the teacher:

(continued)

Task 3.9 *(continued)*

- the progress of pupils against the ILOs;
- how this will impact on the lesson planning and the ILOs for the next lesson in the sequence for the different groups.

These focused observations can be added to your PDP for future reference.

Task 3.10 Reflecting on a unit of work

Reflecting on a unit of work you have taught in your placement school, consider how the evidence acquired (through, for example, assessment outcomes and evaluations) from lessons taught during the first half of the unit has been used to inform pupils learning in the second half of the unit. Ensure you use all the evaluation and assessment evidence developed to conduct this reflection. Store this information in your PDP as evidence of Masters level work.

A general framework for planning schemes of work

Although you are unlikely to be involved with developing schemes of work on school placement, it is important to understand the broader picture they represent so you can see where the units of work and lessons you plan and teach fit in. Well-planned schemes of work are long-term curriculum-planning documents which are used to outline expectations for learning across a period of time, for example, a KS or year. They form the basis for planning units of work. Thus, an understanding of the mechanics of effective long-term curriculum planning should help you to understand the relationship of long-term planning with medium- and short-term planning of units of work and lessons.

Schemes of work need to provide a range of opportunities for breadth and balance of experience to enable the requirements of the curriculum framework in which you are working to be met. Careful attention should be paid to how progression and continuity are planned for across years and within and between KSs. Thus, to achieve progression and continuity, increasing demands and expectations are placed on pupils. These can be broken down into four aspects:

1   a gradual increase in the complexity of the sequence of movement;
2   an improvement in the demonstrated performance qualities;
3   greater independence in the learning context;
4   a gradual challenge to the level of cognitive skills required.

These can be tracked through assessment of pupils.

Task 3.11 enables you to look in detail at some schemes of work.

Task 3.11 Schemes of work

Obtain a copy of the schemes of work for one KS in your placement school. Compare these with those obtained by another student teacher in another school. Discuss with your tutor the coverage of the requirements of the curriculum (e.g. NCPE) for this KS.

Store the information in your PDP to refer to when you are developing a unit of work from one scheme of work or, later, when you start your teaching career and you are writing your own schemes of work.

Summary and key points

The priority placed on planning in your development as a teacher is no accident; rather, it is a firm intent to prioritise the need to recognise the responsibility you have as a teacher for the learning and progress of each pupil. The chapter has prioritised the need to know your pupils and build learning on established knowledge of their prior attainment. It has considered in detail short-term planning of individual lessons, then sequences of lessons which fit into medium-term planning of units of work. It has also focused on the relationship between planning in the short, medium and long term.

When faced with planning PE learning and teaching experiences for the first time, it is natural to want to rely on your own previous experiences and the advice and guidance of those you view as more experienced. Whilst it is important to take account of both of these, you should avoid passively planning to match what and how you were taught at school or implementing ideas absorbed from other sources without critiquing their origins and how they relate to your ILOs, objectives and aims.

Effective planning requires you to be proactive, flexible and both critically aware and evaluative in order to provide appropriate learning opportunities for all your pupils, thus moving their learning forward. As a teacher, you are central to the process of promoting change and development in pupils' learning. The emphasis placed on a reflective approach through the cyclical process of planning, teaching, assessing and evaluating helps to reinforce the need for criticality which is important for enhancing both pupils' learning and your teaching. Reflection should challenge your expectations and existing practice and presents creative alternatives within the planning process.

As you extend your experience, the opportunity to reflect enables you to explore your own attitudes, values and beliefs which, according to Gibbs (1988), play a significant part in the development of professional skills, such as planning and evaluating for pupil progress (Chapter 16 looks at beliefs in more detail).

Check which requirements of your ITE you have addressed through this chapter.

Further reading

Anderson, L.W., Krathwohl, D.R., Airasian, P.W., Cruikshank, K.A., Mayer, R.R., Pintrich, P.R., Raths, J. and Wittrock, M.C. (eds) (2001) *A Taxonomy for Learning, Teaching and Assessing: A Revision of Bloom's Taxonomy of Educational Objectives*, complete edition, New York: Longman.

Formulating effective and differentiated ILOs is a skill which requires practise, reflection and feedback. This revised consideration of Bloom's taxonomy (Bloom *et al.* 1956) helps develop understanding of the most effective way to build confidence with language appropriate to building learning outcomes based upon attainment levels.

Capel, S., Leask, M. and Turner, T. (eds) (2013) *Learning to Teach in the Secondary School: A Companion to School Experience*, 6th edn, Abingdon, Oxon: Routledge.

This book introduces the professional knowledge, skills and understanding required by teachers, including principles of effective planning and teaching.

Cohen, L., Manion, L. and Morrison, K. (2004) *A Guide to Teaching Practice*, 5th edn, London: RoutledgeFalmer.

This book is a comprehensive consideration of teaching and learning with a specific focus on planning.

Grout, H. and Long, G. (2009) *Improving Teaching and Learning in Physical Education*, Maidenhead, Berks: Open University Press.

This book, designed for student PE teachers, focuses on the 'real' PE lessons they plan and teach. It is a very practical book about the core business of teaching PE.

McGregor, D. and Cartwright, L. (2011) *Developing Reflective Practice: A Guide for Beginning Teachers*. Maidenhead, Berks: Open University Press.

Reflective practice is fundamental to a teacher's professional development. This book is well suited to supporting reflective practice during your student teaching and early years as a teacher.

Additional resources for this chapter are available on the companion website: www.routledge.com/cw/capel.

Acknowledgement

The authors would like to thank Cathy Gower for her contribution to earlier versions of this chapter in previous editions of the book.

4 Observation in PE

Maggie Killingbeck and Margaret Whitehead

Introduction

Observation is at the heart of effective teaching of PE. It is an essential skill for you to develop if you are to promote learning. Observation enables you to see how the pupils are responding to your teaching and provides you with the information on which to base your feedback and guidance. Observation as a skill develops with experience but crucially depends on your knowledge and understanding both of the material which pupils are exploring and of the nature of the pupils themselves. Observation also gives you the information on which you can base your next lesson, information needed to record pupil progress and information concerning the effectiveness of your teaching.

Objectives

At the end of this chapter you should be able to:

- understand the importance of observation;
- understand why observation is essential to effect learning;
- appreciate that effective observation depends on knowledge and understanding of the nature of the material which pupils are exploring and the basic principles of movement;
- understand what other influences there might be that affect your observation.

Check the requirements of your initial teacher education (ITE) to see which relate to this chapter.

The importance of observation

Observation is a fundamental and essential skill for those teaching PE. Observation permeates all teaching in respect of the establishment of an orderly and safe environment and in relation to promoting learning to achieve your short-term and long-term aims (see later in this chapter and Chapter 16 for a discussion of teachers' long-term aims and beliefs).

Observation in lesson organisation, management and safety

It is very important that at all times you are alert to pupil activity in respect of on-task and off-task behaviour and the safety aspects of the lesson. While effective planning should ensure that these aspects of your teaching have been thought through carefully, it is your 'in-lesson' observation that will confirm all is going well. Without effective class management in a safe environment it is unlikely that you will be able to promote learning. Chapter 6 looks in detail at lesson organisation and management and Chapter 11 considers safety issues.

On account of the importance of observation in respect of organisation and management, it is recommended that you use the following strategies:

1   Be sure you position yourself at all times so that you can readily observe the whole class.
2   Before you begin to observe learning, check that your organisational instructions have been followed – particularly in relation to all aspects of safety, such as use of space and the correct assembly of apparatus and equipment.
3   As the lesson proceeds take time to stand back periodically and observe the class. This will give you essential information about whether your instructions, particularly in relation to safety, are being followed and if pupils are on task. Problems concerned with inappropriate behaviour are best dealt with as they begin to appear, rather than waiting until the situation is out of hand.

Task 4.1 asks you to gather information from an observer about how often you stood back to observe the class and what action you took as a result of this observation.

Task 4.1 Observation of the whole class related to organisation and management

Ask your tutor or another student teacher to:

- observe a lesson you teach and record each time you stand back from the class to survey the pupils;
- note what action you took after this whole-class observation;
- note times when additional whole-class observation could have been valuable.

Discuss these findings with the tutor or student teacher and then repeat the exercise with another class. Put the notes relating to this task in your professional development portfolio (PDP).

Observation and the promotion of learning

Typically learning is achieved through interaction between the pupils and the teacher. As the teacher you will select the intended learning outcomes (ILOs) of the lesson, plan episodes for the lesson that will facilitate the achievement of the ILOs and then guide the pupils through these episodes.

As the pupils engage in the tasks set, your role as the teacher in promoting learning begins. Critical here is your observation of the movement responses of the class and of individual pupils: in other words, the information pupils are sending to you, as shown in their movement activity. Again it is very useful to stand back periodically to survey how the pupils are progressing in the task set. Information may indicate that the task is too easy or too hard or it may reveal that some pupils are having a particular difficulty. What the teacher sees will initiate action in one of a number of ways, as appropriate. For example, the teacher may:

- repeat the task;
- simplify the task;
- remind the class of a key feature of movement;
- make the task more challenging;
- move on to the next task;
- give individual guidance to a pupil;
- remind the class of the level of application to the task that is expected.

Task 4.2 asks you to discuss with another student teacher the nature of the information you would have gathered to take each of the above actions. For example, if it was clear that the pupils were bored on account of the task being too easy, you would introduce a more challenging task.

Task 4.2 Interaction between the teacher and the pupil

Working with another student teacher, discuss the nature of the information you would have gathered to initiate each of the above bullet point actions.
   Put your notes in your PDP.

All of the actions listed above are instrumental in promoting learning. Without this interaction between pupil response, teacher observation and teacher guidance, learning is unlikely to occur (see Chapter 5, which goes into more detail about the importance and nature of feedback to promote learning).

Knowledge and understanding that support effective observation and thus learning

The ability to see what is happening in a lesson is, of course, at the heart of effective observation. As mentioned above, it is a skill that develops over time. However, the ability to see with accuracy and clarity depends on the knowledge that the observer brings to a situation. To take an example away from the teaching situation, if an individual has no knowledge or understanding of the vast range of species and habits of butterflies, all an observer would be able to recognise would be that a particular butterfly was, for example, large and yellow. However, someone who had spent many years studying butterflies would recognise and be able to describe its distinctive features, maybe its wing formation or colour of its antennae, and might express surprise that it was feeding from a particular flower. In the physical activity context, if you were a rugby expert you would immediately notice an unusual formation or an effective execution of a particular technique. On the other hand, if you had never seen rugby being played you would have little to say about what you were seeing in relation to, for example, the interpretation of the rules or the range of techniques being called upon. Your knowledge and experience in an area of activity will not only enable you to see more clearly; it will provide you with a bank of information from which to draw to guide pupils and thus promote their learning.

Observation, language and learning

The knowledge you have in respect of what you are teaching not only gives you a wide and deep understanding of the activity being undertaken; it will, crucially, give you the language to describe to pupils which aspects of the activity or movement are being well performed and those that need further attention. The butterfly example above shows this quite clearly. The knowledgeable observer would have a wide vocabulary of words to describe the butterfly, its habitat, structure and behaviour. In contrast the novice is likely to have only a very restricted vocabulary to describe the attributes of the specimen. Teaching is based on communication between the teacher and the pupil and, without a sound vocabulary related to the task at hand, it will be all but impossible to promote learning. The four aspects of knowledge discussed below (Figure 4.1) will each provide you with a wealth of understanding that will facilitate observation, provide you with essential vocabulary and thus enable you to be more effective in promoting learning.

Types of knowledge that underpin effective observation

The four types of knowledge listed in Figure 4.1 can be seen as a series of layers. Layer 1, the outer ring, indicates that the first task for you is to understand the nature of the activity that you are teaching, i.e. those features of one activity that distinguish it from another activity. Layer 2 proposes that you need to be knowledgeable of the nature of the specific techniques that constitute the content of any particular activity. These are perhaps the first two areas for you to work on. Understanding of the two innermost layers is the next step to master. Layer 3 details components of the activities in layer 1 and layer 4 provides an analysis of the techniques set out in layer 2. As will be seen later, there are further ways in which these layers are related.

Task 4.3 asks you to use the example for hockey in Table 4.1 and select two further activities, identifying key words in relation to each knowledge layer.

Task 4.3 Identifying layers of understanding in different activities

To give you a general idea of the material in each of the layers, using the example given below in Table 4.1 for hockey, select two further activities, only one of which can be a competitive game, and add key words to Table 4.1 in relation to these activities. Store in your PDP.

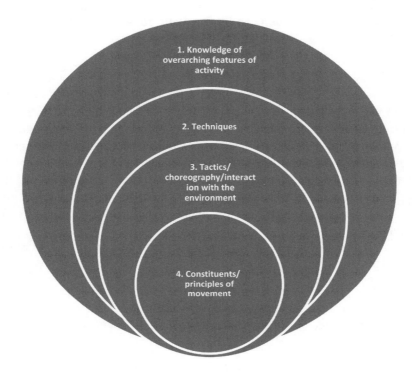

Figure 4.1 Knowledge and understanding required for effective observation.

Table 4.1 Identifying layers of knowledge and understanding

Layer	Hockey (two examples in each box)		
1 Overarching features/form and procedures	Invasion game of 11 a side Dangerous-hitting rule		
2 Techniques	Hitting Dribbling		
3 Tactics, choreographic/ interactive elements	Sudden change of speed Passing backwards		
4 Movement constituents	Controlled follow-through in the execution of a hit Ball kept close to the stick in dribbling		

Layer 1: Using your knowledge of the form and procedures of the activity/material being taught to inform your observation, language and teaching

Knowledge of the rules of any activity you teach is essential for you to plan and present work with authority. For example, you need to know procedures in athletics about what counts for a jump/throw or a no-jump/throw, rules in swimming about the way turns have to be executed and what constitutes an acceptable bowling action in cricket. You need to be confident of the current rules in any competitive game you teach. An up-to-date rules book in your pocket can be an asset. In this way you will recognise infringements and deal with them appropriately. Pupils are often exercised by what is/is not fair; good observation accompanied by a clear explanation will enhance your pupils' confidence in you. In addition, in some activities, such as trampolining and orienteering, there are safety rules to be followed; again you must be aware of these and take all steps to minimise risk (see Chapter 12 on safety).

Task 4.4 asks you to identify from your current timetable activities with which you are familiar and those with which you are less familiar, and consider strategies you could take to become better informed about the latter.

Task 4.4 Knowledge of the form and procedures of activities

Consider your current timetable and list activities: (1) about which you are confident regarding form and procedures; and (2) about which you know less and need to become better informed.

Identify strategies that will enable you to become more familiar with those activities listed under (2) above. Discuss these strategies with your tutor.

Put these lists in your PDP and revisit the list every time your timetable changes.

Layer 2: Using knowledge of the breakdown of a technique as essential to inform your observation, language and learning

In your own learning with teachers and coaches it is likely that you have been working with practitioners who have a good grasp of the techniques they are teaching, thus enabling them to have a clear understanding of the nature of these movement patterns. This type of knowledge is essential for your planning, effective observation and feedback. In this chapter we use the notion of technique to describe the movement pattern in isolation from a game/dance/sequence or context of an activity. When these techniques are applied within an activity we refer to them as movement skills.

Using the example of an overarm throw from a deep fielder to the wicket keeper in cricket, the following is a simple example of the knowledge that is desirable to have before teaching a technique. The throw should start with a run-up, which leads into the adoption of a wide base with feet planted sideways to the direction of the throw, with the opposite foot forward to the throwing arm. This is followed by taking the throwing arm back, the transference of weight from the back foot to the front foot, followed by the whipping-through of the throwing arm and then the release of the ball. After the release there is a follow-through of the arm.

The level of detail in technique analysis with which you should be familiar will depend on the expertise of the pupils in the group. Set out below in Table 4.2 is a slightly more complex analysis that would be appropriate for pupils beyond a beginner stage. This is presented in the form of three phases of technique: preparation, action and recovery. The preparation is that part of the technique where the mover prepares to execute the throwing action. This is followed by the action that propels the ball away from the mover. Once the ball has been thrown the technique is completed by a final rebalancing recovery stage. This way of analysing a technique can be very valuable to guide your selection of ILOs, planning, task setting, observation and feedback. More specifically, it can provide you with the teaching points you need to pinpoint key aspects of a technique to observe. It is very valuable for you to create a grid such as that in Table 4.2 before you teach a particular technique. Further examples of technique analysis can be found on the companion website (www.routledge.com/cw/capel).

Task 4.5 asks you to create an analysis grid in the form of Table 4.2 with reference to a technique other than the overarm throw, and Task 4.6 asks you to observe pupils working on techniques and consider the nature of the supportive feedback you might give them.

Task 4.5 Creating an analysis grid

Create an analysis grid in the form of Table 4.2 with reference to a technique other than the overarm throw. Discuss your analysis with your tutor and put it in your PDP.

Table 4.2 Preparation, action, recovery: analysis of the overarm throw

Overarm throw from a deep fielder to the wicket keeper in cricket	
Preparation	Preparation for the throw should comprise a run-up, which leads into the adoption of a wide base, with feet planted sideways to the direction of the throw with the opposite foot forward to the throwing arm. The shoulders should be open so that the body is also sideways in relation to the intended direction of the throw, with the weight over the back foot.
Action	The action phase commences with the transference of weight successively through the body, starting from the back foot, through the hips into the shoulders. The arm is taken back behind the torso and as the weight is transferred there is the whipping action through of the arm and the release of the ball at the optimum angle, ideally 45 degrees from the shoulder if thrown for best distance. The non-throwing arm is used to balance the body.
Recovery	Recovery involves the continuation of weight transference in a forward direction where the trailing leg comes forward to 'catch' the momentum and to stop the body falling forwards. The upper body usually bends forwards to absorb the force from the throwing arm. After the release there is a follow-through of the arm. The recovery phase is completed as the mover takes action to regain balance and stability.

Task 4.6 Observation of techniques

Create an analysis grid in the form of Table 4.2 with reference to a technique other than the overarm throw. Discuss your analysis with your tutor and put it in your PDP.

1   In a class taught by another teacher, observe one pupil who is performing a technique with minimal success. Identify and record one or two teaching points that could help to correct the error.
2   Observe a class learning a technique that is being taught by another teacher. Identify an error common to all or most of the group. Identify and record one or two teaching points that could help to correct the error.

Discuss your observations with your tutor and put the notes into your PDP.

Layer 3: Knowledge and understanding of tactics/choreography/ interaction with the environment to inform your observation, language and learning

This layer builds principally from layer 1 as it details components of the activities in the outer layer, such as strategies and tactics within a game, choreographic forms related to dance and environmental features in outdoor activities.

For example, in a competitive team game such as tennis singles, a valuable tactic is to return the ball into an area of the court as far as possible from the current position of the opposing player. This requires shot selection and pupils need to be alert to the position of the opponent in the court space before executing, for example, a drop shot or a lob.

In dance, choreographic skills are required to generate motifs. As a PE teacher you will need to be able to help pupils select the appropriate techniques to create movement/dance motifs that express their dance intention with an element of originality. Your knowledge and understanding of choreography and choreographic devices will enable you to observe and guide your pupils to achieve a satisfying and creditable product.

In water sports there are likely to be constantly changing environmental features, such as wind, water depth and obstacles in the water. Here you need to be aware of how pupils can apply techniques to perform the skills to accommodate these challenges.

As you can see from the examples above, layer 3 provides further challenges to the execution of techniques and is thus also related to layer 2. Once the pupils have a reasonable grasp of the techniques of an activity, you will be moving them on to the next challenge of applying these techniques in the context of an activity. These applied techniques can now be described as movement skills in that they have to be modified in relation to the demands of the activity. Your knowledge of the elements of an activity will enable you firstly to observe how far the pupils are successful in applying techniques and secondly to provide appropriate guidance.

Task 4.7 asks you to watch an experienced teacher and note down observation and feedback given in respect of this layer of knowledge.

Task 4.7 Teachers' observation and guidance regarding tactics, choreography or interaction with the environment

Watch an experienced secondary PE teacher. Depending on the activity being taught: (1) identify aspects of tactical, choreographic or interactive challenges referred to in the lesson; and (2) note instances of teacher feedback to the pupils relating to these, and note the impact this feedback had on the pupils.

After the lesson, discuss your notes with the teacher, particularly the observations that initiated the feedback. Ask the teacher to observe you in a lesson and record your references to situational differences and demands. Again, discuss this lesson with the teacher and put all these notes in your PDP.

Layer 4: Knowledge and understanding of constituents of movement to inform your observation, language and learning

Layer 4 is most readily seen as a development from layer 2 in that it provides you with detailed analysis of the constituent aspects of movement that together make up a technique.

While there are a number of approaches to analysing movement, such as from biomechanical or anatomical perspectives, one of the most useful approaches is that created by Rudolf Laban (see Killingbeck 2012). Laban's approach generates what are known as principles of movement. These identify four key aspects of movement.

The first aspect relates to what action the whole body and body parts should perform within a technique. For example, actions of the whole body or parts of the body could be that of travelling, turning, jumping, contracting, extending or being held still. Transference of weight may be a critical component in the technique. The role of particular body parts or the shape of the body might be significant.

The second aspect looks at whether the positioning of the body in space or the spatial relationships between the body parts themselves are critical in the execution of the technique. For example, is the level on which the movement is being carried out a key feature? Are either the shape of the travelling pathway taken by the mover or the pathway through space taken by the arm(s) or the leg(s) critical?

The third aspect considers the dynamics of the movement or how the technique is performed. For example, is speed, acceleration or deceleration key to the movement? How much force needs to be produced for the technique to be effective? Should movement be flowing or carefully controlled so that it can be stopped at any time?

The fourth aspect is concerned with the essential relational aspects of the technique. For example what should be the relationship between the mover and the ball/shuttlecock/ribbon? Where should the mover be positioned in the court at each stage of the game? What should be the spatial relationship between the players in a team game? What would be the ideal group shape in dance to convey a particular image/message?

Looking at movement in this way readily reveals the characteristic make-up of any movement. Taking the example of putting the shot, we can use Laban's principles to paint the following picture.

- What is the mover doing? The mover is standing balanced on two feet, shoulder length apart, with the shot in one hand held high up against the neck. From this position the arm is extended forwards to direct and release the shot.
- Where is the movement taking place? The movement of the arm follows a straight path forward and slightly upward, away from the neck.
- How is the movement performed? The movement uses maximum strength or force, particularly in the arm, as this part of the body is extended before releasing the shot. The force is also generated successively through the body from a firm base via the legs and the trunk to the shoulder and arm.
- In what relation is the body to other people and/or the environment? The original stance is sideways to the direction of the put and the put itself is directed into the designated area.

Task 4.8 asks you to carry out an analysis of two techniques using Laban's principles, following the approach used above for putting the shot.

Task 4.8 Analysing a movement using Laban's principles

Carry out this analysis for a leap from one foot to the other with the intention of covering as much ground as possible and then repeat it with a movement of your choice. Discuss your analyses with your tutor and keep them in your PDP.

Movement analysed: A leap from one foot to the other	
What?	
Where?	
How?	
Relationship	

Knowledge and understanding of Laban's analysis are extremely valuable in that this enables you to recognise aspects of the movement, and, very importantly, put into words what has been seen and what needs to be developed. Of particular significance is that the analysis provides you with teaching points for your planning and in-lesson observation. Having acquired this language, you will be able to provide specific detailed feedback. In so doing you will be able to individualise pupil guidance, identifying more or less challenging goals for pupils to ensure effective differentiation in your teaching. Indeed, it could be said that if you have not understood the movement components described above, you will be without some of the essential tools to promote learning. An analysis in this detail is of value in preparing to teach a technique or movement.

Whilst layer 4 clearly throws light on techniques in layer 2, it also provides an insight into ways in which skills need to be developed in the context of the tactical and choreographic areas of the activity – as spelled out in layer 3. It is the case that the knowledge and understanding in layer 4 relating to movement constituents go right to the heart of teaching in a movement context. The constituents of movement identified here are based on principles that are relevant to all movement, whatever the context.

The brief introduction above provides only a glimpse of the richness of Laban's analysis. A more detailed analysis is presented in Table 4.3 and further detail is given on the companion website (www.routledge.com/cw/capel).

Role of knowledge and understanding to inform your observation and language and thus pupils' learning

The section above has considered four layers of knowledge and understanding that will enhance your observation and therefore your teaching and pupil learning. All these layers are important, as without these layers of understanding you will not be able to recognise and describe features of the movement activity that you are teaching. Each in their own way is essential. Without awareness of the form and procedures of an activity you will not be able to recognise, for example, infringements of the rules or the roles of different players

Table 4.3 A basic outline of the content of Laban's analysis of movement

Aspect of movement	Examples of analyses
What is the body doing?	*The body and its parts* can bend/stretch/twist (fundamental to all movement) *Actions* of the whole body: Travel, e.g. run, dash, gallop, sprint Turn, e.g. pivot, spin, spiral, rotate Jump, e.g. skip, leap, vault, bound (five varieties of footwork) Gesture, e.g. contract, extend, spiral, arch Transfer the weight of the body, e.g. roll, cartwheel, fall, slide Hold still, e.g. stop, freeze, balance, halt *Body parts* can lead a movement, be used in isolation from the rest of the body, be used simultaneously or successively *Body shape* may need to be narrow, wide, twisted, symmetrical or asymmetrical
Where is the body moving?	General space/personal space Size of movements Levels: low, medium, high Shape in space: curved/straight Directions: up/down, forward/backward, right/left
How is the body moving?	Time: slow/sustained/lingering; fast/sudden/rapid/quick; accelerating/ decelerating Weight/tension: strong/firm/maximum tension; light/soft/fine/minimal tension; relaxed/no tension In space: direct/piercing/focused; multidirectional/flexible/unfocused Flow: bound/restrained/stoppable; free/unrestrained/ongoing
In what relationship is the body to others and to the environment?	Relating to the space: floor; walls; pitch; arena; court; stage Relating to objects: balls; hoops; goals; weights; benches; mats; horse; climbing frame Relating to people: positioning in relation to a partner/team members/ opposing team members

See the companion website (www.routledge.com/cw/capel) for more details of Table 4.3, particularly in relation to dance.

in a game. Without awareness of the effective performance of the techniques involved in an activity you will be hard pressed to see where pupils need help to improve their performance. Without an awareness of the tactical, choreographic or environmental contexts of activities you will not be alert to situations in which pupils are having problems in applying their techniques in a particular situation. Without a grasp of the constituents of movement out of which all techniques are created you will not be able to pick out specific strengths or weaknesses in movement and give appropriate guidance.

It is a daunting challenge to develop the range of knowledge suggested above, and it is not expected that you will have mastered all layers until you are well into your teaching career. The layers offer you the possibility of drilling down/probing/analysing in increasing detail to inform the content of your ILOs, your observation and your feedback. The layers provide the substance of your teaching points, the incremental nature of which enables you to meet the needs of all pupils and facilitate the achievement of high-quality outcomes as appropriate to each pupil. Initially it might be helpful for you to separate the layers. Layers 1 and 3 require you to become familiar firstly with the overall forms and then the more specific elements of an activity and thus conduct lessons with a sound understanding of the significant features of an activity. Layers 2 and 4 are related, with layer 4 going into more detail than layer 2. A logical approach here is to start with skill analysis in layer 2 and then to move on to movement analysis, as set out in layer 4. However, the layers are mutually informative. As such, as an experienced teacher you may move between the layers in a more flexible manner. For example, you may note that a tactic is breaking down as a result of a loss of group formation, inappropriate timing or the need for greater disguise. In this case layer 4 informs the teaching points related to layer 3. Figure 4.2 provides a diagrammatic representation of the complexity of the relationships between the layers.

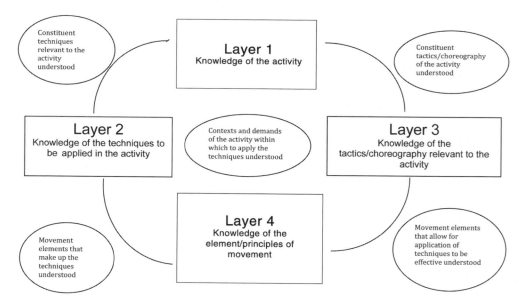

Figure 4.2 Diagrammatic representation of the relationship between the knowledge layers.

Knowledge and understanding as underpinning planning as well as observation

Knowledge, planning and observation are closely related in teaching. The material discussed above in all four layers is likely to be the backdrop to your lesson planning in respect of identifying ILOs and teaching points. The key task of lesson observation is to monitor progress, selecting and using your teaching points to enable all pupils to achieve the ILOs. Teaching points are the bridge between planning and observation, as they identify to what you will direct your attention and give guidance. It is sound advice as you start to teach to observe one teaching point at a time, giving class feedback on this point before moving on to another teaching point.

It is useful at this stage to make two further brief points. The first relates to using pupils working in pairs to observe and give feedback to each other. In adopting peer teaching, as explained in Chapter 5, where pupils work together to improve, for example, a tactic or a technique, it is well to remember that observation is a very challenging aspect of teaching and that pupils will need considerable guidance and practise before they can carry out these tasks effectively.

The second relates to observation of ILOs that work towards whole-school aims. There will be situations in PE when you will be expected to promote whole-school aims such as developing pupil independence, social skills or communication skills. It is important to remember that in these situations these ILOs should be the focus of observation and feedback. For example, if cooperation, leadership or creativity is identified as an ILO, it is essential that you observe and give feedback on the progress pupils are making in this particular aspect of the lesson. You need to suspend attention purely on movement and look at pupil behaviour in line with these broader aspirations of PE. Task 4.9 asks you to note down teacher feedback in relation to ILOs that are not directly associated with movement performance.

Task 4.9 Observation and teaching points for non-movement ILOs

Observe a games or outdoor and adventurous activities lesson taught by an experienced teacher in which cooperative learning is an ILO. List the teaching points made by the teacher in an attempt to facilitate/develop cooperation. Ask the teacher what pupil behaviour triggered the feedback you identified. Keep a note of the observations that gave rise to the listed teaching points and comment on their effectiveness. Keep these notes in your PDP.

Further knowledge and understanding that will inform your observation

While the principal focus of your observation will be on an understanding of the nature of the physical activity you are teaching and its constituent techniques, your ability to observe perceptively with precision and empathy can be affected by other areas of your experience and knowledge. For example, an indepth knowledge of biomechanics, psychology or sociology may enable you to be particularly sensitive to aspects of pupils' work. A sound knowledge of the pupils as individuals can also help you to pick up valuable key information. Finally, it is as well to realise that your personal aims of PE and beliefs may also affect your observation.

Applying biomechanical, psychological and sociological knowledge to your observation

Knowledge of biomechanics can make a very valuable contribution to your observation of techniques and of movement. For example, an awareness of the influence of the location of the centre of gravity in attaining a balance or the importance of a stable base from which to generate power will help you to observe why a skill is being more or less successful. A sound knowledge of the psychology of learning will alert you to possibilities such as pupils who have a short attention span or those whose lack of motivation is impeding progress. An understanding of the sociology of interpersonal relationships will alert you to pupils who appear to find it difficult to relate to others or who make cooperative group work a problem. In these last two cases it may well be that it is the learner's overall behaviour as well as the movement response that is indicating that all is not well. The observation of pupil behaviour in the form of non-verbal communication is an important aspect of your 'reading the class'. Examples of books focusing on biomechanics, psychology and sociology are included in the further reading for this chapter.

Task 4.10 asks you to video/film an experienced teacher and to view part of this lesson from a particular knowledge base such as biomechanics, psychology or sociology.

Task 4.10 The value of drawing on knowledge of biomechanics, psychology or sociology in observation in PE

Seek permission to record a lesson taught by an experienced teacher. After the lesson, watch for ten minutes, without the sound, adopting the perspective of one of the disciplines mentioned above. Note down how knowledge of this discipline helped you to observe with particular clarity.

Watch the filmed episode again with the sound on and note any instances of the teacher's observation that show use of any of the disciplines mentioned above.

Discuss your observations with the teacher and put the notes from this exercise in your PDP.

Observing pupils as individuals

Although all pupils are broadly on the same journey in respect of physical, cognitive and social development, they will all be at a different stage and will have their own personal characteristics. You need to be aware of these differences in your observation. For example, a very shy and apprehensive pupil, a pupil with low self-esteem or confidence, a pupil going through a rapid growth spurt or a pupil who is recovering from injury will all need to be monitored carefully and given particular feedback (see Chapter 11 for more on confidence and self-esteem). An appreciation of individual differences and particular needs should play a part in your observation of pupils and in how you respond appropriately to their work. It is reassuring to note that most schools will be able to provide guidance to help you respond appropriately to particular physical, cognitive or social needs that pupils in your lessons may exhibit (see Chapter 10 for more on inclusion).

Task 4.11 asks you to watch an experienced teacher and identify feedback specific to individual pupils.

> ### Task 4.11 Identification of observation and subsequent feedback to individual pupils
>
> Observe a lesson taught by an experienced teacher and record instances when feedback was provided that demonstrated the teacher's knowledge and understanding of the needs of individual pupils. Discuss your observation with the teacher after the lesson to ascertain the information on which the teacher's observation was grounded. Put a record of this discussion in your PDP as evidence of Masters level work.

Your personal beliefs and how these can influence your observation

As a teacher of PE you need to be aware that your personal frame of reference can influence observation. It is salutary to reflect that personal experience, knowledge and beliefs colour what we see and how we interpret this information. For example, a priest, an estate agent and a farmer are very likely to view a particularly beautiful area of the natural world differently (Best 1985).

Indeed, it is also worth querying what you do not notice (Sanders 2012)! If you are a teacher for whom winning is all, you will observe differently from a colleague for whom inclusivity is a priority. It is salutary to consider the stance that you are taking when you observe in PE. Realising this stance and the effect this has on your observation may surprise you. Carry out the following task to begin to understand the effect of different stances and to get a sense of your own particular stance.

Task 4.12 asks you to watch a filmed episode of ten minutes of a lesson taught by another teacher or student teacher to help you to be aware how particular perspectives can affect your observation.

> ### Task 4.12 Observation of pupils from different frames of reference
>
> Watch a filmed episode of ten minutes of a secondary PE lesson a number of times (this can be a lesson you have taught or one taught by another teacher or student teacher). Each time you watch, do so from a different perspective, as listed below. As you watch, make a note of your observations.
>
> *(continued)*

Task 4.12 *(continued)*

You are:

- ambitious for good examination results;
- concerned for your pupils with special educational needs;
- anxious about discipline;
- determined to challenge all pupils;
- eager to ensure that pupils enjoy the lesson.

It would be useful for another student teacher to carry out the same task, observing the same filmed episode, independently of you. After viewing, discuss together what you noted in respect of the outcome of observing from different perspectives. Consider from which perspective you felt most comfortable in your observation, and why, write a 2,000-word account on the experience of carrying out this task. Store this in your PDP as evidence of Masters level work.

Observation in reporting and recording

While observation is generally undertaken in a lesson so that you can respond immediately to give pupils support, there will be occasions when you will be expected to gather information via observation to complete an assessment or a report (see Chapter 9 on assessment). This might be for writing an annual report, making judgements in an examination situation or for monitoring standards generally in the department or school.

In these cases the focus of the observation will have been provided in the form of criteria and it is your job to observe objectively what is required. Working alongside another colleague is useful in these situations so that preconceptions of pupil ability do not colour judgement on pupil performance. It is all too easy to see only what you expect (Child 2007: 160).

Using observation in lesson evaluation to monitor the effectiveness of your own teaching

While the focus of this chapter has been on observing pupils in the teaching situation, your observation throughout the lesson can provide you with the material to complete your lesson evaluation and to make judgements about the effectiveness of your overall teaching.

For example, you could ask yourself some of the following questions.
In respect of organisation:

- Was the way I organised the space appropriate?
- Did the pupils have enough space to work safely?
- Did I have enough apparatus and equipment of the correct size/weight that the pupils knew how to use?
- Did pupil behaviour indicate that appropriate rules and routines have been established and standards of behaviour have been clearly set out?

In respect of your planning of ILOs and tasks:

- Were the ILOs an appropriate challenge or were they too easy or too hard?
- Were the tasks I set appropriate to help the pupils achieve the ILOs?
- Did my teaching points enable the pupils to make progress?
- Do I need to do more work on movement analysis?
- Was the teaching approach I used effective in promoting the achievement of the ILOs?
- Was the grouping of pupils effective?
- Did I give pupils too much or too little opportunity to make their own decisions?

By 'reading' the class in these ways you can pick up how effective your teaching and planning were and, of course, set yourself goals to improve aspects of your work. These observations should feature in your lesson evaluation (see Chapter 3). Constructive self-criticism is the platform from which improvement takes place and observation provides you with the information for this development in the short term and the long term.

Task 4.13 asks you to reflect on your lessons to identify priorities for your development.

Task 4.13 Learning about your teaching from reflecting on observations during lessons
After teaching a lesson ask yourself the questions above and identify three aspects of your teaching that you feel are priorities in your development. A video or filmed recording of the lesson would be helpful. After more than a week, ask your tutor to observe a lesson you are teaching focusing on the three goals you identified. Discuss with your tutor how far you have made progress. Keep these notes in your PDP as evidence of Masters level work.

Summary and key points

This chapter has looked widely at issues concerned with observation in teaching PE. The underlying importance of observation with respect to lesson organisation and management, learning and language development were outlined. The suggestion that effective observation depended to a great extent on the knowledge that you bring to the lesson was then discussed in detail. This was presented as comprising four layers that cover both the structure and form of activities being taught and the nature and constituents of movement. Additional areas of knowledge that are valuable were identified, such as that from biomechanics, psychology and sociology. To this list was added the need to know each pupil as an individual and to be aware how your own personal beliefs about PE can affect your observation. The skill of observing in PE is as important as it is challenging. It is challenging as your pupils are distributed over a large area and are seldom still. It is important as observation, and the feedback it generates, is at the heart of promoting learning. Observation warrants very serious consideration and is a fundamental skill for teachers of PE.

Check which requirements of your ITE you have addressed through this chapter.

Further reading

Gallahue, D.L. and Donnelly, F.C. (2003) *Developmental Physical Education for All Children*, 4th edn, Champaign, IL: Human Kinetics.

Chapter 16 'Movement skill development through movement concept learning' reinforces the value of Laban's analysis of movement for the PE teacher. In particular, Laban's analysis is commended for its usefulness in providing a language with which to identify and articulate/discuss movement. In addition there is recognition of the potential of the analysis to provide pupils with a tool kit that will enable them to take greater responsibility for their own learning.

Observing Children Moving (OCM) CDRom and Observing and Analysing Pupils' Movement (OALM) CDRom. See: The Movement Observation Series OCM and OALM at http://www.tacklesport. com/s/movement-observation/ (accessed 8 December 2014).

These two CDRoms are very useful resources for student teachers. Each includes over 70 video clips of children and young people performing a range of movement patterns from a wide range of activities. OCM looks at the younger pupil and OALM at the top primary and early secondary pupil. Both are extremely useful for practice observation, with shots taken from different camera angles. Tasks are set to challenge the viewer to describe what is observed, compare movements of different pupils and identify areas for development.

Sanders, L. (ed.) (2012) *Dance Teaching and Learning: Shaping Practice Youth Dance*, London: Youth Dance England.

Chapter 4 provides more detail regarding Laban's analysis of movement. Whilst the examples refer to dance, the additional detail concerning what, where, how and with whom/what is of value to all students of human movement.

The following books provide information about biomechanics, psychology and sociology:

Bartlett, R. (2014) *Introduction to Sports Biomechanics: Analysing Human Movement Patterns*, Abingdon, Oxon: Routledge.

Delaney, T. (2009) *The Sociology of Sports: An Introduction*, Jefferson, NC: McFarland.

Jones, R., Potrac, P., Cushion, C. and Ronglan, L. T. (2011) *The Sociology of Sports Coaching*, Abingdon, Oxon: Routledge.

Tod, D. (2014) *Sport Psychology: The Basics*, Abingdon, Oxon: Routledge

Watkins, J. (2014) *Fundamental Biomechanics of Sport and Exercise*, Abingdon, Oxon: Routledge.

Weinberg, R.S. and Gould, D. (2011) *Foundations of Sport and Exercise Psychology*, 5th edn, Champaign, IL: Human Kinetics.

Additional resources for this chapter are available on the companion website: www.routledge.com/cw/capel.

Acknowledgement

The authors would like to thank Elizabeth Marsden for some of the material included in this chapter, that was taken from the chapter in the third edition of the book.

5 Communication in PE

Paula Nadine Zwozdiak-Myers

Introduction

This chapter is concerned with effective communication in PE. Clearly, communication is crucial in all teaching. Without communication, teaching cannot take place and poor communication leads to confused/garbled and incomplete messages which result in inadequate learning.

Each subject makes specific communication demands. The PE teacher has to contend with a variety of contexts (classroom, gymnasium, sports hall, swimming pool, playing field), and must also recognise the intrinsically practical nature of the subject. Although good use of spoken language is essential, excessive talking is unforgivable because it can deny the pupil valuable activity time. Explanations and instructions should be succinct. You have almost certainly had the experience of listening to a teacher drone on when what you wanted to do was to get going on a physical activity. Pupil talk can also be used effectively in PE lessons to deepen and extend learning but, again, talk must not dominate in practical sessions where your objective is to get the class moving.

Like all subjects, PE has its own technical vocabulary and part of the pleasure of being an expert in a discipline is knowing subject-specific words and phrases and using them with other experts. Most pupils, however, are not experts and your teaching language must not confuse them. Of course, if you have General Certificate of Secondary Education (GCSE) or General Certificate of Education (GCE) Advanced (A) level classes, pupils will expect to hear subject-specific language, but with a year 7 group, you must use a way of speaking appropriate to their level of understanding. If you are going to include a technical term, it must be carefully explained or have an obvious meaning in context.

Objectives

At the end of this chapter you should be able to:

- understand the central role of communication in all teaching;
- have a good idea of the quality and flexibility of your voice;
- understand the role of teacher language in the teaching and learning of PE;

(continued)

(continued)

- understand the key role of questioning in PE lessons;
- understand the importance of teacher feedback to promote learning;
- understand the role of pupil language in PE lessons;
- have an increased awareness of modes of communication through which to convey messages;
- explore the use of demonstration to communicate effectively to promote pupil learning.

Check the requirements of your initial teacher education (ITE) to see which relate to this chapter.

The PE teacher's voice

As a PE teacher you need a good voice which can be adapted to a variety of settings, some of which are difficult and demanding. It is sensible to get to know what your voice sounds like by recording yourself talking on a dictaphone or tape recorder. Task 5.1 asks you to listen to your own voice.

Task 5.1 Evaluating your voice

Record yourself reading a piece of text in a natural voice or having an ordinary conversation with a friend. If you have not heard yourself on tape before, prepare for a shock. You may sound quite different from what you expect. Remember though that you hear your voice coming 'back' from your mouth whereas most people hear it coming 'forward'.

Listen to your voice positively and discover your strengths. Is the tone pleasant? Do you vary the pitch to give interest? Do you sound like a friendly individual?

Vary the recording context to include different spaces where you teach. How do you sound in the classroom? gym? sports hall? swimming pool? outside?

Note down what you perceive as the strengths and weaknesses in your voice, share these thoughts with your tutor and put these notes in your professional development portfolio (PDP).

When you have become accustomed to the sound of you speaking and have grown to like what you hear, think about ways in which you could vary your voice. You can experiment with the following elements of paralanguage:

- pitch
- speed
- pause

- stress
- volume
- enunciation.

Now complete Task 5.2.

Task 5.2 Voice variation

It is worthwhile practising voice variation. Use a tape recorder to explore pitch and speed variation. Read a passage from a book and use pause for effect. Add stress to highlight certain words or phrases. You will probably feel silly doing this but the practise is invaluable. It has been said that somebody who can tell a story well will make a good teacher. This may be an exaggerated claim, but certainly an expressive and flexible voice is a tremendous asset in teaching.

You should also use real lessons for voice practise. A radio microphone would be ideal but you could ask your tutor to concentrate on your use of voice during some lessons and to provide you with feedback. You want positive comments as well as suggestions for improvement.

Put your tutor comments in your PDP. It is useful to repeat this task later in your ITE, at which time you can refer back to these notes.

All of these variations have an effect on the pupils you teach. A high voice generates more excitement; a deep voice is calming and is useful when disciplining a class. Your normal voice can vary considerably in pitch without discomfort. A lower voice is usually better indoors whereas a higher tone will carry better outside.

Speed can give pace to a lesson, whereas a slow delivery has the opposite effect. If you are teaching gymnastics with a large class using apparatus in a small space, you may choose to speak slowly to create a safe, careful environment. A speedy delivery might be needed with a small group in a sports hall if you want to generate enthusiasm and evoke an energetic response.

Pause can be an effective strategy for teachers. Very often, instead of allowing a brief silence, a teacher uses a filler like 'er' or 'um'. One filler, much loved by PE teachers, is 'right', said with purpose and emphasis. There is nothing wrong with that but over-use of the same filler can be damaging. Pupils may concentrate on how many times you say 'right' and could ignore any important teaching points you make! Pause is also valuable as a gentle form of discipline. If you are talking to the class and a pupil is not listening, a pause in your delivery linked to a pointed look can bring the offender onside.

Stress is a useful tool because it is a way of highlighting important information. Stress must be used sparingly though. It is tiring to listen to somebody who is continually stressing words. Instructions about safety and key elements in a skill can be stressed so they stand out from the normal, more relaxed delivery. This 'baseline' voice should be audible, pleasant to listen to and unforced.

It is obviously vital that what a teacher says is audible and audibility is sometimes linked to volume. PE teachers have to cope with large spaces and classes outside where wind and traffic noise compete. A simplistic deduction suggests that you should shout or roar to be heard by your pupils. It is certainly helpful to have volume available if needed, but audibility is based on a number of factors. If you have a lot to say to your class, then they should be close to you, not dispersed. You should always position yourself so all the pupils are in front of you. It is very hard to hear somebody whose back is to you. In general, if you are behind somebody, audibility is reduced by 75 per cent.

Sometimes, even when pupils are gathered round, you have to gain silence by a loud 'quiet, please'. Once you have silence, the golden rule is not to shout into it. Moderate your voice and speak naturally to the class. You do not want to become the sort of PE teacher who *always* speaks loudly, even in social settings.

Enunciation is important for PE teachers. You should speak precisely so pupils can hear easily the words you speak. In ordinary conversation, careful enunciation is not normally necessary but when you are talking to a dispersed group of pupils in a large space, care is essential. In addition, some of your class may learn English as an Additional Language (EAL) or have Special Educational Needs and/or Disabilities (SEND), such as mild hearing loss, so you must ensure that no words are lost, otherwise your message may be confused or incomprehensible. (For more information on supporting pupils learning EAL, see Department for Education and Skills (DfES) 2002; National Association for Language Development in the Curriculum: www. naldic.org.uk; and the Physical Education Initial Teacher Training and Education (PEITTE) network via the Association for Physical Education website: www.afpe.org.uk.)

> If you do have to talk to a scattered class, you must first ensure that they are quiet and attentive. You then use good projection to make yourself heard by the pupils furthest from you. Projection involves careful enunciation and a concentration on reaching the remotest pupils by pushing the voice out with conviction. This sounds somewhat painful, but good projection becomes a habit and then it is easy to make even a whisper carry a long way.

It is important to recognise that how you use your voice reinforces the meaning behind the message you want to convey. Pupils often take more notice of how something is said rather than what is said. If you praise a pupil but deliver the praise in a flat, unenthusiastic way, the pupil will not be convinced you mean it. Equally, if you discipline someone, your voice should indicate firmness or displeasure at some unacceptable behaviour. To use your voice effectively, each element of paralanguage or non-verbal communication needs to be woven together sensitively like a finely tuned instrument (see Unit 3.1 (Zwozdiak-Myers and Capel) in Capel *et al.* 2013; Robertson 1996; Goldman 2004; Hastings 2006).

The technical language of PE

As with all disciplines, PE has its own specialist language. This language is invaluable because it helps experts in PE to communicate succinctly with each other. Part of the development of any discipline is this accumulation of subject-specific terminology.

PE teachers are familiar with the words and phrases of their subject, but their pupils may not have met the vocabulary before or may have only a hazy idea of what the various terms mean. These should be introduced gradually and explained or, better, exemplified in practical situations. If the class see a lay-up shot performed and labelled, they will have learnt the phrase and the meaning in the most effective way. Of course, many pupils need to have the learning reinforced by questions or repetitions. Carry out Task 5.3 to analyse technical vocabulary in an aspect of PE.

Task 5.3 Technical language

Select one activity which you are teaching (for example, cricket or gymnastics) and make a list of technical terms associated with that activity. Do not forget that you are an 'expert'. What seems to have an obvious meaning to you may well be much less obvious to a pupil in year 7 (for example, a straight drive or a headstand). When you have completed your list, which in both the activities cited would be very long, consider how you might explain some of the key terms to pupils. With a verbal description? By a demonstration? By use of a diagram? A chart? A video excerpt? Try this out in one of your lessons teaching this activity.

Reflect on the effect of your particular awareness of language in a lesson and put these notes in your PDP.

Specific forms of language use in the teaching of PE

This section reminds you that your use of voice will be influenced both by where you are teaching and what you are teaching. It also looks at questioning and feedback as specific forms of language use in PE.

PE covers a range of activities taught in a variety of contexts and each particular blend of activity and context should have an effect on your use of language. One of the simplest polarities is indoors/outdoors. If you are teaching a games lesson outside on a cold winter's morning, your instructions and explanations must be concise, in order for pupils to start moving as soon as possible, to keep warm throughout the lesson. It might even be advantageous to consider how much of your verbal input could be given in the changing rooms beforehand.

Some activities taught in PE (for example, swimming) are very skills-based and also potentially dangerous. The swimming pool is also a difficult setting acoustically. Language is likely to be command-style in tone and wording, associated with a strong motivational element – praise linked to skill acquisition.

Dance, on the other hand, is about creative movement, and the risk factor in a well-organised class is small. This does not mean that as a teacher you have a licence for verbosity but rather your language is likely to be more metaphorical and expressive, based on stimulating description and open questions to encourage diverse pupil responses to tasks given.

Questioning is a universal feature of teacher language in all disciplines. It also helps pupils to learn the subject-specific terminology of PE, develop their listening and thinking skills, and monitor their knowledge and understanding of key concepts, skills and processes.

Research has shown (Brown and Edmondson 1984) that teachers spend about 30 per cent of their time asking questions and ask about 400 questions a day. A majority of these will be checks on knowledge recall. For example:

- How many players are there in a volleyball team?
- What do we call a tennis shot made before the ball bounces?

In a PE lesson, the response to such a question could be linked to a pupil movement or demonstration. For example:

- Which part of the foot do you use to pass the ball?
- At what point do you release the discus?

All the questions quoted above are closed: there is only one correct answer, which the pupils should already have been taught. It is inappropriate to ask pupils closed questions on topics they have not covered.

There are other questions you can ask which demand more thought of the pupils. These are generally open questions. It is not sensible to make all the questions you ask searching ones because if you do, the pace of lessons will move slowly as pupils need time to prepare and deliver their responses. However, in one-to-one contexts and as pupils progress in PE, you should encourage them to think and become reflective learners. You might use evaluative questions such as:

- What do you think is more effective in football, the cross cut back to the forwards or the pass lofted forward to them?

or questions which call for understanding, such as:

- Why do you pass with the side of the foot, not the toe?
- What is the point of the follow through?

Task 5.4 requires you to analyse your lesson talk and questioning in lessons you teach.

Task 5.4 Analysing your lesson talk and questioning

Ask your tutor or another student teacher to observe one of your lessons and check on the amount of time you talk in lessons using a stop watch. This might seem a fairly crude measure, but it gives you an idea of how much you talk and whether you want to try and reduce the verbal input. Of course, some talk is to static pupils (for example, giving instructions) while some is to active ones (for example, giving feedback to pupils while working on a task). You might like to differentiate these.

(continued)

Task 5.4 *(continued)*
On another occasion ask an observer to write down all the questions you ask. This is not easy and some are likely to be missed. That does not matter because the record obtained should still give you a flavour of your questioning approach. Check how many questions you ask and what type of questions they are. Who answers them? You? Nobody? A range of pupils? Just one or two pupils? After each lesson discuss the findings with your observer. Identify what aspects of your teacher talk you need to work on. Put these notes in your PDP and repeat this exercise later in your ITE.

The effective use of questioning is a complex process. Table 5.1 illustrates how different types of questioning might be used to support the development of pupils' higher-order thinking skills in relation to Bloom's taxonomy of educational objectives (Bloom *et al.* 1956). The companion website includes further information on Bloom's taxonomy (www.routledge. com/cw/capel).

Black and Wiliam (2002) provide further insights on the use of Bloom's taxonomy in relation to questioning and Wragg and Brown (2001) classify the content of questions related to learning a particular subject as one of three types: empirical questions, conceptual questions and value questions. You might like to refer to this literature for more information.

Table 5.1 Linking Bloom's taxonomy (Bloom *et al.* 1956) to the development of higher-order thinking skills

Cognitive objective	What pupils need to do	Use of questioning to develop higher-order thinking skills
Knowledge	Define, recall, describe, label, identify, match	To help pupils link aspects of existing knowledge or relevant information to the task ahead
Comprehension	Explain, translate, illustrate, summarise, extend	To help pupils to process their existing knowledge
Application	Apply to a new context, demonstrate, predict, employ, solve, use	To help pupils use their knowledge to solve a new problem or apply it to a new situation
Analysis	Analyse, infer, relate, support, break down, differentiate, explore	To help pupils use the process of inquiry to break down what they know and reassemble it
Synthesis	Design, create, compose, reorganise, combine	To help pupils combine and select from available knowledge in order to respond to unfamiliar situations
Evaluation	Assess, evaluate, appraise, defend, justify	To help pupils compare and contrast knowledge gained from different perspectives as they construct and reflect upon their own viewpoints

Adapted from DfES (2004a), Unit 7: Questioning, pp. 13–14.

The capacity to ask questions effectively is a skill you can develop during your ITE and into your teaching career. It is important that you ask clear, relevant questions and use pause appropriately so that pupils have time to think about their answer before they respond. Muijs and Reynolds (2011) suggest that three seconds or slightly longer is a reasonable time for any such pause, although up to 15 seconds might be required for open-ended, higher-level questions. You can use closed or open-ended questions or combine the two into a series of questions depending upon the nature of the task at hand and context. Devising a series of questions is an effective technique for extending pupils' knowledge and understanding about a particular task or topic you might have introduced earlier.

If pupils encounter problems answering your questions you should find alternative ways to ask the same question. Muijs and Reynolds (2011) identified three types of prompts which can be used for this purpose:

1   verbal prompts – cues, reminders, tips, references to previous lessons or giving part of a sentence for the pupil to complete;
2   gestural prompts – pointing to an object or modelling a behaviour;
3   physical prompts – guiding a pupil through movement skills.

These prompts, used alone or in combination, can be useful devices in getting pupils both to understand and answer questions. The latter two types of non-verbal prompts are important elements of questioning and must relate directly to the words that you use. By incorporating a range of prompts and different stimuli into your teaching, the questions you ask can be more easily understood by pupils who are visual, auditory and/or proprioceptive/kinaesthetic learners.

The protocol of answering questions needs to be defined and enforced. Some teachers ask named pupils and redirect unanswered questions to other named pupils. Another technique is to ask a pupil who puts a hand up. The problem with using this strategy is that some pupils never put their hand up, possibly through fear that a wrong response could result in criticism or ridicule from you or from their peers, whereas others do so without knowing the answer because they wish to be seen as keen or knowledgeable.

Pupils also ask you questions. Sometimes a brief response suffices. In some instances, you can relay the question to the class and get them to think about possible answers. On occasion, the question will be a challenge to your authority and you will have to use techniques like humour or deflection.

Questioning that is used during lesson episodes to review guided practice and as a plenary activity to mark the closure of a lesson provides opportunities for interaction between you and your pupils that should be sensitively orchestrated to create a positive, non-threatening working environment. The questioning techniques you adopt should be varied to accommodate the different learning/teaching strategies you are using and the learning needs of all your pupils.

Bailey (2002) provides further insights on 'questioning as a teaching strategy in PE' and, Spackman (2002) discusses the importance of questioning in PE in relation to 'assessment for learning'. Task 5.5 is a Masters task to complete near the end of your ITE.

Task 5.5 Reflecting on your use of questioning

Write a 2,000-word essay closely examining the cognitive processes pupils would need to carry out in order to realise the objectives identified in Table 5.1. Select one of the classes you teach and carefully consider how you:

- currently use questioning;
- could use questioning;

to develop your pupils' higher-order thinking skills. Consider the implications of this analysis in relation to the future development of your teaching. Put this essay into your PDP as evidence of Masters level work.

Teacher feedback

Teacher feedback is an essential component of the teaching process as it is a key element in learning. Feedback is fundamental to learning in that it directs pupils' attention to specific intended learning outcomes (ILOs) and informs them of their progress, where they have mastered an aspect of a movement/skill/composition/game and where they need to focus their attention to improve. The feedback must therefore highlight this aspect of learning *and no other*. For example, if you are working to develop choreographic skills, but all your feedback is focused on individual movement performance, it is unlikely that the ILO will be achieved. On the other hand, if you want to achieve a polished performance of a sequence, feedback focused on choreography is distracting. (See Chapter 13 for a detailed discussion on matching feedback to ILOs.)

You give feedback in a number of situations in lessons. For example, you may call a class to gather round you, you may ask pupils to stand where they are and listen, or you may give feedback while the class is working. Further, you may give feedback to a group or to an individual. However, whenever feedback is given, when, how and to whom you give the feedback, it must be clear and accurate. This means that you must have a sound knowledge and understanding of what is to be mastered. Clear knowledge of the material enables you to observe effectively and use appropriate terminology as well as give productive feedback. This is important because if the teacher gives incorrect information this can inhibit rather than promote learning.

Certain types of feedback have been found to be more effective than others, depending on the characteristics of the skill and the learner. Mawer's (1995: 183-191) work on feedback is of value as it includes considerable discussion about types of feedback. He proposes that general feedback such as 'good' can do little to reinforce learning as pupils do not know what aspect of the task is being referred to. He advocates the use of positive feedback that also identifies which aspect of the work is being performed well - for example, 'Good work, Peter, you remembered to keep your back rounded as you moved into your forward roll.' As a teacher of PE you should avoid negative critical comments as this can be humiliating to pupils whose efforts are on show for all to see. Where a pupil is having difficulty, encouraging constructive and informative feedback should be used – for example, 'Well tried, Clare, you need to remember to keep your fingers together as you practise your breaststroke arm action.' From a more general perspective it is always better to draw attention verbally or in a demonstration to what *is* to be done, rather than what *is not* to be done and what *is* correct or appropriate rather than what *is not* correct or appropriate. A pupil who is not wholly attentive may miss preliminary comments and believe the wrong example is the one to emulate.

Feedback which includes advice on how to improve is most effective if you are able to stay with pupils to see if they can act on the advice given and improve. You can then give wholly positive feedback to the individual pupil. This is excellent for motivation. With a large class, however, it is difficult to give constructive feedback to each pupil and you may want to use pupils to provide feedback to each other. This approach is incorporated into the Reciprocal Teaching Style (Mosston and Ashworth 2002). If you try this approach, which has a great deal to offer, remember that pupils may be unfamiliar with the role of commenting directly on a partner's work. Pupils need to be introduced to peer feedback in a step-by-step approach, as it demands observational, verbal and social skills. It is not unknown for reciprocal teaching to have the opposite effect to that intended. For example, pupils inexperienced in giving feedback can be negative, critical and dismissive.

Mosston and Ashworth (2002) identify four forms of feedback, which are not dissimilar to those discussed by Mawer. These are value statements, corrective statements, neutral statements and ambiguous statements. They discuss the strengths and weaknesses of these forms of feedback. For example, corrective statements are seen as essential elements in promoting learning, whereas ambiguous statements are viewed as confusing and unhelpful to the learner.

Research undertaken by the Assessment Reform Group (ARG) (1999) identified feedback as a key element in their work to promote assessment for learning. The underlying message behind this research is that all assessment, including feedback to pupils, should be formative. That is, it should be designed to point the way to achieving or enhancing the learning of each pupil. This is a challenging notion but is surely valid. Simply to tell pupils what they *have* or *have not* achieved is hardly likely to promote further learning. (See Chapter 9 for further discussion on assessment for learning.)

The most valuable feedback is given to an individual, is encouraging, specific, informative and constructive and should lead the pupil on to further learning. Feedback given to a whole class is not without value, but is less effective in the learning process as it is, of necessity, non-specific and seldom directly relevant to every pupil.

Task 5.6 is a Masters level task and should be completed near the end of your ITE.

Task 5.6 Main purposes for using different types of feedback

The main purposes of using different types of feedback, as identified in Unit 12: Assessment for learning (DfES 2004b: 12), are to:

• acknowledge what pupils have learned and encourage them to reflect on and extend their learning still further;

(continued)

M
W

Task 5.6 *(continued)*

- recognise that pupils need time to reflect on their learning;
- encourage pupils to pose further questions to clarify or further develop their own or each other's thinking;
- encourage pupils to make next steps.

Critically evaluate how these purposes are translated in your own teaching. Identify aspects of feedback you would like to develop further and plan appropriate opportunities which enable you to realise these goals.

Put these reflections in your PDP as evidence of Masters level work.

Written language in PE teaching

Because PE is seen as a practical subject involving a great deal of movement from teachers and pupils, talk might be viewed as the exclusive medium of teaching. This would be a pity because there are many instances where the written word is appropriate and useful and can support the development of pupils' reading skills. It is important to use written language which is appropriate and can be accessed and understood by all those for whom it is intended.

If there is a whiteboard or an overhead projector (OHP) in the gymnasium or sports hall, you can write up the key terminology, teaching points or the elements of a practice for pupils. Transparencies can be prepared beforehand and filed for individual or department reference. If you are writing in the lesson, it needs to be clear (see below). Diagrams can also be drawn or displayed. A flexible jointed 'figurine' can be used on an OHP or visualiser to illustrate body positions.

Of course, with examination classes, there is more emphasis on writing. You have to develop an acceptable board-writing style – clear, neat, even and of a size which can be read by a pupil at the back of the class or one with poor eyesight. Avoid misspellings. If you are not sure how to spell a word, check it before the lesson. Your pupils should also be encouraged to write accurately and legibly.

Many PE teachers use work cards and these can be valuable resources. It is important that they are well presented, user-friendly and preferably laminated to last. You should check your spellings and grammar. Written materials, including handouts, can also be valuable in wet-weather lessons, or with pupils who are not participating in lessons or who are off school for an extended period. Again, get into the habit of filing all your written materials and resources for easy access and future use.

Another writing task for you as a PE teacher is the production of notices and posters. Again, the clarity, correctness and presentation quality are very important as these modes of communication send out non-verbal messages to pupils, colleagues and visitors to the school (like Office for Standards in Education (Ofsted) inspectors). You will want to ensure these are the messages you want to convey.

Wall displays and posters on the notice boards in a PE department should be vibrant, colourful, topical and updated regularly. Pupils identify with numerous sporting 'heroes' and 'heroines' across a range of physical activities. Visual images which reflect their diverse interests can be an inspiration and act as a stimulus to promote healthy active lifestyles and the personal pursuit of physical challenges.

ICT can be invaluable and greatly enhance the production of written and graphical materials. See Chapter 8 in Capel and Breckon (2014) for more information on the use of ICT in PE teaching. Task 5.7 asks you to pay particular attention to your writing to convey information.

Task 5.7 Using written language

In one of your next indoor lessons, see if you can use a whiteboard or OHP to illustrate and reinforce/support your teaching. You might want to list the sections of the lesson, provide appropriate terminology that may be new, stress the teaching points or display some pupil ideas.

Ask your tutor or another student teacher to observe and comment on how the strategy worked. Were you at ease with the writing role? Was your writing clear? Did the pupils react well? Did any look at what was written later to check? Did it take up too much physical activity time? How could you improve your use of the board or OHP in future? Put these comments in your PDP and use them to improve your technique next time you use such resources.

Pupil talk in PE lessons

Pupils inevitably talk in all lessons. It is part of the socialising process. They talk subversively when the teacher is not watching, but it is clearly better to direct the need to talk into a constructive channel. Silence, of course, is important too. Pupils should watch a demonstration in silence and they should not talk when the teacher is giving instructions or explanations. You should not start talking until all pupils are silent and attentive.

Some activities taught in PE make pupil-to-pupil talk very difficult. Pupils in the swimming pool tend not to talk to each other because the setting is not conducive. They might squeal when they enter the cold water or shout with the pleasure of the experience. A strenuous game of football or hockey can also make pupil conversation difficult. Language tends to be used to call for the ball or to indicate the proximity of an unseen opponent. Indeed, if you find there is a lot of pupil talk going on that is not related to the activity, you might need to condition the game in some way to enhance pupils' concentration and increase their participation level.

Pupil talk, however, is a very valuable aspect of PE. Talk can be used in a variety of ways to assist learning, deepen understanding, identify misconceptions and provide opportunities for pupils to express their opinion.

One obvious way for pupils to learn is by asking the teacher questions; but they are generally reluctant to do that. Asking questions can make pupils seem 'stupid' and could be interpreted as 'creepy' behaviour by their peer group. Answering questions can help learning, especially if the pupil is encouraged by being given time to think and if initial answers are followed by further probing. Such a process is best done at an individual or small-group level but can be time-consuming. It is to be encouraged and all pupils should benefit from such focused attention from time to time, but the reality of PE and of teaching in large spaces where vigilance is essential means that it cannot happen more than once or twice a lesson.

Discussion is the most available form of pupil talk to encourage learning. A number of activities can benefit from pupil discussion – the construction of a group sequence in gymnastics; a problem-solving exercise in outdoor education; the planning of a trio dance as the development of a motif. All of these inevitably demand pupil interaction with ideas being voiced; perhaps tried practically; then refined and developed with the help of further discussion. The problem for you as a PE teacher in such situations is to control the balance between pupil talk and physical activity and to ensure that the talk is task-directed and not merely social.

The composition of a group is important. Friends may work well together and discuss productively; they may, however, be tempted to chat, as friends do. A mixed-ability group may operate effectively, but there is the danger of the able being held back or the less able being ignored. There is no formula guaranteed to achieve results. You must monitor the progress of groups and mix and match accordingly. Remember, though, that if you define a number of groups over a period of time, there will probably be a marked reluctance to change that system. This may be appropriate in some situations, for example, if using sport education (Siedentop 1994) as a means of teaching a particular game. It may not be appropriate in other situations. If you want flexibility, tell the pupils that you intend to vary groupings and establish the principle by making regular changes.

Another important factor in achieving a good discussion environment is the clarity and nature of the tasks set. Imprecisely defined tasks lead to woolly and unfocused discussion. That does not mean that all tasks need to be closed. PE has a number of areas which require open-ended tasks, especially with older and more experienced pupils; for example, a group sequence in gymnastics or discussing issues in the sociological aspect of GCE A level. However, open-ended tasks can still be couched in precise accessible language, for example, in a dance lesson a teacher could say:

> This music is called 'The Market Place'. Listen to it carefully and then discuss in your group what could be going on in this market. Use your ideas to create a short dance work based upon your interpretations of the mood and rhythm of the music.

Task 5.8 asks you to pay particular attention to pupil talk in a lesson.

Task 5.8 Group talk

Plan to include a group task in one of your next lessons. Your specific observation task is to check on the discussion pattern of individual groups. Is there a dominant pupil? Is there a non-contributor? Is talk task-focused? Is there enough physical activity? Should you think of rejigging the groups next time to improve the quality of discussion? How can you improve the quality of the discussion in the groups in future? Discuss this with your tutor and try to put any changes identified into practice. Put these notes in your PDP.

In PE, talk has a valuable role in testing hypotheses, suggesting tactics and exploring the consequences of physical initiatives. The imagination is an important element in successful physical activity and, although skills learning is fundamental, pupils should be encouraged to use their imagination, to make suggestions and, where possible, to test ideas in practice.

Reciprocal learning can be used to good effect in PE lessons. In this situation pupils work in pairs with one acting as the teacher and the other as the learner. The 'teacher' needs to be clearly briefed about what aspect of a skill is to be worked on. It is general practice to give the key teaching points and the best ways to do this may be on a wall poster or a work card. Inevitably, this process involves pupil talk, with the 'teacher' giving instructions, providing feedback and praising effort and competent performance. Interaction between you and the pair of pupils is with the pupil acting as 'teacher' to reinforce this role. See Chapter 13 for more information about teaching strategies.

When pupils are engaged in group tasks and are talking constructively about what they will do, the teacher has a monitoring role. It is important to give the groups some initial time to get their ideas going. If you intervene too quickly in a group, you may hinder rather than help. Your role is to assess when a group has stalled or broken down and to support by question or advice.

An example of communication and its link to observation: demonstration to promote pupil learning in PE

An often-quoted cliché, 'a picture speaks a thousand words', suggests that, as sighted people, we gain much information through our eyes. In practical subjects such as PE, demonstration can be an invaluable teaching aid. There are many reasons why demonstrations are used – for example, to explain, to encourage, to reinforce and to evaluate. The following exemplars give possible reasons for deciding to use demonstration as a teaching aid to promote pupil learning:

- to *set a task*. A demonstration can be more effective than a lengthy verbal explanation and is a more economical use of your time. A good strategy to use is: set up the activity with one group while the rest of the class is working, then stop the class to show the demonstration;
- to *teach a new skill/activity*. Here demonstration can focus on specific teaching and movement observation points, such as where to place hands in relation to the head for a headstand in gymnastics or the point at which you lose contact with the ball for a push pass in hockey;
- to *emphasise a particular aspect/help pupils' understanding*. For example, use of demonstration to show a change of speed, direction, flexibility or strength;
- to *improve quality/set standards*. Use of demonstration can focus pupils' observations so that you can show what is expected and educate them to look more closely at each element that builds into the competent performance of a skill. For example, body tension used to perform a vault in gymnastics, the fluency of transitions in dancing from one movement phrase to another or the placement and use of fingers when dribbling the ball in basketball;

- to *show variety*, especially to show *creativity*. Demonstrations allow pupils to observe the different responses pupils make to given tasks in, for example, gymnastics, dance and manoeuvres used in games to create space;
- to *reward improved/well-done work*. Use of a demonstration can be particularly important when you call on a pupil or group of pupils who may not be outstanding but always work to the best of their respective abilities and deserve recognition;
- to *stimulate/motivate*. Demonstration can show pupils' flair and individuality, to motivate all pupils and to challenge the more able to set personal targets – for example, to work toward achieving a slice serve in tennis or master the Fosbury flop technique in the high jump;
- to *show completed work*. At the end of a unit of work demonstrations provide opportunities to show and reward the individual pupil, pairs, small groups and half-class groups. Knowing that they could be called upon to demonstrate often stimulates and encourages pupils to work at refining the quality of their physical movements.

There are many factors you need to consider when setting up a demonstration.

You have to decide *who* is going to demonstrate and *why* (Figure 5.1). Generally it is more motivating for the class if a pupil demonstrates, but it may be more appropriate for the teacher to demonstrate particularly if there is not a pupil who is sufficiently skilled, or if a new or difficult skill is being shown. Consider which pupil(s) you could ask to demonstrate and be mindful not to use the same ones each time. Do not always ask the most able pupil as this may demoralise others. It is important that sometimes you select a mid-ability level pupil to demonstrate. A group can show their expertise, or to save time half the class may demonstrate. Visual aids such as posters of good gymnastic movement, work cards for games tactics and video excerpts of swimming techniques can also be effective tools in showing good form and movement to a class.

Before you engage pupils in demonstrating to the class, consider the following:

- Have you asked the pupils if they mind demonstrating in front of the class?
- Do the pupils know what is expected of them? Have you briefed them? Have they practised the demonstration? Do they feel confident in demonstrating?
- What role is the pupil to take in the demonstration? You need to know your pupils and recognise their strengths – for example, if they are taking on the role of the feeder in a practice.
- Are the environment and situation safe?

Figure 5.1 Who is going to demonstrate?

- If pupils make an error give them the opportunity to try again and do not allow other pupils or yourself to laugh at mistakes.
- Always remember to praise the demonstrators and to thank them afterwards.

How can pupils get the most out of a demonstration?

In the exemplars of reasons identified for using demonstration above, the word 'show' recurs, which indicates that an important component part of demonstration is *observation* (see Chapter 4 on observing pupils in PE). The pupils who are 'looking at' the demonstration need both to *see* and *understand*. It is important to educate pupils to *observe* intelligently by using such techniques as:

- directing their attention to specific aspects of the demonstration;
- asking them well-structured questions about the demonstration;
- focusing their attention on the quality of the work being shown;
- helping them to perceive similarities and differences in the work being performed.

Figure 5.2 illustrates important factors that you need to be aware of when pupils *observe a demonstration*. The first priority is safety (Chapter 12 addresses safety issues in PE). You must also consider the best position for the pupils to view the demonstration. A number of considerations should be taken into account – for example, whether the demonstrator is right- or left-handed, the position of the sun if outdoors (you should be facing/looking into the sun, with the sun behind the pupils so that they can see the demonstration), or whether there are any distractions (pupils should not be facing any distractions, therefore should have their backs to another group or to a classroom). You also need to consider the speed of the demonstration (beginning slowly) and that some pupils may need to see the demonstration more than once.

Before you set up the demonstration consider the environmental conditions, particularly as these will affect the pupils' ability to *hear the explanation of the demonstration* (Figure 5.3). Is it very windy? If so, bring the group in close to you so that they can hear the accompanying explanation. As the demonstration is performed, state the most important teaching points in clear, concise language. Always remember to follow the demonstration up with a question-and-answer session and positive, constructive feedback on the pupils' performance.

You must *focus the pupils' attention* on a specific aspect of the demonstration (Figure 5.4) to ensure that they know what they are looking for. Once identified, all pupils should listen to verbal explanations and observe the demonstration carefully. Following this up with a

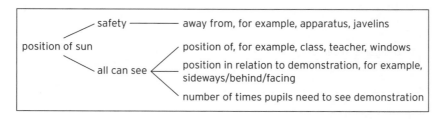

Figure 5.2 Observing a demonstration.

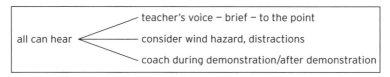

Figure 5.3 Hearing the explanation of a demonstration.

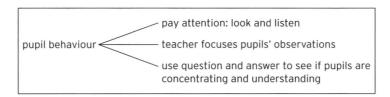

Figure 5.4 Focusing pupils' attention in a demonstration.

question-and-answer session ensures that pupils have been concentrating and understand the teaching points being made. This is vitally important for improving pupils' evaluative skills.

Now carry out Task 5.9 to monitor your management of demonstrations.

Task 5.9 Observation of a demonstration

Devise an observation sheet that focuses on the use of demonstration. Use the information above to identify important aspects of demonstration that you want to include and/or develop further. Ask your tutor to use this observation sheet to monitor your use of demonstration in a lesson. Discuss the outcome of this observation exercise with your tutor after the lesson. Put these observations into your PDP. In future lessons endeavour to put into practice what you learn from this experience. Also, try to incorporate the feedback received into future observation sheets to support use of demonstration further in your observation of teaching and learning.

It is important for you as the teacher to be knowledgeable and to be able to demonstrate well, because pupils imitate good practice in order to become more proficient. Sometimes this process is called 'modelling'. Also remember that 'practise' makes 'permanent', so demonstrations do need to be 'perfect'! Now carry out Task 5.10 to clarify your rationale for using a demonstration.

Task 5.10 Clarifying your use of demonstration

Design a lesson that incorporates demonstration. Use the following questions to clarify key factors that you need to consider when setting up a demonstration:

(continued)

Task 5.10 *(continued)*

- *What* is the nature of the demonstration?
- *How* will this promote pupil learning?
- *When* during the lesson could this be introduced most effectively?
- *Where* in the teaching space will the demonstration take place?
- *Who* is going to demonstrate?
- *Why* am I using this demonstration?

Discuss your responses to each question with a tutor or another student teacher. Use these questions to clarify your use of demonstration in future PE lessons. Put these notes in your PDP for later reference.

Cautionary endnote – what not to demonstrate and when not to use demonstration!

It is strongly recommended that you avoid demonstrating *what not to do*. Occasionally pupils misunderstand and think what they see is what they should do! And there are times when it is not appropriate to use demonstration – for example, at the beginning of a lesson when the class needs to be active quickly and on a very cold day when standing still to watch a demonstration is not appropriate.

Summary and key points

This chapter has explored language skills in relation to communication in PE lessons. It has stressed the importance of audibility and the appropriate use of your voice in different situations and contexts. The importance of your grasp of, and accurate use of, technical language has been stressed. The use of questioning has been considered in some detail, with the challenge for you to use different types of questions to challenge pupils in a variety of ways. Feedback has been highlighted as a key aspect of communication that has a significant effect on pupil learning. The need to ensure that all written work sets pupils a good example and is of a high standard has been discussed and the role of pupil talk has been introduced as an issue to be considered. By developing these aspects of language skills you are well on the way to becoming an effective communicator.

The chapter has also explored demonstration as one exemplar of communication in practice. You should now appreciate how effective, purposeful demonstration can be used to set tasks quickly and to help pupils understand the task better. The value of demonstrations in the learning process has also been outlined.

As was recognised in the introduction to the chapter, communication is at the heart of teaching. The teacher is, above all, a communicator. Language is one of the most significant tools of the teacher's trade. Communication is the vehicle through which knowledge is passed from the teacher to the pupils. Without effective communication, ILOs will not be achieved. Desired learning will not take place. Many other aspects of teaching rely on effective communication, such as feedback, organisation and class management. To bring together all the important aspects of communication, complete Task 5.11 below.

Check which requirements of your ITE you have addressed through this chapter.

Task 5.11 The place of communication in teaching

Write a 2,000-word essay on the following topic: 'Critically consider the claim that communication is the most significant of the teacher's tools in the promotion of learning.'

Put your essay in your PDP as evidence of Masters level work.

Further reading

Fisher, R. (2009) *Creative Dialogue: Talk for Thinking in the Classroom*, Abingdon, Oxon: Routledge.

This book emphasises the development of critical and creative thinking through questioning and dialogue between pupils and teachers and between the pupils themselves. It introduces a special form of dialogic teaching based upon an approach called Philosophy for Children, which helps to enhance communicative skills as well as develop the habits of intelligent behaviour.

Muijs, D. and Reynolds, D. (2011) *Effective Teaching: Evidence and Practice*, 3rd edn, London: Sage.

Chapter 3 discusses the important relationship between pupils' learning and interactive teaching. Components of effective questioning techniques are highlighted and examined in relation to class discussion.

Robertson, J. (1996) *Effective Classroom Control: Understanding Teacher–Student Relationships*, 3rd edn, London: Hodder and Stoughton.

Chapter 4 discusses how gestures and speech, vocal behaviour and meaning, and eye contact and speech can be used to convey enthusiasm to sustain pupils' attention. The bibliography provides a rich resource for classroom management and control.

Rogers, B. (2011) *Classroom Behaviour: A Practical Guide to Effective Teaching, Behaviour Management and Colleague Support*, 3rd edn, London: Sage.

The author describes some of the real challenges teachers may encounter when working in today's classrooms and offers advice on how building positive rapport with pupils and colleagues can support good practice. He draws on a range of case studies to exemplify the importance of developing effective verbal and non-verbal communication skills.

Spendlove, D. (2009) *Putting Assessment for Learning into Practice*, London: Continuum.

The author argues that 'part of emotional literacy in schools lies in recognising the vulnerability of children in the learning process' (p. 10). Against this backdrop, he examines the relationship between feedback and learning in Chapter 1 and between questioning and dialogue in Chapter 2, offering suggestions of how to create an emotional environment in which trusting relationships exist and children feel safe.

Other resources and websites

National Association for Language Development in the Curriculum: www.naldic.org.uk.

This website provides a professional forum for the teaching and learning of EAL, supporting bilingualism and raising the achievement of ethnic minority learners. The ITE link enables you to access short summaries of EAL research in the UK and internationally as well as the resource archive, ITE network and forthcoming events.

Additional resources for this chapter are available on the companion website: www.routledge.com/cw/capel.

Acknowledgement

The author would like to acknowledge the significant input of Roger Strangwick to the first two editions of this chapter.

6 Lesson organisation and management

Julia Lawrence and Margaret Whitehead

Introduction

Pupils need to be actively engaged in the learning experiences, which is evidenced by the amount of time they are deemed to be 'on task'. In a PE context this is reflected by the amount of time they are involved in motor and other activities related to the subject matter in such a way as to produce a high degree of success, with intended learning outcomes (ILOs) of the lesson more likely to be met. Thus the organisation and management of pupils during a lesson are key factors in ensuring that effective learning takes place. As the 'manager' of the learning experience you have control over many factors which are reflected in your planning (see Chapter 3), the teaching and learning approaches you adopt (see Chapter 13) and how you review the learning that has taken place (see Chapter 3). You also need to manage the environment in which you are working and the people who may support you.

The development of organisation and management skills occurs over a period of time (Richardson and Fallona 2001) and is closely related to the confidence and competence of the individual teacher. With this in mind you need to accept that different contexts and situations may result in different outcomes. Further, effective leadership and management of the learning environment have a significant impact on pupil learning outcomes (Allen 2013). Thus the development of these aspects of your teaching is likely to be ongoing and worthy of focused reflection throughout your teaching career. However, potentially, they may be one of your main concerns when you first start teaching lessons on school placement. The aim of this chapter is to give you some guidance regarding the development and application of organisation and management skills. Further, it will seek to provide examples of when and where such skills can be applied effectively within the teaching environment to enhance pupil learning.

Objectives

At the end of the chapter you should be able to:

- organise people, the space, the equipment and time, before, during and after lessons;

(continued)

(continued)

- establish effective rules and routines;
- understand how to increase the time pupils spend on task in lessons.

Check the requirements of your initial teacher education (ITE) to see which relate to this chapter.

Organisation and management of the learning environment

Your ability to organise and manage your classroom will reflect your ability to lead the learning of your pupils. Thus, effective planning is essential to the process. In Chapter 3 support and guidance were provided regarding the principles and processes associated with planning. In this chapter consideration is given to organisational strategies that allow the implementation and management of the teaching plan. What is important to remember is that how you organise and manage the learning environment impacts on the success of the lesson itself.

Organisation is not only about planning how to achieve ILOs but also about being prepared for the unexpected that can take place before, during and after the lesson. A well-organised teacher is better able to respond to situations during lessons than one who has not prepared fully. Your organisation should focus on people (your pupils and others who may be supporting you; for example, teaching assistants) and yourself, the space, the equipment and the best use of time.

Whilst you will need to organise and manage throughout the lesson, three key organisational points can be identified: activities you should undertake before the lesson starts, those that will occur during the lesson and final activities you should consider once the lesson has finished. A summary of some of the key activities/areas can be found in Table 6.1.

Table 6.1 Some organisational tasks that need to be completed before, during and after a lesson

Before the lesson	During the lesson	After the lesson
• Plan the lesson • Mark homework • Check the space • Check the resources • Check equipment • Set work for pupils not doing the lesson • Establish any specific roles and responsibilities within the lesson	• Oversee entry into the lesson – what routines will you implement? • Monitor changing, collect valuables, take the register – are there any specific roles and responsibilities? • Organise space • Organise equipment • Establish teaching tasks/activities – include success criteria • Give instructions • Organise groups • Progression between activities • Review of learning opportunities • Oversee exit from the lesson	• Evaluate the lesson • Plan the next lesson (see Chapter 3)

Organisation before the lesson

The planning and organisation of a lesson prior to the arrival of a class are very important. You may find it useful to discuss your lesson organisation with your tutor in order to identify potential stress points and receive guidance on how you might prepare for and respond to problems that may arise. If you are looking to receive feedback on any planning, make sure that you provide sufficient time for staff to provide this. What is key is that the more confident you are with the material and how you are going to organise and teach the lesson, the more able you are to deal with any situations that may arise during the lesson.

Within your planning you should identify where activities will take place and familiarise yourself with any potential hazards (issues concerned with safety are covered in Chapter 12). It is always worth confirming with other staff the areas you are going to use. Do not assume that just because you have planned to use the field someone else might not want to use it too. You should also check when examinations or other events, e.g. a school play, are being held and whether this changes the space that is available for use. Finally, consideration needs to be given to any provision. While most lessons tend to carry on regardless of the weather, be aware that in some cases you may need to double up groups indoors if the weather is very poor. Pupils quickly pick up if you have failed to plan effectively, and this may result in disruptive behaviour. It is always worth planning for both an indoor and outdoor lesson if there is some doubt about the venue, or as a minimum have a series of pre-planned indoor lessons based around your scheme of work.

Any space in which you work has a variety of aspects that can be used in your teaching, for example, walls, lines, markings, grids and apparatus. Try and get as much information as you can before your placement starts so that these can be integrated into your planning. (You should have collected such information on your preliminary visits to the school: see Chapter 1.) Some schools have appointed groundskeepers, who may be based on site, who may be able to provide additional markings if given the appropriate amount of notice. You should plan to use the working space as appropriate for a specific lesson – for example, using grids for practices or setting up equipment for a circuit. If you are in a confined space using apparatus/equipment your organisation has to be planned carefully to ensure that:

- the environment is safe at all times;
- the apparatus is not too close to walls;
- you are aware where misplaced balls/shuttles may go;
- it accommodates large groups for activity (e.g. badminton);
- equipment/apparatus is stored and accessible;
- you are using the space most effectively for the activity and the pupils.

Most off-task activity occurs during the transitions between activities within a lesson. When planning, be clear how these will be dealt with to ensure maximum learning opportunities. For example, do you need to collect in equipment in order to set up for the next activity or can the working area be used in different ways? Can the next activity be set up while the previous task is being carried out? Can you involve pupils in setting up their own practice areas?

Within your planning, consideration should be given to the nature of the class being taught, including the number of pupils in the class, their motivation, their gender and how well they cooperate together. This may influence how you group pupils, or the roles you give them within the lesson. You also need to consider how much equipment/apparatus is available for a particular activity (e.g. rugby, athletics or hockey) as this determines how you can organise tasks/practices/games.

Your planning therefore links numbers of pupils with resources and equipment that are needed and available for the lesson. Thought needs to be given in your planning to the collection of equipment at the start of the lesson and/or getting out equipment during the lesson, its location and use during the lesson, and the methods employed to put it away at the end of the lesson. Further consideration also needs to be given to the placement of equipment and where those not participating are positioned. By organising resources and equipment prior to the lesson, you give your class a sense of readiness and organisation that should filter through to the lesson itself.

The following is a checklist for you, the PE teacher, for organising the lesson *before* it starts. You should have:

- *planned and prepared the lesson*. It is essential to plan each lesson well before it is taught. In this way you have a clear understanding of what you want to achieve in each lesson you teach (see Chapter 3);
- *checked the working space*. Is it available and safe for use? At the beginning of the day it is important to check your working space so that you have a smooth start to your lesson. For example, it may have been used for evening classes and equipment (e.g. badminton posts/nets) may not have been put away;
- *checked and counted all equipment*. Is it readily available and in good order? You may delegate this task to pupils, but it is important to ensure the equipment is ready (e.g. basketballs are inflated for your lesson). Consider setting aside time in which this is done every week;
- *have prepared team lists, bibs, visual aids, work cards and spare whistles*. As part of your preparation it may be advantageous to prepare team lists for when you move to the game section of your lesson, visual aids to give pupils more ideas, work cards to help pupils complete a task and spare whistles so that pupils can take on the role and responsibility of umpiring/refereeing in your lessons. This makes for smooth transitions and little wasted time;
- *set work for pupils not participating practically in the lesson through injury, illness or for other reasons*. It is useful to check your school policies and procedures regarding these non-participants. Ideally these pupils play a constructive role in the lesson rather than 'sitting out'. For example, they may be able to give useful feedback to pupils who are active, or umpire or score. On some occasions these pupils may be asked to make notes on aspects of the lesson. Lessons outdoors may be a problem if the weather is very cold and it may be appropriate for pupils who are 'off practical' to do some theory work indoors on the specific activity being taught. Tasks set for these pupils can address some of the broader aims of PE;
- *marked homework*. It is important that you meet deadlines and return homework with appropriate feedback for pupils. This is also very important for pupil motivation (see Chapter 7).

Task 6.1 is designed to alert you to the ways in which teachers prepare for lessons.

Task 6.1 Teacher preparation before a lesson

Shadow an experienced PE teacher in your placement school for a morning and record the way each lesson is prepared for in advance of the pupils arriving. Record these observations in your professional development portfolio (PDP). Check back to the list above as you begin to take more responsibility for lessons.

Organisation and management during the lesson

Organisation and management during a lesson begin when the pupils arrive in the changing room to start the lesson and conclude when they leave the PE area. During this time you are expected to respond to many situations, both planned and unplanned. One way to improve organisation and management during this period is to establish routines with which both you and your pupils are familiar. Primarily pupils need to know what is expected of them in terms of behaviour, effort and task completion. Establishing routines, therefore, plays a vital role in the success of lessons. If you provide pupils with terms of reference, in the form of rules and routines, they have a framework on which to base behaviour. The use of appropriate sanctions to reinforce inappropriate behaviour must also be identified. If you need to issue sanctions, make sure that they are consistent, appropriate and enforceable. In most schools, home-school contracts now exist, providing teachers, parents and pupils with information on what each can expect from the other. Do not be surprised to see codes of conduct displayed in the school environment, again providing terms of reference for both staff and pupils. Further support for the management of pupil behaviour can be found in Chapter 8. Tasks 6.2 and 6.3 require you to look at some of the expectations and routines that may be useful for you to employ.

Task 6.2 Expectations and PE

Read the school and PE department expectations for your placement school, then discuss these with your tutor. Ask if there are any additional expectations for specific activities you are teaching. Put your findings in your PDP. Add to these notes as you implement these in your lessons.

Task 6.3 Routines in PE lessons

Routines in PE are valuable and important. Examples of aspects of PE lessons for which routines are advantageous are: entering the changing rooms, changing, taking the register, entering the working space, giving instructions, collecting equipment, starting work, gaining attention, finishing a task, moving into different groups, moving from one task/activity to another, putting equipment away, leaving the working area/space, leaving the changing rooms.

(continued)

Task 6.3 *(continued)*

Can you think of any more? If so, add them to this list.

Observe two different members of the PE department in your placement school teaching lessons, looking specifically at the way they enforce the rules and what routines they have for those tasks and behaviours which occur frequently. How are the routines different? How are they the same? Can you suggest why this might be? How can you apply these in your lessons? Put your observations in your PDP.

Expectations, routines and procedures are very often specific to particular activity settings, for example, swimming, athletics and outdoor and adventurous activities. Table 6.2 sets out some examples of activity-specific rules, routines and procedures and Task 6.4 asks you to add further examples.

Task 6.4 Expectations and routines for specific activities

Table 6.2 identifies some expectations, routines and procedures for specific activities. Add to this list rules, routines and procedures for three activities you are teaching on school placement.

Activity 1
Activity 2
Activity 3

Discuss these suggestions with your tutor and put these notes in your PDP.

General organisational situations: the changing rooms

As has been indicated previously, the success of a lesson invariably stems from how pupils first arrive at, and prepare for, the lesson. Ensuring pupils are focused on the learning objectives of the lesson as soon as possible will limit the time pupils are off task, thereby increasing the time available for learning to occur. Being present when pupils arrive is a good aspiration to

Table 6.2 Some examples of expectations, routines and procedures

Activity	Expectation/routine/procedure
Gymnastics	No large apparatus to be used until the teacher has checked it for safety. No running at times when apparatus is being put out or dismantled
Swimming	No one to enter the pool without permission. No running on poolside. No screaming in pool
Hockey	One short sharp whistle: stand still, face the teacher and listen
Javelin	Always walk when carrying a javelin. Have the sharp end pointing down. Never throw unless given permission by the teacher

have; it will set the tone for the lesson as well as reinforcing expectations around punctuality and arriving prepared. Different schools have different policies regarding what to do on arrival. Task 6.1 has alerted you to the strategies employed within your placement school.

As well as allowing you to set the tone of the lesson, being present in the changing rooms while pupils are changing helps to prevent inappropriate behaviour and encourages pupils to change as quickly as possible. In some cases it also provides the opportunity to take the class register, thereby reducing the need to have this as a separate activity, as well as allowing you to share the objectives for the lesson. This gives you the opportunity to outline the focus of the lesson, to set up the first task the pupils are to undertake or to organise some of the key aspects of the lesson – for example, what size groups pupils are going to work in during the first part of the lesson or which pupils are responsible for taking out the equipment. It is important, however, to remember that you should not go into the opposite-sex changing rooms. If you are teaching a mixed class, you have to adopt a different approach. Check with your tutor the procedure adopted in your placement school.

Be aware of when and how notes to be excused from the lesson are dealt with and how such pupils are integrated into the lesson. Consider what happens to those pupils who arrive late or without the appropriate kit. Again your department should have procedures to be followed in these situations.

Below is a checklist of procedures that you might wish to use in the changing room:

- Establish pupils' entry into the changing room. This should be orderly and quiet. Schools/teachers have their own routines (see Tasks 6.2 and 6.3, above).
- Establish routines for attending to tasks such as collecting pupils' valuables and excuse notes and giving out kit to pupils who have forgotten theirs. Routines prevent time being wasted at the beginning of a lesson.
- Take the register. This can be done while pupils change without wasting too much time. However, there may be times when it is better to take the register in the working space before the lesson starts, e.g. for a mixed-gender class.
- Establish routines for organising taking out equipment. There are many different methods for doing this (see below).
- Set a task from the work in the previous lesson so that pupils start working quickly. For example, in hockey, you can ask pupils to 'remember the practice of beating your opponent that we covered in last week's lesson; practise this when you get to the pitch'. Pupils can therefore start as soon as they are ready.
- Check all pupils are out of the changing room and lock the door. Most changing rooms are locked for security. It is your responsibility to check all pupils are changed and have left the changing room.

Organising and managing people: pupils, others and yourself

Pupils

As has already been identified, you begin the organisation of pupils in the changing rooms at the start of the lesson. However, during the lesson itself, you organise pupils when setting up and/or to change the activity, to collect or put away equipment or put pupils into groups or teams. There are many reasons for specific groupings of pupils, for example:

- mixed ability: where pupils of a wide range of abilities work together. This type of grouping is a good context for fostering leadership and cooperative skills;
- similar ability: for specific activities such as swimming;
- contrasting ability: here you may consider utilising the strengths of more able pupils to support other pupils' performance, effort or behaviour in positive ways;
- social friendship: this is useful with older pupils as it can promote motivation.

It is your responsibility to devise methods of putting pupils into groups and to check all pupils have a group, as quiet, shy pupils may not tell you if they have not found a group with which to work. Your method of grouping pupils should take as little time as possible. Generally try and avoid the pupils picking groups, which can result in a lot of wasted time and poor self-esteem for some pupils.

Although it is more efficient to maintain grouping throughout a lesson there can be situations, such as needing to differentiate between pupils, in which changing group structure is important. This change constitutes a significant transition and needs to be planned by you before the lesson. If you do change the grouping in a lesson you need to plan how this can be carried out swiftly. Where possible, try to build from current groups into the next grouping, for example, develop groups from 1s to 2s or 3s; 2s to 4s or 6s; or 3s to 6s, so that there are smooth transitions and continuity in the lesson. This is particularly important outside on cold days. Some methods you may use for grouping pupils are:

- calculate the number of pupils participating from the register taken in the changing room, or count heads as the pupils are warming up, so you know the number in the class and can think of any adaptations you may need to make to your planned groups during the lesson;
- in 2s of similar height and build for a warm-up task;
- pupils jogging; teacher calls a number, for example 2, 3, 5 or 7. Pupils quickly get into groups. Eventually the stated number go into first practice/apparatus/team group;
- if you know the class you may devise appropriate groupings/leaders/team lists before the lesson;
- into 2s; number yourselves 1 and 2; number 2 gets a ball. Have balls in a designated area central to the working area;
- develop above practice to 4s with one ball. Join with another 2 and put one ball away as quickly as possible (the teacher may number pupils 1 and 4 and state a number, for example, 3, who puts the spare ball away);
- mixed ability – 28 pupils split into teams of 7 – find a partner (into 2s), join with another 2 to make a 4 – in your 4s number off 1 to 4, all 1s together, all 2s together, all 3s together, etc. to form teams of 7.

Wherever possible, organisation between activities should be kept to a minimum (see Figure 6.1, which shows progression in groupings in volleyball as well as use of work space). The same principles for developing grouping can be used in other activities.

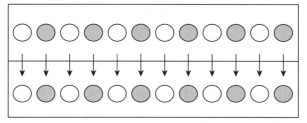

1 v 1 warm up activity – volleying to partner over net down centre of space

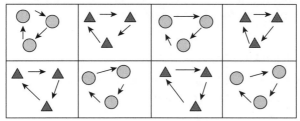

Into 3s – divide space equally. Set a practice for continuous volley, dig, etc.

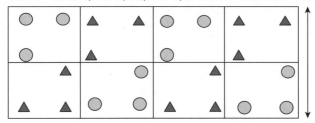

3 v 3 – set up a conditioned game – serve, receive, set, spike, etc.

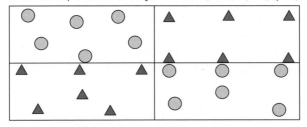

6 v 6 – join with another 3 and set conditions of play

Figure 6.1 Progressions in groupings and use of working space in volleyball (adapted from National Coaching Foundation 1994).

Others

It is possible that during some of your lessons, additional support for some pupils may be provided in the form of teaching assistants. Such additional resources offer opportunities to reflect on what you wish to achieve for the pupils for whom this support is provided, and should encourage you to think creatively about how this can be implemented. The role of support staff may vary according to the experience of the individual, but what is essential is that these assistants are fully aware of what is expected of them within the lesson. Therefore every effort should be made to talk to them prior to the lesson, so that they have a clear understanding of their role and your expectations of their contribution within the learning process. Over time, they might be able to offer specific guidance around planning for the support of a particular pupil or pupils. Key aspects you may therefore wish to consider in relation to others are as follows:

- Planning of the lesson:

    o   Can you work with the support staff during the planning of the lesson?
    o   If you are planning alone, how will you share the plan with the support staff prior to the lesson?

- Supporting the learning of pupils:

    o   What role will the support staff take during the lesson?
    o   Which pupil(s) will support staff work with?

- Assessment of pupils:

    o   How will support staff work with you to assess pupil progress?

- Evaluation of the lesson:

    o   How will you use support staff to evaluate the learning achieved?
    o   Can you use support staff to evaluate your own teaching?
    o   How will support staff support subsequent planning?

Yourself

Most teachers work in a classroom with seating and the teacher needs to plan the most effective seating for the task in hand. As a PE teacher, however, you more often work in spaces without pupils in set places/seats. Good teacher positioning and movement are vital in establishing and maintaining learning, discipline and safety in your lessons. You need to position yourself so that your voice is audible, with the appropriate volume for the specific environment – for example, a swimming pool, hockey pitch on a windy day or a sports hall with poor acoustics. You must always be aware of the whole class and avoid having your back to the group, standing in the middle of a group of pupils or having pupils behind you. Good positioning enables you to observe effectively so that you can monitor, for example, pupils' progress or behaviour and give them feedback either as individuals, groups or as a whole class (Chapter 4 focuses on observation of pupils in PE). The same principles hold for a classroom setting when you are teaching theoretical aspects of PE. Try not to stay in one place throughout these lessons. Move among the pupils and monitor their work and give feedback as you pass pupils.

In a practical setting your positioning changes constantly depending on your working space and the purpose of a task (e.g. setting up a practice or demonstrating). You need to be aware of your positioning in relation to the class and also of the class in relation to you, other groups, the sun and any other important factors. For example, if it is sunny, you should be positioned so you are looking into the sun so that the pupils can see you. The following are some examples of the many different situations you experience when teaching PE in which effective positioning is important in your lesson organisation and management:

- When getting the equipment/apparatus out, establish set routines and give the class clear instructions, then make the pupils responsible, stand back where you can see everyone and watch, only helping when and where necessary.
- When setting up a demonstration: see Chapter 5.
- When setting a class task you need to be able to see everyone and to ensure that all the class can see and hear you. This is much easier to do in a smaller indoor space than in an outdoor space. In your outdoor lessons, define the working area for pupils – for example, refer to the use of lines on the court or pitch, so that you do not lose contact with your class.
- Monitoring your class. This is best done from the perimeters – for example, from the corners of an indoor space, from the back of a tennis or badminton court. From your observations you are able to assess whether the whole class understands the task. If most of the pupils are doing one thing incorrectly or the task is too easy or too difficult, you need to stop the whole class and give further guidance or clarify instructions.
- Helping individuals/small groups. Here you may be supporting a pupil in gymnastics or dividing your attention between several small 4 v 4 football games. At all times you must be able to see the rest of your class as you work with a particular pupil or pupils. This is best achieved by monitoring from the perimeter and looking in towards the class.
- When setting a class competition ensure that you are in a position, before you begin the competition, where your peripheral vision enables you to see all the pupils as well as who wins.
- Be near to a misbehaving pupil or pupils. It is important to circulate and be close to a potential trouble zone. Knowing your pupils and their names helps you control potential disruption (see Chapter 8). Take steps to learn pupils' names so that you can establish contact from wherever you may be in the working space (see Chapter 8 and particularly Task 8.8 for further information on learning pupils' names).
- It is important to be aware of any pupils with special educational needs and the nature of their specific needs, for example, poor hearing or eyesight, so you can position them advantageously in your lessons (see Chapter 10).

In Task 6.5 your tutor or another student teacher observes you and notes down how effective your positioning was in a number of different lessons.

Task 6.5 Teacher positioning

Ask your tutor or another student teacher to observe and record how effectively you position yourself when teaching three different activities – for example, gymnastics, swimming and outdoor games. Keep these records. At the end of these observations you should be able to draw up a list of ways in which teaching position influences pupil learning and behaviour. You also appreciate how different activities in PE require different teaching positions. Try to use this knowledge to improve your positioning in your next lessons. Put the information in your PDP.

Organising and managing the space

As a PE teacher you work in a number of spaces (e.g. gymnasium, sports field, swimming pool, classroom). During your ITE you gain knowledge regarding the health and safety requirements of each area and the need to conduct an appropriate risk assessment (see Chapter 12) and this aspect of your work must never be forgotten. Much organisation of space occurs before the lesson starts (this has been covered earlier in this chapter) and should be reflected in your planning. However, it is also important that you are able to organise and manage the work space efficiently and effectively to maximise safety, pupil involvement and activity.

There are a number of ways to identify your work space. Line markings in a sports hall or field/court area are useful, as is the use of cones, although consideration needs to be given here to risk management and safety in respect of the type of cones used. Where possible, cones should be set out prior to the practice to be conducted. This might be while the pupils are involved in a warm-up, or by using those who are not participating. It is also possible to allow pupils to set up their own work areas once they have received a practical demonstration.

Some examples of how to use the available space are given in Figure 6.2. Although focusing on netball, the same principles for using working space can be applied to other activities. Task 6.6 then asks you to focus specifically on space management in a PE class.

Task 6.6 Organisation of your working space

Design an indoor circuit for a class of 30 pupils for an activity and year group of your choosing, the use of which is planned to achieve specified ILOs. In your planning consider safety, activity levels of the pupils and methods of recording pupils' results. After completing this task, teach the lesson. In your evaluation identify how far the space organisation enabled you to achieve the ILOs. Note areas requiring further development and use this information to design further circuits. Put this information in your PDP.

Organisation and management of equipment

Use of equipment is central to most work in PE and is an important area of organisation. You need to decide what equipment is needed for pupils to achieve the ILOs and ensure that this is available. As identified in the introduction, pupils learn most effectively when engaged on a task. Therefore to achieve maximum activity and learning, you should, wherever possible and appropriate, provide each pupil with an individual piece of equipment (e.g. when working on individual skills in football or basketball). This increases the number of opportunities for practise and should promote skill development. Also, when pupils are working with others, group sizes should be kept as small as the amount of equipment allows so that they are actively engaged in the activity. The use of small-group practices reduces the time spent waiting, thereby increasing the amount of actual activity time per pupil. Equally, the use of small-sided games allows for increased opportunities for pupils to apply the skills they have

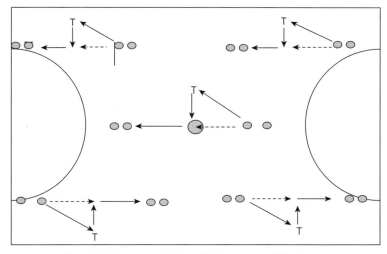

Organisation on netball court: five groups of 5 players

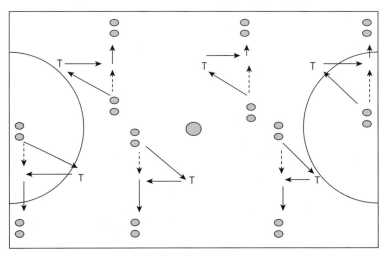

Organisation on netball court: six groups of 5 players

Figure 6.2 Organisation of your working space in netball (adapted from Crouch 1984: 123).

learnt during practices in larger game situations. All these strategies ensure that pupils are actively involved, increasing the opportunities for learning and reducing the opportunities for inappropriate behaviour.

Your lesson should develop logically so that you are not putting equipment away and getting it out again. Some general aspects to consider are where the equipment is stored and the best or most appropriate methods for getting it out and putting it away. Some methods you may use are:

- first pupils ready take equipment out – remember that equipment should always be counted;
- pupils line up outside store room individually or in groups and collect equipment when told;
- certain groups always take equipment out, others always bring it in;
- as groupings change, any spare equipment must be put away for safety reasons. Have containers near to the working area. Decide how/who is to put equipment in these containers;
- at the end of a lesson make sure you count the equipment again, organise its collection and/or involve pupils in these tasks.

These are general principles for organising equipment but you should appreciate that you need specific rules and routines for organising equipment for each activity (see Task 6.4). In gymnastics, for example, line up in 2s by the mat trolley, the first mat to go to the furthest part of the gym. Pupils should be made responsible for caring for the equipment and at all times safety procedures must be adhered to.

The same principles apply when you are taking a classroom lesson as there are books and other resources to be managed. Organisation is just as important in this setting and poorly planned management of resources can mar the effectiveness of a lesson. For example, if textbooks are not available or access to online resources is limited, certain ILOs will not be achieved.

Organisation after the lesson

Once the lesson has finished, you need to evaluate it as soon as possible. This might initially be verbally with the member of staff observing you, but should also be written so that you can return to this self-assessment and reflect on what you have learnt. Your evaluation should focus on progress in pupils' learning (be sure that you include within your planning how this will be assessed, specifically what you might hear, read, see) as well as the specific personal goals you wanted to achieve (for example, the teaching standards on which you were focusing/being observed). However, it is also important to reflect on whether your organisation and management could be improved, particularly in order to create more time for learning (you may wish to have this as a focused target). This evaluation informs the planning of your next lesson. Chapter 3 discusses both planning and evaluation in more depth. Activity 12.3 in Capel and Breckon (2014) is a useful exercise to do at this point to review the areas covered in this chapter so far.

Managing time

Throughout the chapter so far frequent mention has been made about how well-planned and efficient organisation can use time to best effect, promote learning and guard against pupils moving off task. In fact, time management is a key element of teaching. This refers both to managing pupils' time and to managing how you spend your time (see also Unit 1.3 (Green and Leask) in Capel *et al.* 2013).

Ideally, in PE, pupils are active most of the time; however, because of the nature of the subject, there are always parts of the allocated lesson time during which pupils are not active. For example, pupils are not active when:

- they change before and after the lesson;
- the register is taken;
- they listen to instructions, watch demonstrations and receive teaching points;
- they wait for their turn on a piece of apparatus;
- they observe a partner's work;
- they read task cards or study criteria to guide performance;
- they consider how to solve a problem;
- they plan together in group settings.

There are, of course, times in the lesson when pupils are, quite legitimately, not physically active, but are nevertheless engaged 'on task'. Examples are identified in the third and last bullet points above. However, care should be taken to ensure that, as far as possible, pupils are active for most of the time. Indeed, the art of effective time management is to ensure only the minimum time is spent on the non-active aspects of the lesson (including organisation). Where overlong periods of time are given to any of the non-active parts, pupils' attention is likely to wander, and they may become disruptive, with resultant behaviour problems. Time taken to deal with these problems is not time well spent! All the guidance given in the chapter so far should help you to use time to best effect.

Lessons can vary from 35 minutes to 70 minutes or longer. In some schools transportation to off-site facilities may also have to be accounted for as part of the overall length of the lesson. This time may be used productively to prepare pupils so that they are ready to start the lesson as soon as they arrive at the facility (e.g. you may recap on previous learning and/or cover some new learning which can then be put into practice). The tempo of the lesson should ensure logical, smooth transitions, avoiding over-dwelling on a particular task. When you are inexperienced it is sometimes difficult to judge how much time to spend on a task. This depends ultimately on the pupils' responses to your material and you, as the teacher, must be aware of pupils who work at different rates. It is important that you monitor pupils' responses to check if they are working satisfactorily or if they are uncertain what to do, perhaps because the explanation was not clear or the challenge set is too hard. This is sometimes known as 'reading' the class. Having 'read' the pupils' response you need to respond appropriately. This may be to do nothing, to explain the task again, to modify the task or to give specific feedback to all or some pupils. During the lesson you also need to manage pupils' movement, noise levels and behaviour.

The allocation of time in your lesson should allow time for:

- pupils to complete tasks and receive feedback from the teacher;
- pupils to use the apparatus and have time to put it away. It is pointless to get apparatus out in a gymnastics lesson if pupils do not then have enough time to put the apparatus away safely, without hurrying;

- pupils to have a game if they have practised skills/small-sided games. Pupils need time to experience how well they can apply their earlier learning to a game situation. This may also inform you of pupils' understanding of tasks set;
- pupils to complete a circuit and to collect scores;
- you to give feedback about the lesson. It is important to highlight the learning you hoped to achieve (e.g. with a question-and-answer session) to conclude your lesson;
- you and the pupils to finish the lesson smoothly;
- the pupils to shower and dress after the lesson;
- you to ensure pupils are not late for their next lesson!

Task 6.7 is designed to make you aware of how pupils spent their time in lessons.

Task 6.7 Monitoring pupils' use of time

Observe a lesson taught by another student teacher and watch one pupil throughout the lesson. Record when this pupil is active or not, and whether this is productive or non-productive activity. After the lesson discuss your observations with the student teacher and debate ways that active time can be increased. Ask the student teacher to conduct the same exercise on one of your lessons. Use the outcomes of the discussion work to improve use of pupil time in future lessons. Put both records in your PDP and use this to increase pupil time engaged in productive activity in future lessons.

Academic learning time in PE (ALT-PE)

Given the importance of active learning time, it is not surprising that considerable research attention has been directed to this aspect of teaching. One such research initiative is known as Academic Learning Time in PE (ALT-PE: Siedentop *et al.* 1982). This research divided activity time in lessons into:

- that time in which pupils are engaged in motor and other activities related to the subject matter in such a way as to produce a high degree of success and for ILOs of a lesson to be met. This has been called time 'on task' (or 'functional' time) (Metzler 1989). It is often seen as a determinant of effective teaching in PE;
- other time in which pupils are engaged in motor tasks but which is not time on task – for example, the task is too hard or too easy or pupils do not apply themselves to learning (e.g. they may hit a shuttle over the net in a badminton lesson but not work to achieve a specific ILO such as the use of a particular stroke or specific tactic).

Siedentop and Tannehill (2000) reported results of research which showed that these two account for, on average, 25–30 per cent of total lesson time. However, time on task may account for only 10–20 per cent of total lesson time (Metzler 1989). Siedentop and Tannehill also identified differences in the amount of time on task in lessons in which different activities are being taught. Least time on task was found in lessons in gymnastics and team games, with time on task rising in lessons in individual activities to highest time on task in dance and fitness activities. More recently, research conducted in Greece (Derri *et al.* 2007) highlighted that, although focusing on academic learning time in PE improved skill retention, success was dependent upon the effective use of managerial and organisational strategies if learning is to be enhanced.

Task 6.8 is a refinement of Task 6.7 and involves an observer noting specifically what the pupils are doing during one of your lessons.

Task 6.8 Time pupils spend on different tasks

Ask your tutor or another student teacher to observe one of your lessons and record the amount of time in which pupils are:

1   actively engaged in motor tasks (e.g. practising a skill, playing a game);
2   actively engaged in non-motor learning tasks (e.g. choreographing a dance with a partner or watching a video of a particular skill being learned, activities to achieve broader goals of PE);
3   supporting others in learning motor activities (e.g. holding equipment, supporting a partner);
4   moving from one task to another;
5   waiting;
6   receiving information;
7   engaged in other organisational tasks;
8   engaged in other tasks or activities and not working towards achieving lesson ILOs.

(The ALT-PE observation schedule (Siedentop *et al.* 1982) is available in Chapter 12 (pp. 154-157) in Capel and Breckon (2014) and on the companion website: www.routledge.com/cw/capel.)

How much time is spent on each of these eight types of tasks (a) individually and (b) on 1-3, and on 4-8, respectively? What is the relative percentage of time pupils spend working directly to achieve lesson ILOs (1-3) and on other tasks (4-8) in the lesson? Do you think this is acceptable? Discuss these with the observer. As appropriate, work to change the time allocation in your lessons. Repeat this task later in your ITE to check if the time spent on different tasks has changed. Put these observations and notes in your PDP.

Task 6.8 should have highlighted the interactions between different aspects of a lesson – for example, the more time you spend organising, the less time pupils can spend on task. Hence, increases in time on task in your lessons cannot be achieved without effective organisation. Task 6.8 should also alert you to managerial and behavioural issues within your classroom, both of which influence the time pupils spend on task. Task 6.9 is an exercise to compare time on task in different lessons.

Task 6.9 Gathering information about time on task in different lessons

Ask your tutor or another student teacher to complete the ALT-PE observation schedule (Siedentop *et al.* 1982; available in Chapter 12 (pp. 154-157) in Capel and Breckon (2014) and on the companion website: www.routledge.com/cw/capel) while observing two lessons you are teaching in different activities, to see if there are any differences in time on task between lessons in different activities.

After each lesson reflect on the results and discuss these with the observer, to inform your evaluation of the lesson(s) and to identify what you can do to increase time on task. Ask the observer to undertake the same observations after you have had time to try and increase pupils' time on task in the lesson. After all the observations, compare the time on task in lessons in different activities. Put this information in your PDP.

The importance of time management in PE is paramount, as without effective use of time, ILOs are unlikely to be achieved. Now complete Task 6.10.

Task 6.10 Application of ALT-PE principles

Derri *et al.* (2007) conducted a small-scale study looking at the relationship between academic learning time and motor skill development. Their findings indicated that, whilst an improvement in skill performance and retention was evident, of greater significance was the limited amount of academic learning time within the lessons observed. Conclusions around the effective use of organisation and management skills were identified as potential reasons for this. Such findings highlight the need for teachers to reflect upon the strategies they employ when teaching.

Having read this article, conduct a small-scale study on your own teaching, focusing upon the enhancement of academic learning time. Identify the strategies you employ and reflect upon any changes you make to you own practice. When reviewing your findings spend some time reflecting upon how your changes in practice impacted upon the pupil experience. Put these notes in your PDP as evidence of Masters level work and use your findings to improve pupil time on task.

Summary and key points

Your management approach will reflect you as an individual, but also the school/setting in which you work. Although all teachers have to organise and manage their lessons, organisation and management in PE lessons need specific consideration as pupils are working in large spaces and using a variety of equipment within a limited time. Taking a step back and thinking about what management is is an important activity which, if done early, applied and reviewed, makes for an easier life. It builds confidence and competence and ultimately will allow you to relax and deliver your best.

It will allow you to identify roles and responsibilities clearly within the lesson and as a result increase opportunities for pupils to take a greater responsibility for their own learning, identifying clear tasks and ensuring that learning objectives are achieved. Although all teachers need to be able to give clear, precise instructions and explanations, PE teachers need to consider how they can give these to pupils who are not sitting in neat rows, behind desks, but moving around in a large space, often at considerable distances from the teacher. As a PE teacher, organising and managing lessons effectively is especially important because of the safety implications of activities and the large space in which you work.

How you organise and manage your class will vary – factors such as age, experience and activity will all play a part. In an effective lesson as little time as possible should be spent on organisation and management. Although effective lesson organisation and management are clearly important and may even be key to the success of a lesson, they are not everything and alone they are not enough. They can create time for learning to take place and an environment suitable for effective learning, but you need to use that time effectively for learning to occur. Effective lessons are those in which the time pupils are on task is maximised. The teacher has planned thoroughly what and how s/he is going to teach and how s/he is going to organise and manage the lessons (anticipating possible situations and having planned especially carefully to prevent problems which may occur in the lesson, but having thought through how to respond to problems if they occur). You must be careful not to focus too much on effective organisation and management (especially in the early stages of your school experiences), but see these as providing time and opportunity for effective teaching and learning to occur.

The way you organise and manage your class is an individual preference. Such skills are based around the establishment of clear expectations and routines, both of yourself and of those you teach.

The aim of this chapter has been to provide an overview of ways in which you can develop your organisation and management skills. For many student teachers, the development of such skills is seen as a high priority. However, such skills develop over time and with experience. Even the most experienced teacher is still learning new ways of dealing with the ever-changing face of the classroom. Take time to reflect on your teaching and identify situations when a different approach may have been more appropriate. Be consistent in both your preparation and planning. Enter each lesson confident about your material. Most of all, be clear about your expectations. Once pupils are aware of these, positive relationships can be established, leading to enhancement of learning.

Check which requirements of your ITE you have addressed through this chapter.

Further reading

Lawrence, J. (2014) Creating an effective learning environment, in S. Capel and P. Breckon (eds) *A Practical Guide to Teaching Physical Education in the Secondary School*, 2nd edn, Abingdon, Oxon: Routledge.

This practical guide provides supporting observation tasks which encourage reflection on personal practice. Chapter 12 provides further development of some of the concepts explored in this chapter and in Chapter 8. Of particular interest may be the section which focuses on the management of the classroom climate, as well as activities which encourage you to reflect on other more experienced teachers' practice.

Mawer, M. (1995) *The Effective Teaching of Physical Education*, Harlow: Pearson Education.

Chapters 6 and 7 in this book focus on aspects of organisation and management. Chapter 6 focuses specifically on how effective learning environments can be created, particularly focusing on interaction with new classes. Chapter 7 focuses more on the maintenance of learning environments, looking at behaviour management strategies.

Siedentop, D. and Tannehill, D. (2000) *Developing Teaching Skills in Physical Education*, 4th edn, New York: McGraw Hill Higher Education.

Chapters 4 and 5 focus on preventive classroom management, discipline techniques and strategies in PE lessons.

The Education Endowment Foundation (2014) Sutton Trust – EEF Teaching and Learning Toolkit (available online at: http://educationendowmentfoundation.org.uk/toolkit/).

This resource provides summaries of existing research across education and summarises the impact of strategies on the attainment of pupils.

Additional resources for this chapter are available on the companion website: www.routledge.com/cw/capel.

7 Motivating pupils for learning in PE

Kevin Morgan, Dan Milton and Julia Longville

Introduction

Teachers' behaviours and motivational strategies play a significant role in shaping pupils' learning, attainment and the quality of their experiences in PE (Vallerand and Losier 1999; Reeve 2009). Presenting challenging and enjoyable learning opportunities that motivate pupils to participate, exert effort and learn in PE should, therefore, be an overriding principle of a PE teacher's philosophy. Motivated pupils typically try hard, concentrate, persist in the face of difficulty, demonstrate a positive attitude and enjoy the activities. Given the vital role of PE in promoting physical activity, your aim, as a PE teacher, is to foster such responses in all pupils in an attempt to motivate them towards learning and participating in physical activity. This is a particular challenge, as it has been suggested that there are few areas of achievement that generate such contrasting motivational responses as PE (Biddle 2001). For some pupils, PE is the highlight of their day, whereas others perceive it as a major source of stress and anxiety. Such varied attitudes are the result of a number of factors, including family background, peers, past experience, school ethos and you, the PE teacher. Some of these factors are outside your control, but the aspects you are able to manage directly are your teaching behaviours, teaching strategies, attitudes and enthusiasm. The aims of this chapter are to introduce the role of motivation in promoting pupils' learning, identify different types of motivation and motivational theories, and suggest teaching approaches that facilitate the development of an effective learning climate which supports the development of intrinsic motivation (see Chapter 8, which focuses on developing an effective learning environment).

Objectives

At the end of this chapter you should be able to:

- understand the definition of motivation and its importance in relation to pupils' learning;
- recognise individual differences in pupils' motivation;
- understand the two most prominent contemporary theories of motivation in PE, namely Self-Determination Theory (SDT) and Achievement Goal Theory (AGT), and be able to implement teaching strategies that can be adopted in line with these theories;

(continued)

(continued)

- appreciate the significant aspects of teaching behaviour that can promote an effective motivational climate;
- understand the role of *pupils' voice* in promoting and enhancing motivation.

Check the requirements of your initial teacher education (ITE) to see which relate to this chapter.

Motivation and learning

Motivation relates to the *why* of behaviour. It has been defined as an internal process that activates, guides and maintains behaviour over time (Schunk 2000). In other words, motivation is what 'gets you going, determines where you are trying to go, and keeps you going' (Slavin 2003: 329). Gervis and Capel (2013: 148) identified the three elements of motivation as:

1   direction (the activities people start);
2   intensity (the effort people put in);
3   persistence (the activities people continue).

It is crucial for you to understand that pupils need to be motivated to learn and that they have different motives for putting effort into your lessons. An important distinction in this regard is the difference between *intrinsic* and *extrinsic* motivation. Intrinsic motivation comes from within the person and is associated with doing an activity for itself, for the pure pleasure and satisfaction derived from participation. Intrinsic motives for participating and putting in effort to learn in your PE lessons could include excitement, fun, enjoyment and the chance to learn and improve skills (Deci and Ryan 1985). Extrinsic motivation, on the other hand, results from external rewards such as praise, recognition, status, approval or acceptance by peers or teachers. Extrinsic motivation involves participating and putting in effort to learn in PE to, for example, gain a tangible or social reward, or to avoid disapproval.

   The *additive principle* suggests that intrinsic motivation can be boosted by extrinsic motivators (Deci and Ryan 1985). However, contrary to popular belief, this is not always a good idea. In fact, in some situations where the task is being performed because of intrinsic motives, extrinsic rewards (such as school merits) can lower the pupil's intrinsic motivation. In order to explain this phenomenon, Deci and Ryan (1985) stated that rewards can be divided into two types: *controlling* and *informational*. Controlling rewards include praise and tangible rewards (e.g. merits) and are given to influence (control) a person's behaviour. Informational rewards (e.g. teacher feedback), on the other hand, convey information about a person's competence at a particular task. According to Deci and Ryan (1985), rewards perceived by the pupils as controlling decrease intrinsic motivation, whereas rewards viewed as informational increase intrinsic motivation. Task 7.1 asks you to observe a teacher in relation to the use of rewards.

Task 7.1 Controlling and informational rewards

With your tutor's permission, observe a lesson taught by your tutor and identify *controlling* rewards given to influence an individual's behaviour (e.g. praise and merits) and *informational* rewards (e.g. feedback given to the pupil on competence, improvement or effort). Discuss the data collected with your tutor and consider how you might influence pupils' intrinsic and/or extrinsic motivation through using these two types of reward. Put these notes in your professional development portfolio (PDP) for future reference.

Whilst all pupils are required to take part in PE, some motives for participating and putting in effort to learn are clearly intrinsic (e.g. because PE lessons are fun) and some are clearly extrinsic (e.g. because I gain rewards); others are less clear. For instance, how would you classify the motive 'because participating in PE helps me to control my body weight and look good'? It seems more intrinsic than extrinsic but it is not totally intrinsic as the motive involves reasons for participation other than fun, enjoyment or learning. For this reason, Deci and Ryan (1985) proposed that viewing motives as either intrinsic or extrinsic is too simplistic and they developed a continuum of motivation called Self-Determination Theory to explain this.

The self-determination continuum

The self-determination continuum distinguishes between *amotivation*, *extrinsic* and *intrinsic* motivation as different ways of regulating behaviour. At one end of the continuum, pupils are *amotivated* (neither intrinsically nor extrinsically motivated and thus experiencing feelings of incompetence and lack of control), whereas at the other end they are intrinsically motivated to learn by the pure enjoyment and pleasure of the activities. In between these two extremes pupils go through differing forms of autonomous (self-directed) and controlling extrinsic motivation (Figure 7.1). *External regulation* is a controlling form of extrinsic motivation which exists when behaviour is completely controlled by external sources such as rewards and constraints. *Introjected regulation* is also considered to be controlling and is evident where pupils participate to please or impress others, or to avoid feelings of guilt (e.g. to please their teachers or parents, or to impress their peers). Although these controlling forms of extrinsic motivation can sometimes regulate or motivate short-term engagement in your PE lessons, they are unlikely to sustain it over time and can have a negative impact on pupils' motivation for physical activity (Teixeira *et al.* 2012). However, not all extrinsic motives are controlling; for instance, if pupils participate and put in effort to learn in your lessons because they see the value in the subject or outcome (e.g. the health benefits attached), they are experiencing a more autonomous form of extrinsic motivation, *identified* regulation. Finally, pupils who participate and put in effort to learn because the activity is a key part of their personal make-up (e.g. they consider themselves to be an athlete or sports person) are displaying *integrated regulation*. This SDT continuum can, therefore, be used to describe the quality of motivation a pupil displays within your lessons.

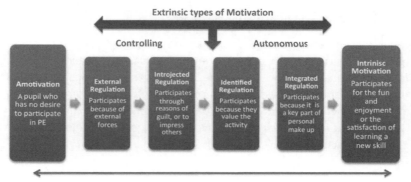

Figure 7.1 Levels of self-determination.

Where pupils are on the continuum depends on a whole range of different factors, including the type of activity, their relationship with you (as the teacher) and their peers, previous experiences and their general health and wellbeing. It is essential, therefore, to get to know your pupils. Task 7.2 asks you to encourage pupils to discuss the nature of their motivation.

Task 7.2 Types of motivation

With the help of your tutor, construct a simple description and example of the six 'levels' of motivation in SDT (Figure 7.1). Hand these out to the pupils and ask them to indicate what they consider to be their primary level of motivation to participate and put in effort to learn in PE. Discuss the information collected with your tutor and consider how you might respond to these different levels of motivation in your teaching. Put these notes in your PDP.

SDT theory is based on the premise that there are three psychological needs that motivate all human behaviour – autonomy, competence and relatedness (these are explained in Table 7.1). By supporting these three needs and creating a supportive climate as a teacher, it is possible to move your pupils along the continuum of self-determination towards more self-determined or intrinsic motivation (Reeve 2009).

Using the basic tenets of SDT can influence your teaching approaches and help to create a more autonomy-supportive (self-directed) motivational climate for your pupils (Van Den Berghe *et al.* 2012). The research evidence on SDT provides strong support for the use of an autonomy-supportive motivational climate in promoting intrinsic motivation in PE (Ntoumanis 2012). However, despite the reported benefits of an autonomy-supportive motivational climate, it is acknowledged that PE teachers still engage in

Table 7.1 Psychological needs

Autonomy	The need to feel autonomous, that is, to make your own decisions and to be in control of your own behaviour, e.g. exercising because you want to, not because you were told to
Competence	The need to feel competent and able to accomplish things, e.g. mastering a physical skill or improving your expertise in an activity
Relatedness	The need to relate to others and feel a sense of belonging, e.g. being part of the lesson, feeling accepted and valued by other pupils and the teacher

controlling behaviours that can impede the three psychological needs (Table 7.1). According to Reeve (2009), some of the reasons for these more controlling teacher behaviours include: a belief that they are more effective; that they demonstrate a higher level of teacher competence; and that without control, you cannot effectively structure a lesson. The suggestion, therefore, is that there needs to be a balance between teacher control and pupil autonomy in your PE lessons in order to facilitate the most effective learning environment. Now complete Task 7.3.

Task 7.3 Balance between autonomy-supportive and controlling teacher behaviours

Arrange for a lesson you teach to be video- and audio-recorded. After the lesson watch the recording and identify if and how you use autonomy-supportive behaviour (e.g. pupil choices) and controlling behaviour (e.g. teacher commands and rewards). Discuss the data collected with another student teacher and consider how you might increase your use of autonomy-supportive behaviour in your lessons. Put these notes in your PDP.

Although closely linked to SDT, the origins of motivational climate are associated with AGT. Therefore, before identifying and explaining the different types of motivational climate in PE, it is important to understand the theoretical background of AGT (Nicholls 1989).

Achievement goal theory

AGT proposes that, in achievement settings, such as PE, the pupils' main concern is to demonstrate ability and to avoid demonstrating incompetence in front of their peers and teachers. Ability or achievement, however, can be perceived in different ways dependent upon two states of goal involvement, known as *task* and *ego* involvement. When pupils are *task-involved* they focus on personal progress with an emphasis on effort, mastery of the task and the learning of new skills. In contrast, when pupils are *ego-involved* they focus on demonstrating superior ability compared to others and on outperforming their class mates, with the minimum effort required (Nicholls 1989). Now complete Task 7.4.

Task 7.4 Goal involvement

With the help of your tutor identify two pupils who would seem to be task-involved and two who would seem to be ego-involved. Conduct two short discussion sessions, one with each pair of pupils, and ask them to share with you what makes them work hard in PE lessons. Enquire if and how they have different or the same views when working in various activities in the PE curriculum. Discuss with your tutor how you could use this information to foster task-involved attitudes in your pupils in PE. Put these notes in your PDP.

According to Nicholls (1989), a pupil's state of goal involvement in your lessons is the combined result of his/her achievement goals (goal orientations) and the prevailing situational factors (motivational climate). Goal orientations are individual differences in pupils' proneness to be task-or ego-involved resulting from childhood socialisation at home or in learning situations such as school. Nicholls (1989) contended that after the age of about 11 years (i.e. secondary-school age), task and ego goal orientations are *differentiated* as independent constructs so that pupils can be high or low in both, or high in one and low in the other.

Elliott and Church (1997) have focused on 'approach' (trying hard in an attempt to achieve) and 'avoidance' (not trying in an attempt to avoid failure) behaviours associated with achievement goals and developed the 'trichotomous' and 'two-by-two' models of goal orientations. The trichotomous model identifies three types of goals: task (approach), ego approach and ego avoidance. The two-by-two model divides both the task and ego goals into 'approach' and 'avoidance' behaviours. Task 7.5 asks you to gather data on pupils' approach and avoidance behaviours.

Task 7.5 Approach or avoidance behaviours

Ask your tutor to watch a lesson you teach and identify approach behaviours in your pupils (trying hard) and avoidance behaviours (not trying). Discuss the data collected with your tutor and use AGT to try to identify why pupils might be adopting such behaviours. Put these notes in your PDP.

Individual pupil differences in tendency towards task or ego goal orientations are not to be denied, but research in PE (e.g. Dorubantu and Biddle 1997) has shown that the motivational climate created by teachers can be more influential than pupils' goal orientations in determining their motivation.

Motivational climate

Motivational climate is defined as a situationally dependent, psychological environment directing goals of action (Ames 1992). When an emphasis is placed on learning, self-referenced goals, improvement and effort, a *mastery* (task-involving) climate is promoted. In such a climate, pupils are more likely to adopt positive behaviours such as trying hard, selecting challenging tasks and persisting in the face of difficulty (Ames 1992). In contrast, when the emphasis is placed on social comparison and winning competitions, a *performance* (ego-involving) climate prevails. In this case (particularly when their perceptions of ability are low) pupils often adopt more negative behaviours, such as a lack of effort and resilience in an attempt to protect themselves from demonstrating low ability (Ames 1992).

Based on Epstein's (1989) original work, Ames (1992) identified the structures of achievement situations that influence the motivational climate as *task, authority, recognition, grouping, evaluation* and *time* (TARGET) (see explanations of the structures below and in Table 7.2 at the end of this section). Manipulating these TARGET structures to be mastery-focused has been found to be associated with higher task orientation, beliefs that effort and ability are the causes of success, improvement in pupils' intrinsic motivation, a more positive attitude, greater feelings of satisfaction, less boredom, higher perceived ability and a preference for more challenging tasks (e.g. Morgan and Carpenter 2002), which is likely to result in greater learning. In contrast, a perceived performance climate has been associated with higher levels of ego orientation, the belief that natural ability determines success, a more negative attitude towards the activity, less enjoyment and higher levels of boredom.

For PE teachers, therefore, understanding and creating a mastery motivational climate is central to improving pupils' learning and motivation. The following section outlines some specific teaching strategies that you can employ for each of the TARGET structures in order to promote a mastery climate in your PE lessons.

Task structure

The intended learning outcomes (ILOs) of your PE lessons should be clearly identified (based on prior learning) and shared with the pupils in order to ensure that they fully understand what is expected of them, and have some ownership over the learning activities (Chapter 3 looks at ILOs in more detail). Additionally, the organisation of tasks designed to help pupils achieve the ILOs is a crucial aspect in engaging the pupils, decreasing the opportunity for social comparison, maintaining pupils' concentration and interest and maximising their effort, personal improvement and learning. Consequently,

Table 7.2 TARGET structures

TARGET structure	Mastery climate	Performance climate
Task	Self-referenced goals Differentiated tasks Varied and multi-dimensional tasks	Comparative goals Undifferentiated tasks Unidimensional tasks
Authority	Pupils involved in decision making and given leadership roles	Teacher makes all the decisions
Recognition	Individual recognition of improvement and effort	Public recognition of ability and comparative performances
Grouping	Mixed-ability and cooperative groups	Ability groups
Evaluation	Self-referenced Individual feedback by teacher based on improvement and effort	Comparative and public
Time	Flexible time for task completion	Inflexible time for task completion

practices should be designed for individual learning, variety (e.g. a multi-activity design), fun and intrinsic appeal. However, differentiation and personal challenge are difficult to achieve in teaching, where significant differences exist in ability, experience, knowledge and understanding; therefore, to ensure that the tasks you set are individually challenging for all pupils, you should encourage and teach pupils how to set their own self-referenced goals and how to monitor their individual progress towards achieving these goals. Using basic goal-setting techniques such as SMART goals (specific, measurable, achievable, relevant and time-bound), based on self-evaluation of performance, would be one way to achieve this in PE. Now complete Task 7.6.

Task 7.6 Learning goals and differentiated tasks

Plan a lesson that shares ILOs with the pupils and also encourages them to set their own ILOs. Reflect upon and ask the pupils how this impacted on their learning and motivation within the session and record your thoughts and their responses. Discuss the data collected with your tutor and, if it had a positive impact on the pupils, together draw up a plan to develop your use of both the above aspects of teaching. Put these notes in your PDP.

Authority

The authority structure relates to the balance of decision making between you and your pupils during the lessons. To emphasise a mastery climate you should encourage pupils to participate in decision making and provide them with the opportunity to take on leadership roles. Research has shown that the degree to which you involve your pupils in decision making is directly related to positive motivational responses such as feelings of self-competence, responsibility, independence and greater levels of determination and engagement in learning (Ames 1992). This aspect of the TARGET structure is closely related to the 'autonomy' need in SDT (Deci and Ryan 1985), as covered earlier, and to 'pupils' voice', which is addressed later in this chapter.

Several teaching styles from Mosston and Ashworth's (2002) spectrum allow for shared decision making in your lessons. The spectrum is a continuum of teaching strategies (called 'styles' in the spectrum) categorised according to the decisions made by the teacher and pupil before, during and after the activity. At one end of the spectrum is the command style, in which the teacher makes all the decisions across all three phases. At the other end of the spectrum is the learner-initiated style, in which the pupil makes almost all the decisions and the teacher acts as a facilitator (this style is very rarely used in schools, as rarely are pupils able to select the activity in which they participate). Between these two styles, Mosston and Ashworth (2002) identified a series of other styles, each categorised according to the decisions made by the teacher and pupil. Styles such as reciprocal, inclusion, guided discovery and problem solving are particularly focused on pupil decision making (or authority) within lessons. Research by Morgan *et al.* (2005) demonstrated that such styles foster a more mastery-involving motivational climate than the more traditionally used teacher-led styles. Task 7.7 asks you to observe and discuss pupil decision making in a lesson.

Task 7.7 Pupils' decision making in a lesson

Ask your tutor to observe a lesson you teach and identify if and how you encourage pupils to make decisions themselves. Discuss the data collected with you tutor and consider ways in which you could increase opportunities for pupils to make decisions within your lessons. Put these notes in your PDP.

Recognition

The type of recognition and rewards, reasons for and distribution of recognition and rewards have important consequences for pupils' learning, interest, satisfaction and feelings of self-worth. To foster a mastery motivational climate, your recognition and rewards should be focused on individual effort and improvement, rather than comparisons between pupils. This ipsative assessment (assessment against previous performance/achievement) provides equal opportunity for all to be recognised for their accomplishments, not just the high achievers, because everyone can try hard and there is always room for improvement.

Although often given with good intention, when rewards are given publicly and on a differential basis they invite social comparison and emphasise a performance motivational climate. To foster a mastery motivational climate, therefore, you should try to give individual recognition to your pupils, so that feelings of satisfaction derive from improving personal standards rather than doing better than others. In PE settings, providing individual feedback and distributing this equally is a significant challenge, but one that you should persevere with. By providing one-to-one feedback the teacher recognises every pupil's individual needs, which is more likely to enhance pupils' confidence and perceived ability. Task 7.8 asks you to consider feedback to individuals.

Task 7.8 Individual recognition of personal progress

Ask your tutor to observe a lesson you are teaching and record if and how you provide individual feedback to pupils, noting to whom the feedback is given and about what (e.g. learning, behaviour). Discuss your observations with your tutor and together make a list of strategies you could use to provide individual feedback and distribute your recognition equally amongst pupils in a class. Put these notes in your PDP.

Grouping

How you group your pupils is particularly salient in determining the motivational climate in lessons. When pupils work in groups based on ability, it is easier to make ability comparisons. On the other hand, when the teacher promotes mixed-ability and varied grouping arrangements, it is more difficult for the pupils to interpret performance comparatively and, consequently, this is more likely to evoke a mastery motivational climate. However, there are circumstances in PE where ability groups may be preferable due to the nature of the activity. For example, in sustained running sessions, pupils of lower aerobic capacity would be unable to maintain the same pace as the more able runners in a mixed-ability group and would, therefore, be more likely to perceive this as a comparative situation in a performance motivational climate.

In order to foster a mastery motivational climate, the most important element to emphasise and promote within your groups is cooperation. Pupils can learn from each other just as effectively as they can learn from you, particularly when there are experienced performers in the groups. This type of learning environment, however, needs to be carefully constructed and facilitated by you, rather than just assuming it will happen by chance. Developing pupil leaders within groups assists this process, as does grouping pupils into units that work well together and complement each other's strengths and limitations. Sport education (Siedentop 1994) is an example of a PE-specific pedagogic model that utilises this grouping strategy effectively and using the reciprocal teaching style (Mosston and Ashworth 2002) is another. Now complete Task 7.9.

Task 7.9 Grouping strategies for effective learning

Make a list of different ways you could group your pupils in PE and consider when mixed-ability and ability grouping might be appropriate. Consider ways in which you could encourage pupils to work cooperatively and how this might impact on their learning. In planning three lessons during the forthcoming week, each with a different class, explore different ways of grouping the pupils and reflect on how this affected their learning. Keep these notes in your PDP.

Evaluation (elsewhere in the book, judgements of this nature are referred to as assessment)

Evaluation is one of the most important features of your lessons and consequently pupils' motivation to learn can be easily undermined by how it occurs. Evaluation that emphasises normative comparisons is identified with a performance motivational climate and evokes a state of ego involvement that can impair pupils' self-worth, intrinsic interest and perceived ability (Nicholls 1989). The mere availability of social comparison information, however, is not the main concern; rather, it is when this is emphasised that motivation can be undermined (Treasure 2001). In contrast, when evaluation is based on improvement, progress towards individual goals, participation and effort, everyone has equal opportunity to achieve.

Consistent with the recognition structure, in order to emphasise a mastery motivational climate, evaluation should be communicated individually without comparison to others. Furthermore, effort should be recognised and rewarded and mistakes regarded as part of the learning process rather than an indication of failure. Effective evaluation strategies for the promotion of a mastery motivational climate include informing your pupils of the criteria against which they are being evaluated and including them in the evaluation of themselves (self-evaluation) through, for example, video analysis or the use of personal diaries. They can also be involved in evaluating others (peer evaluation), for example, within the reciprocal style of Mosston and Ashworth (2002). By becoming more aware of their own and others' strengths and weaknesses, pupils are more likely to understand their achievement/performance and to be able to set themselves targets for improvement.

This is called evaluation/assessment *for* learning. Now complete Task 7.10 to consider the use of evaluation/assessment *for* learning.

Task 7.10 Assessment *for* learning

Ask your tutor to observe a lesson you teach and record: (1) how you use evaluation strategies to encourage individual progress and effort and (2) situations in which you encourage self and peer evaluation. Discuss the data collected by your tutor, particularly in respect of how these strategies promoted pupil learning. Consider with your tutor changes you might make in your teaching as a result of this reflective discussion. Put these notes in your PDP.

See Chapters 9 and 16 in Capel and Breckon (2014) and unit 6.1 (Haydn) in Capel *et al.* (2013) for more information on assessment.

Time

The pace of instruction and the time allotted for completing tasks significantly influence motivation. Strategies for promoting a mastery motivational climate in your lessons include the use of *extension* tasks, for those that finish the task early, and additional time for those who require it, thus allowing all pupils to progress at the rate of learning appropriate for/in line with their potential. However, depending on the maturity and experience of the pupils, allowing them flexibility in time to complete a task also has the potential to result in a loss of focus and for the pace of your lessons to drop to unsatisfactory levels so that learning is not maximised. You should, therefore, closely monitor tasks that allow pupils flexible time to ensure that they remain on task and are progressing at a rate that is optimum for their learning. Time is covered in Chapters 4, 5 and 12 in Capel and Breckon (2014). Now complete Task 7.11.

Task 7.11 Allowing flexible time to learn

Arrange for a lesson you teach to be video- and audio-recorded. After the lesson watch the recording and identify if and how you provided pupils flexible time to learn at their optimum rate. Note if you used an extension task for pupils who had completed a task very quickly and easily. Take these considerations into account in planning your next lesson with this class and ask your tutor to observe how effective you are being in this respect. Discuss your teaching with your tutor and put your notes in your PDP.

Consistent with a mastery motivational climate (Ames 1992) and SDT (Deci and Ryan 1985), adolescents have a strong desire to be independent from adults, to be autonomous, and to have an element of control over their own learning. The final section of this chapter on pupils' voice focuses specifically on this important aspect of developing an effective motivational environment in your PE lessons.

Pupils' voice in PE

The value of listening to young people in different contexts in society is well documented (Sandford *et al*. 2010). Increasingly, young people are perceived as capable of reflecting accurately on their own experiences (Christensen and James 2008; Heath *et al*. 2009) and, as such, they should be considered a key source of information for you, in terms of what engages them in PE lessons (Alderson 2008). *Pupils' voice* is about empowering young people to be involved in the process of learning and for teachers to value the contribution they have to make. This is important because it gives pupils responsibility and ownership of their learning and enables them to promote good relationships with peers and adults (Davies 2013). In addition, it is widely accepted that pupils engaging in discussions about their own and others' performance is a significant learning process for them (Sandford *et al*. 2010), enabling them to develop important skills such as listening to others, working collaboratively and making choices and decisions (Davies 2013). Furthermore, hearing what pupils have to say develops a shared culture and informs them of what is expected of them in the PE environment. As a consequence, attendance, participation, behaviour, attitudes, self-esteem and achievement often improve as pupils take ownership of what is happening around them and feel more engaged and valued (Davies 2013). It is, therefore, considered essential to create opportunities for pupils to be heard in your PE lessons and for their voices to be respected and valued.

Research in PE by Xiang *et al*. (2003) found that pupils liked to have choices, such as an activity choice day, but that PE teachers rarely allowed this. Further, Prusa *et al*. (2004) reported differences in self-determination between groups that were given choices in PE lessons and groups that were not, with the groups that were given choices reporting lower levels of *amotivation* and *external regulation*, and higher levels of *intrinsic* motivation. Therefore, increasing pupil choice within the curriculum can have a positive impact on pupils' motivation within your PE lessons (Ntoumanis 2001). Considering this relationship, and the fact that levels of physical activity start to decline after adolescence (Sallis *et al*. 2000), it would seem critical to listen to your pupils regarding their preferred activities within your lessons (Graham 1995; Hopple and Graham 1995). Indeed, pupils' voices and observations accurately reflect the experiences they are having and provide invaluable information toward understanding their experiences in the activities offered in your PE classes (Berstein *et al*. 2011). Now complete Task 7.12.

Task 7.12 Encouraging pupils' voice
Write a list of ways in which you might give pupils a *voice* in your lessons. In your teaching explore the use of some of the ways you listed and keep a record of pupil reactions to this opportunity, particularly changes in their engagement in the lesson. Discuss your findings with your tutor and consider reasons behind the effectiveness or otherwise of the different approaches you used. Continue to try out possibilities and then write a 1,000-word reflection on your experiences and findings. Put this writing in your PDP as evidence of Masters level work.

O'Sullivan and MacPhail (2010) identify some innovative ways of representing pupils' voices in PE (including photography, personal biographies, free writing, pupil drawings, scrap books, video diaries, poster sessions and physical activity timelines) and present a strong argument for including their perspectives in challenging accepted practices and implementing change to shape the curriculum. They argue that listening to and collaborating with your pupils will help you to understand their perspectives and implement changes to transform inequities that threaten participation and learning. Creating this type of collaborative learning environment is more likely to achieve the primary goal for all pupils to be active and, more importantly, to help pupils become motivated enough to want to learn and begin their own pattern of lifelong participation in physical activity (O'Sullivan and MacPhail 2010). Task 7.13 asks you to engage pupils in the evaluation of your lessons.

Task 7.13 Inviting pupil feedback on your lessons

At the end of a lesson, ask each of your pupils (anonymously) to complete the lesson evaluation pro-forma in Table 7.3 below (and also on the companion website: www.routledge.com/cw/capel), to provide you with feedback on their experiences in your PE lesson. Ask them to place these in a 'feedback box'. Use these to reflect on your teaching and, where appropriate, the content. Take particular note of consistent messages and also of contrasting messages. Write a 1,500-word piece setting out what you have learnt from this exercise, which might recommend changes in your teaching and interaction with all or some of the pupils. Put this writing in your PDP as evidence of Masters level work.

Table 7.3 Lesson evaluation for Task 7.13

Which aspects of the lesson did you enjoy?

....
....

What did you learn from the lesson?

....
....

Which aspects of the lesson would you like to change?

....
....

How could the lesson be improved?

....
....

Summary and key points

This chapter has attempted to demonstrate that you can develop a positive motivational climate in your lessons through fostering pupils' self-determination and implementation of the TARGET structure. Furthermore, it has emphasised the importance of the value of developing a mastery motivational climate in your PE lessons and of listening to your pupils' voice. The evidence presented in the chapter suggests that the promotion of a mastery motivational climate will assist you in enhancing pupils' motivation for learning. Finally, it is important to identify that, in addition to implementing the motivational theories and strategies covered in this chapter, your pedagogical and social skills as a teacher are crucial in motivating pupils for learning. Indeed, skills such as caring, nurturing, connecting, engaging, drawing out, stretching and reaching out to pupils, along with positivity and enthusiasm, are key aspects of working with your pupils and in developing their love of being active (Almond and Whitehead 2012c; Gano-Overway and Guivernau 2014). Now complete Task 7.14.

Task 7.14 Observing your teaching behaviours

Ask a colleague to video- and audio-tape a lesson you teach, specifically focusing on your interactions with the pupils. Focus on your pedagogical and social skills as well as your TARGET behaviours in the lesson. Write a 2,000-word piece evaluating your work from a number of perspectives covered in this chapter and create a development plan to strengthen your teaching. Put this writing in your PDP as evidence of Masters level work.

Check which requirements of your ITE you have addressed through this chapter.

Further reading

Ames, C. (1992) Achievement goals, motivational climate, and motivational processes, in G.C. Roberts (ed.) *Motivation in Sport and Exercise*, Champaign, IL: Human Kinetics, pp. 161–176.

This chapter argues that teachers need to pay particular attention to the motivational climate they create and that the promotion of a mastery motivational climate will lead to effective learning strategies being adopted by the pupils.

Biddle, S.J.H. (2001) Enhancing motivation in physical education, in G.C. Roberts (ed.) *Advances in Motivation in Sport and Exercise*, Champaign, IL: Human Kinetics, pp. 101–128.

This chapter presents results from a set of studies conducted mainly in European school PE settings, with the aim of discussing the enhancement of motivation in PE.

Morgan, K. (2011) *Athletics Challenges*, 2nd edn, Abingdon, Oxon: Routledge.

This PE teaching resource specifically implements the TARGET structures (Ames 1992) in athletics. It aims to foster a mastery motivational climate and to encourage all pupils to have a positive learning experience through a climate of inclusion and personal challenge.

O'Sullivan, M. and MacPhail, A. (eds) (2010) *Young People's Voices in Physical Education and Youth Sport*, Abingdon, Oxon: Routledge.

This book highlights the importance of young people's voices in understanding how they experience and understand PE, sport and physical activity.

Additional resources for this chapter are available on the companion website: www.routledge.com/cw/capel.

8 Developing and maintaining an effective learning environment

Kerry Whitehouse, Lerverne Barber and Vanessa Jones

Introduction

Developing and maintaining an effective learning environment in your lessons supports other aspects of your teaching by providing the best possible conditions to promote and support each pupil's learning, progress and achievement and to prevent misbehaviour. This chapter is designed to help you develop and maintain an effective learning environment for effective pupil learning.

Developing and maintaining an effective learning environment which promotes positive behaviour does not happen by chance. There are a multitude of factors to consider; in this chapter these are organised around the *ART* of positive behaviour management:

- *awareness* of: yourself (self-awareness) in the way you present yourself; the lesson climate; why pupils misbehave;
- *relationships*: knowing pupils as individuals; communicating effectively; promoting positive interpersonal relationships between teacher and pupils, and between pupils; and understanding the impact of praise and rewards on behaviour and the learning environment;
- *thoughtful planning* to use time effectively, ensuring all pupils are challenged and can achieve the intended learning, and the management of the working space.

The chapter is structured using the ART model.

Your ability to understand how to create an effective learning environment and promote positive behaviour develops as you gain experience and practise a variety of approaches. These are strengthened as you get to know your pupils and develop supportive and respectful relationships.

The UK government pledge to support teachers and head teachers in promoting positive behaviour and sanctioning behaviours which are unacceptable means that schools must ensure that they have a strong behaviour policy, which includes advice on the use of rewards and sanctions which are applied consistently (Department for Education (DfE) 2014d). It is important that you understand and are aware of the school behaviour policy as a starting point when you first begin school placement and later as you start to teach. School policies however are a small part of the big picture; effective and positive learning environments go much deeper.

Effective non-verbal communication is an important factor in developing an effective learning environment. In developing aspects of your teaching designed to create an effective learning environment, you will use some of the skills identified in other chapters in this book. You should therefore refer to other chapters where appropriate.

Objectives

At the end of this chapter you should be able to:

- understand the importance of creating an effective learning environment and a positive lesson climate;
- appreciate some aspects of self-presentation that are important to PE teachers;
- understand the importance of building positive and respectful relationships with pupils;
- understand the importance of purposefulness in a lesson;
- appreciate how to use time and space effectively to engage all pupils in a stimulating learning environment;
- understand the role of an effective learning environment in promoting positive behaviour as a means of preventing misbehaviour;
- understand the importance of non-verbal communication in developing and maintaining an effective learning environment.

Check the requirements of your initial teacher education (ITE) to see which relate to this chapter.

ART: Awareness

This section looks at awareness of: yourself (self-awareness) in terms of the way you present yourself; the lesson climate; and why pupils misbehave, including the importance of consistency of pupil expectation.

Self-awareness: How you present yourself and how you are perceived by the pupils

Task 8.1 asks you to identify the message you think the teacher is sending to pupils through the examples of good practice identified.

Task 8.1 What message is the teacher sending?

Read the statements below and identify what messages you think the PE teacher is sending through these examples of good practice.

(continued)

Task 8.1 *(continued)*

- The teacher arrives at the lesson before the pupils in order to meet them outside the changing room.
- The practical space is set up ready for the lesson when the pupils enter.
- The teacher greets all of the pupils by name as they enter the space.
- The teacher dresses appropriately for the type of activity being taught, e.g. bare feet for gymnastics/dance; smart clothes for classroom lessons.
- The changing rooms and indoor working spaces are well maintained and have resources on the walls to support and enhance learning.
- Pupils are included in other aspects of PE when they are unable to take part practically, e.g. as coach, performance analyst, choreographer.
- Sporting achievements are recognised and celebrated via the appropriate channels, e.g. on the walls of the PE department; during assemblies; in newsletters; on the web.

What message do you communicate to the pupils in each of these scenarios? How does this influence their perception of you? Are the aspects of good practice a true reflection of the teacher you aim to be? Discuss your responses with your tutor or another student teacher. Store your findings in your professional development portfolio (PDP) for reference later.

All the statements above relate to the teacher being well prepared for the lesson and creating a positive working environment for the pupils. These are attributes of an effective teacher. Task 8.2 asks you to consider other attributes of an effective PE teacher.

Task 8.2 Key words to describe an effective PE teacher

Write down 12-15 adjectives or phrases you might use to describe an effective PE teacher, for example, 'patient', 'well organised'. Underline all those that refer to how you might *present yourself* as a PE teacher. Compare your list with that of another student teacher doing the same task.

Store this information in your PDP.

Although teacher attributes are related to the personality of each individual, it would be surprising if your list of adjectives or phrases to describe an effective PE teacher differed radically from that of another student teacher doing the same task. Such is the particular nature of the subject of PE that to be successful you need to exhibit key attributes or characteristics. These enable you to gain the respect of pupils, motivate them to work and promote the learning of each individual pupil. In turn these promote positive behaviour.

As an enthusiastic and committed teacher you plan and prepare each lesson thoroughly, identifying obtainable, appropriate and challenging but achievable intended learning outcomes (ILOs) for pupils and differentiating learning tasks to accommodate the needs of each individual pupil. In addition you arrive early for the lesson, provide a quick pace to the lesson and do not allow minor interruptions to interfere with the lesson. You have a positive approach and teaching style, smile a lot, praise pupils for effort or performance, give specific, positive feedback whenever possible and encourage pupils to achieve the ILOs, therefore developing a positive lesson climate. Further, you dress and act as though you are enthusiastic about, and participate in, physical activity yourself. It is also an advantage to be a positive role model in your skilful execution of movement skills, and it is certainly the case that teacher demonstrations can help to inspire and enthuse pupils. There are three fundamental aspects of effective teacher self-presentation. These are discussed below.

First, a PE teacher needs to be *confident*, *authoritative* and clearly *in control of the situation*. These self-presentational attributes are necessary because you frequently work in a large space, at some distance from many of the pupils and in an environment that may contain safety hazards (see Chapter 12). To retain your authority you must convey clearly an assured and business-like self-presentation. Elements that contribute to the teacher's authority have been identified by Kyriacou (2009: 103) as 'subject knowledge; interest in and enthusiasm for the subject; and, the ability to set up effective learning experiences'. Appropriate and smart clothing is also essential. You are in part an organiser and a safety manager and your presentation must reinforce these roles.

Second, a PE teacher needs to be *energetic* and *enthusiastic*. While all teachers have to engage and interest pupils, you also have to motivate pupils to expend considerable effort in order to benefit fully from the lesson. A lethargic teacher is hardly likely to have a dynamic and determined class. In everything you do, you need to be alert, lively and encouraging. Do you convey to your pupils your enthusiasm for your subject content, for them and their learning, for improved performances and expenditure of effort? How do you accomplish this?

Although it is difficult to define precisely how enthusiasm is shown, as this is unique to each of you, it is important that as an enthusiastic and committed physical educationalist you convey your enthusiasm to the pupils, enthusing and motivating them to participate. However, it is worth remembering that enthusiastic teachers vary their voice, gestures and expressions; move around the teaching space; and maintain a quick pace to the lesson that involves high levels of interaction with pupils.

Third, a PE teacher's self-presentation needs to convey more than an authoritarian, able sports person. The movement skills that are often the focus of the lesson are performed by the pupils for all to see, and so there is a danger of self-consciousness, as the pupil's very selves, their bodies, are the subjects of observation and evaluation. The work in PE is therefore of a very personal nature and you need self-presentational skills that demonstrate a dimension of *understanding* and *sensitivity*. Furthermore, you need to convey to the pupils that you are approachable, sympathetic and caring. You should show both verbally and non-verbally that concern for pupils and their respective efforts is at the heart of the lesson.

Caring is revealed both in interactions between teachers and pupils and between pupils. A *caring pedagogy* (Noddings 1992, cited in Siedentop and Tannehill 2000) embraces pupils' personal and social growth and achievement to try to 'create a synergy between the learning goals and social goals of physical education' (Siedentop and Tannehill 2000: 106). Thus, teachers care that pupils learn and improve. It is based on the belief that if pupils feel respected and accepted by the teacher and their peers, they are more likely to apply themselves to their learning. A caring pedagogy includes:

- pupils who are supportive, responsible, accountable, cooperative, trusting, empowered, who identify with the class and who are committed to fairness and caring;
- learning communities which have boundaries, persist over time, share common goals, value cooperative practices, identify with community symbols and rituals, and are committed to fairness and caring;
- strategies for sustaining fairness and caring, such as collaboratively developed class procedures and discipline codes, class meetings to solve problems and develop class norms, challenging learning activities emphasising respect, opportunities to know one another and willingness to deal with values in the curriculum;
- investment in the development of pupils and sustaining conditions within which pupils protect the rights and interests of classmates;
- teacher practices such as helping, valuing pupils, treating pupils respectfully, being tolerant, encouraging and supporting, which are viewed by pupils as caring;
- caring teachers who plan challenging and significant activities and help pupils achieve important outcomes;
- caring teachers with skills and knowledge that relate to diversity issues in pedagogy and in the content being taught.

(adapted from Siedentop and Tannehill 2000: 115)

Your self-presentation should at all times demonstrate your professionalism and genuine concern for each individual pupil. Units 1.2 (Allen and Toplis) and 3.1 (Zwozdiak-Myers and Capel) in Capel *et al.* (2013) cover aspects of self-presentation. Task 8.3 focuses on self-presentation.

Task 8.3 Effective self-presentation

Return to Task 8.2 and compare the three aspects of self-presentation identified above (confident, authoritative and clearly in control of the situation; energetic and enthusiastic; understanding and sensitive) with your list and those aspects you underlined. Discuss with another student teacher how far you agree with the priority given to these three. Set yourself the challenge of conveying these three attributes during your next week of teaching. Ask your tutor to give you feedback on your mastery of each. Record your success, or otherwise, in your PDP.

It is worth taking time to check aspects of your non-verbal communication in relation to your self-presentation, for example, use of your voice (see Chapter 5), the clothes you wear, confidence and your movement in a lesson. You might also want to check other aspects of how you present yourself; for example, whether you have any habits or mannerisms such as the overuse of certain words and phrases (such as 'OK') or flicking the hair back from your face, which may detract from your ability to communicate with pupils effectively.

You might find pupils spending more time counting how many times you say 'OK' or flick your hair back than they spend listening to you. Your own habits and mannerisms are the focus of Task 8.4.

Task 8.4 Your habits and mannerisms

Ask another student teacher or your tutor to film you teaching one of your lessons. After the lesson observe the footage and try to detect any habits or mannerisms which could be hindering learning. Aim to reduce any such habits or mannerisms. Repeat the task at a later date to see if there is any difference. Record in your PDP how you reduced/eliminated the habit or mannerism.

Awareness of the lesson climate

A lesson with an effective learning environment has a positive climate. When we talk about the climate we are referring to the prevailing mood of the lesson. Pupils and their learning are placed at the centre of both the lesson planning and delivery. The lesson has a relaxed but purposeful atmosphere in which the pupils have a clear understanding of the ILOs. Pupils are expected to learn and to be on task (see Chapter 6), supported by a caring, enthusiastic teacher (see above). The teacher uses a positive teaching style, identifying and providing feedback on appropriate work; the positive reinforcement motivates pupils to learn and enhances their self-esteem (see Chapters 7 and 11 and Units 3.2 (Gervis and Capel) and 4.2 (Jepson and Walsh) in Capel *et al.* 2013). A positive climate in which specific feedback is provided about pupils' performance on a task, along with information about how to be more successful, in a way which is encouraging and supportive, is more likely to motivate pupils. Thus, much of the interaction in the class is positive, creating effective interpersonal relationships. A climate is not positive if it has all of the above, but no learning is taking place. You have, no doubt, experienced lessons in which there was a good atmosphere and pupils were 'busy, happy and good' (Placek 1983) but no learning was taking place.

Being at ease in your teaching

In a lesson with a positive climate you are likely to be at ease. If you are at ease, your pupils are likely to be so too. When pupils are at ease they are likely to be more confident, able to concentrate on the learning tasks and more likely to behave appropriately. When you are at ease you are more likely to smile, conveying that you are confident and enjoying the work you are doing with the pupils. This can be aided by using humour effectively.

Using humour

As with other teaching skills, humour must be used appropriately. In the early stages of learning to teach you may wonder whether, when and how you should use humour. However, as you develop as a teacher, you should become more confident. Humour can be used to laugh at yourself when you have said or done something silly, to reassure a pupil who is anxious, to defuse a situation in which there is potential conflict, to laugh with pupils at something they find amusing (as long as that is appropriate for you as a teacher); for example, a hockey ball breaks in two and the pupils laugh about which part to use. Such scenarios reveal the more approachable and human side to your nature.

Although using humour well can be effective, using humour inappropriately can make lessons go terribly wrong. You must not use humour at a pupil's expense, for example to humiliate through sarcasm. If you use humour too much pupils may perceive you as trying to be their friend, therefore you may become too familiar with pupils (see below). It may also make the lesson and pupils' learning seem unimportant. Thus, effective use of humour can help you to establish a warm, caring, positive climate in your lessons, but if you do not use it effectively, it can destroy your working relationship with your pupils and undermine your authority. It should therefore be used with care and treated as a teaching skill to be developed as you do with any other skill.

Task 8.5 asks you to focus on the lesson climate.

Task 8.5 Lesson climate

Observe two or three lessons, each taught by a different teacher. Focus on how the teacher establishes and maintains a positive lesson climate. Record examples of good practice in your PDP so that you can incorporate some of them into your own teaching, where appropriate.

Awareness of why pupils misbehave

It is important to be aware of possible internal and external situations and factors which may result in pupils misbehaving in your lesson. This provides information from which you can consider changes you can make to ensure there is a positive learning environment, reducing the likelihood of misbehaviour. Before continuing, reflect upon your past experiences and consider why pupils might misbehave in lessons by completing Task 8.6.

Task 8.6 Why pupils misbehave in lessons

Try to think of at least ten possible reasons why pupils might misbehave in lessons and then classify these under the headings below or create your own headings.

- events happening outside the classroom, at home, during break or lunch time;
- organisation of the class and the learning environment;
- tasks set within the lesson;
- the relationships between the pupils in your lesson;
- verbal and non-verbal communication.

Compare your list with those of another student teacher. Store your list in your PDP for future reference.

The interactions you have with pupils are based on your expectations, which in turn influence the way the pupils respond. If you expect pupils to misbehave, based on previous experience or reports from other teachers, they will probably fulfil your expectations. If you have high, but obtainable, expectations, it is likely to lead to pupils performing well and behaving appropriately. Thus, expectations can be self-fulfilling and you should:

- have consistent, realistic yet high expectations of all pupils, and set obtainable, appropriate and challenging but achievable ILOs and tasks for them;
- focus on current performance rather than previous performance on an activity or task;
- avoid comparing one pupil's performance with that of other pupils;
- endeavour to motivate all pupils by providing positive, constructive feedback which helps pupils to improve and raise standards.

See Unit 3.2 (Gervis and Capel) in Capel *et al.* (2013) for further information about teacher expectations.

Likewise, if you use positive verbal communication you encourage positive behaviour. Strategies you may wish to try with your classes to develop a positive and effective learning relationship include the following:

- Make a casual comment rather than a reprimand. For example: 'I didn't realise that we needed three basketballs in this game; can you make the changes please?'
- Framing questions: Rogers (2000: 27) suggests using the four Ws when framing questions to pupils about a behaviour problem:

  o   What's the problem specifically?
  o   What rule or right is being affected by this problem?
  o   Why do you think this problem is occurring?
  o   What can you do to fix the problem? It may also be useful to ask: how can I help?

- Use rule reminders: For example, 'Let's just recap that it is unsafe to chew gum in PE lessons. If anyone would like to put gum in the bin, please use this opportunity.'
- If-then statements: These can be a great help in allowing pupils a little time to consider the consequences of their actions, e.g. if you do not follow the instructions given by the referee, I will ask you to leave the pitch to complete a 'rules awareness' task.
- Partial agreement: Agreement is an essential strategy for avoiding or resolving conflict. It means teachers not trying to have the last word, or asserting their power in a situation when a pupil disputes their judgement.

  For example: Pupil: 'I wasn't talking, I was doing my work.'
  Teacher: 'OK, maybe you were but now I want you to press on to finish the task.'

ART: Relationships

This section looks at relationships: knowing pupils as individuals; communicating effectively; actions that promote positive interpersonal relationships between teacher and pupils, and between pupils; and understanding the impact of praise and rewards on behaviour and the learning environment.

Building positive and respectful relationships

Relationships play a key role in developing an effective learning environment and positive behaviour. Good relationships are at the heart of good behaviour. You need time and capacity to develop effective relationships with the pupils in your classes, which Rogers (2011) refers to as an 'establishment phase'. This usually occurs in the first few weeks of knowing a class and Rogers contends that this largely determines the relationships developed from then on. He argues that 70 per cent of pupils in any given class will work with a teacher providing the teacher is engaging, confident and respectful, and when a class meet a new teacher for the first time they will be looking at how the teacher deals with what Rogers refers to as the 'early defining moments', i.e. the first interactions with pupils that will determine the relationships dynamic of the class in the future. Non-verbal communication is important when developing relationships, for example, making eye contact with pupils, considering your facial expressions and varying your proximity to pupils, moving closer if you suspect a behaviour issue is about to arise. You can also strategically ignore a specific behaviour if you believe the pupil is seeking your attention. Now complete Task 8.7.

Task 8.7 Early defining moments

After you have taught your first lesson(s) with a number of classes, list the types of pupil behaviour that may be deemed 'defining moments' (both positive and challenging) in those early lessons with those classes. Now consider how you dealt with them and if in future you would repeat or change your actions. You may wish to use Table 8.1 to complete this task.

Table 8.1 'Defining moments' for developing relationships

What was the pupil behaviour?	What are your reflections upon the actions you took?	What have you learned from this early defining moment?
e.g. In the first lesson, I organised a starter activity which involved checking pupils' prior learning by writing their answers to questions on the whiteboard. This enabled pupils to engage in thinking before all had arrived in the sports hall. Some pupils did not engage with this and were off task, using practical equipment in the sports hall inappropriately.	I called over the small group of pupils who were off task and asked them firmly to return equipment to the 'safe' area, and to continue with the task. I recapped the task and my expectations and added information about using equipment safely and the loss of valuable learning time. Pupils responded by saying they had completed the task.	I do not think that my initial instructions and expectations were clear enough; I gave pupils too much time to complete the activity. In future I need to ensure that pupils are fully aware of what to do next if they believe a task has been completed. I will also ensure that timings of activities are appropriate.

Store the table/list of both those actions you would repeat, i.e. that you felt supported the development of positive relationships, and how (and why) you would change any future actions to lead to a better outcome in your PDP for use later.

Knowing your pupils

In establishing relationships it is important to learn pupils' names. If you learn pupils' names quickly, you send a message that you care about them as individuals and for their learning. However, it is not easy to learn pupils' names in PE lessons, as they are not sitting at desks. As a new teacher in the school you need to make a special effort to learn pupils' names. Many schools produce lists of photos of all pupils in a class. It can be very impressive to learn the names of the pupils before you meet them! You can learn names by talking to pupils at the beginning of the lesson when taking the register and at the end of the lesson. Teachers often use techniques such as asking pupils to say their names when they talk to them; set a goal of using pupils' names in, say, 50 per cent of interactions with them or set targets of learning, say, six names each lesson. However, it is difficult to hear what is being said in, for example, a swimming pool or when pupils are scattered in a large area; therefore you need to find techniques appropriate for the situation. Whatever technique you use, it is important that as a student teacher you learn pupils' names. Task 8.8 asks you to try techniques to learn pupils' names.

Task 8.8 Learning pupils' names

As soon as you can, get a register of all pupils in your classes. Ask experienced PE teachers what techniques they use to learn names. Make a particular effort to learn the names of pupils as soon as you can. If one technique is not working, try another one until you have found a technique that works for you. Record in your PDP why a specific technique did or did not work.

In addition to learning names, you need to know pupils personally in order to build relationships with them. It is useful to know a little information about each pupil, e.g. something they are proud of, their interests, as this provides a point of contact in interacting with them. It is also important to know about any particular needs, for example, high achievement, learning difficulties or emotional difficulties. The school can give you information and advice on considerations you should make when interacting with pupils.

You and your pupils must develop mutual respect for each other, accepting each other and valuing each other's viewpoints. All aspects of your teaching are important in showing you value pupils, including aspects such as questioning techniques. Asking open-ended questions, as well as developing pupils' higher-order thinking (see, for example, Bloom *et al.* 1956; see Chapters 3 and 5 and the companion website: www.routledge.com/cw/capel), are useful techniques for valuing pupils' contributions. A teacher may, for example, ask a question such as 'how can you get over a box without putting your feet on it?' If you only want and accept one possible answer 'a vault', you may discount an answer from a pupil who answers the question but does not give the answer you wanted. Hence, the pupil's answer is not valued and the pupil is not given the opportunity to make an effective contribution to the lesson. If you do only want one response, try not to totally discount an incorrect answer from a pupil; rather, prompt the pupil to think again and guide the pupil to give the correct answer. However, you need to think about whether the question is worded in the right way and whether you can ask questions which encourage more than one response.

Knowing the pupils in your class and how they react is vital in creating an appropriate climate for learning and to promote positive behaviour. Learning is multidimensional and often context-dependent, e.g. pupils may respond differently in various activities and when working with different groups.

Within your lessons, what you say and do, your body language, verbal communication and expectations all impact upon the way pupils respond to you. You should show both verbally and non-verbally that concern for pupils and their respective efforts is at the heart of the lesson. Task 8.9 is designed to help you consider the positive and negative aspects of your communication with pupils.

Task 8.9 Positive and negative verbal communication

What you say to pupils, *why* you say it, *how* and *when* you say it has a direct influence on the climate you create in your lesson and on the learning of your pupils. Record one of your lessons. Play the recording back and, as you listen/watch it, consider the following questions:

- Was your communication mostly positive or mostly negative?
- Were there any patterns to communication, for example, positive/negative feedback to some/all? positive about work but not about behaviour? different to able pupils compared to less able pupils? different to boys than to girls?
- How did your pupils respond to the communication?

Discuss with your tutor the pattern of your verbal communication, your pupils' response and the implications of this. Identify how you can increase the amount of positive communication, if appropriate.

Record your findings in your PDP. Try to put this into practice in your next lessons.

'You cannot control other people's behaviour, only your own, yet you can influence and manage pupils' behaviour' (Whitehouse 2014: 174). Although you want to establish a good rapport with pupils, some student teachers on their initial school placement adopt a friendly approach to their pupils and then they have not been able to establish their authority. You must maintain your status as a teacher so that your authority is not undermined and so that pupils do not lose respect for you. If you establish a good relationship with your pupils you can exert your authority when you need to. Siedentop (1991: 132) identified the following components of good relationships:

- Know your pupils.
- Appreciate your pupils.
- Acknowledge their efforts.
- Be a careful listener.

- Include pupils in decisions.
- Make some concessions when appropriate.
- Always show respect for pupils.
- Show honesty and integrity.
- Develop a sense of community, of belonging to the class.

Thus, it is important that you find a balance between controlling the class and placing a heavy reliance on punishment and being over-friendly and familiar with pupils so that boundaries become blurred, potentially making some pupils feel socially excluded. If you establish a good relationship this will mean that you are establishing mutual decision making and equality within the classroom. That is not to say you should let pupils run riot but you should support their part in the learning process. Roffey (2011: 103-104) lists a series of actions to support this:

- Greet pupils by name and smile so that you look pleased to see them.
- Show an interest; find out something about their life and ask the occasional question without interrogating them.
- Find something that you have in common, for example a team you both support or sport you both like playing.
- Find something that you can genuinely admire and comment positively on these qualities.
- Give regular positive feedback which is specific, genuine and brief.
- Let them know you believe they are worth the continued effort.
- Consistently show that their success, safety and wellbeing are of concern to you.
- Model courtesy – open a door for them; say please and thank you.
- Tell pupils what you enjoy about teaching them.

(adapted from Roffey 2011: 103-104)

As with all other aspects of your teaching, you need to monitor your relationship with your pupils. Now complete Task 8.10.

Task 8.10 Relationships with pupils

Both observe the lesson of another teacher and ask your tutor to observe you towards the beginning and then at the end of the placement, focusing on pupils' reactions to the teacher and the lesson. Make comments on and give examples for the following:

- Do pupils get to class early? Do they change quickly? Are they enthusiastic?
- Do pupils do things quickly and willingly?
- Do pupils ask questions to enhance their learning?
- Do pupils follow established rules and routines?
- Do pupils treat the teacher and other pupils with respect?
- Do pupils help one another without being prompted and feel positive about the class identity?

(continued)

Task 8.10 *(continued)*

Reflect on your observation of the teacher and on your tutor's observations of you. Discuss what these suggest about establishing positive interpersonal relationships with pupils. Reflect upon any progress you have made between the two observations. Keep the findings in your PDP to help you further develop your relationships with pupils in your classes.

Rewards

Pupils prefer to be praised rather than criticised. Praise can provide positive reinforcement, make pupils feel better and valued and want to work to achieve more in the lesson. You should use praise when pupils do something well, put effort into their work, show persistence and exhibit appropriate behaviours. Remember that it is important to praise *effort* as well as *achievement*. To be effective, praise needs to be positive, encouraging and specific. The general points to remember when using praise are not to over-praise as it becomes meaningless; make sure praise is earned and *sound* and *look* as though you mean it. Rewarding effort/desirable behaviour, and ignoring undesirable behaviour, 'rewards' and positively reinforces the behaviour you expect in lessons that have an effective learning environment and shifts the focus away from any bad behaviour (Kyriacou 2009). It is important, therefore, to focus on the positive, not condoning the unacceptable, but giving praise when appropriate and applying consequences which are fitting for the behaviour when necessary. Task 8.11 helps you understand the praise that you use in lessons.

Task 8.11 Use of praise

Ask your tutor or another teacher to observe a lesson and identify your use of praise during the lesson. Identify aspects such as the balance between praise to individuals, groups and the whole class; for effort/achievement/behaviour. Who gets the praise, how often and why? Discuss how effective your use of praise was and what you can do in your next lesson to increase its effectiveness. Record this in your PDP to refer to in developing your use of praise in future lessons.

ART: Thoughtful planning

This section looks at thoughtful planning in terms of how to use time effectively, ensuring all pupils are challenged and can achieve the intended learning, and management of the working space.

Thoughtful planning of time

In a purposeful lesson a teacher must create as much time as possible for learning (see time on task in Chapter 6). You can achieve this by good organisation and management skills (see Chapter 6) and by establishing a good pace to the lesson. It is important when planning that you look for ways in which you can save time, e.g. take the register whilst the pupils are changing.

You should also make sure that the lesson starts as promptly as possible and that your organisation enables each task or lesson episode, including changing from one task or lesson episode to the next, to proceed smoothly and efficiently. Establishing a prompt and clear start to a lesson means that you are able to maximise lesson time and focus pupils' attention on the learning environment from the outset, immediately eliminating any opportunities for disengagement that could lead to misbehaviour. You also create a sense of urgency in the lesson, encouraging pupils to do things quickly rather than dawdling. For example, pupils should jog to the outside space in which they are working, perhaps as part of the warm-up, rather than walk along chatting to a friend. Organise pupils within the group to take responsibility for taking out equipment maybe on a rota; make them feel it is an important and responsible role. They should also have been set a task to start when they get to their activity space.

Having a consistent approach to the start of every lesson means that pupils know what to expect and react quickly to instructions. Clear expectations help create an effective learning environment and maximise your lesson time. Avoiding situations where pupils are waiting around for the teacher to organise them has a positive impact on learning and on behaviour as pupils are engaged in the lesson from the outset. You should not allow the pace of the lesson to slow, for example, by taking too long to explain what pupils are to do next or spending too much time on one task, which could lead to boredom and possible disruption. When grouping pupils, plan who will work with whom in advance if possible. Use a logical sequence of numbers for small-sided practices, such as 2-4-8; reorganising pupils from groups of three to pairs, for example, can take longer and can cause problems when breaking up friendship groups (see Chapter 6).

Task 8.12 looks at purposefulness of a lesson.

Task 8.12 Purposefulness of a lesson

Observe two or three lessons taught by experienced teachers, focusing on the purposefulness of the lesson; for example, how long it takes for pupils to change for the lesson; what techniques the teacher uses and what is said to maintain a good pace to the lesson; how the teacher deals with unnecessary interruptions; how long pupils spend on each task; how long it takes to move from one task to another and how the teacher keeps this time to a minimum.

How do these compare with your own lessons? Ask another student teacher or your tutor to observe one or some of your lessons in relation to the same points. Do you need to change your practice to create a more purposeful lesson or plan more thoroughly for this to happen? Are there aspects of good practice you can adopt in your lessons? Identify what you need to do and try these out in your lessons. Record the teacher's and your own techniques in your PDP to refer to in planning further lessons.

Thoughtful planning of learning for all

A well-organised approach to planning at three levels – detailed and well-structured lesson plans (short-term planning), units of work (medium-term planning) and, later, schemes of work (long-term planning) – enables you to maximise opportunities for pupils to achieve the

ILOs. Careful planning should ensure that ILOs are clear and concise and, when presented at the start of the lesson, should give pupils an overview and understanding of the lesson focus and help to keep the pupils on task. Your lessons should be planned on a weekly basis, with each lesson evaluation feeding into the planning of the next lesson, identifying any individual or personalised learning needs. It is better to over-plan than under-plan and it is important to reflect critically on your completed lessons and units to inform future planning. However, your lesson plans should be suitably flexible to allow for adaptations in response to pupil achievement and needs, using the unit of work as a guide or indicator. Capel and Blair (2013) note the danger of being too rigid in planning, as this may lead to a routine or rigid approach to teaching that does not enable you to respond to the progress in learning needs of pupils in any one lesson. Planning is covered in Chapter 3, as well as in Chapters 4 and 5, in Capel and Breckon (2014).

In order to allow all pupils to achieve success, the appropriate and challenging but achievable ILOs you set for pupils should be differentiated to meet the needs of different pupils and be meaningful to each individual. In England the inclusion statement for the National Curriculum (DfE 2014a) states that teachers should set high expectations for every pupil, plan extension work for pupils whose attainment is significantly above the expected standard, and plan, in greater depth, lessons for pupils with low levels of prior attainment and for those from disadvantaged backgrounds. You are also expected to use appropriate assessment to set ambitious targets for pupils. Inclusion is addressed in detail in Chapter 10.

Pupils' learning is affected by a number of factors, including their previous knowledge and experience of an activity, their individual needs and the learning situations which the teacher organises. An understanding of theories of learning, for example, Piaget (1960), Vygotsky (1962) and Bruner (1966), helps you to develop teaching tasks which are appropriate to pupils' learning needs and which actively engage them in their own learning. See Units 5.1 (Burton) and 5.2 (Lowe) on learning in Capel *et al.* (2013) and try to apply the information to PE. You may also wish to consider the link between theories of learning and your teaching and learning strategies so that you can plan interesting and varied tasks to suit the range of different learning needs in any one class. Kolb's (1984) experiential learning cycle (cited in Jones and Barber 2014: 137) is also relevant here. We recommend adopting teaching and learning strategies that actively involve pupils in their own learning and which help them achieve a specific ILO (see Chapter 13). Chapter 11 in Capel and Breckon (2014) provides some practical examples.

It is especially important to set appropriate and challenging, but achievable, ILOs in PE because pupils' performance is on show; therefore failure in PE is particularly obvious. Physical actions and the success or otherwise of a pupil in accomplishing a task can be seen immediately by the rest of the class. ILOs and tasks that are too easy or too difficult will impact on pupils' achievement. Likewise, if a task or skill is too complex, or if it is not challenging enough, pupils may disengage. It is at the point that a pupil stops trying or 'goes off task' that behaviour issues can start. There is plenty of literature on teaching points for particular skills you might teach and, indeed, you include these in your lesson plans. An ability to 'read' what is happening during lessons and flexibility in adapting to changing circumstances are important (see Chapter 4 on movement observation). Modifications to your planning as the lesson progresses – including teaching strategies, content, material, approach to pupil learning – may be needed to enhance an effective learning environment.

It is also important to plan for positive behaviour. This can be done through collaboration, consistency and consequences, i.e.:

- Teacher/pupils: A mutually agreed behaviour checklist is a starting point for lessons and classroom routines. Chapter 14 in Capel and Breckon (2014) offers some good advice and practical strategies for implementing these.
- Teacher/teacher: School behaviour policies are written so that teachers have a consistent approach when dealing with negative behaviour and pupils are aware of the consequences of their actions. It is important therefore that you are aware of the policy and enforce it consistently.
- If you state a consequence, you must ensure that you follow through, e.g. if you warn pupils that a consequence of their behaviour will mean that they will lose five minutes of their lunchtime, then you need to be prepared to carry this out.

Thoughtful planning of the environment

The working space is an important consideration when planning, as the facilities and the equipment available in a particular space impact on pupil learning. The general appearance of the working space is an important factor in creating an effective learning environment. The space should be clean and tidy and convey a sense of care and attention to pupils and their learning. It is obviously hard to keep working spaces clean and tidy if a large number of groups and teachers are using the space, or if a space is used as a multi-purpose facility, such as lunch served in the hall followed immediately by a dance or gymnastics lesson. In dance and gymnastics pupils are, for the most part, required to work in bare feet and often engage in floor work; thus, cleanliness and tidiness are of paramount importance for reasons of health and safety. Further, be mindful of potential hazards to your outdoor working spaces such as a long-jump pit littered with drink cans and broken glass where pupils eat their lunch on the playing fields. This situation is made more difficult if a space is let to outside users. If you arrive for a lesson in a space that is unclean or untidy, it is worth cleaning or tidying it up before the lesson starts. You should also mention this to your tutor or head of department so that they can take steps to ensure that it does not happen again.

Each time you use a space you must check that it is safe (see Chapter 12). This requires equipment to be well maintained and in good order. There should not be any equipment left lying around in a working space. Likewise, as your lesson progresses, you should make sure that spare equipment is put away safely and not left lying around. Also, ensure that equipment is put away properly after the lesson so that it is tidy and easily accessible and that the space and the changing rooms are left in a suitable state for the next group. Engage the pupils in looking after their learning environment in order to take responsibility for it.

You can enhance the space by using neat, tidy and well-presented visual displays, such as posters and notices. Ensure, as far as possible, that these are informative, current and meaningful to *all* pupils by, for example, changing the displays seasonally and featuring male and female role models from different cultural backgrounds. Posters are very useful in gymnasiums or sports halls for providing visual displays of skills. Examples of actions and balances are particularly useful when introducing partner work/sport acrobatics. Literacy skills can also be developed by displays of key words associated with an activity or lesson focus. Again, these need to be changed regularly as the activity or focus changes. There are several books and websites that you can refer to for advice on how to create good visual displays. All of these should help to create a positive feeling among pupils about the lesson and about the environment in which they are working as well as aiding pupil learning.

Task 8.13 asks you to look at the PE spaces and Task 8.14 (on the companion website: www.routledge.com/cw/capel) identifies a range of strategies designed to support an effective learning environment for you to try out.

Task 8.13 The PE spaces

Are the PE facilities in your placement school attractive? clean? tidy? well looked after? Do they invite participation? What can you learn that you can apply when you are in your own school? How can you create an attractive, motivating PE environment in your school? You might like to offer to create a display, for example on an activity or an event, and keep this information in your PDP for reference when you are in your first post.

Non-verbal communication

Throughout this chapter the importance of non-verbal communication in developing and maintaining an effective learning environment has been highlighted. Non-verbal communication is the process of communication through sending and receiving messages and cues between people which do not involve words or speech. Non-verbal communication includes a range of things, including, for example, the way you present yourself, such as your appearance, gestures, posture, facial expression, habits and mannerisms, body language, touch, listening to pupils, distance, informal space around the body, the use of time and a clean and tidy workspace. It also includes the use of voice (see Chapter 5). For example, eye contact is a form of non-verbal communication which comprises actions of looking while talking and listening, frequency of glances, patterns of fixation, pupil dilation and blink rate. Non-verbal signals are important for good communication, classroom management and control. Thus, it is important that you are aware of what non-verbal messages you are sending out yourself and through the learning environment and to be sure these are the messages you want to convey.

Non-verbal communication can have a considerable impact, without any verbal communication, in creating an effective learning environment and promoting positive behaviour, e.g. looking at a pupil slightly longer than you would normally communicates your awareness that that person is talking or misbehaving. This may be sufficient to gain the pupil's attention. It can also have as great an impact, if not greater, than verbal communication, depending on whether or not verbal and non-verbal signals match each other; for example, if you are sending a consistent message by praising someone and smiling and looking pleased or reprimanding someone and looking stern and sounding firm, you are perceived as sincere. On the other hand, if you are smiling when reprimanding someone or looking bored when praising someone, you are sending conflicting messages that cause confusion and misunderstanding. Likewise, the appearance of the changing rooms, or posters on the wall, is a form of non-verbal communication; if the changing rooms are untidy, or the walls contain out-of-date lists or torn posters, for example, what message are you sending to pupils?

It is important to recognise the central role of non-verbal communication in all aspects of the ART model in developing an effective learning environment, as illustrated throughout this chapter.

Summary and key points

A positive climate in your lessons helps to create an environment in which pupils can learn, supporting the other aspects of your teaching. In creating a positive climate it is important to realise that a wide range of messages are sent out in a variety of ways, including your self-presentation and the presentation of the working space, as well as the purposefulness of the lesson. In a purposeful lesson with a positive climate, pupils are actively engaged in learning, motivated by appropriate and challenging but achievable ILOs to enable them to experience success and enhance their self-esteem. Suitable praise, feedback and guidance provide information and support to enhance further learning. This requires you to differentiate your material to cater for the needs of individual pupils (see Chapter 10) and to treat pupils in a way that shows you are interested in and care about them as individuals and about their progress. In order to create an effective learning environment, as an enthusiastic and committed teacher you should:

- plan and prepare each lesson thoroughly;
- identify appropriate and challenging but achievable ILOs for pupils, differentiating learning tasks to accommodate the needs of each individual pupil;
- arrive early and provide a quick pace to the lesson, not allowing minor interruptions to disrupt the flow;
- have a positive approach, praising pupils for effort or performance, giving specific, positive feedback whenever possible and encouraging pupils to achieve appropriate ILOs;
- dress and act as though you are enthusiastic about, and participate in, physical activity yourself;
- act as a positive role model in your skilful execution of movement skills wherever possible;
- be aware of the impact of all aspects of non-verbal communication.

Check which requirements of your ITE you have addressed through this chapter.

Further reading

Marland, M. (2002) *The Craft of the Classroom*, 3rd edn, London: Heinemann Educational.

A readable book that looks at classroom interaction.

Whitehouse, K. (2014) Teaching to promote positive behaviour, in S. Capel and P. Breckon (eds) *A Practical Guide to Teaching Physical Education in the Secondary School*, 2nd edn, Abingdon, Oxon: Routledge, pp. 166–179.

This chapter looks at strategies to promote positive behaviour within the PE classroom.

Additional resources for this chapter are available on the companion website: www.routledge.com/cw/capel.

Acknowledgement

The authors would like to thank Peter Breckon, Susan Capel, Margaret Whitehead and Paula Zwozdiak-Myers for their contribution to previous editions of this chapter.

9 Assessment *for* and *of* learning in PE

Angela Newton and Mark Bowler

Introduction

Assessment is integral to learning and teaching and thus is an essential part of your role as a PE teacher. You need to recognise where pupils are in their learning, communicate strengths and areas for development and identify the steps required to improve further. This might involve assessing pupil performance in PE, or broader aspects of learning such as their ability to make informed decisions and assess themselves and others. Examples of assessment can range from informal comments such as 'good shot' to the more formal assessment involved in examinations.

There are two principal types of assessment. One is known as formative. This type of assessment is designed to help pupils to progress their learning. The other is known as summative and provides information at the end of a lesson or unit of work concerning what pupils have achieved. In one sense, formative assessment looks forward while summative assessment looks back. Another way to differentiate between these two types of assessment is to refer to the first as assessment *for* learning and the second as assessment *of* learning. Both of these types of assessment are covered in this chapter.

There is a current consensus that more attention should be paid to assessment *for* learning. For example, telling a pupil that s/he has attained a 'good hang position in the air' provides little information to enhance learning. More information and guidance are given if the feedback goes further than this and indicates that the pupil performed a good hang position and continues with 'now try and drive your knee up higher in take-off to gain more height'. Similarly, an examination awarded just a mark gives little guidance as to how pupils can improve their work. Written comments giving feedback on strengths and areas to work on are far more productive and are again an example of assessment *for* learning.

Assessment was identified by the Office for Standards in Education (Ofsted) (2003) as a weakness for student PE teachers. Ofsted (2008, 2013b) has suggested that assessment practice is an area for development in our subject. This chapter identifies the reasons why we assess and how we do it. It aims to improve your ability to use the principles of assessment *for* learning as well as assessment *of* learning to enable all pupils to achieve their full potential. There are opportunities throughout the chapter to reflect upon and critically analyse assessment in practice.

Objectives

At the end of this chapter you should be able to:

- identify the broad principles and purposes of assessment in PE;
- understand the role of assessment *for* learning in improving teaching and learning in PE;
- apply shared intended learning outcomes (ILOs), questioning, feedback and pupil peer and self-assessment in your lessons;
- critically evaluate the success of assessment in helping pupils to achieve their full potential;
- understand the role of assessment *of* learning.

Check the requirements of your initial teacher education (ITE) to see which relate to this chapter.

Principles and purposes of assessment

Assessment is an integral part of teaching and learning, whether your focus is formative, as in assessment *for* learning, or summative, as in assessment *of* learning. As with every other part of your work, it needs to be done well in order to be effective. Pupils and parents, in particular, are concerned that assessment is carried out rigorously and fairly. This is true both of the very informal assessments you make in a lesson and of the most formal, as in giving a course work grade. Parents may complain if they feel their child's work is being unfairly judged by a teacher; for example, that the child always receives criticism, but never praise. Appeals may also be made to awarding bodies against grades awarded by accredited examination courses.

Good assessment adheres to certain principles:

- It should have a clear purpose and should be fit for that purpose.
- It is clear what the attainment – practical or written – is being measured against.
- It should be valid and reliable.

Purposes of assessment

Assessment fulfils a number of functions and these are discussed in the next section. Some researchers categorise these functions under two main headings. These are formative and summative. The purpose of formative assessment is to provide pupils with guidance as to how they can move on from their current stage of understanding or mastery. Typically, formative assessment is given in the ongoing teaching situation and may not be formally recorded. Formative assessment is also given in the comments written on a piece of homework or an examination script. The purpose of summative assessment is to record attainment at a particular time, usually the end of a unit, term or year, to record learning. This is often a formal process and records are kept of these marks or grades, such as in pupils' school reports.

As you work through the next section, decide whether the purpose of the assessment described is summative or formative. In order to make this decision you must consider whether the assessment promotes learning (assessment *for* learning) or merely assesses the current level of learning (assessment *of* learning).

Guidance or feedback

Pupils require information about their attainment to help them to understand what you are looking for in their work, to challenge them to greater achievement and to motivate them. This is most likely to take the form of verbal comments to pupils, although you may also be required to provide written feedback on occasion, for example, when pupils are 'on report' or when you are marking written work.

Diagnosis and evaluation

When first meeting a group of pupils or when beginning a new unit of work, you may wish to make a preliminary assessment of the pupils' strengths and needs, in which case you are assessing for the purpose of *diagnosis*. This information guides your subsequent planning. On a lesson-by-lesson basis you want to know what or how much pupils have learned in a lesson so that you can judge to what extent the ILOs of the lesson have been achieved and then plan the next lesson on the basis of this evaluation. In this case you are assessing for *evaluation*.

Grading and prediction

You may be required to provide grades for an annual report to parents. The grading system may be designated by the school or the department. With respect to examination classes, you need to grade the work in accordance with the requirements of the awarding body. Many of the sixth-form pupils you teach will be making applications for university. You may need to assess their attainment prior to the completion of application forms to provide a predicted grade and to give information for a reference concerning potential for their chosen course of study. These assessments are for the purposes of *grading* and *prediction*.

Motivation

The nature of the assessment and the way it is communicated to pupils can have a significant effect on their motivation, particularly when it is given publicly. More able pupils thrive on being recognised as running the fastest or jumping the furthest; however, for less able pupils it is never appropriate to draw attention to their attainment relative to others. An alternative approach to motivate pupils may be, on occasion, to focus on broader goals, such as how well they can reflect on their work, their leadership skills or their ability to work cooperatively as part of a team. All pupils benefit from positive feedback on effort and application, and on recognition of how much they have improved against previous attainment. Measuring attainment against an individual's previous work is called ipsative assessment and is covered later in this chapter.

As you get to know the pupils you realise that individual pupils respond differently to different types of feedback. For example, some may relish a challenge, others may need to be reminded that they are not performing up to their potential, while others may be very sensitive to less than positive comments. Lesson-based informal feedback is the means by which pupils are made aware of the continuous process of assessment you carry out in each of your lessons. Your observations of pupil attainment and of their responses to assessment, and the way you respond via feedback, are key aspects of your teaching which you need to monitor and use sensitively to maximise pupil motivation and learning.

Selection of pupils for grouping

There may be a school or department policy to group or set pupils according to their ability in PE. You therefore need to provide the relevant information for the groups you teach. These assessments are being carried out for *selection* purposes.

There are other assessment demands made of PE teachers. For example, you may be asked by your head of department or another colleague to conduct trials in an extracurricular activity in order to select pupils for school teams, or to decide which pupils may benefit most from an invitation to take part in an outdoor activity expedition. On occasion PE teachers may use certain criteria for selection, but the selection process could depend on the teacher making judgements about which pupils perform better than others. The first form of assessment mentioned above is called criterion-referenced and the second is known as norm-referenced. These types of assessment are explained further later in the chapter. Team selection criteria may not take account of the really keen rugby player who turns up every week at the beginning of the season but does not make the progress or have the necessary physical attributes required for the team. Thus PE teachers have to be clear about how they justify their criteria for team selection. The keen, but non-selected player may lose motivation and self-esteem as a result of the process and you need to consider the effects of such decisions. Self-esteem is addressed in Chapter 11.

Formal reporting

Awarding bodies usually require teachers to assess pupils formally. Examination boards may have elements of teacher-assessed coursework for both practical and theoretical elements. This assessment needs to be planned and carried out systematically and the criteria being used need to be very clearly identified (see assessment *of* learning, later in the chapter). Careful assessments of all pupils must be made and recorded in some way. These assessments, collected at intervals from selected units and lessons over a period of time, or from teacher-graded coursework, provide evidence for you to make judgements about pupils. This can form the basis of termly/annual reports to parents.

Task 9.1 asks you to work with another student teacher to observe and analyse assessment in different settings.

> **Task 9.1 Observing assessment in action**
>
> Observe a PE teacher or fellow student teacher in at least two lessons. Record all instances of assessment in each session. Following the observation, answer the following questions:
>
> - What *methods* are used for assessing pupils? This answers the question of how pupils are assessed (e.g. teacher or peer observation, listening to answers to questions, writing down scores/comments, written comments by pupils or assignments).
> - *What* is the teacher assessing? (e.g. attitudes, planning, attainment, knowledge, understanding, evaluation, cooperation)
> - *Who* is doing the assessment? Is it always the teacher? Are pupils involved in the process?
> - *Why* is the assessment being carried out? Is the purpose to give feedback to the pupils/parents/governors/others? Is it to motivate? Is it to identify the best performers? Any other reasons?
> - *How* are pupils given the results of assessment? Is it through an informal process such as a brief comment giving constructive feedback? Is it through a mark given for a specific attainment or evaluation? Any other ways?
>
> Identify which of your examples involve assessment *for* learning and which involve assessment *of* learning. Some could involve both. Put these observations in your professional development portfolio (PDP) and draw on them when you are planning assessment in your lessons.

Measuring pupils' achievement

The purpose for which you are carrying out the assessment should determine the yardstick against which you measure achievement. All assessment involves comparison and there are three types of comparison usually associated with assessment:

1   comparison with the attainment of others (*norm-referenced* assessment);
2   measurement against predetermined criteria (*criterion-referenced* assessment);
3   comparison with a previous attainment in the same activity or task (*ipsative* assessment).

Units 6.1 (Haydn) and 6.2 (Youens) in Capel *et al.* (2013) provide further information.

A race is an obvious example of a *norm-referenced* assessment. Each runner's performance is being judged in relation to the performance in the race of the other competitors. Many school examinations and class tests are also norm-referenced, the aim being to create a rank order of achievement.

Many awarding bodies produce precise descriptors against which pupil attainment is assessed (e.g. General Certificate of Secondary Education (GCSE) practical work). The statements may be associated with a corresponding mark that contributes to a final grade.

These statements are the criteria against which pupils' attainment is judged, making the assessment *criterion-referenced*. Awards of many governing bodies (e.g. British Gymnastics Award Schemes) are made on the basis of criterion-referenced assessments.

Where a pupil or athlete is judged to have achieved a 'personal best' then the assessment is being made against previous attempts by that individual to jump, run, swim, etc. This is an *ipsative* assessment. Much informal assessment carried out by both pupils and teachers in lessons is of this nature, for example, when a teacher praises work which is of a higher standard than in previous lessons. Such assessments are made of any aspect of pupil activity or behaviour. When a teacher tells a pupil, 'You have behaved better this lesson than ever before', or a pupil reports that, 'It's the first time I've swum a whole length without stopping', then ipsative assessments have been made.

If you wish to assess for the purpose of *grading* pupils' achievement, for *selecting* pupils or deciding who would benefit most from a particular opportunity, that is, *predicting* their future attainment, you may well want to compare pupil attainments and thus you are using *norm-referenced* assessment. In making a *diagnosis* of pupils' needs and strengths you need criteria for determining their level of competence. In this case a *criterion-referenced* assessment is most useful. Pupils may well be motivated by the teacher's acknowledgement that their attainment is improving and an *ipsative* assessment provides this. Future improvement of their skill or behaviour is assisted if you are able to offer *guidance* about what the pupils need to work on to develop their attainment further. This is an essential element of assessment *for* learning. The mode of assessment must always be appropriate for what is being measured and why it is being measured. This makes it fit for purpose.

Validity and reliability

An assessment is of little value if it does not assess what you want it to assess. If you give a group of pupils a written examination which requires them to show their knowledge of the rules and tactics of basketball it only provides you with information about pupil knowledge of rules and tactics. It does not help you to decide if pupils are able to apply decisions in a game, as no indication is given of their ability to play the game. If an assessment does not provide you with the information that you want then it is not a valid assessment. The assessment may, however, be reliable. This means that the assessment, e.g. a written examination, would achieve the same range of results if the assessment was carried out by another teacher. If you marked a set of examination scripts on another occasion, or if another teacher marked the scripts, the marks awarded to each pupil would be the same as those you gave originally. Good assessments should be both valid and reliable. It is possible for an assessment to be reliable and not valid, as in the case of the basketball examination. Likewise, in a GCSE class studying the skeletal and muscular systems, an essay set on an aspect of work that is not on the syllabus could be reliable but is not valid. However, an assessment is not valid if it is not reliable. For example, a situation in which class members were given the responsibility to grade peers without explicit criteria has the potential to be valid but is unlikely to be reliable on account of the variation in pupil knowledge and understanding. Assessment reliability and validity can be improved with the use of assessment criteria.

It is the case that assessment in the form of assessment *for* learning is integral to and closely related to the normal lesson activity. In this situation, as a teacher, you are likely to use informal methods of assessment very frequently which rely on observation and verbal interaction and take place in the usual working space. This form of assessment is essential in lessons to gather information on a class's overall response and attainment, and is integral to all teaching (see Chapters 4 and 6 on observation and organisation, respectively). However, these methods can be unreliable in assessing pupil progress as they often rely on fleeting snapshots of pupils performing. Much more systematic assessment is needed if grades are to be awarded. Written tests which include multiple-choice items and are carried out in formal examination conditions with the whole cohort of pupils sitting in the same room and being given identical instructions are far more likely to elicit reliable results. However, this type of assessment has limited use. These two examples reveal that the type of assessment must match what is being assessed.

The perfect assessment is yet to be developed. Validity may be increased by using a number of different assessment methods, for example, direct observation, study of video recordings and written work. You should try to make your assessments as valid and reliable as possible within the overall aim of ensuring that any assessment you use is fit for the purpose you have in mind. This will involve authentic learning contexts rather than atomising elements of skill, tactics/composition and decision making. For example, in games a teacher should assess pupils' performance in the game itself rather than through practices that isolate individual skills. Task 9.2 asks you to reflect back on your own experience in PE and consider the reliability and validity of assessment practices to which you were subject.

Task 9.2 Reflecting on your own assessment experiences

Consider your own experience as a pupil of being assessed in PE. What assessments took place in your PE lessons? Were you aware of being assessed? Were assessments closely related to normal lesson activity? Do you know on what basis the grade or comment on a report was made? Consider whether the informal/formal methods of assessment that you experienced in PE were valid and reliable. Record your examples of assessment on the diagram below.

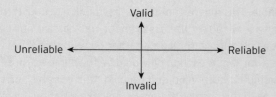

Put these notes into your PDP and consider them when you are planning assessments in your lessons.

The constituents of assessment *for* learning

Assessment *for* learning has been referred to earlier in this chapter. It is useful now to look into this aspect of assessment in more detail. Research led by the Assessment Reform

Group (ARG) (2002) into classroom-based practice (e.g. Black and Wiliam 1998; ARG 1999) resulted in the production of ten research-based principles of assessment *for* learning to guide practice.

These identify that assessment should:

1 be considered as part of your planning;
2 focus on pupil learning;
3 be a central part of your practice as a teacher;
4 be regarded as a key professional skill for teachers;
5 be sensitive and constructive to take account of the emotional impact on pupils;
6 foster motivation in pupils;
7 promote understanding of the criteria for assessment and pupil commitment to the goals they need to attain;
8 provide pupils with guidance about how to improve;
9 enable pupils to reflect and self-assess so that they can become independent learners;
10 recognise a full range of educational achievement for all pupils.

(adapted from ARG 2002)

The work of Black and Wiliam and the ARG has had a far-reaching impact throughout education in England. It has significantly influenced assessment practice and policy in schools for more than a decade. Whilst the work of the ARG has now finished, the Association for Achievement and Improvement through Assessment website (http://www.aaia.org.uk/) provides a good source of information on best practice in relation to assessment, recording and reporting.

The role of assessment *for* learning

As stated above, assessment *for* learning is a type of assessment that promotes pupil learning, understanding and attainment. It refers to feedback that builds from pupils' current level of mastery and identifies how further progress can be made. It is essentially constructive and forward looking. Understandably, it is a vital element of your work as a teacher. Effective use of assessment *for* learning requires good observation skills which give rise to accurate assessment and the provision of effective feedback to pupils. Most of your observations focus on pupils' actions in performance, or contributions whilst adopting different roles such as official, coach or choreographer. They may also focus on pupils' work towards achieving the broader goals of education towards which PE contributes. Many of these actions are fleeting and you have to rely on your ability to observe and judge instantaneously. This is a skill that you need to develop throughout your ITE and beyond and is linked to your knowledge and understanding of the contexts in which pupils are working. You need to know what you expect to see in pupil attainment and develop the ability to compare this to what you observe. Positioning and the ability to scan your class are other related teaching skills (see Chapter 4 for further guidance on observation). Once you have established sound observation skills, assessment *for* learning helps to determine the progress being made by pupils, indicate their strengths and weaknesses and identify their future needs.

Black *et al.* (2003) found that implementing specific assessment strategies can greatly improve pupil learning and increase enthusiasm and motivation in classroom subjects. These strategies provide a useful framework for your work in assessing for learning. In relation to PE, Spackman (2002) has identified four characteristics of assessment *for* learning that are applicable in our subject. These are shared ILOs, questioning, feedback and pupil peer and self-assessment. This is a useful text to study. Now complete Task 9.3.

Task 9.3 Investigating the nature of the assessment you are using in your teaching

Ask a teacher to complete a focused lesson observation that notes down instances when you used each of the four assessment strategies identified by Spackman. After the lesson discuss the results with the teacher and set yourself a target to work towards using all four strategies as appropriate.

Repeat this exercise again to note your progress in the use of these strategies. Record your progress in your PDP.

Shared ILOs

ILOs should be shared with pupils so that they are clear about what is to be learned and why they need to learn it. Statements should model the expectations that guide pupils towards the expected learning. When sharing ILOs in a gymnastics lesson, for example, you might say:

> By the end of today's lesson you will be able to adapt your movement sequence from floor to apparatus and refine your shapes and changes in speed and direction to perform more fluent sequences. This will help you to produce precise and controlled sequences with some originality.

It is important when sharing ILOs that the learning is clearly identified, in terms of what pupils will know, understand or be able to do, rather than simply the tasks that the pupils will be carrying out. These ILOs should be revisited throughout the lesson and assessed at appropriate times. When reviewing ILOs, you should ensure that pupils understand how well they achieved the ILOs and the potential they have for further improvement. Guidance for writing clear and differentiated ILOs is given in Chapter 3 and also in Chapter 16 (Bowler, Bassett and Newton) in Capel and Breckon (2014), which also has some useful activities (e.g. 16.1, 16.2, 16.3) to help you to plan and assess learning outcomes.

Questioning

Effective questioning techniques are essential in order to assess pupil knowledge and understanding accurately. Whilst pupil attainment can demonstrate knowledge and understanding, questioning allows a more comprehensive and rigorous assessment, being able to reveal pupils' intellectual grasp of an issue or problem. In the gymnastics example given above, teacher questioning would focus on appreciation of what is being learned, that is, the effects that changes in direction and speed have on a pupil's composition. For example, questions that might be posed are 'When is it appropriate to increase speed?' or 'At which point in the sequence can changes in direction be made?' Questions should be carefully planned and pupils should be given time to answer; you may even devise a situation in which there is a discussion of the answer with a peer. Teacher questioning, probing and prompting and peer discussion of questions allow pupils to think about their responses more deeply. (See Chapter 5 on the teacher's use of language for more discussion of questioning techniques.) To ensure that all pupils remain engaged during questioning episodes, a no-hands-up policy is advisable. This is where the teacher asks all pupils to consider a question and then selects pupils to answer at random. It is also important to foster a supportive environment in which pupils understand that an incorrect answer is part of the learning process.

The questions you use should be directly applicable to what is being learned and appropriate to the cognitive level of the pupils. In addition you need to be clear about the purpose of asking questions: whether a question is being asked for recall, to require pupils to analyse a task or to give pupils the opportunity to make innovative suggestions. A closed question is one that requires a single answer while an open question allows more variable and detailed responses, demanding higher-order thinking (see Unit 3.1 (Zwozdiak-Myers and Capel) in Capel *et al.* 2013). Bloom's *Taxonomy* (Bloom *et al.* 1956) (see Chapters 3 and 5 and the companion website: www.routledge.com/cw/capel) provides a framework from which you can design and evaluate learning and therefore distinguish between lower- and higher-order thinking skills. Lower-order thinking is usually required in answering closed questions, while higher-order thinking can be activated with open questions. Depending on the nature of the learning you are intending pupils to achieve and thus the domain you are tapping into, you need to phrase questions in an appropriate way.

Anderson *et al.* (2001) later revised the taxonomy and replaced the nouns used by Bloom with verbs. These describe actions which are easier to measure and therefore help planning, delivery and assessment. Table 9.1 summarises these two categorisations.

For example, a low-order (remembering) question might ask pupils if they can recall the name of the muscles in the front of the thigh or the correct learning points for a practical skill or technique. Higher-order questions might ask pupils to identify, for example, a movement/ part of a skill that requires the use of that muscle (applying) or to design a practice to develop the skill or technique (creating).

Table 9.1 Comparison of Bloom and Anderson's taxonomies

Bloom's taxonomy	Anderson's taxonomy	
Evaluation	Creating	Higher-order
Synthesis	Evaluating	↑
Analysis	Analysing	
Application	Applying	
Comprehension	Understanding	
Knowledge	Remembering	Lower-order

Task 9.4 is designed to help you to realise the different sorts of question that are used in teaching.

Task 9.4 Observing and analysing questioning

Observe a teacher for a lesson in your placement school.

1   Record all the questions that the teacher asks over a 20-minute period.
2   Identify the number of closed and open questions that the teacher uses during the lesson.
3   Evaluate the closed questions and rewrite any you feel could be expressed as open questions.
4   Categorise the level of cognitive demand within the questions using Anderson's taxonomy as a guide.
5   Select one question from either remembering or understanding and consider how it could be made more demanding in order to trigger higher-order thinking skills.

Put your observations and notes in your PDP and refer to it when developing questions to use in your lessons.

Feedback

Feedback is one of the most effective aspects of assessment *for* learning when it is focused on learning needs (Black *et al.* 2003). Feedback should focus on providing information to enable pupils to improve and therefore 'close the gap' between where they are in their learning and where they need to go or be. This involves effective teacher observation, discussed earlier. ILOs should be the focus of all feedback.

In PE most feedback is provided verbally. This is commonly divided into descriptive and prescriptive forms (Schmidt and Wrisberg 2008). Descriptive feedback describes the attainment of a pupil, whereas prescriptive also gives the pupil points for improvement. A piece of descriptive feedback might be, 'You contacted the ball with the inside of your foot', while a piece of prescriptive feedback would be, 'You contacted the ball with the inside of your foot – to gain more power you need to use the laces.' Feedback can also be a powerful tool for motivation (see motivation in Chapter 7 and also Unit 3.2 (Gervis and Capel) in Capel *et al.* 2013).

Positive, encouraging feedback incorporating the expectation that a pupil is capable of improving motivates the pupil to further effort. On the other hand, dismissive, negative feedback can leave a pupil demoralised and with little interest in continuing to work on a task. It is therefore important to ensure that as far as possible your feedback is positive as well as constructive and personalised for the needs of each pupil. Another point to bear in mind is the need to be objective in observing pupils. Try not to let expectations based on previous work influence your judgements. There is a good deal written about teachers' perceptions of pupils and the way that teachers tend to see what they expect to see. This is called the self-fulfilling prophecy (see Unit 3.2 (Gervis and Capel) in Capel *et al.* 2013).

It is also necessary to provide written feedback on essays and other projects that pupils who are following examination courses write. Written feedback to pupils should always include comments and not simply a grade. Comments need to identify what has been done well, what needs to be improved and guidance on how to implement changes. Opportunities to discuss and follow up these comments must be planned into your lessons in order to ensure that pupils interact with the feedback given. Feedback is also covered in Chapters 7 and 8. Now complete Task 9.5.

Task 9.5 Critical reflection on research into the effect of feedback on learning

Review the article by Hattie and Timperley (2007) (below) and consider the impact of the findings in relation to your own practice. In doing this you should reflect on which feedback strategies are most important to you as a PE teacher and which you currently consider to be central to your own development. Put your notes in your PDP as an example of Masters level work.

Hattie, P. and Timperley, H. (2007) 'The power of feedback', *Review of Educational Research*, 27, 1: 53–64.

Peer and self-assessment

While it is the case that teachers carry out most of the assessment, it is usual for broad education guidelines to recommend that pupils themselves begin to make judgements on their own and others' attainment and progress. Peer and self-assessment are useful in providing additional feedback to that which a teacher alone can offer. It is essential to remember that pupils' ability to assess themselves or others is in itself a skill that has to be learned, as pupils may not find it easy to critique their own or others' work (see below).

Peer evaluation is a very valuable exercise and should occur prior to self-evaluation. The use of criteria sheets is helpful so that pupils know what they are looking for (see the reciprocal teaching style of Mosston and Ashworth (2002), which involves peer assessment/ teaching). Pupils need to develop the trust and confidence necessary to carry out this kind of assessment. This requires careful planning and a willingness to devolve responsibility to the pupils. In situations of self- or peer assessment it is not your role to give direct feedback on pupil attainment. Instead you should enquire how they feel they or their partner is progressing, and what next steps need to be taken for improvement. This is where questioning can be used to good effect (see above, Chapter 5 and Unit 3.1 (Zwozdiak-Myers and Capel) in Capel *et al.* 2013). The role of the teacher is also to commend the pupil on astute assessment or to give guidance on how assessment techniques can be improved.

When assessing practical performance, it is easy to see if a peer or self is successful in some activities, e.g. it is easy to see if a ball bowled in cricket is near to the wicket. However, it is not easy to know why it was successful. Peer assessment should be developed before self-assessment because pupils cannot see themselves perform unless they have access to video playback. Observing and assessing a peer can have a positive effect on pupils' own attainment as it deepens their understanding of the activity/task. The development of visual analysis software provides the opportunity for immediate visual feedback that allows pupils to assess their own and others' attainment more readily. Pupils should not be aiming merely to judge each other's work. The peer assessment process should provide pupils with the opportunity to reflect upon the requirements of a performance, and to begin to appreciate the nature and constituents of movement. This can be linked to pupils using proprioceptive feedback to assess self, but they need time and help to develop this.

Developing peer and self-assessment involves careful planning, time and patience. Pupils need plenty of opportunities to practise this skill. Their ability to evaluate attainment and provide constructive feedback must be developed gradually and with pupil maturity in mind. You might begin by providing pupils with prompts or basic criteria. For instance, pupils may be asked, using a work card or criteria sheet, to identify the strongest aspects of, for example, a performance or piece of written work as well as a key area for development. Eventually you want pupils to make their own decisions about what needs to be improved and also how this progress can be effected.

Using assessment for learning to inform teachers' in-lesson decisions

You also draw on assessment *for* learning skills in the ongoing teaching situation to judge the appropriateness of the ILOs of a lesson. This requires good skills, including good observation and sound knowledge of the activity being assessed. If this 'in-lesson' assessment indicates that the ILOs are too ambitious you may need to modify your aspirations for the lesson. This is not unusual, even with experienced teachers. Classes sometimes do not respond as anticipated. There is no point in staying with your plans if there is clearly no way that pupils can reach the intended levels of work. Normally this means dropping one ILO or making an ILO less demanding.

Now complete Task 9.6.

Task 9.6 Action research

Select one of the four characteristics of assessment *for* learning identified by Spackman (2002: see above) that you feel will improve your practice. Identify two or three goals to focus on in relation to your chosen characteristic, e.g. questioning: improving the use of open questions; ensuring that all pupils are engaged during questioning; employing higher-order questions to stretch more able pupils.

Plan a short unit of work for four lessons and using the action research cycle conduct a small research project aimed at improving your practice. To help you with this, read Chapter 15 and Zwozdiak-Myers, Action research in Capel and Breckon (2014) (Activities 20.1a, 20.1b, 20.2a, 20.2b, 20.3a, 20.3b, 20.3c, 20.3d should also be useful). You may also wish to do some further reading to help identify your goals and to understand the research literature.

After each lesson carefully review and evaluate progress against your goals, making adjustments to your planning as necessary. Some researchers call this plan-do-review (Elliott 1991). You will find it much easier if your tutor or another student teacher acts as an observer. Evaluate the results and identify how you might apply the findings to other lessons/groups of pupils.

Further guidance on reflective practice is provided in Chapter 15. Put your plans and notes in your PDP as evidence of Masters level work.

Assessment *of* learning

As indicated at the start of the chapter, the purpose of assessment *of* learning or summative assessment is to record attainment at a particular time, usually the end of a unit, term or year. Summative assessment records learning. This is often a formal process and records are kept of these marks or grades. Summative assessments often appear in pupils' school reports. In both these cases assessment is in the interest of subsequent pupil learning.

Assessment *of* learning may be carried out for evaluation, grading, prediction, selection or formal reporting (see earlier in the chapter in the section on purposes of assessment). Assessments for awarding bodies require you to work with specific assessment criteria. These will most commonly be for 14–19 examination courses, leadership courses and governing body award schemes. You are expected to make judgements about pupils' learning in order to inform a grade or level or indicate progress towards a goal. Assessment of pupils on a particular unit of work needs to be carried out against the unit objectives. Assessment of an individual, small group or whole group in a lesson needs to be carried out against the ILOs of that lesson.

Although summative assessments are primarily used to confirm learning, they also provide an opportunity for you to reflect on your practice and make adaptations for future lessons in the light of the changing needs of your pupils. Summative assessments, such as an in-class test, can also be used to help pupils identify areas which require further development and plan for improvement. When used in this way summative assessments can promote reflective learning and help pupils to prioritise areas for development. Black *et al.* (2003) refer to this process as the formative use of summative assessment. Further examples might include pupils applying marking criteria to assess their own and others' work, pupils setting their own questions and developing their own assessment criteria.

Building assessment into unit planning

Having worked through this chapter you should understand fully that assessment is not a 'bolt-on' process but is integral to effective teaching and learning. Therefore, it is helpful for you to consider the range of assessment that PE teachers undertake in their day-to-day teaching. As a student teacher you are probably not involved in mapping assessment across units and schemes of work. However, even at this early stage it is useful to be thinking about this. You must first be clear about what you want your pupils to learn. This is expressed as your unit objectives. You must also consider the context in which you are teaching. At the planning stage you must clarify which of the unit objectives you are going to assess and record for individual pupils. These objectives are the focus of your evaluation. Once these have been identified you must then decide on the strategy to be used for each objective. All assessment that you intend to carry out should be built into the structure or framework of your units of work and should be carried out throughout the unit.

All objectives from the unit should also be evaluated from a class perspective in order for you to be able to assess the quality of your teaching relative to pupil achievement. This follows the same process as evaluating lesson ILOs, that is, an evaluation of what the pupils achieved, material and challenges they should move on to next and how your teaching affected their learning (see Chapter 3).

Summary and key points

After working through this chapter you should now understand the principles and wide range of purposes of assessment, including the need to ensure assessments are valid and reliable. You should also understand the role assessment plays in improving teaching and learning in PE and how it can develop your competence in assessing pupils in your day-to-day teaching. This includes assessing the broader goals of education as well as pupil performance. It is recommended that you specifically focus on assessment *for* learning strategies such as shared ILOs, questioning, feedback and peer and self-assessment, as these enhance pupil learning and improve your teaching.

This chapter has indicated the need for appropriate and specific assessment criteria, whether the assessment is formal or informal. Judgements can then be made and feedback provided in order to move learning forward. You should also be familiar with the need to assess against unit objectives or ILOs of a lesson in order to inform pupil learning, as well as your own planning and teaching. Given Ofsted concerns about assessment, you should now realise the importance of assessment and be in a position to place it at the centre of the learning process.

Check which requirements of your ITE you have addressed through this chapter.

Further reading

Black, P. and Wiliam, D. (2002) *Working Inside the Black Box: Assessment for Learning in the Classroom*, London: Kings College.
Black, P. and Wiliam, D. (1998) *Inside the Black Box: Raising Standards through Classroom Assessment*, London: Kings College.

These two publications give detailed information on the use of assessment *for* learning in improving the understanding of how assessment can enhance and improve the teaching and learning process. Although not PE-specific, they can add to your understanding of assessment.

Black, P., Harrison, C., Lee, C., Marshall, B. and William, D. (2003) *Assessment for Learning: Putting it into Practice*, Maidenhead, Berks: Open University Press.

This text is based on a two-year study involving school teachers. It provides a review of the assessment research followed by a discussion on the implementation of the chosen strategies. The strategies are evaluated and guidance for implementing change is provided.

Gardner, J. (ed.) (2012) *Assessment and Learning*, 2nd edn, London: Sage Publications.

This book contains chapters authored by members of the ARG, a group of researchers who focus on ensuring policy and practice take account of current research evidence. The book concentrates on the use of assessment in supporting learning. It provides practice-based theory about assessment in the classroom, developing motivation and assessment in relation to learning theory.

Wragg, E.C. (2001) *Assessment and Learning in the Secondary School*, London: RoutledgeFalmer.

This book looks at the different purposes of assessment, then describes and analyses the different means of assessing progress. Another purpose is to relate assessment to learning. The book is designed to help you reflect on assessment and then take action to improve teaching and learning in your own classroom.

Additional resources for this chapter are available on the companion website: www.routledge.com/cw/capel.

10 Planning for an inclusive approach to learning and teaching

Philip Vickerman, Barbara Walsh and Julie Money

Introduction

Teachers have a fundamental responsibility to maximise the learning of all pupils. Teachers are, therefore, required to work flexibly and creatively to design environments that are conducive to learning for all. This involves identifying potential barriers to learning, teaching and assessment, whilst using strategies that offer full access and entitlement to PE. As part of this process you need to develop strategies for working in partnership with pupils, parents, teachers and external agencies to ensure equality of opportunity in PE. A central aspect of this involves active consultation with the pupils themselves, listening to their views, opinions and perceptions of PE.

This chapter provides you with an overview of issues pertinent to an inclusive agenda whilst offering opportunities to reflect upon your practice and learn to use strategies to ensure equality of opportunity in PE. In England in recent years notions of inclusion and diversity have risen up the agenda to such an extent that there is a plethora of policies, legislation and statutory guidance. The National Curriculum (NC) (Department for Education (DfE) 2014a: 9) states that in relation to inclusion teachers should 'set high expectations for every pupil'. They should plan stretching work for pupils whose attainment is significantly above the expected standard. They have an even greater obligation to plan lessons for pupils who have low levels of prior attainment or come from disadvantaged backgrounds.

This requirement is supported by other statutory and policy directives such as: the Special Educational Needs (SEN) and Disability Rights Act (Department for Education and Skills (DfES) 2001), and the Equality Act (UK Legislation 2010). Currently, the Children and Families Act (UK Legislation 2014) is about reforming services for vulnerable children in order to give every child an equal chance, whatever their start in life, to make the very best of themselves. These acts all intend to tackle entrenched inequalities, with the contribution of all pupils and groups now being signalled as an important part of a modern society. Naturally, this has significant implications for you as a PE teacher in ensuring you meet the full diversity of pupils' needs.

Statistical evidence from the DfE (2013d) suggests that around 19 per cent of pupils across all schools have SEN and of this, 53 per cent are within mainstream schools. However, this number is likely to rise with the introduction of the Children and Families Act (UK Legislation 2014), where schools will be expected to accommodate pupils with SEN through appropriate differentiation. Thus, if we combine this data with other diverse and/or marginalised groups (in relation to, e.g. race, gender, English as an additional language, class and poverty, to name but a few), the need to have a commitment to supporting inclusive education is well evidenced. This, matched by the increasing focus on the individual within the NC and a greater focus on personalised learning (Lewin and Solomon 2013), emphasises the requirement for you as a teacher to embrace this agenda within your strategies for learning, teaching and assessment in order to maximise opportunities for all pupils to participate, perform and reach their full potential. As an example of the practical implications of these policies, PE teachers are required to review the suitability of learning objectives, the nature of activities and the assessment strategies in order to ensure all pupils learn and develop.

Objectives

At the end of this chapter you should be able to:

- appreciate the philosophy and practice of inclusive PE that follows the personalisation agenda;
- identify core values which enable you to plan, deliver and review your strategies for inclusive PE;
- understand the principles of the National Curriculum for Physical Education (NCPE) (DfE 2014c) related to inclusion and its implementation within PE settings;
- consider a range of learning, teaching and assessment strategies that equip you with the knowledge, skills and understanding to plan and deliver effectively for inclusive PE.

Check the requirements of your initial teacher education (ITE) to see which relate to this chapter.

Including all pupils in PE

Runswick-Cole (2011) asserts that inclusion has become part of the global agenda and, as part of a modern society, equality of opportunity in all aspects of life is a social and moral right for all citizens. They propose that schools offer ideal opportunities to learn mutual understanding and respect for diversity. In order for you to begin to consider planning for inclusion in PE lessons, it is essential first to clarify that pupils have a fundamental right to an inclusive education, supported in England through statutory legislation and guidance. In beginning to interpret this, you should recognise that success depends on teachers having an open mind, positive attitude and willingness to modify and adapt learning, teaching and assessment strategies and practices (Morley *et al.* 2005).

It is crucial to appreciate this does not involve trying to support all pupils in the same way. As Rogers (2007) indicates, in order to facilitate full access to the PE curriculum, you need to develop skills to identify individual pupils' needs, and then devise plans appropriate to their particular circumstances. As such, Mouratidis *et al.* (2008) and Vickerman (2007) support this view, suggesting equality of opportunity and inclusiveness should focus on celebrating difference whilst creating systems in which pupils are treated equally, but differently. This ensures their particular needs are met through gaining accessibility to all aspects of PE and school sport.

When planning for inclusion, Goodley (2014) supports the promotion of the social model of disability (Watermeyer 2012) as a means of removing emphasis from pupils with SEN, focusing rather on the roles teachers and non-disabled pupils can play. The social model of disability recognises that often the greatest restrictive factor to a barrier-free PE curriculum is not the pupil who is being perceived as different, but the lack of flexibility and commitment to modify current practices by schools and teachers. Similarly, according to Kelly *et al.* (2014), a move towards fully inclusive education will require cultural and flexible shifts in ideologies and practices in schools. For example, if a pupil in a wheelchair struggles to shoot a netball into a high hoop, schools should consider purchasing alternative shooting rings that move up or down. Another example may be where a pupil, because of cultural beliefs, cannot take part in strenuous physical activity when fasting; PE teachers should consider involving the pupil in an officiating or coaching role, in order to ensure s/he can participate in the lesson. In order to develop an inclusive PE curriculum you should therefore consider strategies that respect difference (Rink and Hall 2008) and offer other pupils opportunities to value and celebrate diversity.

Planning for inclusion requires responsive and flexible approaches that recognise all pupils are on a continuum of learning in PE (Vickerman and Coates 2009). Vickerman and Blundell (2012) advocate the need to consider new ways of involving all pupils, drawing on the teacher's skills of experimentation and reflection as well as collaborating with other colleagues and external agencies to maximise learning potential. Task 10.1 asks you to observe another teacher and note down ways in which pupils with particular needs are catered for.

Task 10.1 Observing the practice of another teacher

Observe a lesson taught by another teacher and note down ways in which the particular needs of pupils are catered for. This may involve, for example, modifying the task or the equipment, or allocating more time for a task to be undertaken. Discuss your notes with the teacher and keep these in your professional development portfolio (PDP).

The assessment of pupils with SEN presents many issues to PE teachers, as the types of activities, specialist environment, equipment and the dynamics and organisation of different group sizes all have to be taken into consideration. It is important that diversity is embraced and that pupils' achievements and progress are recognised. You therefore need to consider adopting flexible teaching and assessment strategies (Cole 2008) to provide opportunities for all pupils to demonstrate knowledge and understanding. Assessment for learning helps to inform you about pupils' learning and guide you in the next steps in planning pupils' learning and lesson planning. Assessment of learning allows you to collect information about what has been achieved over a period of time. Both assessment for learning and assessment of learning have pedagogical functions that support pupil achievement. However you need to decide on which type of assessment best suits the learner, intended learning outcomes (ILOs) and the purpose of the lesson (see Chapter 9). A pupil with cerebral palsy, for example, participating in a games activity involving sending and receiving, may need assistance with modified equipment to help the pupil demonstrate propelling a ball (i.e. a plastic gutter or shoot). In this situation your assessment is particular to that pupil and is in no way comparable with your assessment of others in the class. This personalised assessment enables an SEN pupil to demonstrate individual success and achievement within the PE curriculum (Hutzler and Levi 2008). An example of modifying teaching in gymnastics may involve restricting or increasing the number of moves in a sequence in order to address the full continuum of learning. Assessment of this task reflects the particular challenge set for the pupil(s).

Furthermore, as part of adopting a systematic process to inclusive PE, schools and teachers should audit their current practices whilst identifying any areas for development. The Equality Act (UK Legislation 2010) is one such method, by which schools and teachers are now being expected to review and evaluate the extent to which they are enabling pupils' full access to the curriculum. As part of this approach there is an increasing emphasis on 'hearing the voices of children' (Coates and Vickerman 2008, 2013) or, in other words, involving pupils in aspects of your planning. In this way pupils' aspirations and interests can be taken into account in devising curricula and lessons. Task 10.2 asks you to reflect on what you have read so far in this chapter, familiarise yourself with key documentation and consider implications for your work in PE.

Task 10.2 Fundamentals of inclusion

Based on your reading of this chapter so far, make some notes on what you consider as key aspects of inclusion policy and practice that impact on your teaching of PE. Familiarise yourself with government and school policies. Reflect upon what strategies you consider essential to removing barriers to achievement for the full diversity of all pupils in PE. As part of this process you should consider the following questions:

- Have I read the key government statutory documentation on inclusion?
- What is the school policy on inclusion?
- What is the PE department policy on inclusion?
- In what ways is PE better able or less readily able than other subject areas to cater for pupils with disabilities?

It may be useful to meet your placement school SEN Coordinator (SENCO) as you carry out this task. Put relevant documents and notes in your PDP.

A diverse continuum of pupil needs

The SEN and Disability (SEND) Code of Practice 2014 (DfE 2014e) addresses young people with SEN. The main change in the SEN Code of Practice 2001 (DfES 2001) is that the age range is now 0-25 years old, and there is a clearer focus on the views of young people themselves.

The Statement and Learning Difficulties Assessment is replaced by the Education and Health Care Plan. The 'Local Offer' is also part of the Bill, where there is a single information point where families can see clearly what services are available for young people aged 0-25 in the area who have SEND in relation to education, health and care.

While it is essential that you are fully aware of the statutory requirements concerned with individualised practices in education and recognise the philosophy behind these, this is only the first step in your playing an active part in the process. The key to accommodating all individuals depends on your adapting your practice to cater for the needs of all pupils (see later in the chapter for more detail). This includes the gifted and talented as well as those with a disability. Thus, pupils with outstanding potential need to receive appropriate guidance and support within and outside the curriculum. In lessons, these pupils may need more challenging tasks and be required to reach higher levels of achievement. Outside the curriculum you should try to direct them to extracurricular activity sessions, clubs and coaches where their potential can be nurtured. (For further information on talent development in PE, see Morley and Bailey (2006); Bailey *et al*. (2009); Chapter 11 in Capel *et al*. (2006); and Chapter 15 in Capel and Breckon (2014).)

Another group of pupils who need specific support are those with English as an additional language. These pupils need specific attention. There may be a bilingual support worker to assist or in some situations the pupil can be paired with a bilingual pupil. If you do not have a support worker in the lesson you could increase the use of demonstration or visual images/posters to explain the ILOs you are trying to achieve (see Association for Physical Education website for further guidance: afPE.org.uk). Pupils who are hearing- or sight-impaired also need to be accommodated in your lessons so that they can take as full a part as possible, learning and thriving in the PE context. The SENCO in your placement school should be able to give you guidance on supporting these pupils, and others with particular needs.

Other groups who need your consideration are those from non-English cultural family backgrounds, girls and travellers. (See Evans (2014) for a full debate about the needs arising from cultural diversity and the different perspectives and characteristics of girls. See Daniels (2008) for research into catering for the needs of travellers and also Bhopal (2004). For research on Muslim women in sport, see Benn *et al*. (2011).)

Key values for including all pupils in PE

The four key principles related to equality of opportunity are *entitlement, accessibility, integration and integrity* (Department of Education and Science and the Welsh Office (DES/WO) 1992). These should remain cornerstones upon which the PE curriculum of a school is founded.

The concept of *entitlement* asserts every pupil's fundamental right to access the PE curriculum. This is of particular relevance to pupils with SEN and has been endorsed by the SEN and Disability Rights Act (DfES 2001), Disability Equality Duty (Disability Rights Commission 2006) and the SEN Code of Practice (DfE 2014d). Indeed, this revised SEN Code of Practice focuses centrally upon the action of schools to implement and deliver inclusive PE. As part of this entitlement, you are expected to take action within the individual school context to plan for inclusive practice in order to facilitate pupils' full entitlement to the curriculum. This recognises the premise of PE teachers adopting positive attitudes and open minds through which potential barriers are minimised via consultation and modification of learning, teaching and assessment strategies (Vickerman and Blundell 2012).

In terms of *accessibility*, it is your responsibility to ensure PE lessons are barrier-free and relevant to the diversity of pupils. This endorses the social model of disability (Watermeyer 2012), which sees it as your responsibility to adjust your teaching in order to accommodate the needs of individual pupils, rather than the pupil being seen as the barrier to participation. For example, a pupil with English as an additional language may require assistance with communication skills in order to be fully included in your lesson, and the school and PE department should plan for this in advance.

In relation to the third principle of *integration*, this recognises the benefits of inclusive education and the positive outcomes that can be achieved for all pupils through such approaches. It also begins to address notions of citizenship in which pupils should be encouraged to develop mutual understanding and respect for individual diversity as part of their involvement and participation within a socially inclusive society (Lambe and Bones 2006). Pupils from different cultural backgrounds could, through the medium of dance, for example, learn to appreciate varying traditions and social customs. In this way teamwork, cooperation, mutual understanding, respect and empathy for difference can be addressed in PE (Vickerman and Coates 2009).

Furthermore, in considering the need to ensure all pupils are integrated into your PE lessons, pupils with SEN should be seen as an extension of your existing mixed-ability teaching, in which you differentiate your work (Vickerman and Blundell 2012). Therefore, as a teacher you should already be developing the necessary skills to facilitate inclusive PE, whatever the need may be, and, as a result, only occasionally require specialist advice and guidance. Thus, the fundamental factor in successful integration is a positive attitude and a readiness to adapt and modify your practice to meet individual pupils' needs. The focus of The Children and Families Act (UK Legislation 2014) is that the views of the children and young people are addressed.

Finally, in relation to the fourth principle of *integrity*, you are expected to underpin your teaching by valuing the adaptations and modifications you make in order to plan effectively for the inclusion of all pupils. As part of this personal commitment, you should ensure that inclusive PE is of equal worth, challenging, and in no way patronising or demeaning to the individual pupil concerned.

Task 10.3 asks you to consider the application of these four principles to your own teaching.

Task 10.3 Key values for inclusive PE

Review the four principles of entitlement, accessibility, inclusion and integrity. To address these principles, identify what you consider to be the key actions you should adopt as part of your inclusive learning, teaching and assessment. It may be useful to consider specific pupils or particular physical activities, e.g. swimming, to undertake this task. Discuss your notes with your tutor and then put these in your PDP.

The National Curriculum and inclusion

Government directives for the NC in England (DfE 2014a: 5) advocate within the inclusion statements that teachers should set 'suitable challenges', where high expectations for every pupil should be set. Teachers 'have an even greater obligation to plan lessons for pupils who have low levels of prior attainment or come from disadvantaged backgrounds'. An effective, inclusive school should be based upon a whole-school approach to the curriculum in which one of the main purposes is to establish entitlement to a range of high-quality learning experiences for pupils, irrespective of social background, culture, race, gender and/ or differences in ability (Hayes and Stidder 2013).

An inclusive curriculum is one in which all learners see the relevance of the curriculum to their own experiences and aspirations whilst enabling sufficient opportunities to succeed at the highest standard. In doing so, the NCPE (DfE 2014c: 6) suggests lesson planning should 'ensure that there are no barriers to every pupil achieving'. The NCPE Framework (DfE 2014b: 5) recognises that many disabled pupils may only require the aids that they use as part of their daily life; however the potential difficulties must be addressed at the outset of the work. Thus, in responding to meet all pupils' needs in PE, the NC (DfE 2014a) Statutory Inclusion Statement identifies two expectations related to: setting suitable learning challenges; responding to pupils' needs and overcoming potential barriers for individuals and groups of pupils. Table 10.1 sets out some examples of how the aspects of the Statutory Inclusion Statement can be realised in your teaching.

Practical examples of inclusive PE

So far, we have established a range of principles you need to consider when setting out to include all pupils in PE. We now turn to some examples of learning and teaching that can support this inclusive approach. In reviewing the diverse range of learning and teaching models designed for inclusive PE, all can be simplified to four common factors. These are based around: curriculum adaptation (changing what is taught); instructional modifications (changing how you teach); devising appropriate assessment strategies (adapting how you assess pupils); and human or people resources (looking at changing who teaches or supports adapted aspects of PE).

What is taught?

When planning for inclusive PE, it is important to start from the premise of full inclusion (Maher and Macbeth 2013) and, where this may not be possible, to consider adaptation and/ or modification of activities or learning and teaching strategies, or both. A central success factor in meeting this is initially to consult, where appropriate, with the pupils and/or relevant professionals as part of a multidisciplinary approach (Fitzgerald 2005; Coates and Vickerman 2008). This enables you to consider at the planning stage any differentiation that may be required. Careful thought needs to be given to the activities to be covered with respect to those with particular needs. While curriculum planning cannot be designed around the needs of pupils with disability, consideration can be given to the most appropriate activities, where

Table 10.1 Taking account of the Statutory Inclusion Statement in PE

Aspect of Statutory Inclusion Statement	Interpretation related to planning for effective inclusive PE	What skills, knowledge and strategies do I need to develop?	What resources do I need to help me to succeed?
Setting suitable learning challenges	Ensure that you know what the individual needs of your pupils are. For example, pupils who have coordination difficulties may require shorter-handled racquets or larger balls	Be clear about the nature of the skill being taught. Recognise different starting points in improving this skill to ensure the pupil succeeds and is motivated to learn and develop	Discuss strategies with previous class teachers, tutors, the SENCO or disability sport organisations such as the English Federation for Disability Sport
Responding to pupils' needs and overcoming potential barriers for individuals and groups of pupils	Ensure that your learning and teaching environment is conducive to individual pupil needs, and offers entitlement to the curriculum. For example, a pupil who has to keep her legs covered for religious reasons may require flexibility in PE clothing policy	Check the school PE policy on clothing and ensure it is sufficiently flexible and inclusive to accommodate individual pupil needs. Ensure there are no health and safety implications of e.g. wearing long trousers in the PE activity to be undertaken	Discuss with the individual pupils concerned how you can be responsive to their individual needs. Discuss the PE clothing policy with relevant parties
	Ensure your learning/teaching approach is accessible, and does not restrict opportunities to demonstrate progression	Ensure that you plan to take a range of equipment into the PE lesson. Ensure there is sufficient space and time for those with disabilities to make progress in the lesson	Be ready to use a variety of teaching approaches to cater for pupils' individual needs
	Ensure your assessment is accessible, and does not restrict opportunities to demonstrate mastery and progression. For example, a wheelchair user who cannot demonstrate a run or a jump in athletic activities may require an adaptation of the assessment task	Recognise the value of baseline assessment. Adopt an open mind to the focus of assessment and consider what the key features are that you wish to assess. Construct an appropriate assessment strategy that involves, for example, verbal rather than physical participation	At the planning stage identify which principles you want to assess, and how they can be modified or interpreted for the particular pupil concerned. Ensure that the modified assessment has integrity and is still measuring athletic knowledge, skills and understanding

options are feasible. For example, basketball may be more accessible than volleyball for a wheelchair user, and it may be easier to cater for all pupils in sports acrobatics rather than in curriculum gymnastics.

In some cases the use of different equipment is the answer to inclusion; alternatively devising a slightly modified form of a game may be the answer. However, in many cases what is taught is best understood by referring to the ILOs that are planned and the tasks that follow from these ILOs. All pupils are involved in the same activity but the specific tasks and outcomes are differentiated according to the needs of each individual pupil. In fact, differentiation, which is the teaching approach designed to include all pupils, is the principal way in which you cater for those with SEN (differentiation is also considered in Chapter 3). In respect of fully inclusive teaching, you may well have to be particularly ingenious and imaginative in creating alternative outcomes and differentiated tasks.

The Youth Sport Trust (YST) (2008) states that the majority of young people with disabilities benefit from having the tasks in 'bite size chunks or stepping stones' (p. 24). The concept of 'STEP' (YST 2008) includes adapting the *space* – where does the activity take place? *task* – what is happening? *equipment* – what is being used? and *people* – who is involved?

In relation to *equipment,* when modifying games activities, such as basketball, adaptations to equipment may initially require lighter, larger or different-coloured balls in order to access the activity. The *task* may be adapted in terms of the rules, such as allowing a player with movement restrictions five seconds to receive and play the ball. In addition, if utilising such a strategy, it is vital that all members of the group understand the need for such an adaptation in order that they can play to this rule during a game. Modifying the *task* in dance for a pupil with a learning difficulty could, for example, involve you setting a task of creating a dance routine exemplifying four movement components rather than the six or seven you have required of the rest of the class (Vickerman 2007). In athletics participation of physically disabled pupils may involve one push of their wheelchair, rather than a jump into the sandpit, or reducing distances to run or travel; this too is addressing the *task*.

Increasing the amount of *space* to play the invasion game as well as using a specified area where an attacking player is unopposed are two examples of how space can be adapted for a pupil with disability. In relation to *people,* teachers need to consider how young learners are arranged in relation to the tasks. For example, are they working individually, in pairs or in groups and are these pairings/groups of similar ability or mixed ability?

How teaching is conducted

Learning and teaching approaches can be modified in a number of ways. As indicated above, differentiated teaching strategies are the key to your effecting inclusion. Other more specific examples could include the use, by you, of more gestures, non-verbal communication and demonstrations or visual prompts (YST 2008), rather than relying purely on verbal communication. These modifications would accommodate both those with hearing impairment and those for whom English is an additional language as well as with visual prompts for pupils on the autistic spectrum disorder. Use of peer support (outlined later in the section on who supports learning) is another way that teaching can cater for a variety of needs. A subtle modification of your teaching could also be in respect of the nature of your feedback. With pupils with SEN your feedback is more likely to be directed towards effort and improvement rather than performance per se. To achieve this involves astute observation (see Chapter 4) and empathetic interaction between you and the pupil, as well as the encouragement of sensitive interaction between others in the class and the disabled pupil. Task 10.4 looks at the ways that you cater for pupils with different needs and abilities.

Task 10.4 Use of different approaches to cater for pupils with particular needs

Select a class that you teach which includes pupils with different needs and ask your tutor to observe you teaching and to note down how you adapt your teaching so that all are catered for. The tutor should note if and how you catered for learners of very different needs and abilities.

Discuss the tutor's notes after the lesson and keep these in your PDP.

Another aspect of modifying learning and teaching approaches could be in relation to a pupil with an emotional and/or behavioural difficulty who may be struggling to fulfil a particular skill on account of an inability to focus and concentrate for any length of time. Through your skilful task setting, encouragement and effective behaviour management, the pupil may still remain on task and be motivated to keep trying to raise his or her physical attainment. For example, where young people make up their own individual warm-ups that may include dynamic stretching, pupils on the autistic spectrum disorder can use this as a form of modelling as they observe good practice from their peer group (YST 2008).

This last example reveals that work in PE can contribute to achieving wider educational goals as well as PE-specific aims. The notion that there are two ways of looking at learning in PE is supported by Hughes and Fleming (2013), who describe two principles of learning: 'moving to learn' and 'learning to move'. They argue that PE has a distinctive role to play, because it is not simply about the education of the physical but involves cognitive, social, language and moral development and responsibilities. One strategy to facilitate inclusion may involve a shift from the traditional (learning to move) outcomes of PE in which skills are taught and learned, to a wider experience of PE (moving to learn) involving opportunities to plan for the social inclusion of pupils across a diverse continuum of learning needs. Above all, as the examples outlined show, it is essential that you modify your learning and teaching approaches to cater for the needs of pupils.

As the inclusion statement indicates (DfE 2014a), responding to the diverse needs of pupils requires PE teachers to acknowledge and respond to difference and diversity amongst pupils, whilst embracing social models of disability through changing learning and teaching styles to fit the pupil rather than the other way round (Watermeyer 2012). Task 10.5 challenges you to devise alternative tasks in the context of two lessons.

Task 10.5 Designing alternative tasks to cater for pupils with a disability

In a gymnastics task asking pupils to travel in a variety of directions on apparatus, create a task for a pupil who can move but is unable to walk or climb.

In a basketball task asking pupils to practise bouncing the ball with both hands, create a task for a pupil who only has use of one hand.

Discuss your suggestions with another student teacher.

Put these notes in your PDP.

For further valuable tasks and more information on differentiation, see Capel *et al.* (2006) Chapter 11 (Activities 11.6, 11.8 and 11.9 are particularly useful) and Capel and Breckon (2014) Chapter 15 (Activities 15.2, 15.3, 15.5, 15.8 and 15.9 are particularly useful).

Devising appropriate assessment strategies

As a PE teacher you set ILOs appropriate to the group and the individual pupils that make up the class, recognising that each pupil is on a continuum of learning. Devising appropriate assessment approaches must be considered when planning alternative tasks. As a corollary of this, you should also offer alternative methods of assessment which maximise opportunities for pupils to demonstrate knowledge and understanding. Assessment strategies need to go hand in hand with ILOs. If these outcomes have been modified for a pupil, it is likely that assessment also needs to be modified. If tasks and learning outcomes are clear, devising assessment strategies should follow and not be too problematic.

For example, for a pupil with movement difficulties that make practical participation impossible, an alternative in a gymnastics lesson may be to observe and identify the principles underpinning a particular skill. The assessment here would involve the pupil verbally describing rather than demonstrating the skill.

Another pupil with limited verbal communication may be able to demonstrate a roll in gymnastics rather than describe the particular principles of that knowledge, skill or understanding orally. As a result the pupil is still evidencing attainment, but is demonstrating rather than describing the process. A group of pupils who may need special consideration in devising teaching approaches are those on the autistic spectrum (see Durrant 2009 for coverage of this area).

Who supports learning?

All schools have a SENCO and this colleague can give you very valuable information and advice about the needs of individual pupils. Another colleague who may be able to help you is the pupil's form tutor, who may know the pupil and the family well. There may also be other personnel in your placement school who can give support and information. It is useful to ask your Head of PE, to whom you might go for guidance.

Depending on the nature of the special need, a pupil may have a support assistant in the PE lesson. These colleagues can be of great assistance. However, many assistants have not had any training in supporting work in PE and it is necessary for you to brief them fully on the role they are to play.

Other support for pupils with SEN can come from their peers. Again, these pupils need careful instruction; however it is often the case that other pupils can enjoy this responsibility and are sensitive, supportive and encouraging. An example could be if you have a pupil with limited vision: you could organise activities such as a 20-metre 'running for speed' activity in which a peer runs alongside the pupil for support. It is perhaps wise not to use the same pupil in a support role too often, both because all pupils should be active in PE as far as possible and because this supportive task can be a situation in which all can develop valuable social skills.

Task 10.6 requires you to reflect on some key issues underpinning inclusive practice.

Task 10.6 Review of inclusive practice

Critically reflect on the practical examples for modifying activities for various pupils' individual needs. As part of this critical reflection, identify what strategies you can use to maximise success in learning and achievement whilst minimising barriers to participation. At the same time, consider the following questions:

- What are your key principles for planning an inclusive PE curriculum?
- Who needs to be involved in planning an inclusive PE curriculum?
- What do you see as the potential challenges and success factors in planning PE lessons that meet the needs of the many, rather than the few?

Put these notes in your PDP.

In summary, these examples demonstrate how the practice of inclusive PE can be delivered if you are prepared to recognise the key principles and values noted earlier in this chapter. A critical success factor is to be flexible and be prepared to try out different learning and teaching strategies to see if they work (Vickerman and Blundell 2012). As part of your developing competence in the area of inclusive PE, you should not be daunted by being unsuccessful in your attempts to create barrier-free lessons. The important point is that you learn from your experiences, then try again, rather than restrict yourself to limited learning and teaching strategies.

Summary and key points

Embedding an inclusive approach to your learning, teaching and assessment

It is evident from analysis within this chapter that inclusive PE is a key issue for government, schools and teachers. The philosophical basis of inclusive PE as socially and morally sound is supported through legislation and the development of practices in the NC (DfE 2014a). Your role, and that of schools, is central to the success or failure of the PE inclusion agenda in ensuring the needs of the many, rather than the few, are met within the curriculum. In order to consider how to meet this agenda, there is a need to establish a clear and consistent framework for stakeholders involved in inclusive PE. 'The Eight Ps Inclusive PE Framework' (Vickerman and Blundell 2012) (Table 10.2) helps clarify the widely held view of inclusion as a combination of philosophy, process and practice, and draws together a number of key points considered in this chapter. As a result, you are encouraged to use this framework as a basis for considering, planning, delivering and reviewing your emerging practice in inclusive PE.

The framework encourages you to recognise and spend time analysing; planning and implementing each of the interrelated factors, to ensure you give yourself the best opportunities for creating barrier-free PE lessons for all the pupils you serve (Smith and Thomas 2006). As such, the first point is to recognise and fully embrace the *philosophy* underpinning inclusion discussed in this chapter as a basic and fundamental human right, which is supported in England through statutory and non-statutory guidance, such as the SEN and Disability Rights Act (DfES 2001), the NC Inclusion statement (DfE 2014a) and the Single Equality Act (Government Equalities Office 2008). In order to facilitate this process you should embrace a *purposeful* approach to fulfilling the requirements of differentiated learning, teaching and assessment. Consequently, you should spend time examining the principles that form the basis of inclusion, while noting the rationale and arguments for inclusive PE. In order to achieve this you should develop *proactive* approaches to the development and implementation of your inclusive learning and teaching and be prepared to consult actively with fellow teachers, pupils and related individuals and agencies in order to produce a *partnership* approach to your delivery.

Inclusion demands a recognition and commitment to modify and adapt your learning and teaching strategies in order to enable access and entitlement to the PE curriculum, and you have an obligation to undertake this through a value-based approach. The development of inclusive PE must therefore be recognised as part of a *process* that evolves, emerges and changes over time, and it is important to acknowledge that it requires ongoing review by all stakeholders.

In conclusion, therefore, it is your responsibility and that of the whole school to ensure inclusion is reflected in *policy* documentation, as a means of monitoring, reviewing and

Table 10.2 Eight Ps Inclusive PE Framework

Philosophy	What are the key concepts related to inclusive PE?
Purpose	What are the rationales behind inclusive PE?
Proactive	What challenges am I likely to face in planning and developing an inclusive PE curriculum, and how can they be overcome?
Partnership	Who do I need to work with to ensure I succeed?
Process	Where is the starting point for my development of inclusive practice, where are the review points and how will I know if I am successful?
Policy	What policies exist in school regarding inclusion?
Pedagogy	What are my own learning and teaching approaches to the development of inclusive PE?
Practice	How can I ensure that I make a difference in practice when I work with the pupils in my class?

evaluating delivery. The critical success factors, however, rely on ensuring policy impacts on your *pedagogical* practices. Thus, while philosophies and processes are vital for schools and teachers, ultimately you should measure your success in terms of effective inclusive *practice*, which makes a real difference to the experiences of all pupils in your PE lessons. Task 10.7 challenges you to consider examples of practice against each of the principles in the Eight Ps Framework and Task 10.8 focuses on the learning, teaching and assessment strategies you would adopt to ensure the individual needs of all pupils are met.

Task 10.7 Developing an inclusive PE framework

Critically review the use of the Eight Ps Inclusive Framework as part of the planning process for including pupils with SEN. Put your completed chart in your PDP as evidence of Masters level work.

Eight P's Inclusive PE Framework	Interpretation of what each stands for in developing your own learning and teaching framework for inclusive PE
Philosophy - What are the key concepts related to inclusive PE?	
Purpose - What are the rationales behind inclusive PE?	
Proactive - What challenges am I likely to face in planning and developing an inclusive PE curriculum, and how can they be met?	
Partnership - Who do I need to work with to ensure I succeed?	
Process - Where is the starting point for my development of inclusive practice, where are the review points and how will I know if I am successful?	
Policy - What policies exist in school regarding inclusion?	
Pedagogy - What are my own learning and teaching approaches to the development of inclusive PE?	
Practice - How can I ensure that I make a difference in practice when I work with the pupils in my class?	

Task 10.8 Developing personalised learning

Read a range of journal articles which focus upon the views and experiences of pupils with SEN in PE. Integrate this research literature to provide a critique (2,000 words) which critically reflects upon the learning, teaching and assessment strategies you would adopt to ensure the individual needs of all pupils are met. Share this with your tutor and put it in your PDP as evidence of Masters level study as well as addressing the standards you need to meet to qualify as a teacher.

Check which requirements of your ITE you have addressed through this chapter.

Further reading

Capel, S. and Piotrowski, S. (eds) (2000) *Issues in Physical Education*, London: RoutledgeFalmer.

This book is written both for student and practising PE teachers and addresses a range of equality issues from differing perspectives.

Coates, J. and Vickerman, P. (2008) 'Let the children have their say: children with special educational needs and their experiences of physical education – a review', *Support for Learning*, 23, 4: 168–175.

This paper is a review of literature on listening to the voices of pupils with SEN related to their experiences of PE. The paper is worth reading to gain insights into empowering young people who may be marginalised and the barriers and challenges they face in gaining access and entitlement to PE.

Hayes, S. and Stidder, G. (2013) *Equity and Inclusion in Physical Education*, 2nd edn, Abingdon, Oxon: Routledge.

This book offers a comprehensive overview of a range of issues related to including diverse groups in PE. The book specifically addresses a multiplicity of issues related to social class, race, ethnicity, gender, sexuality, SEN and ability and is a valuable resource for all working to include pupils in PE.

Winnick, J. (2011) *Adapted Physical Education and Sport*, 5th edn, Champaign, IL: Human Kinetics.

This book offers a range of theoretical and practical strategies for inclusion in physical activity. It provides an extensive resource for reviewing differentiated strategies for including a range of pupils in physical activity.

11 Learner-centred teaching – a physical literacy perspective

Margaret Whitehead

Introduction

This chapter aims to remind you that, notwithstanding your challenge to master the range of teaching skills you need to be an effective teacher, your principal focus should be on the pupils and their needs. It is worth remembering that learning is not necessarily the outcome of teaching. Teaching can be conducted without any learning taking place. You are a facilitator of learning, first and foremost. This chapter therefore asks you to stand back and take stock of your development as a teacher and consider the impact you can make on pupils and their learning. Teaching, to be effective, must be a learner-centred enterprise.

The concept of physical literacy was introduced in Chapter 2. It is used in this chapter to provide a rationale for learner-centred teaching. Pupils who are making progress on their physical literacy journey will evidence improvement in confidence, physical competence, motivation and knowledge and understanding, thus enabling them to value physical activity and take responsibility for maintaining this activity for life. It should be understood that all pupils are on their own individual journey. All can make progress. Comparison with others is irrelevant; it is personal progress which is to be nurtured and celebrated. In this context the teacher should know each pupil as an individual and, as far as possible, tailor teaching to meet individual needs. Physical literacy is clearly a learner-centred concept.

Working in the context of physical literacy, this chapter focuses on two aspects of learner-centred teaching. The first section on 'learning in PE to develop physical competence' highlights the physical competence element of the concept and is based around a series of key propositions. The second section, 'fostering confidence, self-esteem and a readiness to take responsibility', builds from the confidence and responsibility elements of the concept.

Objectives

At the end of the chapter you should be able to:

- understand that physical literacy is a concept that puts the learner at the heart of teaching;
- appreciate that all elements of teaching are significant to promote learning;

(continued)

(continued)

- recognise the key aspects of teaching covered in Chapters 1–10 that are crucial for learning in the physical domain;
- appreciate the importance of teacher behaviours that enable pupils to develop confidence, self-esteem and a readiness to take responsibility;
- recognise the key aspects of teaching covered in Chapters 1–10 that are crucial to the fostering of confidence, self-esteem and a readiness to take responsibility.

Check the requirements of your initial teacher education (ITE) to see which relate to this chapter.

Learning in PE to develop physical competence

This section highlights some key aspects of learning related to physical competence that are addressed in the foregoing chapters. Key propositions are proposed in relation to these aspects. Each of the foregoing chapters has its own focus but the underlying rationale common to all is to give you guidance and advice about how to promote learning. Developing physical competence is a central element of physical literacy and should be understood as an individual journey. Each pupil will have a particular cluster of endowments and each pupil will need to be catered for if optimal learning is to be achieved by all. It would be valuable to read some of the foregoing chapters again, focusing your attention particularly on the impact on pupil learning of the constituents of teaching being discussed.

The first aspect of teaching that influences learning is the design of the lesson in terms of its intended learning outcomes (ILOs), the tasks set and the teaching approach used. The lesson should be designed to cater for the needs of all pupils. As far as possible, tasks should both build on previous achievement/knowledge and lay the ground for progress, refinement and application. Learning is more likely to occur where the lesson presents an incremental challenge both from earlier lessons and within itself. Lessons should be clearly fit for purpose, thoughtfully and imaginatively planned and provide opportunities for all pupils to experience success. Lessons should be logically structured, with the introductory section laying the ground for the work of the lesson and the final plenary drawing the work together. This aspect of teaching is the focus of Chapter 3 but the importance of planning is also referred to in Chapters 4, 6, 7 and 10 on observation, organisation and management, motivation and inclusion respectively. This aspect of teaching generates key proposition 1.

> *Key proposition 1 is that learning is more likely to occur if lessons are logically structured to lead the learner on to further success*

The second aspect of teaching that is important to facilitate learning in the physical domain links to planning and is concerned with the preparation and management of the context of the learning. The context should provide pupils with an appropriate and safe environment in which time, space and equipment are well organised and used. Routines are established and time is not wasted. Groupings are logically developed and equipment is readily available. An ordered setting is likely to provide a learning environment that will support pupil application, understanding and learning. Good overall organisation will also enable the teacher to have time to monitor the class, notice where pupils differ markedly in their response and unobtrusively introduce appropriate differentiation procedures. This aspect of the promotion of learning is set out in Chapter 6 but is also recognised as important in Chapters 3, 5, 7 and 8 on planning, communication, motivation and an effective learning environment respectively. This aspect of teaching generates key proposition 2.

Key proposition 2 is that learning is more likely to occur if learners are working in well-managed settings and have the time, equipment and space to carry out the set tasks.

The third aspect of teaching that is significant in promoting learning is effective communication between the teacher and the pupils. Learning can best be described as the result of effective communication of relevant information. You as the teacher will, in most cases, know more than the learner and it is your job to share this knowledge with the learners. Clarity of purpose and confidently delivered instructions are essential if pupils are to be clear about the nature of the task and the particular aspects of a movement or an activity on which they are to focus. Forms of communication should be chosen that are accessible to the pupils – their age, experience and language facility. Communication is central to the whole process of promoting learning. Information can be imparted in a range of ways but in all cases it should be audible and/or visible to all, brief, specific and readily understood by pupils. Effective communication is the focus of Chapter 5 but is also mentioned in Chapters 3, 7, 8 and 10 on observation, motivation, an effective learning environment and inclusion respectively. This aspect of teaching generates key proposition 3.

Key proposition 3 is that learning is more likely to occur when you use a variety of forms of communication, all of which are clear, concise and accessible to pupils.

Now carry out Task 11.1.

Task 11.1 Recognising teaching that promotes learning (a)

Videotape 20 minutes of a lesson you teach and after the lesson identify teacher actions which are exemplars of key propositions 1, 2 and 3. In subsequent lessons concentrate on that aspect of teaching among these three which was least in evidence. Ask your tutor to monitor your teaching and give you feedback regarding the aspect you are working on. Keep these records in your professional development portfolio (PDP).

The fourth aspect of teaching that influences learning in the physical domain is the teacher's use of observation of pupil responses. Whereas communication (discussed above) can be seen as principally explaining the task and setting out the organisation of tasks, observation is the foundation of ongoing feedback from the teacher to the pupil. Knowledgeable and astute feedback to an individual pupil, a group or the class provides essential in-lesson information and support for learning. Via observation you can apply your understanding of pupils and of material so that detailed aspects of the pupil(s) response can be highlighted for praise or further guidance. Feedback based on observation is a critical element in the promotion of learning, not least to cater for the needs of each individual pupil. Observation is the subject of Chapter 4 but is also referred to in Chapters 3, 5, 6, 7, 9 and 10 on planning, communication, organisation and management, motivation, assessment and inclusion respectively. This aspect of teaching generates key proposition 4.

> **Key proposition 4 is that learning is more likely to occur when you use observation to give personalised feedback to reinforce, guide and advise pupils.**

The fifth aspect of teaching that is fundamental to promoting learning is your effectiveness in motivating the pupils to engage in the tasks at hand. To learn, pupils must apply themselves fully to the task and persevere in repeating and applying the movement or knowledge as guided by the teacher. Motivation is more likely to occur if tasks are designed to enable each pupil to succeed and where pupil effort, progress and achievement are recognised. Enthusiastic teaching and variation in teaching approach also stimulate motivation. Motivation and learning can often be enhanced if pupils play a part in planning and monitoring their own learning and experience the satisfaction of making progress through their own efforts. Teaching that promotes motivation is explained in Chapter 7 but its value is also signalled in Chapters 3, 4, 5, 6, 8, 9 and 10 on planning, observation, communication, organisation and management, an effective learning environment, assessment and inclusion respectively. This aspect of teaching generates key proposition 5.

> **Key proposition 5 is that learning is best fostered where pupils are motivated to apply themselves to the tasks at hand and, as appropriate, take responsibility for their own learning.**

The sixth aspect of teaching that is important if learning is to be achieved is the recognition that every pupil is different. Teaching should be inclusive. In most cases this will involve differentiated teaching. Pupils will not learn unless the tasks set are appropriate to their potential and capacity. Every pupil is unique, with their own characteristics, experience, perceptions and endowment. As far as possible tasks should be meaningful and achievable by all pupils. While it is a challenge for you to know each pupil as an individual, this is a goal that should be kept in mind. Using your observation skills and the knowledge you have of the material, you should be able to give specific feedback and guidance to each individual pupil. Discussion of catering for individual differences should be understood not only as concerning pupils with significant potential or those with specific challenges, but should be appreciated as referring to each and every pupil. Inclusive teaching is the subject of Chapter 10 but attention to individual needs permeates many other chapters, for example, 3, 4, 5, and 8 on planning, observation, communication and an effective learning environment respectively. This aspect of teaching generates key proposition 6.

Key proposition 6 is that, as learning is a process unique to each individual, it is more likely to occur where pupils' potential, abilities and characteristics are recognised and their individual needs met.

Now carry out Task 11.2.

Task 11.2 Recognising teaching that promotes learning (b)

Videotape 20 minutes of a lesson you teach and after the lesson identify teacher actions which are exemplars of the key propositions 4, 5 and 6. In subsequent lessons concentrate on that aspect of teaching among these three which was least in evidence. Ask your tutor to monitor your teaching and give you feedback regarding the aspect you are working on. Keep these records in your PDP.

The seventh aspect of teaching that will have a profound influence on learning in the physical domain is the nature of the atmosphere or ambience of the lesson. Learning depends on there being an ordered, safe environment without distractions. It also depends on a climate of mutual respect between the pupils and the teacher and between the pupils themselves. In a situation in which pupils are asked to try new tasks and to create their own ideas, both of which are on show for all to see, they need to be confident that their efforts will be appreciated. It is not unusual for pupils who doubt if they will make any progress to opt out of a set task or even of PE altogether, not wanting to put themselves in a position where they are likely to fail. Learning will not occur if there is a fear of failure or of humiliation. These conditions are best achieved in settings where pupils feel both that the teacher is perceptive, appreciative and encouraging and that their efforts will be recognised and rewarded. The development of an effective learning environment is the subject of Chapter 8 but recommendations concerning the creation of a climate conducive to learning are elements of other chapters, for example, Chapters 6, 7 and 10 on organisation and management, motivation and inclusion respectively. This aspect of teaching generates key proposition 7.

Key proposition 7 is that learning is more likely to occur if pupils feel secure in the environment - physically, socially and emotionally, confident that their efforts will be valued and their achievement, however modest, will be appreciated.

The eighth aspect of teaching that plays a significant part in promoting learning relates to your use of assessment. A critical part of learning is for pupils to have a clear picture of their achievements, to know how far they are being successful and how they can make progress. Assessment is best seen as charting individual progress. It therefore requires teachers to comment on the progress of each individual pupil. Pupils should not feel that they are constantly being compared with others. Assessment *for* learning, criterion-referenced assessment and ipsative assessment are all likely to be powerful tools to motivate pupils and promote learning. Given the importance of assessment, it should be seen as integral to all learning and teaching rather than being an exercise that is introduced to a lesson or unit at a specific time. Assessment is the subject of Chapter 9 but issues concerning use assessment are flagged up in Chapters 3, 4 and 8 on planning, observation and an effective learning environment respectively. This aspect of teaching generates key proposition 8.

Key proposition 8 is that learning is more likely to occur if assessment is used at all times as a motivational tool.

The ninth aspect of teaching that plays a part in learning is concerned with the confidence with which you present yourself and in the clarity of your interest in and commitment to physical activity. In a sense this aspect encompasses all that has been explained already in this chapter. You as the teacher send out crucial messages in all you do: in the way you are prepared for the lesson, in the standards you set, in the interest you have in your pupils and in the way you transmit the value of the work of the lesson. The assured teacher with clear intentions and beliefs provides a sound role model and creates a calm, assured and confident climate which has the potential to inspire and empower pupils to learning. The discussion of purposeful teaching that evidences clear aims is the subject of Chapter 2 but is also seen as important in Chapters 4, 5 and 8 on observation, communication and an effective learning environment respectively. This aspect of teaching generates key proposition 9.

Key message 9 is that learning is more likely to occur if it is led by a teacher who is confident and committed and is a role model in relation to attitudes towards the value of physical activity.

Now carry out Task 11.3.

Task 11.3 Recognising teaching that promotes learning (c)

Videotape 20 minutes of a lesson you teach and after the lesson identify teacher actions which are exemplars of key propositions 7, 8 and 9. In subsequent lessons concentrate on that aspect of teaching among these three which was least in evidence. Ask your tutor to monitor your teaching and give you feedback regarding the aspect you are working on. Keep these records in your PDP.

Learning that promotes the development of physical competence is one of the core purposes of PE and is a crucial element in fostering physical literacy. As can be seen throughout the first part of this chapter, there have been repeated references to the importance of your understanding and knowledge of the pupils as individuals and the need for you to cater for every participant whatever their endowment and potential. Teaching, seen as facilitating learning, must have the pupil at its heart.

Fostering confidence, self-esteem and a readiness to take responsibility

The second section of the chapter considers ways in which teaching can be conducted to foster the development of pupil confidence, self-esteem and readiness to take responsibility.

These are all core elements of physical literacy. It is proposed here that confidence is founded on the development of self-esteem that enables individuals to feel empowered in the future to put themselves in physical activity situations in which they are confident they will have rewarding and meaningful experiences. Branden (1995: 27) writes that 'self-esteem is the disposition to experience oneself as competent to cope with the basic challenges of life and worthy of happiness'. He proposes that self-esteem has two interrelated components, self-efficacy and self-respect, and continues (p. 26) by explaining that 'self-efficacy means the confidence in the functioning of my mind, in my ability to think, understand, learn, choose and make decisions' and that 'self-respect means assurance in my value, an affirmative attitude towards my right to live and be happy'.

The section reconsiders the material in the foregoing chapters of the book and highlights aspects of teaching that can foster confidence, self-esteem and the readiness to take responsibility. Again, as above, this is not a 'one size fits all' issue. The development of confidence, self-esteem and the readiness to take responsibility is as unique to the individual as developing physical potential. You therefore need to think very carefully about how you can create a class atmosphere in which there is demonstrable interest in each individual pupil as you work to achieve the development of these significant characteristics in each pupil.

While this section highlights key aspects of teaching that foster the development of confidence, self-esteem and readiness to take responsibility, you need to remember that learning which promotes the development of physical competence is also likely to have an impact on developing these characteristics. However, there is no necessary relationship between these two aspects of pupil development. In most cases, developing physical competence will receive positive feedback and praise, thus building pupil confidence. However, there may be improvements in physical competence that go unrecognised by the teacher and there may be a very competitive regime in which modest achievement in comparison with others may be dismissed as insignificant and not acknowledged as noteworthy.

If your goal is that all pupils continue to participate in physical activity outside school and after schooling is completed, it is essential they leave lessons having had experiences in which they have been recognised as successful and which they have experienced as rewarding. Positive, supportive feedback from you will enhance the perceptions they have of themselves, enabling them to feel valued and thus grow in confidence and self-esteem. Experiences in PE should be positive, pleasurable and meaningful if pupils are to value physical activity and take the responsibility to take part in physical activity beyond PE. If pupils leave a lesson feeling inept, inadequate or humiliated there is little likelihood they will voluntarily put themselves in similar situations in the future. As indicated in the definition of physical literacy, i.e. 'the motivation, confidence, physical competence, knowledge and understanding to value and take responsibility for engagement in physical activities for life' (Whitehead 2014a), participation in physical activity in the future is the underlying rationale for PE; therefore this aspect of teaching should have serious consideration.

The challenge for the teacher

This is a real challenge for you as it means that you have a responsibility to get to know pupils as individuals and interact with each one during the lesson. In fact there should be a particular sort of ambience in the lesson. Implications for the ambience of lessons to promote confidence, self-esteem and a readiness to take responsibility can be seen as coming under four headings. These are to:

1   create an atmosphere of encouragement, challenge and celebration;
2   engender a sense of optimism – a 'can do' culture;
3   encompass the development of mutual respect in which each individual pupil is valued;
4   include opportunities for pupils to take responsibility for their own learning and thus feel ownership and pride in their progress.

Each of these, in their different ways, contributes to a growth in pupils' positive self-image, thus enhancing their self-esteem. This overall ambience can give pupils the confidence to take the initiative to be involved in physical activity – in PE and beyond. Now carry out Task 11.4.

Task 11.4 Recognising teaching that fosters confidence, self-esteem and a readiness to take responsibility

Observe another student teacher and identify teaching characteristics that promote confidence, self-esteem and pupil readiness to take responsibility. Ask the student teacher to carry out the same exercise in observing you. Discuss both observations with this student teacher and consider how you might develop these aspects of teaching. Put both observations in your PDP to refer to as you work to develop relevant elements of teaching.

Teaching that creates an atmosphere of encouragement, challenge and celebration

The teacher's approach and self-presentation in lessons play a significant part in the development of pupils' confidence. Enthusiastic teaching is stimulating and engaging and sends out a message that the activity of the lesson is exciting, worthwhile and has the potential to be a positive experience. The confidence shown by the teacher in the value and potential of the lessons is readily picked up by the pupils, who themselves develop respect for and confidence in the activity. The teacher who is adept at providing material that can challenge pupils, and at the same time provide opportunities for all to make progress, will engage pupils. The teacher who genuinely celebrates effort, progress and achievement can spur pupils on and give them the confidence that the activity is within their reach and promises rewarding experiences wrought from the pleasure of success.

Aspects of teaching that create an atmosphere of encouragement, challenge and celebration and thus promote confidence include:

•   demonstrating enthusiasm and encouragement towards all pupils;
•   setting tasks that challenge, but are within reach of, all pupils;
•   recognising and rewarding effort, progress and achievement;

- using praise as appropriate with all pupils;
- celebrating improvement, however small;
- avoiding negative messages at all times.

These aspects of teaching are discussed in Chapters 3, 4, 5, 7, 8 and 10 on planning, observation, communication, motivation, an effective learning environment and inclusion respectively. Now carry out Task 11.5.

Task 11.5 Recognising teaching that creates an atmosphere of encouragement, challenge and celebration

Observe another student teacher and identify teaching characteristics that create an atmosphere of encouragement, challenge and celebration. Ask the student teacher to carry out the same exercise in observing you. Discuss both observations with this student teacher and consider how you might develop these aspects of teaching. Put both observations in your PDP to refer to as you work to develop relevant elements of teaching.

Teaching that engenders a sense of optimism – a 'can do' culture

Teachers' expectation of success and their belief in pupil ability are powerful tools to foster the development of self-esteem. The use of feedback gives guidance that the teacher expects to be within reach of pupils and reassures pupils that they can make progress. This enables pupils to realise that the teacher has confidence in them and values their efforts. This teacher confidence is instrumental in pupils developing a positive attitude to their abilities and potential. In addition, where the teacher devolves some responsibility to the pupil, this again demonstrates trust in and respect for the pupil. These two teaching approaches together should enable pupils to feel valued and build confidence in their own ability. As a result pupils should develop self-esteem in respect of participation in physical activity, which can engender the confidence that is so central to pupils making progress in their physical literacy journey.

Aspects of teaching that engender a sense of optimism in pupil potential and thus foster self-esteem include:

- adopting a 'can do' approach with each pupil;
- selecting and using the most appropriate feedback for each individual pupil;
- ensuring that all pupils experience success, being challenged as appropriate;
- demonstrating optimism and expecting high, but realistic, standards;
- enabling pupils to self-assess and take pride in their own performance.

These aspects of teaching are discussed in Chapters 3, 4, 7, 8 and 10 on planning, observation, motivation, an effective learning environment and inclusion respectively. Now carry out Task 11.6.

Task 11.6 Recognising teaching that engenders a sense of optimism – a 'can do' culture

Observe another student teacher and identify teaching characteristics that engender a sense of optimism – a 'can do' culture. Ask the student teacher to carry out the same exercise in observing you. Discuss both observations with this student teacher and consider how you might develop these aspects of teaching. Put both observations in your PDP to refer to as you work to develop relevant elements of teaching.

Teaching that demonstrates respect for the individual and encourages mutual respect among pupils

Teacher concern for the individual lies at the very heart of learner-centred teaching. All pupils are different and should not be compared with others. Normative assessment is not appropriate given the very different potentials that every pupil brings to PE. Pupils need to feel valued for who they are and what they can achieve. They need to feel that they are known and understood by the teacher in their own right. They need to be helped to understand and accept their potential in the confidence that they will be respected, not ridiculed or humiliated. The teacher should ensure that each pupil feels part of the group and that other pupils respect and value them. The confidence and self-esteem that these various attitudes engender are hugely important if pupils are to continue their participation in physical activity throughout life.

Aspects of teaching that will demonstrate respect for the individual and encourage mutual respect among pupils and foster confidence and self-esteem include:

- ensuring you know all pupils as individuals, both by name and in respect of where they are on their physical literacy journey;
- adopting a caring, empathetic approach with all pupils;
- ensuring that each pupil feels valued and is included at all times;
- enabling each pupil to develop self-awareness and pride in their personal performance;
- adopting ipsative assessment, recognising individual progress;
- ensuring that pupils respect each other and are encouraging and supportive of other class members.

These aspects of teaching are discussed in Chapters 4, 7, 8, 9 and 10 on observation, motivation, an effective learning environment, assessment and inclusion respectively. Now carry out Task 11.7.

Task 11.7 Recognising teaching that demonstrates respect for the individual and encourages mutual respect among pupils

Observe another student teacher and identify teaching characteristics that demonstrate respect for the individual and encourage mutual respect among pupils.

(continued)

Task 11.7 *(continued)*

Ask the student teacher to carry out the same exercise in observing you. Discuss both observations with this student teacher and consider how you might develop these aspects of teaching. Put both observations in your PDP to refer to as you work to develop relevant elements of teaching.

Teaching that provides opportunities for pupils to take responsibility for their own learning and thus feel ownership and pride in their progress

This aspect of pupil development is generally less well addressed in teaching but is worthy of serious attention if we are to achieve the long-term goal of physical literacy, being that pupils take responsibility for continued participation in physical activity for life. Experiences of pupils in PE are critical in achieving this end. A lesson ambience that facilitates learners to take responsibility includes opportunities for pupils to work on open-ended tasks and in problem-solving situations. It also involves their playing a part in planning, selecting and evaluating tasks and experiences in PE. It also includes teacher willingness to hear their views and discuss and debate the value of participation in physical activity beyond schooling. Group discussion with their peers is also valuable so that pupils confront and reflect on a range of views.

Aspects of teaching that provide opportunities for pupils to take responsibility for their own learning and thus feel ownership and pride in their progress and lay the ground for future participation include:

- using open-ended tasks and problem-solving situations which require pupils to make their own decisions;
- involving pupils in planning aspects of lessons and allowing them to select tasks and challenges on which to work;
- respecting and acting on pupils' views;
- encouraging pupils to ask questions and taking time to engage in discussion;
- encouraging pupils to reflect on their experiences and discuss with teachers and their peers approaches to maintaining active participation for life.

These aspects of teaching are discussed in Chapters 3, 5, 7 and 8 on planning, communication, motivation and an effective learning environment respectively. Now carry out Task 11.8.

Task 11.8 Recognising teaching that provides opportunities for pupils to take responsibility for their own learning and thus feel ownership and pride in their progress

Observe another student teacher and identify teaching characteristics that demonstrate opportunities for pupils to take responsibility for their own learning and thus feel ownership and pride in their progress. Ask the student teacher to carry out the same exercise in observing you. Discuss both observations with this student teacher and consider how you might develop these aspects of teaching. Put both observations in your PDP to refer to as you work to develop relevant elements of teaching.

To reiterate, to foster confidence, self-esteem and a readiness to take responsibility in pupils you should aspire to:

- create an atmosphere of encouragement, challenge and celebration;
- engender a sense of optimism – a 'can do' culture;
- encompass the development of mutual respect in which each individual is valued;
- include opportunities for learners to take responsibility for their own learning and thus feel ownership and pride in their progress.

Underlying these recommendations is the need to recognise pupils as individuals and help each one to experience success, grow in confidence and feel valued. In many ways your teaching skills are the 'tools of the trade' to promote physical competency, while your ability to reach out to every pupil, in respect of each developing the personal qualities about which the second section of this chapter has been concerned, depends on how you use these tools. Reflect on the material in the second section of the chapter by completing Task 11.9.

Task 11.9 Fostering confidence, self-esteem and a readiness to take responsibility
In the light of the material and tasks in the second section of the chapter write a short essay (1,600 words) in which you consider the challenges you will face in working to promote confidence, self-esteem and a readiness to take responsibility in *all* your pupils. Share this with your tutor and keep it in your PDP as evidence of Masters level work.

Summary and key points

This chapter has aimed to help you to look at teaching through new eyes – not to see teaching as comprised of a cluster of knowledge and skills that you learn and use, but rather to view all that you are learning as providing a rich source of information and practices on which you can draw to cater for whichever class or individual with whom you are working. As has been demonstrated in the two sections of this chapter, the practices to promote physical competence and those to foster confidence, self-esteem and a readiness to take responsibility are very closely related, and in some ways impossible to separate. Nevertheless, it is important to be alert to nurturing each of the elements of physical literacy to ensure that all are achieved.

Teaching, to be effective, is a learner-centred activity. Pupils may all be on a similar pathway but each will be at a different place and will encounter different hurdles. Each will be at a different point in their physical literacy journey. If you can so engage the pupils you teach that each one both develops their physical competence and grows in confidence, self-esteem and the ability to take responsibility to maintain physical activity, you will have succeeded as a teacher and as someone who has changed pupils' lives for the better.

Check which requirements of your ITE you have addressed through this chapter.

Further reading

Branden, N. (1995) *The Six Pillars of Self-Esteem*, New York: Bantam.

This seminal book provides a sound treatise on self-esteem. Of particular interest are Chapter 2 'the meaning of self-esteem', Chapter 12 'the philosophy of self-esteem' and Chapter 14 'self-esteem in the school'. Interestingly, there are also references to the importance of teacher self-esteem.

In addition, as the content of this chapter has been drawn from those aspects of Chapters 1–10 that focus on two aspects of learner-centred teaching in the context of physical literacy, please refer back to the further reading at the end of Chapters 1–10.

12 Teaching safely and safety in PE

Anne Chappell

Introduction

PE, by its very nature, involves challenges, adventure and inherent risks. Being able to teach safely in PE is a requirement for you to be able to qualify as a teacher as well as an ongoing expectation. In England these expectations are outlined in the Teachers' Standards (Department for Education (DfE) 2011) and other DfE publications (DfE 2014f). The Office for Standards in Education (Ofsted) School Inspection Handbook makes judgements about schools based on 'the success in keeping pupils safe' (Ofsted 2014b: 54). A school considered 'outstanding' in relation to behaviour and safety is one in which: 'all groups of pupils are safe and feel safe in school and at alternative provision placements at all times. They understand very clearly what constitutes unsafe situations and are highly aware of how to keep themselves and others safe in different situations' (Ofsted 2014: 55; see also Ofsted 2014c). It is worth noting that, in the most recent survey of all secondary initial teacher education (ITE) subject inspections in England between 1999 and 2002, Ofsted reported that: 'strong features of most PE lessons were the trainees' organisation, control of resources and their high expectations of pupils' behaviour; these were, in part, driven by the safety consciousness of most trainees' (Ofsted 2003: 12).

The importance of teaching safely and safety in PE is highlighted in numerous publications (e.g. Kelly 1997; Raymond 1999; Severs 2003; Whitlam 2005; Beaumont 2007; Association for Physical Education (afPE) 2012; Chappell 2014). As Whitlam (2005, p. 15) identifies, 'totally safe or risk free situations do not occur in PE and school sport because they are practical activities involving movement, often at speed and in confined areas shared with others'. Beaumont (2007: 31) goes on to say that this is what makes PE and school sport 'an exciting and challenging aspect of school life' and that without 'a perceived element of risk, activities . . . would cease to attract and stimulate . . . and fail to provide a genuine opportunity for personal and social development', alongside preventing high-quality learning through and about the physical. Your role as a PE teacher is to ensure that you develop a culture of teaching safely and safety in PE (and, by implication, pupils learning safely and about safety), thereby creating and managing a safe learning environment that controls and minimises potential risks and maximises pupils' learning experiences in PE (Raymond 1999). Every accident or injury that occurs highlights the importance of safe practice and the need to adopt procedures that minimise the likelihood of a recurrence of such incidents. The Free Dictionary (2014: http://www.thefreedictionary.com/safe) defines 'safe' as: 'free from danger or injury' and 'free from risk'.

The DfE identifies that it 'is important that children learn to understand and manage the risks that are a normal part of life' (2014g: 4). The aims of the National Curriculum in England with specific reference to PE include support for young people in developing an 'active, healthy lifestyle' (DfE 2013a: 237). Alongside this, the Teachers' Standards require all teachers to 'establish a safe and stimulating environment for pupils' (DfE 2011: 10). Therefore, it is crucial that you plan your lessons to ensure pupils are acquiring appropriate knowledge and understanding of health and safety matters and consider 'what pupils should know' (Beaumont 2008; afPE 2012).

Objectives

At the end of this chapter you should be able to:

- understand key health and safety legislation, regulations and policy, as well as your professional responsibilities and issues for maintaining safety in all aspects of teaching PE;
- use resources to support your practice in school;
- develop pupils' knowledge and understanding of, and ability to create and manage, their learning environment to ensure the health and safety of themselves and others;
- create a safe environment for teaching and learning in your lessons.

Check the requirements of your ITE to see which relate to this chapter.

Health and safety legislation and regulations

Given the essential requirement to teach safely and safety in PE, it is necessary for you to acquire an indepth knowledge and understanding of health and safety issues. This section provides an overview of key health and safety organisations, legislation and regulations (see Figure 12.1 and Table 12.1, below); your professional responsibilities; issues of teaching safely and safety; how to develop pupils' knowledge and understanding of safety; and how to teach pupils to create and manage their learning environment to ensure health and safety of themselves and others. You also need to understand: concepts and principles underpinning safe practice in the different physical activities and teaching environments in which you are teaching; how to assess the safety of specific activities/exercises; the associated safety procedures for specific activities being taught; first aid/emergency procedures; particular medical conditions (e.g. asthma, diabetes), and know how to plan and/or adapt exercises/ activities to minimise risk to pupils with these conditions; class management/organisation skills in relation to the positioning of you, the placement and use of equipment, and the orientation of the activity or exercise. To this end we advise you to read *Safe Practice in Physical Education and Sport* (afPE 2012) which looks in depth at safety issues. This is a key document supporting the work nationally in the UK within the PE subject area which is updated every four years to take account of developments in the area, including a response to recent case law.

It is important for you to recognise that the law provides checklists, procedures and frameworks to safeguard professionals who may be exposed to risks in the workplace. You should, therefore, familiarise yourself with health and safety organisations, legislation and regulations, particularly their interrelationships and interconnections, to understand better your professional responsibility in teaching safely and safety in a PE context.

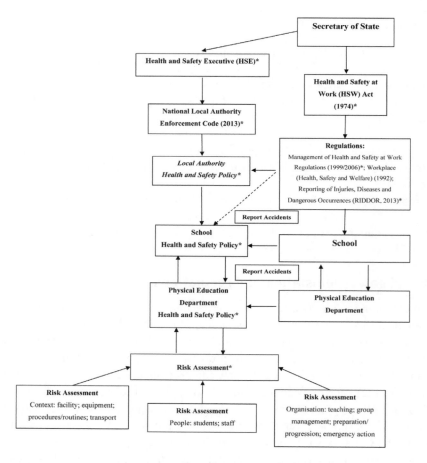

* See Table 12.1 for a description of this organisation, legislation or regulation.
Italics indicates the position of the Local Authority relative to maintained schools.

Figure 12.1 Overview of health and safety organisations, legislation and regulations (adapted from Elbourn 1999).

Table 12.1 Descriptions of selected health and safety organisations and associated legislation and regulations

Health and Safety Executive (HSE)	This is the national independent watchdog for work-related health, safety and illness established under the Health and Safety at Work Act (UK Legislation 1974). Its role is to secure the health, safety and welfare of people at work; to protect the public against risks to health and safety arising from work activities; and to control dangerous substances. The HSE is responsible for proposing and setting necessary standards via policy; securing compliance with those standards; and undertaking other forms of activity designed to stimulate or support necessary action on the part of people and organisations that create potential harm (HSE 2011). This action includes: (a) inspecting workplaces (including schools and universities); (b) investigating accidents and cases of ill health; (c) enforcing good standards, usually by advising people on how to comply with the law; (d) publishing guidance and advice; (e) providing an information service; and (f) carrying out research (Elbourn 1999: 8).
National Local Authority Enforcement Code	This outlines the role of the Local Authorities (LAs) in supporting, encouraging and advising employers to manage occupational health and safety. It seeks to promote good health and safety standards and practice. It ensures that health and safety legislation is enforced in a consistent way across LAs, and between LAs and the HSE (HSE 2013a).
Health and Safety at Work (HSW) Act (UK Legislation 1974)	Health and safety is about preventing people from being harmed at work by taking the right precautions and providing a satisfactory working environment. The HSW Act (UK Legislation 1974) requires that: (a) employers look after the health and safety of their employees; (b) employees look after their own health and safety; and (c) employers and employees care for the health and safety of others (e.g. members of the public).
Management of Health and Safety at Work (MHSW) (1999) Regulations	This outlines the requirement for employers to manage health and safety, including the assessment and management of risks arising from work-related activities to their employees and others.
Reporting of Injuries, Diseases and Dangerous Occurrences Regulations (RIDDOR) (HSE 2013b)	'Reporting certain incidents is a legal requirement' (HSE 2013b: 1). Those which must be reported include deaths; major injuries; injuries where an employee or self-employed person is away from work or unable to perform his or her normal work duties for more than seven consecutive days; injuries to members of the public or people not at work, where they are taken from the scene of an accident to hospital; some occupational diseases; some dangerous occurrences and reportable gas incidents (HSE 2013b). These occurrences must be reported via the RIDDOR database without delay. This reporting process 'informs the enforcing authorities about deaths, injuries, occupational diseases and dangerous occurrences so that they can identify where and how risks arise, and whether they need to be investigated' (HSE 2013b: 2). It also facilitates the investigation of serious accidents and advice 'on preventative action' (Raymond 1999: 16).

(continued)

Table 12.1 (continued)

Local Authority health and safety policy	LAs are responsible for producing a broad health and safety policy statement which should ensure that all employees know what is expected of them and what they need to do to discharge their legal liabilities. Additionally, each maintained school is required by its LA to produce a school health and safety policy statement covering local organisation and health and safety arrangements. This is then attached to the LA document to form a complete response to the requirements of the HSW Act (Elbourn 1999). Non-maintained schools are not required to refer to LA policy but may choose to do so.
School and PE Department health and safety policy	All schools are required by the DfE to have a health and safety policy (DfE 2014e). This should include content such as: (a) 'the policy's aims in relation to the law; (b) the responsibilities of the governing body, headteacher, school health and safety officer and safety representatives; (c) duties and obligations of staff; (d) what is expected of pupils; (e) the composition and duties of a safety committee; (f) arrangements for risk assessments; (g) emergency procedures (including first aid) and fire drills; (h) accident recording and reporting procedures; (i) safety training; (j) security issues; (k) review and monitoring procedures' (Elbourn 1999: 11). Headteachers are responsible for health and safety matters in a school. Heads of department (HOD) are responsible for the health and safety within their department. Teachers are responsible for the immediate area of their work. If teachers discover a hazard, the law requires them to take all reasonable steps within their power to eliminate this and to refer the matter to their HOD or headteacher, if the limits of their authority preclude a permanent solution. The headteacher needs to ensure that PE teachers are: (a) trained in risk assessment and making quality and justifiable decisions; (b) provided with quality information; (c) monitored so that they can learn from their successes and can be helped to minimise the seriousness of harmful outcomes; (d) provided with a framework for making high-quality decisions that minimise the seriousness of harmful outcomes; (e) supported if they follow the LA's/school's decision-making framework, even if harm results (Elbourn 1999. See also afPE (2012).
Risk assessment (people, context and organisation)	afPE (2012) provide a useful structural and contextual framework (comprising people, context and organisation) for educating both teachers and pupils in the importance of risk management (Figure 12.2; afPE 2012).

Task 12.1 asks you to study the health and safety documentation in your placement school.

Task 12.1 Health and safety policy statements and processes in your placement school and PE department

Familiarise yourself with the health and safety policy statements and processes of both your placement school and PE department.

Find out: (a) who is the school's designated Health and Safety Officer; (b) who is the PE department's designated Health and Safety Officer (or equivalent); (c) who are the certified and trained first aid personnel in the school and in the PE department; (d) where both the first aid box and travelling first aid kit can be found; (e) what risk assessment form is used in the PE department; (f) what form should be filled in to record an accident or injury and where it can be accessed; (g) who is involved and what the stages of the process are in relation to accident forms; (h) where relevant, the role of the LA in supporting the policy and process of health and safety.

Record this information in your professional development portfolio (PDP), for future reference.

Professional responsibilities for and issues related to teaching safely and safety in PE

Your professional responsibilities for and issues related to teaching safely in PE include: duty of care and acting in loco parentis; negligence; risk management and control, risk assessment and safety; dealing appropriately with injuries or accidents and accident reporting; first aid training, first aid boxes and travelling first aid kits. Figure 12.2 provides an overview of the factors involved in effective risk management and guides the key considerations for enabling safe working conditions.

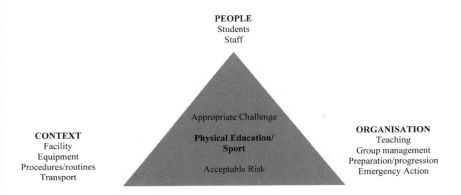

Figure 12.2 The risk-management model (afPE 2012, p. 16, courtesy of Beaumont, Eve, Kirkby and Whitlam).

Duty of care and in loco parentis

All teachers are responsible for the health and safety of pupils in their care. You should take reasonable care in any situation to: safeguard pupils; anticipate and manage risks to ensure they are at an acceptable level (Whitlam 2005); and ensure that pupils are not harmed by the actions of themselves or others. This is called 'duty of care'. The term 'in loco parentis', which literally means 'in place of the parent', underpins this duty of care for teachers when responsible for pupils. Whilst pupils are in a teacher's care, some of the privileges of the natural, caring parent are transferred to the qualified teacher. Thus, teachers with this legal responsibility must exercise the same duty of care as a 'reasonably prudent parent', judged not in the context of the home but in that of a school situation. Crucially the 'higher duty of care' is applied in the professional context and qualified teachers, by virtue of their skills, training and experience, are expected to have 'greater insight' and 'awareness of the consequences' of their practice. Teachers are required to undertake practice which is recognised to be 'regular and approved' within the profession (afPE 2012). This is only possible for you if you keep up to date through on-going professional learning and continuing professional development (CPD) activities (see Chapter 17 for guidance on CPD), as outlined in the Teachers' Standards (DfE 2011).

As a student teacher you cannot legally take on the responsibility for the health and safety of pupils; that responsibility lies with the qualified and experienced teacher in charge of the class/group. When you are teaching, a qualified and experienced teacher must always supervise you in the teaching environment in the same way as they supervise any adult without qualified teacher status (afPE 2012). Likewise, you cannot act as a supply teacher to fill in if the regular qualified teacher is absent. If the qualified teacher is not available, you must not proceed to teach (see Unit 8.3 (Leslie and Collins) in Capel *et al.* 2013). Similarly, if you are running a lunchtime and/or after-school club, you must always have a qualified teacher present.

Negligence

afPE (2012: 57) states that: 'everyone has a duty of care not to cause harm to others. Where the expected professional standards are not met, and this results in damage (injury in PE contexts) and this was reasonably foreseeable, an allegation of negligence may apply'. An allegation of negligence requires four elements, which relate to: the nature of the responsibility undertaken for the claimant; carelessness by 'act' or 'omission' whilst undertaking that responsibility; resulting injury to the claimant; and information that the potential for the incident could have been foreseen.

> It is the element of carelessness that may impose a liability of negligence. The use of reasonable foresight, anticipation and forward planning is expected, set at the level of guarding against the possible consequences of a failure to take care, to avoid acts of omissions that could reasonably be foreseen as likely to cause injury to other people.
>
> (afPE 2012: 58)

Claims for negligence are normally made against employers and 'significant levels of protection exist against allegations of negligence by staff as individuals'.

(afPE 2012: 57)

Accusations of negligence can be minimised considerably if it can be shown that:

- a teacher is sufficiently qualified, experienced and confident to teach the activity and appropriate supervision is provided;
- teachers keep themselves up to date on health and safety issues and recent developments, through reading, research and other activities such as attendance at relevant courses. Furthermore, they undertake the 'regular and approved' practice that operates within policy guidelines;
- planning takes full account of the people involved, the context of the activity and the associated organisation to ensure that risk management is comprehensive;
- equipment is used for the purposes that it was intended for and is well maintained;
- in a manner appropriate to their age, ability and experience, pupils are taught about safety; have safe practice modelled for them; and are always expected to demonstrate safe ways of working;
- pupils are systematically prepared for the activities being undertaken and the tasks are progressive, ensuring appropriateness for the pupils' experience, ability, age and physical maturity;
- appropriate footwear and clothing are worn, all adornments are removed and safety equipment is used where appropriate;
- any local or overseas visits (including activities at other schools or offsite locations) are preceded by prior agreement of parents by means of information and signed participation documentation. The DfE (2014e) produces a form for this but a member of a school's senior management team is normally responsible for providing documentation and supporting teachers with the process;
- record keeping, such as attendance registers, lesson plans and assessment information, is efficiently documented and stored. These documents record pupil experience and indicate what they are capable of;
- regular and accurate risk assessments are undertaken, documented and reviewed;
- adults other than teachers (AOTTs) are well informed and given a clear role in the lesson.

(for further information, see afPE 2012 and DfE 2014e)

Risk management and control

Risk management is the 'umbrella term given to the whole process of identifying risks and then taking action to eliminate them' (Raymond 1999: 49). The law does not expect you to eliminate all risk, but you are required to protect people as far as is 'reasonably practicable' (HSE 2011: 1). In relation to risk control:

if any significant risk is identified which current practice does not eliminate or minimise, then that risk must be controlled by taking some sort of action ... the action may involve: removing the risk completely; trying a less risky option; preventing access to the hazard; re-organising the group, activity or procedure to reduce the likelihood of the hazard causing harm; providing or requiring protective equipment to be used; improving the staff/pupil ratio or providing more information, tuition or training.

(Raymond 1999: 57)

In simple terms, the decision about action to be taken or not relates to the manner in which the benefits of an activity 'outweigh the risks' or the 'risks outweigh the benefits' (Beaumont 2007: 31).

To ensure that you do all that is reasonably practicable to safeguard the health, safety and welfare of pupils, you need to recognise and eliminate the hazards (or anything that can cause harm, such as equipment or environment) and reduce the risks (or the chance that someone will be harmed by a hazard). You are expected to foresee a substantial risk and take steps to avoid it or reduce it to an acceptable level. As outlined above, you are also expected to possess a greater than average knowledge and understanding of the risks involved in the activities you teach and to take precautions in accordance with that knowledge and understanding (afPE 2012). This can be challenging where practices have been undertaken for many years and are perceived to be the norm and acceptable. It is in this type of environment that you need to be particularly aware, and ensure that you stay up to date with national guidance. Task 12.2 requires you to carry out an analysis of the risks in setting up and managing a circuit.

Task 12.2 Risk management

You have been asked to teach a lesson to a year 8 mixed-sex class involving the setting-up and use of a circuit of activities. You have been told that the lesson will take place in a gymnasium; the pupils will be using dumbbells and mats, benches and skipping ropes; and will be required to complete as many repeats as possible (in one minute) at each station. Pupils will be working in bare feet. The circuit includes push-ups, sit-ups, skipping, step-ups, shuttle runs, squats, biceps and triceps curls. The warm-up comprises sprint relays, windmills and hurdle stretches.

Using Figure 12.2 and the material covered so far in the chapter, list your recommendations to minimise risk. Record your reasons for this selection of recommendations and discuss these with your tutor. Record this discussion and put all elements of the observation into your PDP.

Risk assessment and safety

One of the challenges for you is to identify accurately the potential level of risk that an activity poses. Risk assessment 'involves identifying what could cause harm to people and appraising whether sufficient precautions have been taken to prevent or minimise harm' (Elbourn 1999: 3). Although it might be easy to identify those situations in which risk is most obvious, you need to be able to assess all situations in respect of the likelihood of accident or injury (afPE 2012: 157-160). Figure 12.2 provides an illustration of an effective method for doing this.

Task 12.3 asks you to complete risk assessments on six of your lessons, using the grading structure from Table 12.2.

Task 12.3 Risk rating

Choose six examples of specific activities that you might teach in a PE and/or school sport programme. Use Table 12.2 to calculate a 'risk rating' for each and rank them in order of the highest to lowest rating. Discuss this with your tutor and put your notes in your PDP.

To assist you in assessing the risks in your workplace or teaching environment, HSE (2011: 2-5 and http://www.hse.gov.uk/risk/fivesteps.htm) recommends the following 'five steps to risk assessment':

Step 1: Identify the hazards

Walk around the teaching environment such as the gym and look at anything that could cause harm; concentrate on significant hazards which could result in serious harm or affect several pupils. Also, ask pupils if they notice anything which may pose a risk.

Step 2: Decide who might be harmed and how

Consider anyone that might be at risk (pupils; yourself; PE teacher/tutor; other teachers or adults; public/visitors).

Table 12.2 Calculating a risk rating (Whitlam 2003: 35)

Hazard severity	Likelihood of occurrence
1 Negligible: near miss/minor injury, e.g. abrasion	1 Improbable: almost zero
2 Slight: injury needing medical attention, e.g. laceration	2 Remote: unlikely to occur
3 Moderate: more serious injury causing absence from school	3 Possible: could occur sometimes
4 Severe: serious injury requiring hospital treatment	4 Probable: may occur several times; not surprising
5 Very severe: permanent injury/fatality	5 Near certainty: expected

Severity × likelihood = risk rating

For example, a hockey lesson on dribbling outdoors on an artificial pitch *might* score 1 for hazard severity and 3 for likelihood of occurrence. Risk rating: 3.

For example, a swimming lesson *might* score 5 for hazard severity and 2 for likelihood of occurrence. Risk rating: 10.

Step 3: Evaluate the risks and decide on precautions

Your aim is to make all risks small. If something needs to be done, draw up an action plan and give priority to any remaining risks which are medium or high. In taking action, ask yourself: can I eliminate the risk completely? If not, how can I control the risks so that harm is unlikely? In controlling risks, apply the following principles: (a) try a less risky option; (b) prevent access to the hazard; (c) organise teaching to reduce exposure to the hazard, e.g. issue personal protective/adaptive resources/equipment; (d) provide welfare facilities. Failure to take simple precautions can be significantly to your disadvantage if an accident does happen. Remember that if you cannot reduce the risks to an acceptable level then you should not undertake the activity.

Step 4: Record your findings and implement them

You need to be able to show that: a proper check was made; you asked who might be affected; you dealt with all the significant hazards, taking into account the number of pupils involved; the precautions are reasonable, and the remaining risk is low. Keep a written record for future reference or use. It can help you if anyone asks what precautions you have taken. It can also remind you to keep an eye on particular hazards and precautions. It also helps to show that you have done what the law requires if you become involved in any action for civil liability.

Step 5: Review your assessment and update if necessary

It is good practice to review your risk assessment regularly to make sure that the precautions are still working effectively.

(See also afPE 2012 for detailed guidance and documentation to support this risk assessment process.)

Task 12.4 challenges you to use the five-step risk factor assessment above to assess one of your lessons.

Task 12.4 Risk assessment of a PE lesson

Complete a risk assessment of one of your PE lessons, following the 'five steps to risk assessment' outlined above. Link this assessment to Task 12.3. Discuss the findings with your tutor and put these notes in your PDP.

All schools should have a risk assessment form. The risk assessment form should prompt the recording of issues associated with people, context and organisation, in relation to the breadth of practice, and whether they pose a 'satisfactory/safe/low risk' or an 'unsatisfactory/unsafe/significant risk'. The form should identify any significant risks, identify who is affected and the details of the proposed risk control (afPE 2012). It is important that the form is signed, dated and shared with the leadership and management team (Whitlam 2003), especially where support is required from outside the department to resolve an issue. Task 12.5 asks you to study the risk assessment form in the PE department of your placement school.

Task 12.5 Risk assessment form

Look at a completed risk assessment form for the PE department in your placement school for one of the activities you are teaching; one of the facilities that you are working in; and an offsite activity (e.g. a local fixture or a larger-scale trip).

Consider the way in which staff have recorded any necessary aspects of risk control where an issue has been identified as being more significant than 'satisfactory/safe/ low risk'. What support/action has been sought from outside the department? Discuss this and the associated processes with your tutor. Put these notes in your PDP.

Injuries or accidents and accident reporting

Wherever there is a risk, injuries or accidents are a possibility. If an injury or accident (minor or serious) occurs in your lesson(s), you should not hesitate to act promptly and effectively. It is essential that you understand and implement your placement school's procedures and guidelines for dealing with injuries or accidents. If an injury or accident happens, the priorities are to: (a) assess the situation; (b) safeguard the uninjured members of the class/ group; (c) attend to the casualty; (d) inform the emergency services, if appropriate, and everyone who needs to know of the incident (Department for Education and Employment (DfEE) 1998). Increasingly schools have made it accepted practice for staff, particularly PE staff, to use mobile phones or have provided radios/intercoms (to overcome potential mobile phone signal problems) when they are working at a distance from the school's main building.

It is important that all accidents and injuries (minor or major) are recorded immediately. Some accidents also fall into the category of 'reportable' (HSE 2013a). A reportable accident is defined as one 'which causes death ... certain serious injuries ... industrial diseases; and certain dangerous occurrences' (HSE 2013a: 1). Major injuries include fractures (other than to the bones of the hands and feet) (for other major injuries, diseases and dangerous occurrences see HSE 2013a and http://www.hse.gov.uk/riddor/reportable-incidents.htm) and also RIDDOR (see Table 12.1). This includes 'accidents which result in the incapacitation of a worker for more than seven days' (HSE 2013b: 1).

All schools should have their own accident report forms. afPE recommends that:

> it is important that accidents are reported on the employer's official report form or accident book as soon as is reasonably possible. This aids the reporting process and is also useful in the event of a complaint or claim. It is also good practice to write down the events surrounding an incident as soon as possible to ensure a clear recall at some later date.
>
> (afPE 2012: 138)

In the past it was a requirement that records were kept for at least three years (Department for Education and Skills (DfES) 2002). However, it has become increasingly important for these records to be kept longer in order to ensure that evidence is available in the case where a retrospective claim is made. A detailed accident report would include the information in Figure 12.3.

Particulars of the injured or affected person
Full name:
Date of birth:
Gender:
Home address:
Postcode:
Telephone number:
Status: employee/pupil/visitor (*please delete as applicable*)
Name(s) of witness(es):

Particulars of the accident	
Date:	Time:
Description of the events leading to the accident (*continue on an additional sheet if required*):	
Description of the action taken immediately after the accident (*continue on an additional sheet if required*):	

Particulars of the injury
Was an injury sustained?: yes/no (*please delete as applicable*)
Cause of injury:
Type of injury:
Part(s) of the body affected:
Outcome
Was first aid treatment required?: yes/no (*please delete as applicable*)
If yes, please provide details:
Was a hospital visit required?: yes/no (*please delete as applicable*)
Date of visit:
Was hospital treatment necessary?: yes/no (*please delete as applicable*)
Please provide details:
Was time off required following the accident?: yes/no (*please delete as applicable*)
If yes, how long?:
Was temporary injury sustained?: yes/no (*please delete as applicable*)
If yes, please provide details:
Was permanent injury sustained?: yes/no (*please delete as applicable*)
If yes, please provide details:

Figure 12.3 Sample accident report form.

Risk management
What action has been taken to avoid/prevent a recurrence?
Recommendations:
Report completed by
Name:
Date:
Signature:

Figure 12.3 (continued)

Together with the accident report, a sketch plan (signed and dated) of where an accident has taken place would be useful, as very often people have different views of what took place, where, how and when. Task 12.6 asks you to investigate in your placement school what actions you should take in the event of an accident.

Task 12.6 Reporting accidents

Find out what you have to do if an accident or injury occurs whilst you are teaching a PE lesson in your placement school. What formal guidelines and procedures must be adhered to? Keep a copy of this in your PDP for future reference.

First aid training, first aid boxes and travelling first aid kits

afPE (2012) suggests that the minimum first aid requirements for each school are: a person(s) appointed to take charge of first aid arrangements; information for employees about first aid arrangements; well-maintained records of any incidents where first aid is administered; an appropriate number of suitably stocked, identifiable and easily accessible first aid boxes and travelling first aid kits. There should be at least one qualified first aider for every 50 members of staff in each school. Furthermore, it is advisable that all PE teachers and AOTTs receive first aid training appropriate to their teaching responsibilities – including you (afPE 2012: 37, 138). In the United Kingdom certificates of qualification in first aid are valid for three years and during this three-year period annual refresher courses are available. After three years a requalification is required. The regulations for first aid at work were changed by HSE on 1 October 2013. The three-day 'First Aid at Work' and one-day 'Emergency First Aid at Work' (St John's Ambulance) are examples of first aid courses (for further information on availability of first aid courses, see the Health and Safety Officer at your placement school or university or make enquiries at your local sport, leisure and recreation centre). Further guidance on first aid processes for schools is available from https://www.gov.uk/government/publications/first-aid-in-schools.

How to develop pupils' knowledge and understanding of, and ability to create and manage, their learning environment to ensure health and safety of themselves and others

With reference to teaching safety or developing pupils' knowledge and understanding of creating and managing a safe learning environment, pupils should:

- learn how to respond appropriately to instructions and signals within established routines and follow rules and codes of conduct in a given activity (e.g. negotiate class rules to ensure a safe teaching environment);
- learn the importance of being dressed appropriately for the activity/exercise they are participating in (e.g. no jewellery/adornment; trainer laces tied; long hair tied back; head scarves secured) and the wearing of protective clothing (e.g. shin pads in football);
- learn about correct forms of exercise, and how performance and safety are improved when preparation is carried out properly (e.g. performing recommended stretching exercises during warm-up and cool-down phases of a lesson);
- analyse, plan and carry out tasks safely (e.g. problem-solving activities in outdoor adventurous activities);
- learn the principles of safe partner support (e.g. progressive skills within gymnastics);
- know the proper use of a range of equipment; the safe handling and storage of equipment and apparatus;
- create their own apparatus layout to suit the tasks set and be aware of the risks and hazards (e.g. setting out medium and high apparatus to carry out a 'rotation' task);
- devise, implement and monitor their own, and/or others', exercise and fitness programmes based on the principles of safe and effective exercise (e.g. at Key Stage 4, pupils plan their own exercise programme to improve aspects of their fitness);
- carry out a risk assessment in a particular activity (e.g. as part of their role as an official, they would check the playing area of a football activity for any potholes, etc.).

In planning activities, it is essential that you not only present an exemplary model of safe practice and safety management to pupils but also take time to discuss safety, thus increasing their awareness and understanding in relation to their safe involvement in physical activities within and beyond school.

A case report of alleged negligence

Below is a case report of alleged negligence (see Swansea Civil Justice Centre 2002). Other cases are also available (see Raymond 1999: 97–104; Whitlam 2005; afPE 2012). This detailed case is presented to highlight some of the complexities of the challenges teachers are faced with in practice, and to help you to understand your professional responsibilities in teaching safely and safety in PE. The case report is presented in the following format to guide you through the important considerations: the relevant parties, evidence available, circumstances of the accident, the issues to be addressed, the facts upon which the expert's opinions are based, the expert's conclusion and lessons to be learned.

The relevant parties

The plaintiff (injured party), Rhian, is a pupil at Dwr-y-Felin Upper School. The defendant (the Local County Council (LCC)) denies negligence.

Evidence available

Individual statements from Rhian; Rebecca, her partner in the PE lesson; and PE teacher, Mrs S in October 1997.

Circumstances of the accident

One day in autumn 1997, Rhian participated in her first, year 8, PE lesson. It was the first period of the day, taken by Mrs S, the teacher in charge of the lesson. Towards the end of the lesson, Mrs S asked the class to do headstands in pairs (whilst one pupil performed the headstand, the partner was to give such support as was necessary). Rhian paired herself with another female pupil, Rebecca. Rhian said that neither she nor Rebecca had ever been shown how to perform or support a headstand or had actually been engaged in attempting one. They had not been shown previously, nor did Mrs S demonstrate or give any instruction as to how to do or support a headstand that day. Rhian said that her partner mentioned this to Mrs S but she insisted that they practise full headstands without further demonstration or instruction. They did so. Whilst Rhian was attempting her first headstand, Rebecca was to her side to support her back. Unfortunately, she lost her footing, causing Rhian to move backwards. As a result, she let go of Rhian, who fell, landing awkwardly on her neck and shoulder. Rhian immediately felt a 'click' between her shoulder blades, and felt some discomfort. However, when she looked around the gymnasium for Mrs S, she had left the gymnasium and Rhian was unable to find her. Rhian consequently went back to the changing rooms, and got ready for and went to the next lesson without telling any member of staff. However, she went to the school nurse at lunchtime that day because she was still in discomfort. That visit to the nurse was the start of considerable intervention on the part of healthcare professionals, over several months. Rhian suffered a musculoligament strain of the soft tissues of the cervical spine. There was stark divergence of medical opinion between two consultant orthopaedic surgeons instructed by each party; Mr G considered that Rhian would suffer indefinite symptoms for an indefinite period. The other consultant considered that symptoms for a period of only 9–12 months were properly attributable to the accident.

The issues to be addressed

Rhian alleges that Mrs S failed to: exercise proper supervision or control over her and the other pupils; instruct her and the other pupils in the proper and safe procedure for carrying out the exercise, in particular, the need to form a secure base with the hands and head on the floor before raising the legs; practise the technique of support appropriately and safely; carry out any proper risk assessment of the activity and demonstrate the exercise in the presence of the class; properly assess the skill level and previous experience of the class; have any proper regard to the relevant publications such as: afPE (2012) *Safe Practice in*

Physical Education and Sport; provide her with a safe place to perform the said activity; and provide sufficient supervision or control of her activities and exposed her to an unnecessary risk of injury.

The facts upon which the expert's opinions are based

Teacher

Mrs S had been a teacher for 12 years, having obtained a degree in Education at a very well-respected college. She had not been involved in any incident in which a pupil had been injured before, or since. Mrs S explained that she began to teach the progressive headstand routine in accordance with the National Curriculum for Physical Education in year 7. However, Rhian did not join the school until Christmas of that year, and therefore missed the first term. Rhian's evidence was that she had never been shown how to do a headstand in any shape or form before 9 October 1997; she had never been in a PE class in which they had been attempted. Rhian's partner said that she had been shown how to perform and how to support a headstand whilst she was in year 7.

Teaching style

Mrs S stated that she demonstrated the various sequential stages leading towards a full, straight-legged headstand, with a pupil (to show method of support) before asking the pupils to perform such a supported headstand. This was confirmed by Rebecca, Rhian's partner; she also confirmed that she fully understood the instructions that had been explained by Mrs S. Whatever Rhian's experience, ability and understanding, her partner fully understood her instruction as to how to support a partner when that partner was attempting a headstand manoeuvre. It was also something which she had done before on many occasions.

Supervision

Rhian's partner, Rebecca, said that Mrs S did not leave the PE lesson and she recalled seeing her at the end of the lesson. Mrs S said that she did not leave the gymnasium and supervised the lesson from start to finish. Mrs S went with the girls to the changing rooms and consequently was available if Rhian had wanted to speak with her about the accident. Mrs S said Rhian did not report any accident.

The expert's conclusion

Mrs S properly instructed Rhian in how to perform a supported headstand and the level to which she should attempt to go and she properly instructed her partner in how to support a headstand. Further, Mrs S did not leave the gymnasium until the end of the lesson, properly supervising the class throughout the period. That supervision included giving Rhian some individual tuition about headstands. Neither Rhian nor her partner expressed unwillingness to attempt headstands in line with the instructions given nor any tendency to go outside or beyond those instructions. Mrs S was not guilty of any breach of the duty owed to Rhian on 9 October 1997. Insofar as the allegations that Mrs S ought to have prepared for the lesson (and assessed the risks inherent in headstands) in a different way, no findings were made. Had Mrs S acted differently, that would not have prevented the accident that in fact occurred. Rhian suffered an unfortunate accident but the LCC was not to blame for it. The LCC was not at fault, and was consequently not liable to compensate Rhian for the injury she suffered (Swansea Civil Justice Centre 2002).

Lessons to be learned

In this case report, the key safety issues were estimations of pupils' sense of responsibility and the level of supervision. It is not so much the activity that causes the accidents, but a combination of factors contributing to accidents. Regardless of differences in pupils' age, the type of school, range of teaching environments and type of activity, Thomas (1994) suggests that there are five factors as to why accidents happen:

1   bad luck – factors outside the teacher's control;
2   poor decision making and subsequent reaction to the situation;
3   lack of adequate and appropriate group management, supervision and organisation;
4   overestimation of (a) teacher's ability (knowledge, understanding and competence) and (b) pupil's sense of responsibility;
5   underestimation of potential risk and hazard.

Thus, a knowledge and understanding of how and why accidents happen can provide a basis for modifying current practice, minimising and anticipating the occurrence of injury or accident and developing a safety culture. In this way PE can continue to offer teachers, student teachers and pupils challenges, adventure and risks safely and in safety. To minimise the risk of alleged negligence, remember to follow the 'five steps to risk assessment', as outlined above (HSE 2011), and refer to afPE (2012) *Safe Practice in Physical Education and Sport*.

A checklist to support you in promoting a culture of teaching safely and safety in PE

The checklist below identifies key elements to consider in promoting a culture of teaching safely and safety in PE:

*   Know and understand the current health and safety legislation and regulations (Table 12.1).
*   Familiarise yourself with the health and safety policy statements of the school and PE department (as well as the LA, where appropriate) and the procedures and guidelines arising from these documents.
*   Have a good up-to-date working knowledge and understanding of legal and professional responsibilities and your liabilities relating to health and safety and duty of care.
*   Have an indepth, up-to-date knowledge and understanding of the concepts, principles and safety implications, guidelines and procedures associated with 'people, context and organisation' (Figure 12.1) in relation to your teaching.

- Ensure that you have a risk assessment framework and receive appropriate training and information updates in order to make accurate and consistent decisions which minimise risk in PE.
- Carry out regular risk assessments in relation to 'people, context and organisation'. In order to do this it is essential that you are up to date with the national guidance for PE as well as each of the activities you are planning for.
- Participate in daily, weekly, monthly and annual risk assessments (e.g. outside agencies such as the Health and Safety Officer, maintenance 'team', manufacturer): it is an expectation of school and PE staff.
- Follow the 'five steps to risk assessment' (HSE 2011: 2–5; http://www.hse.gov.uk/risk/fivesteps.htm) fully and clinically.
- Cultivate an ability to perceive and anticipate risks, and become competent in checking for potential hazards. Use this information to make appropriate adaptations to reduce risks to an acceptable level.
- Plan for all eventualities and especially for emergency action, and ensure that you have first aid training appropriate to your level of responsibility.
- Maintain and retain detailed records of your practice.
- Involve pupils fully in the process of safe practice by teaching them safely and about safety. It should be embedded in your teaching.

Furthermore, as safety in PE is a vast subject and one beyond the remit of this chapter, we urge you to read afPE (2012) as well as checking for regular updates with afPE and other relevant professional associations (see further reading). Now complete Task 12.7.

> **Task 12.7 Embedding teaching safely and safety in your teaching**
>
> Undertake a professional learning conversation with your tutor, HOD or other experienced colleague and discuss in detail the professional role and responsibility of the teacher in embedding teaching safely and safety as a fundamental aspect of his or her practice. Consider the challenges faced in undertaking this role and responsibility, and suggest ways of overcoming these. Store this material in your PDP to refer to at a later date.

Summary and key points

This chapter has presented an overview of key health and safety guidance, legislation and regulations in England. It discussed some of your professional responsibilities, and issues of teaching safely and safety. The chapter then considered how you can develop pupils' knowledge and understanding of, and ability to create and manage, their learning environment to ensure the health and safety of themselves and others. This was supported with a case report of alleged negligence in a gymnastics lesson to highlight some of the problems teachers face in trying to ensure pupils' safety and the associated accountability. Finally, the chapter provided a checklist to support you in promoting a culture of teaching safely and safety in PE.

Health and safety considerations are embedded in good practice and, on this basis, this chapter has sought to help you approach your teaching with greater knowledge and confidence, rather than uneasiness and concern. We strongly urge you to take responsibility for your own professional learning and development, and to keep up to date with recent developments, approved practice and research evidence concerning the provision of health and safety in PE.

Check which requirements of your ITE you have addressed through this chapter.

Further reading

Association for Physical Education (2012) *Safe Practice in Physical Education and Sport*, 8th edn, Leeds: afPE/Coachwise.

This key text provides comprehensive up-to-date advice and information for PE teachers and other staff involved in teaching PE and school sport safely and safety in schools.

Chappell, A. (2014) Safe practice, risk assessment and risk management, in S. Capel and P. Breckon (eds) *A Practical Guide to Teaching Physical Education in the Secondary School*, 2nd edn, Abingdon, Oxon: Routledge, pp. 101–125.

This chapter provides a range of activities (10.1–10.16) which can be undertaken in the teaching context to support the ongoing development of up-to-date subject knowledge across aspects of health and safety in PE and school sport.

Raymond, C. (ed.) (1999) *Safety Across the Curriculum*, London: RoutledgeFalmer.

This text provides an overview of responsibilities and interpretation of the main legislation and statutory requirements. It offers background information to help you interpret general principles and apply them to your practice.

Whitlam, P. (2005) *Case Law in Physical Education and School Sport: A Guide to Good Practice*, Leeds: Coachwise/BAALPE.

This text uses examples from case law to identify and reinforce the principles of good practice and standards of care in PE and school sport.

Relevant organisations

Association for Physical Education: www.afpe.org.uk

The Association for Physical Education supports the delivery of PE in schools and in the wider community, seeking to promote and maintain high standards and safe practice in all aspects and at all levels. The website contains regular updates and advice, with links to a helpline for health and safety, and legal advice. They have a health and safety advisory panel who provide support and frequently asked questions.

Health and Safety Executive: www.hse.gov.uk

The Health and Safety Executive's role is to protect people against risks to health or safety arising out of work activities. They offer information, advice and training in relation to regulations and codes of practice, inspection, investigation and enforcement. They also provide frequently asked questions.

Acknowledgement

The author would like to acknowledge the significant input of Geoff Edmondson and Will Katene to the earlier editions of this chapter.

13 Designing teaching approaches to achieve intended learning outcomes

Richard Blair with Margaret Whitehead

Introduction

This chapter is aimed at helping you to understand the complex relationship between your intended learning outcomes (ILOs), your lessons and the learning tasks and learning environment you and your pupils create (Leach and Moon 1999). It supports the proposal that, to achieve any longer-term learning aim in respect of a scheme of work, you are required to develop medium-term objectives for units of work and short-term ILOs for lesson plans (see Chapter 3). Achieving lesson ILOs are the essential building blocks in reaching long-term goals. Having a clear understanding of the key elements of your teaching that have an impact on pupils' learning and achieving ILOs is therefore very important to the whole enterprise of effective teaching of PE. The chapter proposes that the pedagogical knowledge regarding how you teach is as important as the content knowledge of what you teach (Shulman 1999). It encourages you to view the significance of combining content knowledge with pedagogical knowledge as the foundation for understanding the importance of all elements of your teaching. The chapter supports you in developing an understanding of how consciously and subconsciously you develop your overall beliefs concerning teaching which, in turn influences your teaching approach and style in order that you can intentionally support pupil learning.

Objectives

At the end of this chapter you should be able to:

- understand the relationship between the concepts of teaching approach, teaching strategy, teaching style, teaching skill and the learning environment;
- understand that teaching strategies are specifically designed teaching approaches comprised of a carefully selected cluster of teaching skills/elements of teaching;
- understand that the appropriate use of teaching skills is essential to achieving ILOs;
- appreciate that aims, objectives and ILOs can be achieved only if the appropriate teaching strategy is used;

(continued)

(continued)

- be aware of a range of classifications of teaching approaches, both descriptive and prescriptive;
- recognise and implement a range of teaching strategies;
- be aware of your own beliefs in relation to teaching PE and supporting pupil learning.

Check the requirements of your initial teacher education (ITE) to see which relate to this chapter.

Teaching approach, teaching strategy, teaching style and teaching skill

With reference to how you teach, there are a number of concepts or terms that are used in the literature. See Figure 13.1, which charts the relationship between the different concepts.

Literature on teaching identifies a variety of basic teaching skills or elements of teaching, such as positioning, organisation and use of voice, that a teacher needs to master to be effective in promoting pupil learning. These skills are covered in various chapters in this

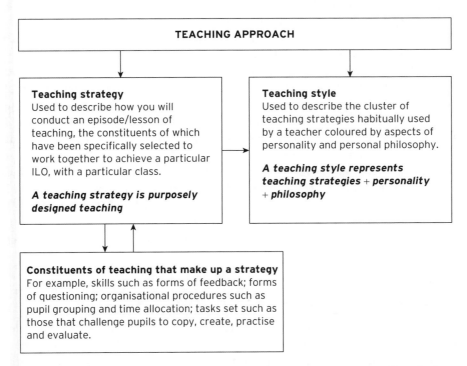

Figure 13.1 Relationship between the concepts of teaching approach, teaching strategy, teaching style and the constituents of teaching.

book. Throughout this chapter the term teaching approach is used to describe the overall pedagogical behaviour of a teacher in a lesson. The term teaching approach therefore encompasses the two types of teaching behaviour described in this chapter – teaching strategies and teaching styles. In this chapter the words strategy and style are used in the following ways.

Teaching *strategy* is used to describe a teaching approach, the constituent elements of which have been selected specifically to work together to achieve a particular ILO with a particular class. Research into teaching strategies has been carried out by, for example, Cole and Chan (1994), Joyce and Weil (1996) and Joyce *et al.* (2002), and specifically within PE by Kirk *et al.* (1996). Additionally, the work of Mosston and Ashworth (2002) clearly identifies strategies, although, confusingly, they call the types of teaching they describe 'styles'. For examples of strategies and a useful debate on this aspect of teaching, see Unit 5.3 (Leask) in Capel *et al.* (2013).

Teaching strategies are powerful learning tools that both promote aspects of learning and prohibit others from occurring. For example, a tightly controlled didactic approach does not foster creativity in dance, nor does an open-ended discovery method result in precision in learning specific techniques such as a swimming stroke or throwing the discus. Likewise, the development of cooperative skills in pupils cannot be achieved if they are always working alone and self-esteem cannot be developed if pupils are always engaged in competitive situations. A teaching strategy is designed to serve an ILO and should be planned after the ILOs of the lesson have been identified.

Teaching *style* is used to describe the general method of teacher–pupil interaction and self-presentation used by an individual teacher. Research into teaching styles was carried out by, for example, Bennett (1976), Galton and Croll (1980) and Oeser (1955). A teacher's style is made up of those skills and strategies used most often, coloured by his/her personal characteristics. For example, teacher A may have an authoritative self-presentation, use few arm gestures, speak with firmness and precision, seldom using humour and expect, rather than praise, effort. Teacher B may have a relaxed self-presentation, frequently use arm gestures and speak with a quiet voice, often using humour and positive body language.

These two teachers could be equally effective, yet each has developed a different style of working with pupils. It would not be impossible for teacher A and teacher B to design very similar strategies to achieve a particular ILO, but for the nature of their interaction with pupils to be distinctive on account of the way their personal characteristics colour their teaching. Task 13.1 asks you to observe two teachers and note how their style of teaching differs.

Task 13.1 Observation of teachers' individual styles

Observe two teachers as they work with pupils and list the behavioural characteristics that each exhibits. How is each style distinctive? The list is likely to include behaviours such as use of humour, use of gesture, amount of interaction with pupils, amount of talking allowed, ways in which order is maintained. Put your notes in your professional development portfolio (PDP).

That all teachers have their own style is both to be expected and welcomed, as this brings variety and colour into pupils' experience in school. However, it would be unacceptable to applaud difference per se. The strategic element of a teacher's style must be devised on a rational and appropriate basis – related to the ILOs, rather than being a matter of personal preference. In addition, it is important that the personal characteristics of a teacher's style are thoughtfully and carefully used, as in different contexts and situations there could be situations where certain characteristics are less appropriate. For example, a teacher's preferred relaxed and somewhat humorous approach may need to be adapted during lessons that include higher-risk activities such as throwing in athletics or water-based activities in outdoor education.

The overall lesson climate or ambience reflects the nature of the interpersonal relationships between the teacher and the pupils and is a significant feature of the learning environment. The ambience of the lesson should, at all times, facilitate learning, creating a positive, productive learning experience (Slavin 2003). The environment and the specific learning tasks should also match the ILOs. For example, in a lesson where you hope to promote innovation and imagination, 'creating an atmosphere that is conducive to interest and inquiry, and permitting activities that engage students' minds and imagination' (Slavin 2003: 367) is an advantage. It should also be remembered that the learning environment includes other aspects of the teaching situation, such as the nature of the working area, the equipment, the time you have available and, in certain situations, the temperature and the weather. All have to work together to support pupils in achieving the ILOs of the lesson.

Elements of teaching that make up a strategy

In designing teaching strategies it is important that you consider all the *elements* that make up a lesson plan and how the strategies work together to support pupils in successfully meeting your planned ILOs. See Chapter 3 for a detailed discussion and guide to lesson planning. Elements that need to be considered include:

- the material to be covered (for example, the swimming strokes);
- the sequencing and packaging of this material into, for example, a series of progressive tasks;
- the time allocation for each lesson episode;
- the extent of the responsibility devolved to the pupils (for example, to follow instructions exactly or to interpret guidance according to ability or imagination);
- the nature of the communication between the teacher and the pupils (for example, teacher questions, work cards, pupil/pupil discussion);
- the grouping of the pupils;
- the focus of teacher feedback (for example, on the acquisition of physical skill or the demonstration of cooperation and tolerance);
- the form and focus of assessment (for example, against previous personal performance or against national standards, formative or summative) (see Chapter 9);
- the organisation of pupils and equipment in the space (for example, highly prescriptive or leaving room for pupil choice).

Many of these skills have already been discussed in earlier chapters; however, the specific way you implement these in your teaching needs careful thought. For example, the way questions are framed has an influence on what can be achieved in a lesson, as can the way pupils are grouped. An understanding that appropriate use and adaptation of teaching skills are essential to promote/achieve particular ILOs is necessary. Activities 2.1, 2.2a and 2.2b in Capel and Breckon (2014) are valuable exercises to carry out to appreciate the relationship between ILOs and constituents of teaching. This is exemplified below through considering the nature of the *learning tasks* set and the specific focus of *feedback*, both of which have a significant influence on what is learned.

A series of lesson plans are a bit like a jigsaw puzzle, each one working with the next to support pupils' learning experience as a whole. If one piece is missing or the wrong piece is selected, then the teachers need to reflect both in and on the action (Schön 1983) and adapt and change strategy and possibly elements of style for the next episode or lesson.

Task 13.2 suggests that you observe teaching, ideally over a 3-6-week period, and begin to identify aspects of planning and teaching that clearly promote achievement of the ILOs. Task 13.3 requires you to look carefully at your lesson planning to see how far you have selected and designed elements to match the ILOs.

Task 13.2 Observation of elements of teaching that facilitate learning

Remembering that all teachers develop their own personal style, it is useful to look more closely at the ways teaching can be planned to achieve a specific ILO. Read and reflect on two units of work and two lesson plans within those units of teachers in your placement school who are working towards different ILOs. Try to observe a minimum of two lessons with each teacher and list those elements of teaching which clearly facilitate the intended learning. Discuss your observations with the teachers in question and put these notes in your PDP.

Task 13.3 Selecting elements of teaching to achieve ILOs

Using your existing lesson plans, select four very different ILOs. In discussion with your tutor, for each ILO identified consider how elements of teaching should be used to ensure it is achieved. For example, if the ILO is that pupils should be able to work together in creating a gymnastics sequence, an element you identify could be 'communication' and the specific use of communication that you plan for would be pupil/pupil discussion. Discuss your thoughts with other student teachers and put these notes in your PDP.

Learning tasks

Learning tasks form the content or material of the lesson that pupils will work on to achieve the ILOs. The design of learning tasks is central to achieving ILOs. Critically, tasks should relate to a specific ILO; for example, their design might require particular work on or attention to:

- replication, e.g. tasks requiring pupils to copy a model exactly;
- precision, e.g. tasks requiring attention to detail in performing a skill;
- developing strength, e.g. tasks that build strength in the arms or legs;
- experimentation, e.g. tasks that ask pupils to explore gymnastic apparatus;
- creativity, e.g. tasks that ask pupils to use imagination in developing a motif in dance;
- intragroup collaboration, e.g. tasks set that demand group discussion and decision;
- self-evaluation, e.g. tasks that ask pupils to compare their own performance with a set model;
- evaluation of a peer, e.g. tasks that require pupils to work together to give feedback to a partner;
- planning subsequent challenges, e.g. tasks that ask pupils to devise how they can progress their own learning.

Also when designing tasks you should consider whether:

- tasks are to be differentiated in design or outcome. Individual pupils can be given different tasks to work on, to match their level of competence or all members of the class can be given the same task, with different expectations according to their ability. For example, in relation to the latter, all pupils may be asked to complete a gymnastics routine. Pupils are given a choice of selecting different-colour worksheets that contain different levels of gymnastic routine. Level 1 contains five out of six movements in a near-complete routine, level 2 contains three out of six movements and level 3 contains two out of six movements (start and finish). The pupils are allowed to self-select which level they would like to try. Previous lessons have guided and supported this self-evaluation process. Additionally pupils are asked to produce a routine including an inverted movement. The physically more able may be expected to include a cartwheel while the physically less able may complete the task satisfactorily using a shoulder stand. Consider how the activity can be differentiated for the cognitively more and less able pupils (see Chapter 3 on planning);
- pupils are to be allowed to select which task they tackle;
- the work set is to be task-oriented, that is, mastering a particular task; or achievement-oriented, to perform a movement challenge at a higher level than others in the class. See Chapter 7 and Unit 3.2 (Gervis and Capel) in Capel *et al.* (2013).

In addition tasks must always:

- be appropriate to the age, maturity, past experience and physical and cognitive ability of the group;
- accommodate aspects of the learning environment, such as the equipment available, the length of the lesson, the working space and perhaps the weather;

- take account of the characteristics of the class, for example, a group who is often reluctant to take part, a group who is boisterous or easily distracted;
- take account of how well the class works together in small groups.

Task 13.4 asks you to design tasks to match ILOs.

Task 13.4 Designing tasks to achieve ILOs

Design a task to work towards each of the following:

- achieving accuracy of passing the ball in hockey;
- promoting group collaboration in gymnastics;
- developing a motif in dance;
- developing endurance in swimming;
- developing self-assessment in athletics.

Discuss your suggestions with your tutor and put the notes in your PDP.

Feedback

Feedback is a key element of any teaching strategy and should relate directly to the task set. Feedback focuses pupils' attention on the ILO underpinning the task set and provides knowledge of achievement and results. In order to learn, pupils need to have knowledge of their progress in respect of the ILO. The feedback must therefore highlight this aspect of learning and no other (Black *et al.* 2003). For example, if you are working to promote teamwork in a game, but all your feedback is focused on individual performance of motor skills, it is unlikely that you will achieve your ILO. Furthermore, pupils will not know if they achieved the ILO as they have not received any specific feedback informing them that this is the case. On the other hand, if you want to achieve a polished performance of a sequence, feedback focused on redesigning the content will be distracting.

It is important that when a task is set, the aspect of the work to be focused on by the pupils is made clear and is followed up by feedback explicitly related to that aspect. For example, a particular practice in hockey could have been set to achieve any of the following ILOs:

- mastery of a new motor skill;
- use of cooperative skills, such as tolerance, communication, flexibility;
- enhanced creativity/imagination;
- consistent rule adherence;
- setting personal goals;
- supporting a partner's learning;
- improved movement observation;
- improved evaluative skills.

Feedback to pupils during and after this practice should be limited to the focus identified. Task 13.5 asks you to consider feedback that matches ILOs from the above list.

Task 13.5 Matching feedback to ILOs

Match the following three examples of feedback to the appropriate ILO above and devise an example of feedback for those ILOs not covered. Compare your answers and ideas with those of another student teacher.

- Well done, Mary, you have scored a goal nearly every time. Do you think the aim that you have set yourself is too easy or too hard?
- Good, Jason, you kept the ball close to your stick throughout the practice.
- You are working hard, Paul. Which part of the practice do you think you are doing best?

Put your notes in your PDP.

Pupils learn better if there is a clear focus in their thinking. This is supported by your observation and your feedback. As PE teachers we are sometimes guilty of giving too much feedback covering a wide range of aspects of the task being carried out. Early in your school placements it is good practice to focus your lesson observations on your ability to give precise and clear feedback against the ILOs of the lesson. The content of your feedback must provide the pupils with information in order to bridge the gap between their current knowledge, understanding and skill and what they need to know, understand or do in order to achieve the ILO successfully (Black *et al.* 2003).

Focus on giving pupils feedback in amounts that they can take in and use to develop their learning and overall performance. Set a task and tell pupils that you are coming round to look for one thing, and one thing only. In other words, you give one teaching point. It is generally the case that pupils find it easier to learn one thing at a time and that your observation and feedback are more specific and thus effective if, at any one time, you are looking at one particular aspect of, for example, a movement skill.

Feedback must be accurate or pupils will be confused and ill informed. Therefore you must have a clear grasp of what is to be mastered, both to explain the task to pupils and to observe and give feedback. This is important because if the teacher gives incorrect information, the feedback can inhibit learning. Appropriate feedback depends on effective observation, which is covered in Chapter 4 and, in addition, it is a key feature of the assessment process. The role of feedback in assessment is discussed fully in Chapter 9.

The above discussion has highlighted the importance of linking teacher feedback specifically to the ILOs of a lesson or particular task or episode. Tasks 13.6 and 13.7, respectively, ask you to monitor your own feedback in relation to ILOs and to consider other aspects of your teaching in relation to ILOs.

Task 13.6 Giving feedback in lessons that matches ILOs

In one of your lesson plans indicate clearly your ILO for each part of the lesson or task. Ask your tutor to observe the lesson, specifically identifying feedback to individuals or the class linked to the stated ILO with a '3' and feedback not linked to the stated ILO with a '1'. Add up your score and discuss your use of feedback with your tutor. Repeat the exercise in another lesson and aim to increase your score. Keep your results in your PDP.

Task 13.7 Matching other aspects of teaching to ILOs

Select a lesson that you have already planned but not yet taught, and consider whether either the mode of communication you plan to use in different lesson episodes or the amount of responsibility you plan to give to the pupils helps you to achieve the ILOs. Modify your plan as appropriate, teach the lesson and discuss with your tutor how far your teaching facilitated the intended learning. Keep these notes in your PDP.

The classification of types of teaching strategies and teaching styles

In the 1960s and 1970s approaches to teaching were the subject of much research and lively debate (see, for example, Oeser 1955; The Plowden Report (Central Advisory Council for Education 1967); Cox and Dyson 1975; Bennett 1976; and Galton and Croll 1980). Researchers analysed teaching and formulated a variety of classifications of approaches. There were two types of approaches identified. One was concerned to recommend how teaching should take place. These are known as prescriptive classifications and align with teaching strategies. The other type was grounded in observing teachers and recording the ways they taught. These are called descriptive approaches and are closely related to teaching styles.

Teaching strategies

One useful prescriptive classification of teaching strategies to support the planning of teaching in PE was created by Mosston in 1966 (see Mosston and Ashworth 2002). The underlying philosophy of the work is that effective learning is only achieved via the appropriate interaction between the pupil and the teacher. They call this the OTLO principle, standing for objectives, teacher behaviour, learning behaviour, outcomes achieved. There are 11 strategies (or styles, in their terms) which are grouped into reproductive and productive clusters. Reproductive strategies are those concerned with pupils replicating and learning established skills and knowledge and include command and practice and reciprocal strategies, while productive strategies provide opportunities for pupils to create their own movement responses and develop their own ideas and include guided discovery and convergent and divergent discovery. The strategies form a continuum or spectrum and are ordered in relation to the pattern of pupil and teacher decision making.

In the first reproductive strategy, command, the teacher makes all the decisions. The strategies then move through, for example, practice, self-check, guided discovery, convergent and divergent discovery to strategies in which pupils select aspects of the activity they want to work on or investigate. For example, pupils may be free to decide which dance style to use to interpret ideas in a poem, or in a classroom situation pupils may be asked to select which aspect of nutrition to research. It is useful to read Mosston and Ashworth's work (Mosston and Ashworth 2002) and to consider both how the overall strategy realises key outcomes and the way in which the constituents of the strategy contribute to this achievement, for example the questioning techniques and the nature of the feedback recommended. Significantly, they are mindful of the broader goals of education as well as the PE-specific goals (see the companion website for more detail of this spectrum: www.routledge.com/cw/capel).

However, it is important to remember that the spectrum Mosston and Ashworth describe contains very broad guidelines for the planning of teaching to achieve a particular ILO. The named strategies in the spectrum do not provide you with ready answers as to how to teach. Rather they give you a useful guide once you have decided on the ILOs of your lesson. Your job as a teacher is to design a strategy tailored to your particular ILO with a particular class. It is valuable here to consider how teaching strategies work within and influence curriculum and the structure of the curriculum.

In considering the notion of a strategy it is important you understand that in only very exceptional circumstances do you plan one strategy for the whole lesson. This is because you are likely to address more than one ILO during a lesson. For example, in a lesson taking a 'Games for Understanding' approach (Griffin and Butler 2005), each part of a lesson needs a different strategy, as different parts of the lesson structure potentially address different ILOs. For example, the focus of the first part of the lesson may be on exploration. This may be followed by discussion of findings and then tasks set to introduce a new movement skill or to improve an existing movement skill. In most lessons the teacher adopts a series of strategies as the lesson progresses and may even implement more than one strategy simultaneously, for example, when groups of pupils need to work towards different ILOs and differentiated learning tasks/challenges are required. An example of the use of a series of strategies used in a succession of lesson episodes, one after the other, is shown in Figure 13.2.

Classifications of teaching styles

The classification of teaching styles is based on the observation of teachers and the subsequent organisation into groups of the types of teachers and teaching witnessed. Each teaching style identified exhibits a cluster of characteristic ways teachers organise their teaching and interact with their pupils. A fairly straightforward descriptive classification of teaching is into two contrasting styles, described as traditional and progressive. The elements of each are set out in Figure 13.3.

While this and the other studies referred to above provide valuable insights into teaching, it has to be realised that the motivation behind the research was to find out either which approach was the most effective or what learning resulted from the use of a particular approach. They were, in fact, considering teaching from the opposite end to that adopted in this chapter. Our focus is, 'How should I teach to achieve this ILO?', not, 'What is the outcome of using this approach?', as was the researchers' focus.

Dance lesson ILOs: by the end of the lesson pupils will have:		
a refined the opening movement phrase in unison; b created a duet movement phrase to include unison and canon; c appreciated duet relationships in dance.		
Intended ILO of lesson episode	**Content/material**	**Teaching strategy**
Body preparation	Warm-up	Whole-class directed work
Precision in movement	Opening movement phrase A, as introduced in previous lesson	Peer teaching in pairs with work cards to check accuracy and detail of movement
In pairs, creative development of a motif	Motif selected from opening movement phrase and developed into a duet to include unison and canon	Problem solving in pairs to develop the motif through discussion, exploration and repetition
Appreciation of duet relationships	Newly created duet movement phrase performed by another pair in the class. Video of a dance duet	Observation of peers and small-group discussion to identify unison and canon. Whole-class observation of a video of a dance duet and discussion with the teacher

Figure 13.2 Possible pattern of strategies that could be used in different sections/episodes of a lesson.

Traditional	**Progressive**
1 Subject matter taught in separate 'lessons'	1 Subject matter integrated
2 Teacher provides all the knowledge	2 Teacher guides educational experiences
3 Pupils in passive role in learning	3 Pupils have an active role in learning
4 All curriculum planning carried out by the teacher	4 Pupils play a part in curriculum planning
5 Rote learning and practice are the favoured ways of engaging with the material	5 Learning often uses discovery techniques
6 Extrinsic motivation using rewards and punishment	6 Intrinsic motivation rather than external rewards and punishments
7 Academic standards important	7 Academic standards not the sole objective
8 Frequent testing	8 Minimal testing
9 Competition used rather than cooperation	9 Includes a good deal of cooperative group work
10 Teaching within the classroom base	10 Teaching within and without the classroom
11 Little emphasis on creative expression	11 Creative expression encouraged
12 Subject matter-centred	12 Pupil-centred
13 Pupils reliant on the teacher	13 Pupils encouraged to develop independence

Figure 13.3 Traditional and progressive teaching (adapted from Bennett 1976).

Understanding your own beliefs and how these influence your approach to teaching

All teachers in the United Kingdom and in many other countries are expected to work to government-designated curricula and are therefore charged with achieving similar aims. However, as indicated earlier in this chapter, all teachers have their individual style of teaching, which is an outcome of their unique personality and socialisation. As you become more experienced, your teaching may be influenced by a developing view of the most important values of PE, for example, how children learn. These views create your underlying beliefs concerning teaching and influence the way you plan your work and interact with the pupils. In the context of you understanding your own approach to teaching, Blair (2013) argues that having an understanding of what you believe and value about teaching PE (what is called 'an ontological narrative') allows you to become more critically reflective in relation to how teaching strategy and teaching style operate together. He sees this understanding as going further than being aware of how strategy and style are synergised, in that it requires you to consider who you are, or indeed who you aspire to be as a teacher, how you view your role in supporting a pupil's learning and how you wish to communicate this view and understanding to pupils, colleagues and other stakeholders, i.e. parents and carers.

While teachers must work to the guidelines set out in government and school policies, there are opportunities for personal beliefs to be expressed. For example, if you view the aim of pupils becoming independent learners as a key mission in your teaching, wherever possible you devolve responsibility to pupils. If you believe learning is best achieved through individual discovery and trial and error, wherever appropriate you use methods to promote this approach to learning. Your beliefs contribute to your personal style of teaching, influencing both the ways in which you characteristically employ a range of teaching skills and the teaching strategies you most commonly use. However, notwithstanding personal philosophies, all teaching is generally guided by the ILOs that are congruent with the broader aims of education and PE.

It is, however, important to differentiate between genuine differences in beliefs and a difference due to lack of thought, which in turn may lead to a lack of planning and preparation. A difference that occurs due to a lack of thought or almost by accident or chance does not relate to any intentional thinking or action on behalf of the teacher. This view is supported by Green (2000), who suggests that PE teachers simply *do* and are not actually philosophising about the teaching of the subject. This position links to developing and understanding your beliefs and values and how these influence the more technical and pedagogical aspects of your teaching, i.e. strategy and style. The strategic element of your style should be devised on a rational and appropriate basis, relating to the ILOs you have planned, as well as to your beliefs and values (Capel and Blair 2013).

Your choice of ILO will involve a degree of personal preference, linked to your personal beliefs concerning the teaching of PE. Teachers have different views and place different emphasis and value on educational processes and practice; additionally all curricula are open to interpretation. For example, one teacher may view the teaching of games in schools as predominantly about the development of technical and physical skills and attributes, whilst another teacher may view the teaching of games in schools being about developing pupils' social, cognitive and affective understanding and skill (Williams *et al.* 2010). Capel and Blair (2013) argue that a teacher's beliefs impact on both what teachers choose to teach but also the way they choose to teach it. To this point we can see the position presented by Green (2000) regarding teachers not thinking about how or what they teach and potentially planning their teaching through the use of bought schemes of work or internet resources.

Capel and Blair (2013) question the origins of an uncritical approach to teaching PE. They are concerned that so much emphasis is placed on trying to meet the requirements to gain qualified teacher status (QTS) by both student teachers themselves and their tutors, which may result in student teachers focusing on short-term day-to-day technical issues. It could also lead to them copying teaching approaches preferred by their tutor and other teachers, as they perceive they are more likely to recognise what they are doing as good pedagogy (Capel and Blair 2013). Although this short-term approach for gaining QTS is understandable and expected, at least initially, this approach may act as a block to thinking carefully about what teaching PE actually means for you as a teacher. It is therefore important that you ask yourself questions such as: why are you using this strategy in this lesson to achieve this ILO with these pupils at this time of day? How does this teaching strategy create a lesson environment that will support intentional learning for all pupils?

You should also refer to Chapter 16, which focuses on teacher beliefs and their impact on teaching.

As you develop a range of teaching strategies and blend them together with your developing teaching style, it is important that you start to think about whole units of teaching as opposed to individual lessons. Consider how you might use a range or indeed the same strategies over a period of six lessons. Which of the strategies are restricted to a specific unit of work and which strategies could be adopted more generally in different units, activities and contexts? Consider how your teaching style might adapt, evolve or stay the same over the more medium-term (6–12 weeks) period.

Now complete the Masters Tasks 13.8 and 13.9. Put these in your PDP as evidence of Masters study.

Task 13.8 Use of teacher questioning or pupil grouping to achieve ILOs

In this chapter setting, learning tasks and giving feedback have been used as examples of ways in which the employment of a particular teaching skill needs to be modified according to the ILOs of the lesson, thus contributing to the nature of the teaching strategy employed. Write 500 words on the various uses of either teacher questioning or pupil grouping in achieving different ILOs. Refer to other chapters in this book as appropriate. Share this work with your tutor and store it in your PDP as evidence of Masters level work.

Task 13.9 Critical consideration of the work of Mosston and Ashworth

Read Mosston and Ashworth (2002) and carry out a strengths, weaknesses, opportunities and threats (SWOT) analysis on using this categorisation of teaching strategies as the principal guide to your lesson planning. See the companion website (www.routledge.com/cw/capel) for an example of a SWOT analysis. Write a 2,000-word essay entitled 'Critically consider if Mosston and Ashworth's spectrum liberates or limits PE teachers'. Share this work with your tutor and store it in your PDP as evidence of Masters level work.

Summary and key points

This chapter has explained the meanings of some key concepts in teaching, with a particular focus on teaching strategies and on selecting the appropriate elements of a strategy to match the ILOs. Teaching strategies are powerful learning tools and must be devised in line with the ILOs of a lesson/part of a lesson. The notion that an ILO cannot be reached without employing the appropriate strategy is very important for you to understand as a PE teacher. It is often claimed that purely through taking part in PE, pupils acquire wider educational goals, such as independence, communication skills or imagination. This view is itself contentious (see also Chapters 1 and 2 in Capel and Piotrowski, 2000), but there is a very powerful argument that, while benefits other than enhanced physical skill *can* be acquired in PE lessons, this *will not* happen unless the teacher adopts the appropriate strategy. A strategy comprises a carefully selected cluster of teaching skills and elements of teaching. It is only through the appropriate design and employment of these building bricks that a strategy can successfully deliver the ILO. Notwithstanding your work to employ appropriate strategies, as a student teacher you are beginning to develop your own teaching style. This arises from aspects of your personality and from your beliefs concerning PE. Your teaching style individualises you as a teacher and adds 'colour' to the wide range of teaching strategies you need to use.

Check which requirements of your ITE you have addressed through this chapter.

Further reading

Capel, S. and Blair, R. (2013) Why do physical education teachers adopt a particular way of teaching? in S.Capel and M. Whitehead (eds) *Debates in Physical Education*, Abingdon, Oxon: Routledge, pp. 120–139.

This chapter discusses teaching as a rational activity and asks if we can identify what makes good teaching? It asks why teachers teach the way they do and presents five factors that influence choice of teaching style and strategy. It questions the implications of teachers not always questioning why they teach as they do.

Capel, S. and Blair, R. (2014) Understanding your views about physical education and how this impacts on your teaching and pupils' learning, in S. Capel and P. Breckon (eds) *A Practical Guide to Teaching Physical Education in the Secondary School*, 2nd edn, Abingdon, Oxon: Routledge, pp. 20–29.

This chapter supports readers to question how and why they have developed their views regarding how PE should be taught and how this impacts how and what pupils learn through PE lessons.

Capel, S., Blair, R. and Longville, J. (2014) Teaching to enable intended learning outcomes to be achieved, in S. Capel and P. Breckon (eds) *A Practical Guide to Teaching Physical Education in the Secondary School*, 2nd edn, Abingdon, Oxon: Routledge, pp. 158–165.

This chapter takes a very practically oriented look at how teaching strategies enable the attainment of intentional learning outcomes. It looks at how learning outcomes inform the choice and content of teaching strategies.

Hardy, C. and Mawer, M. (eds) (1999) *Learning and Teaching in Physical Education*, London: Falmer Press.

Chapter 5 reviews research developments concerning teaching styles and teaching approaches in PE. Emphasis is placed on: the nature and results of studies examining Mosston and Ashworth's spectrum of teaching strategies/styles; approaches to teaching critical thinking skills in PE; direct and indirect approaches to teaching games; and, cooperative teaching and learning in PE.

Joyce, B. and Weil, M. (1996) *Models of Teaching*, 5th edn, Boston, MA: Allyn and Bacon.

Models are identified to provide a frame of reference for describing a variety of approaches to teaching. These models are grouped into four broad families – social; information processing; personal; and behavioural systems – that share orientations toward human beings and how they learn. Each model is discussed in relation to its underlying theory and educational uses and purposes in real learning situations to encourage reflective thought and inquiry.

Macfadyen, T. and Bailey, R. (2002) *Teaching Physical Education*, London: Continuum.

Chapter 4 focuses on Mosston and Ashworth's (2002) spectrum of teaching strategies/styles and provides general guidance when teaching with each approach. It compares the advantages and disadvantages of the direct, teacher-centred teaching with the indirect, pupil-centred teaching and reflects upon why a variety of teaching strategies/styles is important in secondary PE. It then considers other factors which could influence the teacher's selection of instructional method.

Mosston, M. and Ashworth, S. (2002) *Teaching Physical Education*, 5th edn, San Francisco, CA: Benjamin Cummings.

A valuable analysis of teaching PE with a focus on the pattern of teacher and pupil decision making in different styles/strategies of teaching. A useful chapter on teacher feedback.

Additional resources for this chapter are available on the companion website: www.routledge.com/cw/capel.

14 Accredited qualifications and principles of classroom teaching

Elizabeth Myers and Stuart Taylor

Introduction

As with all qualified teachers, you are a teacher first and a subject specialist second. This means that, by the very nature of gaining qualified teacher status you possess the appropriate teaching skills, personal and professional conduct to be an effective practitioner in a variety of educational environments. Classroom teaching forms a significant aspect of the work of many PE teachers, largely through teaching accredited courses. Thus it is essential that, as PE teachers, you are able to teach effectively in both practical and classroom contexts. This chapter explores some of the key factors associated with teaching and learning in the classroom in relation to accredited qualifications in PE, in both academic and vocational examination formats in England, Wales and Northern Ireland. For those student teachers learning to teach elsewhere, we advise you to find out about any accredited qualifications you might be involved in teaching. However, much of the chapter is focused on active learning strategies for teaching in the classroom which are relevant for any PE teacher teaching in the classroom.

Objectives

At the end of this chapter you should be able to:

- understand the Qualifications and Credit Framework (QCF) in England, Wales and Northern Ireland and the place of the 14–19 curriculum in it;
- have an overview, and understand the diversity, of accredited qualifications available in PE and PE-related areas within the 14–19 curriculum;
- be aware of teaching and learning approaches for teaching classroom-based theoretical aspects of accredited qualifications in PE;
- understand the range of assessment procedures for accredited qualifications;
- be aware of the need to strive to continually engage and encourage pupil attainment and progress through effective teaching and assessment.

Check the requirements of your initial teacher education (ITE) to see which relate to this chapter.

Although this chapter explores some aspects of planning and delivery of classroom teaching of accredited qualifications within PE, it does not provide all the answers; many of the issues you may face as a student teacher are likely to emanate from the specific environment in which you find yourself. That said, the principles highlighted are broad enough to act as a catalyst for you to drive your learning forward and to promote professional discussions with your tutor, school staff, other student teachers or as a mode of self-reflection. Now complete Task 14.1.

Task 14.1 Practical and classroom-based theoretical PE lessons

Briefly reflect on your own experience of classroom teaching in PE. This may be some teaching you have done, teaching you have observed or your own experiences as a pupil. Write some notes in answer to the following questions:

- How does a classroom-based lesson differ from teaching a practical lesson?
- What similarities do a classroom-based and practical lesson share?
- Should the teaching of a classroom-based lesson be approached in the same way as a practical lesson?

Compare your reflections with those of another student teacher. Store the information in your professional development portfolio (PDP) to refer to as you teach accredited qualifications in your school-based work.

14–19 qualifications in the Qualifications and Credit Framework (QCF) in England, Wales and Northern Ireland

The QCF is a national framework developed by the Qualifications and Curriculum Authority (England), Department for Education, Lifelong Learning and Skills (DELLS) in Wales and the Council for the Curriculum, Examinations and Assessment (CCEA) in Northern Ireland. The QCF is shown in Table 14.1. The 14–19 curriculum forms levels 1–3 of this framework. It is the opportunity for pupils to gain qualifications in one of three routes of learning:

1   General qualifications: General Certificate of Secondary Education (GCSE), General Certificate of Education Advanced (GCE A) level, the International Baccalaureate (IB) (IB Middle and IB Diploma) and the Welsh Baccalaureate. General qualifications are designed to provide candidates with knowledge and understanding of their chosen subject.

2   National Vocational Qualifications (NVQ), Business and Technician Education Council (BTEC), National Diploma/Certificate and Cambridge Technical Diploma/Certificate (levels 1 and 2). These are designed to combine theoretical study with practical experiential learning of a range of widely applicable skills and knowledge, set within a 'specialised' context, e.g. sport and active leisure.

3   Foundation learning tier: high-quality credit-based qualifications at entry level and level1. These are designed to increase participation, achievement and progression for pupils working below level 2, e.g. English for speakers of other languages (ESOL) skills for life and functional skills, focusing on English skills of speaking, listening, reading and writing.

Table 14.1 The Qualifications and Credit Framework (QCF)

QCF level	Examples of qualifications in each level*	
	Academic	*Vocational*
Level 8	Doctorate Specialist awards	Vocational qualifications level 8
Level 7	Masters degree Postgraduate certificates and diplomas	NVQ level 5 Vocational qualifications level 7
Level 6	Honours degree Graduate certificates and diplomas	Vocational qualifications level 6
Level 5	Diploma of higher education Foundation degrees Higher national diplomas	Vocational qualifications level 5
Level 4	Certificate of higher education	Vocational qualifications level 4
Level 3	A levels IB Advanced diploma Advanced Welsh Baccalaureate	NVQ level 3 BTEC level 3 National diploma/certificate level 3 Cambridge technical diploma/certificate level 3
Level 2	GCSE Grades A*-C IB Middle Intermediate Welsh Baccalaureate	NVQ level 2 BTEC level 2 National diploma/certificate level 2 Cambridge technical diploma/certificate level 2
Level 1	GCSEs Grades D-G Foundation Welsh Baccalaureate	NVQ level 1 BTEC level 1 Introductory diploma
Entry level	Entry level certificate	ASDAN† (e.g. 'Employability')

NVQ, National Vocational Qualification; IB, International Baccalaureate; BTEC, Business and Technician Education Council; GCSE, General Certificate of Secondary Education.
*The lowest qualification is entry level and the highest is level 8. Levels 4–8 are part of the framework of higher education.
†ASDAN is approved as an awarding organisation for qualifications within the National Qualifications Framework and the QCF, regulated by the Office of Qualifications and Examinations Regulation (Ofqual) in England, DELLS in Wales and CCEA in Northern Ireland. As a guide, all Ofqual-, DELLS- and CCEA-approved ASDAN qualifications carry points comparable to GCSEs (25 points equal a level 1, that is comparable to a GCSE grade E/F and 46 points equal a level 2, that is comparable to a GCSE grade B).

The Scottish Credit and Qualifications Framework (SCQF) is the equivalent in Scotland (http://scqf.org.uk/the-framework/). Both the QCF and SCQF are referenced to the European Qualifications Framework (EQF). The EQF is a meta-framework intended as a reference so that qualifications in European Union member states, including the QCF and SCQF, are understood across member states.

The QCF helps you as a teacher to navigate your way through the numerous examination boards and their qualifications. It is important that you know how this progressive framework is designed so that you can see where any qualification which you are involved in teaching fits in.

Qualifications vary in content, delivery and assessment methods. It is important that you familiarise yourself with the course specification and fully understand what is to be delivered and how it is to be assessed. Further, throughout their 14-19 education, pupils are entitled to information, advice and guidance to help them make the most suitable choices. Thus, it is also important to know about the range and diversity of qualifications so that, after you qualify, you are able to offer advice and guidance to pupils to enable them to make informed choices about the courses on offer in your school or other educational establishment. Where possible, try and attend professional development courses to extend your understanding of the qualification and its accreditation process. Now complete Task 14.2.

Task 14.2 The 14-19 curriculum

Search accredited qualifications in the QCF, using http://www.accreditedqualifications. org.uk/index.aspx. Find a selection of different qualifications at each of entry level, level 1, level 2 and level 3.

Obtain a copy of the 14-19 curriculum and range of qualifications that are on offer in your placement school. What is offered as part of the 14-19 curriculum and at what levels?

Compare what is offered in your placement school with what is offered in another school in which another student teacher is placed. Store your findings in your PDP.

Mapping content to the syllabus

Understanding the whole qualification in terms of its content and assessment strategy is vital in ensuring that pupils are not only prepared with the knowledge required for the course but are also suitably prepared for how this knowledge will be examined. Having an understanding of the qualification will enable you and the pupils to apply the content in controlled assessments and examination contexts. Now complete Task 14.3.

Task 14.3 Compare examination specifications for GCSE

Obtain a copy of the GCSE PE specifications from two different awarding bodies: AQA (www.aqa.org.uk), Edexcel (www.edexcel.com), OCR (www.ocr.org.uk), CCEA (www. ccea.org.uk) or WJEC (www.wjec.co.uk).

- Identify the differences in percentage of marks given for the following components: coursework, final examination and practical.
- With reference to the structure of the examinations, examine how and when different components of each specification are assessed.
- With reference to the content of the curriculum, identify which theoretical aspects are examined, what practical options are available and how the coursework is selected.

You can repeat this exercise for A level examinations from the same awarding bodies. Record this in your professional development portfolio (PDP) for reference when you start teaching.

Teaching and learning in the classroom

Whatever the accredited qualification you are teaching on, once you have your class in front of you, you can assume that by making a choice to take this course (that is, for those schools in which pupils have a choice; some schools have a policy of entering all of their pupils for a particular course), the pupils who have chosen the course have done so because they have an interest in PE and sport. On the whole, most pupils probably like PE, play sport, watch sport and sometimes maybe even talk or read about sport. However, it is quite common that some pupils may not have realised that studying PE is much more than just doing PE or 'playing' sport, but in order to be successful they actually have to study. However, often some of the theoretical aspects of PE and sport engage, challenge and inspire pupils and therefore it is important that lessons captivate pupils, regardless of their reasons for choosing the course and their background.

Unfortunately, due to the attainment-driven nature of education in general and accredited qualifications in particular, for some pupils and teachers, the outcome (the pupils' grade) becomes the focal point and therefore affects how both view lessons and learning. When you teach accredited qualifications, therefore, you may experience pressure to meet progress and attainment targets which feed into your own/school statistics. Further, there are tensions between the pressure to cover the large amount of content within the examination specification and that of providing an engaging and creative environment. However, it is important that this does not detract from providing a stimulating and enriching learning experience for pupils; there must be a balance to be successful. You must ensure that you are best preparing pupils to be successful in the long term and not just within the accredited qualification which they are studying. Ultimately, your prime goal as a teacher is to prepare your pupils to become the most effective learners that they can be, as by doing so not only will they gain their optimum grades, but they will also develop skills that are essential as they move through life, whether that is through furthering their education or by entering the workplace. Thus, it is important that you avoid spoon feeding pupils as this may create issues further down the line as, for example, your pupils will have knowledge of the content but may not be able to remember this once the examination is over or may apply this information to an abstract task.

This section looks at how, as a teacher, you can create a stimulating and engaging learning environment to develop and maintain pupils' enthusiasm when teaching a theory topic in the classroom. In order to achieve this, it is essential that you place the pupils at the centre of your planning and in doing so consider how you can develop classroom lessons that:

- *review*: How much do your pupils already know about the topic they are studying? What opportunity is there to recap on a previous lesson on the topic or a different topic?
- *relate*: Can the pupils see the relevance of the content with regard to modern-day PE or sport and/or their own sporting experiences?
- *revise*: Can you be creative and use examination papers and mark schemes so that pupils know what is expected of them and engage in how they will be assessed? Can you promote key skills to develop revision/examination techniques that will benefit pupils across all of their studies?

In order to achieve these three Rs you must place pupils in an effective learning context, by making learning active (practical, hands-on, fun and creative – see Unit 5.2 (Lowe) in

Capel *et al.* 2013), changing the environment (regular changes in activity, delivery methods and resources) and overall by developing effective learners who develop independence and autonomy and become inquisitive about the topic (see below). Now complete Task 14.4.

Task 14.4 Review, relate and revise

Select a topic from one of the accredited qualifications you are teaching or observing on school placement. Consider how you could deliver it using the review, relate and revise principles. How can you build on prior knowledge, relate to a sporting example and then revise how this information will be examined? Discuss this with another student teacher and keep both your own ideas and theirs in your PDP to help inform your future teaching of a range of topics in accredited courses.

Teaching strategies

In order to meet the needs of your pupils it is essential that you select the most appropriate methods to create an optimal learning environment for them. It is not the intention of this chapter to delve into the vast amount of learning theory that you should be aware of in order to select the teaching strategies or approaches to enable pupils to progress and achieve, but it is vital that you subscribe to the notion of 'learner independence'. You may want to refer to Unit 5.1 (Burton) in Capel *et al.* (2013) for further information about learning theories. In order for your pupils to become successful learners in examination PE and effective learners in life, they must be taught to become autonomous learners, where possible. Such characteristics are seen in greater or lesser amounts in all pupils; it is your job to foster and develop this so that each pupil can cope with the progressive nature of education. Becoming autonomous or independent means moving from teacher-led to a more scaffolded approach, whereby the teacher supports the learning process which is tailored to the needs of each pupil, with the intention of helping the pupil achieve his/her learning goals (Sawyer 2006). With guidance, the aim is then for pupils to reach a level of independence where they are in control of their own achievement and utilise the teacher as more of a 'quality assurance' or reviewing tool, as opposed to the main source of information.

This is obviously a very advanced skill and therefore may not be achievable with pupils working on qualifications at level 2 or below. However, at level 3 independence will be a valuable skill for higher education or for the workplace. From a professional standpoint, it is essential that your classroom practice focuses on developing these characteristics so that your pupils are prepared to access further education, higher education, training or employment and be successful in these environments. Failing to do so will ultimately cause your pupils to rely on teacher input, and without such direction, will be ineffective and unsuccessful in their future life experiences. With this in mind, look to well-known/familiar examples, such as Mosston and Ashworth's (2002) spectrum of teaching styles, to provide some structure for your initial attempts at classroom delivery (there is more information about the spectrum on the companion website: www.routledge.com/cw/capel). Consider how using a differing teaching style leads you to plan a variety of tasks for those in your class, sometimes with you (the teacher) being in sole charge of the content, known as the command style, through to a divergent approach where pupils take on the role of setting their own learning tasks, in relation to the specification or qualification syllabus.

Now complete Task 14.5.

Task 14.5 The 'successful' pupil: learner characteristics

Consider one level at which you are delivering classroom or theory lessons (e.g. level 2 or 3 of the QCF). What characteristics would you deem essential for your pupils to be successful in their studies at this level? Create a 'job description'-style document outlining the essential and desired characteristics of a successful pupil in your subject at this level, as shown in the examples in Table 14.2. Discuss the characteristics with your tutor and other student teachers. Add to your own list. Identify what teaching strategies you might utilise to enable these characteristics to be developed in your lessons. Store the information in your PDP for future reference.

How pupils can learn effectively: learning activities

The current examination system in England, Wales and Northern Ireland provides a linear style of assessment with terminal examinations at the end of the taught course (as opposed to a 'bite-sized' learning approach with modular assessment) (Ofqual 2013). Making learning last, or the 'stickability' of knowledge, understanding and application, is very important if your pupils are to be successful within this terminal structure. To gain attention, keep engagement and make learning last, you must develop and use a range of learning activities that assist pupils in making a strong bond or association to both content and concept. For example, you may make the concept being learnt emotive or personal to each pupil, e.g. by using 'fake' competitive environments to bring about emotional responses. Likewise, you can use a piece of music to structure the time allowed for a practise examination question; provide sports experiences so that concepts can be learnt/experienced kinaesthetically; provide a novel practical task where everyone is a beginner; or enable pupils to experience 'trial-and-error' learning (see, for example, the cognitive stage of Fitts and Posner's (1967) Learner Model).

Using a variety of learning activities can change the learning environment to maintain pupil engagement in learning. Learning activities that can be used to vary the learning environment may include, for example:

Table 14.2 Essential and desirable characteristics for learning at level 3 of the Qualifications and Credit Framework

Essential characteristics level 3	*Desired characteristics level 3*
Takes appropriate notes in a form that is suitable and can adapt information with a sense of audience	Refines appropriate notes to personalise the information, aiding retention
Looks for reasons for learning. Capable of linking ideas together so that the 'bigger picture' becomes clear	Makes assumptions and suggestions as to how topics and ideas may relate

Adapted from Developing Effective Learners, Department for Education and Skills (DfES) (2004c).

- Read or write a newspaper/article/magazine report/chapter of an autobiography (develop literacy skills through small bite-sized tasks).
- Create a model (feel/touch and manipulate).
- Draw a picture (represent a topic through a sketch).
- Role play (get inside someone's role or character).
- Complete crossword/anagrams/puzzles (pre-made or created using website generators).
- Carry out a roblem-solving task (with one outcome, but a number of solutions).
- Watch a DVD/movie clip (sound on and sound off/narrate).
- Produce a podcast (summarise a topic/share revision).
- Generate a heated debate (be controversial!).
- Produce an advertisement (show understanding of the marketplace).
- Pitch an idea (*Dragon's Den* style).
- Use music (structure or time a task or set a mood/tone).
- Teach a friend (overlearn through a reciprocal teaching method; see Mosston and Ashworth 2002).
- Use movement (answer a long-answer question in groups; after a set time, move to another question that has been part-answered by the previous group).
- Use a case study (apply theory to practice).
- Design an examination question (what does the examiner *really* want?).
- Do an experiment/investigation (create a hypothesis and carry it out).
- Be a reporter (research and reflect to provide a short response).
- Create a video diary (use an elite athlete's video diary to create a synoptic response).
- Do a competition (short- and long-term, as a team or individual).
- Act as a committee (delegate roles and responsibilities – judge the impact).
- Replicate an event (small- or large-scale).
- Write a letter (from a participant's or organisational point of view).
- Do a sports commentary (use a depth of knowledge to speak fluently).

This is by no means an exhaustive list but provides some ideas to help create an environment conducive to learning. Other examples are on the companion website (www.routledge.com/cw/capel). Which teaching strategy or learning activity you chose will depend on what you want the pupils to learn and how your pupils would respond to learning in this way (see Chapter 13 on teaching strategies to achieve specific intended learning outcomes (ILOs)).

Now complete Task 14.6.

Task 14.6 Plan it twice (at least!)

Chose a topic from an accredited course and explore how different teaching strategies and learning activities could be used to deliver the content. Discuss with another student teacher the advantages and disadvantages of different teaching strategies and learning activities both for the pupils and with regard to the resourcing required (e.g. items needed, teacher preparation time). Store this information in your PDP to refer to when teaching this topic and to generate some ideas for other topics.

In order to achieve an environment conducive to learning, it is essential that you have a good grasp of your pupils' abilities, have planned suitably stimulating activities and can appropriately match the two. As with all lessons, evaluate the success and reflect on how you could make the environment more suited to your learners. Chapter 3 covers planning and evaluating and Chapter 8 covers effective learning environment in more detail.

Learning styles

Imparting knowledge to maximise learning is the ultimate aim of teaching (McKeough *et al.* 1995). Pupil engagement in learning can be promoted through the careful consideration of learning activities in relation to a specific learning outcome (see Chapter 13). However, it is also thought by some that learning may be less successful if teaching does not take into account the preferred learning styles of pupils.

Learning styles can be defined as personal qualities that influence a pupil's ability to acquire information, to interact with peers and the teacher, and otherwise participate in learning experiences (Pask 1976; Entwistle 1992; Grasha 1996). The concept of learning styles stems from the observation that individual pupils prefer to learn in different ways. Some pupils prefer to work independently, whereas others prefer to work in groups; some pupils absorb information while others like to experience activities actively (Davis 2009). In the Visual, Auditory and Kinaesthetic (VAK) model of learning, visual learners prefer visual input and tend to maintain eye contact with the teacher. They can create accurate mental pictures and models. They like to have handouts and prefer to read than to be read to (Jensen 2009); auditory learners prefer to take in information by listening. They often have conversations with themselves (both aloud and in their head) and others. They can recall information from discussions accurately, often mimicking the tone and tempo of the conversations (Jensen 2009), whereas kinaesthetic learners prefer learning by experiencing and doing, with physical input. Kinaesthetic learners are usually physically active, they are affected by teacher expression, posture and proximity and they place much more emphasis on how something is said, not what was actually said (Jensen 2009). The Visual, Auditory, Read/Write and Kinaesthetic (VARK) model is similar to the VAK model, but it also suggests that some people may prefer to take in information through reading and writing.

Note: When referring to the term kinaesthetic within the VAK and VARK learning models, it is written with the interpretation that kinaesthesia is concerned with, and relates to, the conscious awareness of the position of the body and movement of the body in space. When the term proprioception is used, it refers to the subconscious mechanism with which the body regulates posture and movement (Floyd 2007). An example of a kinaesthetic learning task could be the actual articulation of the knee when discussing the range of motion at a hinge joint. Encouraging pupils to explore the range of motion and planes of motion available at the knee joint will allow them to experience the movement and thus develop a conscious awareness of the position of the body in space.

There is, however, some conflict between researchers of the value and use of learning-style theories and models. Kratzig and Arbuthnott (2006) and Leamnson (1999) suggest that learning styles and models have little practical application and use in teaching. Dunn and Griggs (2000), however, argue that there is an overwhelming amount of credible data that demonstrates that teachers can increase pupil academic attainment by focusing on learning styles. Nonetheless, an appreciation for the range of possible ways in which pupils prefer to receive information within your classroom is beneficial so that you design tasks and experiences that cater for and engage all pupils in their learning and, hence, create a conducive learning environment.

The use of learning styles and the VAK and VARK learning models can be useful in ensuring that lessons are planned to utilise a variety of strategies that encourage active engagement and learning. Active learning is a process in which learners strive for understanding and competence and seek out knowledge about the world (Piaget 1972; Rogers 1975). This is something that should be promoted as an ethos, to encourage pupils to take ownership of their own learning, fostering curiosity and interest. In turn, this facilitates the notion of active engagement, whereby it is deemed that pupils learn most effectively when they are interested, involved and appropriately challenged (DfES 2004c). Allowing pupils to test out their knowledge in practise situations results in them understanding it more thoroughly. By fostering opportunities for learners to apply and relate theoretical principles in practice, they become better at remembering these principles (Davis 2009). In essence, to involve pupils in their learning you can, for example, outline the ILO and pupils can decide by themselves how they demonstrate their knowledge. Active learning is covered in Unit 5.2 (Lowe) in Capel *et al.* (2013). Table 14.3 gives some examples of learning activities which utilise visual, auditory, read/write and/or kinaesthetic ways of presenting information in order to provide variety and also to cater for different learning preferences or styles of pupils in the group.

How to use the classroom

Your classroom is a resource that is often overlooked in relation to promoting effective learning. How you set out the teaching space can aid teaching and learning. The careful use of seating plans and working groups can promote peer and collaborative learning. For example, simple strategies like placing easily distracted pupils near the front of the class can have an impact on whole-class learning. The use of 'home' groups (working with peers of similar ability) and 'away' groups (working with peers of differing ability) allows you to vary the working groups and level of support and to differentiate accordingly (e.g. through the use of differentiated worksheets or by offering a set number of questions that a particular group are allowed to ask either you or their peers). Keywords, sentence starters, teaching and learning prompts and taxonomy pictorials (Bloom *et al.* 1956; see Chapters 3 and 5 and the companion website: www.routledge.com/cw/capel) and SOLO taxonomy (structure of observed learning outcomes, in which there is a level of increasing complexity in a pupil's understanding of a subject, through five stages, which it is claimed are applicable to any subject area (Biggs and Tang 2007); see http://www.learningandteaching.info/learning/solo.htm#ixzz3CLOtqyW6) can promote higher-order thinking skills and increase the quality of written and discussion work, with support available if required.

Home learning

Many accredited courses require some non-contact learning hours and home learning can be used to achieve this. Home learning needs to be a valuable endeavour. Completing

Table 14.3 A range of learning activities which present information visually, auditorially, by reading/writing and kinaesthetically

Strategy	Visual	Auditory	Read/write	Kinaesthetic
Computer presentations	✔	✔	✔	✘
Debate	?	✔	✘	?
Demonstrations	✔	✔	✘	✔
Dictation	✘	✔	?	✘
Discussion	?	✔	✘	?
Drawing and sketching	✔	✘	✔	✔
Explanations	✘	✔	✘	?
Feedback (verbal and written)	✔	✔	✔	✘
Games	✔	✔	✘	✔
Group exercises	✔	✘	?	?
Handouts	✔	✘	✔	✘
Internet research	✔	✘	✔	?
Listening	✘	✔	✘	✘
Mind maps	✔	✘	✔	✔
Observing	✔	✘	✘	✘
Photographs/pictures	✔	✘	✔	✘
Practical activity	✔	✘	✘	✔
Presentation	✔	✘	✔	✔
Question and answer	✘	✔	×	?
Questionnaires	✔	✘	✔	?
Reading	✔	✘	✔	?
Recording data	✘	✘	✔	✔
Resource card-based learning	✔	✘	✔	✔
Video	✔	✘	✘	✘
Worksheets	✔	✘	✔	✔

✔ Learning activity which presents information in a visual, auditory, reading/writing and/or kinaesthetic way.

✘ Learning activity which does not present information in a visual, auditory, reading/writing and/or kinaesthetic way.

? Learning activity which may or may not present information in a visual, auditory, reading/writing and/or kinaesthetic way. It is dependent upon the way in which the strategy is used and the situational circumstances.

work not finished in the lesson can be criticised from this point of view, as suitable time should have been allocated for such tasks and the expectation that work can be completed at home if not finished can be detrimental to the work ethic of pupils within the lesson. Home learning should consist of suitable tasks that are related to the lesson sequence. Home-learning tasks need to be relevant, set with the suitable amount of challenge and designed to develop knowledge further, promote independence and prepare pupils for future learning. Through the extension of learning through setting suitable, relevant and challenging activities, home learning can also be a useful tool to consolidate and reinforce learning. A good example of how home learning can be used effectively is in the flipped classroom model, whereby the learning of content is undertaken as home-learning tasks by pupils independently or collaboratively using podcasts, videos, presentations, books and other media; then this knowledge is applied and reinforced in the classroom during the next lesson.

It is good practice to model what home learning should look like to set clear expectations of the quality of work to be produced. Completing the home-learning task yourself or modelling previous pupils' work gives pupils a clear idea of the expectation of the quality of home learning. The use of a virtual learning environment (VLE) can also assist pupils by structuring home-learning tasks or providing more detailed information, so that if they only write PE homework in their planner they still remember what they have to do, as it is outlined on the VLE. Make sure that the appropriate amount of time is allocated to home-learning tasks. Always acknowledge the completion of home learning, mark and give feedback personally where possible (when time allows), and if time or marking load is difficult, plan self- and peer-marking lesson tasks.

Now complete Task 14.7.

Task 14.7 Virtual learning environment (VLE)

Find out from your school tutor who is the central contact for organising the school's VLE. Discuss with that person what capabilities the system has: for example, can you embed videos, set timed quizzes, track who engages with content? Attempt to use these interactive tools to engage your pupils with follow-up homework or flipped learning content. Store this information in your PDP to use as appropriate when setting home-learning tasks and to use as evidence to support your achievement of standards for gaining qualified teacher status.

Assessment

Two aspects of assessment of accredited qualifications are outlined below. Firstly, you and the pupils assess their progress, attainment, understanding and application of content (assessment *for* learning) to inform future learning, and secondly, you and the pupils understand how the accredited qualification is going to be assessed summatively (assessment *of* learning).

The principles that guide assessment *for* learning (see Chapter 9) should underpin learning and ongoing assessment for 14–19 accredited qualifications. Assessment *for* learning activities should be a natural part of teaching; thus, when used effectively and appropriately, this should maximise learning potential for pupils. Some assessment *for* learning strategies that can be used to monitor the progress, attainment, understanding and application of content are outlined below:

- Set high expectations from the start and have a policy for missing, late or inadequate class work or home learning.
- Have a clear assessment strategy. How will you assess progress and attainment, e.g. marked work, practise examinations, tests? What intervention strategies can be offered throughout the year to aid learning, e.g. revision tutorials, topic seminars?
- Get to grips with pupil data. Understand median scores (what pupils should achieve at GCSE based on their Key Stage 2 Scholastic Assessment Test (SAT) scores) and target values. Understand what is required to add value and to achieve their median. Discuss with the other class teachers or head of department how target grades are set and on what information they are based.
- Differentiate to support and extend learning activities, e.g. consider what different ways you need to plan, deliver and feedback to individual pupils within your group.
- Use questioning to gauge understanding and use as hinge points within the lesson, e.g. when planning your lessons, consider what the 'crunch' moments are where learning could move forward or stall.
- Organise the qualification content into topics. Throughout, and at the end of each topic, conduct continuous assessment in relation to class work and home learning and conduct end-of-topic tests to ensure that pupils understand and can apply the course content. This will help you identify weaknesses in content knowledge or application of this knowledge, which will allow you to re-teach elements of that topic that are still misunderstood. It will also allow you to identify quickly struggling pupils and provide a targeted intervention. An end-of-topic test and red, amber, green rating of topics will also help you prioritise which topics to re-teach, or revise first during examination season.
- Praise pupils regularly and above all, share your passion for our fascinating subject and inspire others to want to learn more.
- Provide regular, timely and accurate feedback to pupils, other staff members and parents/carers regarding progress, attainment and barriers to success, e.g. discuss pupil progress with the class teacher, identify and quantify how you know. Take the opportunity to experience a parents' evening and engage in the feedback where possible.

Some strategies that can be used to ensure you and your pupils understand how the accredited qualification is going to be assessed summatively are outlined below:

- Understand the assessment process. Is there an examination, controlled assessment or moderation process? What is the proportionate weighting of each assessment method (e.g. 60 per cent examination and 40 per cent practical)? Understand and identify the implications of these weightings.
- Practise the assessment processes; have mock moderations, examinations and controlled assessment to prepare pupils for the real assessment regularly (in various guises) to reduce the anxiety and induced stress.
- Balance teaching to prepare pupils for the assessment processes, including examinations with teaching content to ensure that pupils are still being educated, and not schooled to pass exams.

Now complete Task 14.8.

Task 14.8 Types of assessment on 14-19 qualifications

Find out the types of assessment which are included on the 14-19 qualifications in your placement school. Ask your tutor what formative assessment (assessment *for* learning) s/he undertakes to help pupils to work towards the objectives of the course and specific aspects of summative assessment (assessment *of* learning).

Observe the assessment taking place and/or read the outcomes of the assessment (e.g. some of the coursework submitted by pupils at different grades) or the teacher's report on practical assessments.

Record your findings in your PDP.

Revision

Revision is very important within a linear model of accredited qualifications with terminal examinations. Revision strategies, such as mock examinations, practising examination questions, learning definitions and terminology, chunking (breaking down large amounts of information into smaller, more memorable chunks of information) and mind maps (creating a visual representation of the information) can all be used to help pupils retain and recall information during examinations. Examination technique is also important, e.g. it is important that pupils understand the command word (e.g. identify, describe, compare) and know how each command word should be answered, the content (what is the context of the question?) and the topic (what topic does it relate to within the specification?), so that pupils are able to apply their knowledge in relation to the question.

Using past papers and mark schemes can prove an insightful learning tool for you as well as the pupils. Make sure that any examination questions that are used for revision purposes are from past papers and use the examination mark schemes to mark work accurately. This allows you to familiarise yourself with how questions may be posed and how to answer these questions, using the mark scheme to understand exactly what the examiner is looking for. It also helps pupils to understand how the examiner marks, which informs how they present their information. It gives pupils a realistic idea of how work is marked, including understanding what the question is looking for, how to structure answers, what is deemed as too vague, correct terminology. Promote the need for the pupils to 'become' the examiner by emphasising that they need to understand what the question requires with regard to a response. Similarly, when marking, always refer back to the assignment brief or outline, and get pupils in the habit of referring back to it. Can they write the question from seeing the mark scheme? Can they create appropriate questions and mark schemes from knowing the content and how it is applied? Does their work reflect what is being assessed?

Summary and key points

This chapter has looked at QCF in England, Wales and Northern Ireland and the place of the 14-19 curriculum within it, as well as the range of accredited qualifications available in PE and the implications of accredited qualifications in PE on teaching and learning approaches. It has also focused on developing your classroom teaching, which is relevant for any classroom teaching, whether or not within accredited qualifications.

The qualifications and certificates towards which pupils are working are the product of their engagement and can act as a passport to further or higher education, training or employment. As a student or qualified teacher it is vital that your pupils' progress and development towards such goals are of fundamental concern to you. It is your responsibility to facilitate learning, motivate and enthuse pupils to want to learn, not only to achieve the qualifications and certificates for which they are studying, but also to achieve and to be successful in the wider goals of education as a whole. Together, these provide the skills for pupils, with the help of teachers and careers advisers, to make their own informed choices about their future. As a student teacher it is your responsibility to develop:

- subject content knowledge to be able to deliver the content of specific qualifications;
- knowledge of individual pupils' attainment and prior experiences and their characteristics and development to be able to respond to the diverse needs of all pupils and challenge them to meet their potential;
- your pedagogic content knowledge, developing a wide array of teaching strategies and learning activities that engage pupils in the process of learning;
- your attitudes to appreciate how the 14-19 accredited qualification fits into the wider educational landscape and how you can promote your subject within it.

However, it is also important that you promote pupil ownership and a growth mind set (continually seeking out new knowledge or furthering/developing existing knowledge/ becoming inquisitive). After all, this is their qualification and it is important that they share in the collective responsibility for their success or potential failure.

Further, as you start your teaching career and have your own groups studying for accredited qualifications, you should ideally try to tie in your topic delivery with that of other subjects your pupils may be studying. Get together with other departments and 'share' a collective responsibility for theory delivery so that your pupils 'overlearn' topics, e.g. factors affecting performance/healthy active lifestyles at GCSE may also be covered in science or personal, social and health education (PSHE) or relating to hooliganism/group dynamics for A level may also be covered in psychology and sociology.

Check which requirements of your ITE you have addressed through this chapter.

Further reading

Grout, H. and Long, G. (eds) (2009) *Improving Teaching and Learning in Physical Education*, Maidenhead, Berks: Open University Press/McGraw Hill.

Chapter 8, 'Teaching Theoretical Physical Education', will provide you with further examples relating to the teaching of examination PE.

Grout, H., Long, G. and Taylor, S. (2011) *101 Classroom Games, Energise Learning in Any Subject*, Champaign, IL: Human Kinetics.

This book provides a wide range of interactive and engaging games; the creative approaches designed to generate motivation and enthusiasm within the classroom and break the constraints of the purely teacher-led classroom setting.

Jarvis, M. (2014) *Brilliant Ideas for Using ICT in the Classroom: A Very Practical Guide for Teachers and Lecturers*, Abingdon, Oxon: Routledge.

This book provides examples of how you can use simple and everyday hardware and software in planning and delivery of classroom PE lessons to enhance pupils' learning.

Additional resources for this chapter are available on the companion website: www.routledge.com/cw/capel.

Acknowledgement

The authors would like to thank Gill Golder for her contribution to the previous edition of this chapter.

15 Teacher as a researcher/reflective practitioner

Paula Nadine Zwozdiak-Myers

Introduction

In recent decades, the concepts enquiry and research have increasingly become embedded within discourse concerning teacher professional development, particularly in relation to performance management, raising educational standards and school improvement planning. Teachers who ask searching questions about educational practice, which arise from their own professional concerns and situational contexts, demonstrate a commitment to continuous learning by seeking new ideas, evaluating and reflecting on their impact, and trying out new practices and ways of working to improve their own effectiveness in the teaching environment. This approach to professional development exemplifies and underpins the concepts of the teacher as a reflective practitioner, as an extended professional and as a researcher. These concepts are closely related, with Stenhouse (1975) arguing that the outstanding feature of extended professionals is their capacity and commitment to engage in autonomous self-development through reflection, systematic self-study and research.

Central to your development as a teacher is your capacity and commitment to observe and analyse what is happening in your own lessons and to use your professional judgement both to reflect and act upon these observations and analyses in order to improve pupil learning and your teaching. This enables you to make informed judgements, which are derived from an evidence base, about the effectiveness of both.

This chapter introduces you to key concepts associated with the teacher as a researcher and reflective practitioner. It also considers how you can make the most of the observation opportunities and experiences incorporated into your initial teacher education (ITE). These include observation by you of teaching conducted by your tutor and other experienced teachers and observation of your teaching by your tutor and other teachers. Other information-gathering techniques are introduced in the context of describing the nature of a method of research often used in teaching – that is, Action Research.

Objectives

At the end of this chapter you should be able to:

- understand what is meant by the teacher as a reflective practitioner, an extended professional and as a researcher;
- understand the role of reflective teaching in developing your expertise as a teacher and improving the quality of pupil learning;
- have some insight into the range of questions which can be addressed through lesson observation;
- know about some techniques available for gathering information about teaching and learning in PE lessons, including Action Research.

Check the requirements of your ITE to see which relate to this chapter.

The teacher as a reflective practitioner, an extended professional and as a researcher

While reflective practice is currently very much part of what is expected of teachers, there has long been a concern for teachers to take responsibility for their own learning and development. The work of key writers in the field, such as Dewey (1933), Hoyle (1975), Stenhouse (1975) and Schön (1987), warrants study (see Activity 19.1 in Capel and Breckon 2014). Dewey identified particular orientations, notably the attitudes of open-mindedness, responsibility and whole-heartedness, that he proposed are prerequisites to reflective action. He built on this and suggested that reflection is associated with a particular mode of thinking, which involves turning a subject over in the mind to give it serious consideration and thought. He identifies five phases or states of thinking: problem, suggestions, reasoning, hypothesis and testing.

Schön's (1987) conceptualisation of the reflective practitioner originated in earlier work (Argyris and Schon 1974). An element of his writing describes two concepts associated with reflection that are useful to you at this stage of your career. These are reflection in action and reflection on action. Reflection in action occurs in the ongoing teaching situation as you survey the class, picking up possibly unexpected responses, which may need an alteration to the lesson as planned. Expressions such as 'thinking on your feet', 'reading the class' and 'keeping your wits about you' aptly portray reflection in action. Reflection in action is a skill that develops over time as your observation improves and you accrue a range of experiences that can inform how you deal with the unexpected. Being ready to modify plans if pupils do not respond as you had anticipated is discussed in Chapter 3 and responding to off-task behaviour was discussed in Chapter 6. Reflection on action involves looking back on action some time after the event. This type of reflection highlights the need for you to think carefully about the outcomes of your teaching and capacity to enhance pupil learning through rigorous and systematic evaluation procedures. This reflection has been discussed in the context of lesson evaluation in Chapter 3, and is returned to later in this chapter.

Hoyle (1975) introduced the notion of the teacher as an extended professional, that is, a teacher who is demonstrating professionalism beyond the baseline of competence in teaching. He describes this teacher as characteristically:

- showing a high level of classroom competence;
- exhibiting a pupil-centred approach;
- having a high level of skill in handling pupils and understanding them;
- deriving great satisfaction from working with pupils;
- evaluating own performance in terms of perceptions of changes in pupils' behaviour and achievement.

Building on Hoyle's (1975) work, and focusing very much on the teacher as a researcher, Stenhouse (1975: 143-144) identifies five key attributes to characterise extended professionals as they research their own practice. Extended professionals:

1   reflect critically and systematically on their practice;
2   have a commitment to question their practice as the basis for teacher development;
3   have the commitment and skills to study their own teaching and in so doing develop the art of self-study;
4   appreciate the benefit of having their teaching observed by others and discussing their teaching with others in an open and honest manner;
5   have a concern to question and to test theory in practice.

These attributes have resonance with many of those aspects of teaching that this book has been introducing to you and on which you have been working. However, your concern with improving your teaching has, to date, been focused on acquiring the basic skills of teaching and has probably been driven by the need to match up to the expectations of your tutor. For example, you may have been encouraged to work on smooth transitions in your lesson management or use pupils more in providing demonstrations. What has been described above, however, is, significantly, led by the teacher's own interest and desire to become ever more effective in promoting pupil learning. Genuine commitment to teacher development arises from critically constructive self-reflection and considered response and has the potential to develop into more systematic research into teaching.

This chapter now reviews those aspects of your ITE which provide the ground for your development as a reflective practitioner and then turns to introducing you to Action Research as one procedure to carry out research into teaching.

Preparing to be a reflective practitioner in ITE

At the heart of reflecting on teaching and of research into teaching is a concern to ensure that pupils learn as a result of your teaching. Much of your ITE requires you to observe, identify and understand the many and complex relationships between learning and teaching. The teacher behaviours, skills and strategies you have been practising have this one goal in mind, for example, planning, observation, communication, organisation and assessment.

The step beyond the execution of these skills in, and of, themselves is to judge if they are effective in promoting learning. Remember that taking a reflective stance on your teaching applies both to the teaching of the content specified in statutory programmes of study and attainment targets (in England, of the National Curriculum for Physical Education (NCPE) at Key Stages 3 and 4 (Department for Education (DfE) 2014b)) and to classroom-based work in General Certificate of Secondary Education (GCSE) and General Certificate of Education Advanced (GCE A) level courses.

There are at least three ways that you can learn first-hand about the relationship between learning and teaching. The first is to observe other teachers and to identify what they do and the effect of their actions. Numerous tasks have been set throughout this book to encourage you to observe teachers at work. The second is to receive feedback on your own teaching from your tutor or another teacher. This feedback is usually focused on how far what you did fostered learning. The third way to learn about the effect of teaching on learning is to conduct a constructively self-critical analysis of your lessons. You will already be familiar with this process through your lesson evaluation.

All three methods mentioned above concerning learning about teaching and about pupil learning depend on some form of observation followed by systematic reflection. Chapter 4 looks in detail at the why, what and how of observation. As observation lies at the heart of becoming a reflective practitioner, practising and acquiring the skills of observation are very important and you are recommended at this stage to reread this chapter.

Learning through observing other teachers

Observing experienced teachers is very valuable and much can be learnt from this exercise. Remember it is a privilege to be present in a lesson; as you move into your career there are seldom opportunities to observe others teach. It is always useful to observe a number of teachers as this helps you to realise that there are many different ways of promoting pupil learning, managing pupils and conducting teaching. As you do these observations you are undertaking the role of what in research is known as a 'non-participant' observer. This means that you play no part in the lesson, sitting unobtrusively in a position from which you can see the whole class, or pupil(s) in question.

In setting up an observation of your tutor or another teacher it is important that an appropriate procedure is adopted. For example, the first step is to talk to your tutor (or another teacher) to confirm his or her willingness to be observed. Following this you need to explain what aspect of teaching you are particularly interested to observe. In your early weeks this may be organisation of the pupils in the space or allocation of time. Later in your ITE you may want to observe pupil learning and see how the teacher caters for the range of different abilities in the class. Alternatively, you may be interested in how the teacher devolves responsibility to pupils. It is valuable at this stage to gather information about the class and the lesson to be observed (see below).

Once you have decided and agreed the focus of the observation you need to draw up a simple observation instrument (to be covered later in this chapter) to direct your attention to key aspects of teaching or pupil learning. For example, your instrument may enable you to document how the teacher uses praise, or it may guide you to observe a small number of pupils and chart their progress in achieving intended learning outcomes (ILOs). You must share this instrument with the teacher in question. If you have the opportunity, it is useful to practise using the instrument, possibly with a video-recorded lesson.

After you have observed the lesson you should arrange to meet the teacher to go through what you observed and discuss this fully with him/her. You will, of course, thank the teacher for allowing you to observe the lesson.

Background information for undertaking an observation

Background information about the class and lesson is important in undertaking any lesson observation. This can be collected from the teacher using a sheet such as that shown in Figure 15.1 (available on the companion website: www.routledge.com/cw/capel) for ease of completion.

It is important that there is a focus for any observation in order to obtain maximum information. What you decide to observe depends on the stage of your ITE, the teaching skills you are finding particularly challenging, for example voice variation, or perhaps an aspect of pupil learning that you are being encouraged to put into effect, such as skill progression. See Chapter 4 on other ideas about what to observe.

What you observe could include:

- the lesson plan and stages of the lesson from the moment the pupils arrive to their dismissal from the changing rooms at the end;
- how the teacher ensures safe participation by the pupils at all times;
- the teacher's use of skills such as verbal and non-verbal interaction, positioning, use of praise and behaviour management;
- how the pupils respond to the challenges set by the teacher;
- how pupils of different abilities are catered for;
- why pupils move 'off task';
- how often pupils ask questions;
- how well the pupils work together in groups.

Class .... Class size .... Boys/girls/mixed ....

Year/Key Stage .... Time .... Room ....

Teacher .... Date ....

Observer ....

Activity being taught ....

Length of Unit of Work .... Lesson number within this Unit ....

What are the intended learning outcomes of this lesson?

1. ....

2. ....

3. ....

You may want to add other information appropriate to the observation.

Figure 15.1 Background information for lesson observation.

The observation in Task 15.1 (see below) is focused on how aspects of teaching can foster pupil learning.

How an observation takes place in a lesson depends on the focus of the observation. If, for example, you are observing a specific management activity, you need to scan the whole environment rather than concentrate on the activity in which pupils are participating. You therefore need to be able to observe all pupils, including those furthest from you. In some situations you may want to focus on one or a few pupils, for example, if a pupil is having particular difficulty or is not on task and is beginning to misbehave. On the other hand, if the teacher is promoting group work you may observe just one group. Further discussion of how to observe can be found in Chapter 4.

Devising an observation instrument

As indicated above, much can be learnt from observation if you have made a record of what you have observed. Systematic documentation of teacher and pupil behaviour is a key aspect of research, and any work you do during your ITE helps to prepare for future reflective investigations. Recording observation is best done on a pre-prepared observation instrument. This instrument does not have to be a complex document, but one that directs attention to the specific issue at hand, as it is all too easy to get distracted by some of the other numerous events that occur in a lesson! Care and attention need to be put into its design to ensure that it is clear and easy to complete. Time taken to map out an instrument is invaluable in facilitating observation. At this stage in your learning to teach it is advisable to keep the instrument simple. Examples of simple observation instruments can be found on the companion website: www.routledge.com/cw/capel. Activity 20.3d in Capel and Breckon (2014) includes two simple and useful observation instruments.

Task 15.1 outlines an observation exercise to match teacher behaviour to pupils working toward pupils developing technique, improving performance or analysing performance. A simple observation instrument is provided in Table 15.1. Table 15.2 is an example of a completed observation carried out.

Task 15.1 An observation schedule for looking at the purpose of tasks set by the teacher

Observe a lesson taught by your tutor or another teacher, using the observation schedule shown in Table 15.1. Identify the ILOs of the lesson with the teacher before the lesson. During the lesson, listen carefully to the teacher and try to relate the tasks set to these ILOs. Make a decision as to whether or not the tasks set are related to developing technique, improving performance or analysing performance. These elements are interrelated and any one task may appear in more than one column. An example is provided (Table 15.2) to show what a completed schedule might look like for a gymnastic lesson. Discuss the lesson with your tutor afterwards to check your interpretation of events in the lesson. Put the completed observation in your professional development portfolio (PDP).

(continued)

Task 15.1 *(continued)*

Table 15.1 Observation schedule for Task 15.1

Part of lesson (see Chapter 3 for identification of parts of a lesson)	Developing technique	Improving performance	Analysing performance

Observing experienced teachers at work and discussing with them, in depth, what you observed helps you to recognise different aspects of teaching and how these relate to learning. You identify and appreciate the appropriate application of a wide range of teaching skills. Furthermore, you begin to learn how to analyse teaching and deduce the reasons for and causes of events in the lesson; in other words, you engage in answering the question 'why', in respect of the way the lesson was taught and how it developed. In talking to the teacher after the lesson you have the opportunity to hear first-hand how the teacher perceived the events in the lesson and to come to understand how decisions were made in the teaching situation that took account of pupil responses. In addition, you can debate other ways that the lesson might have been conducted and how the next lesson can take account of the progress, or otherwise, of the pupils' learning. In this debate you need to listen carefully to what the teacher says, as she/he is sharing with you the process of reflection that you are expected to develop in your ITE. The cognitive processes of analysis and deduction in which you engage here are a valuable foundation for becoming a reflective teacher.

Learning through others observing your teaching

Throughout your ITE you are likely to have a teacher observing all or part of your lessons. As a student teacher you should not be left alone in sole charge of a lesson, particularly in a potentially hazardous subject such as PE. On many occasions the observing teacher takes notes on your teaching in order to support your developing expertise; these are then discussed with you after the lesson. These feedback documents are very important and should be kept either alongside the lesson to which it refers or in a clear section of your PDP. In the early stages of your ITE these documents provide key information on your progress. Once you are established in your school placement you are encouraged to take more responsibility for your own learning, particularly in respect of the overall expectations in your gaining qualified teacher status. As the onus moves to you for your development as a teacher, you begin to practise the critical self-reflection inherent in adopting a research approach to pupil learning and approaches to teaching. Your weekly meetings with your tutor look at the expectations of your ITE and it is likely that, in discussion, priorities for you to work on are agreed. It is therefore appropriate for you to ask your tutor or observing teacher to give you specific feedback on a particular focus. The provision of a simple observation sheet for the teacher to use ensures that you receive the information you need. Examples of foci could include:

- your picking up and responding to early signs of off-task behaviour;
- your use of praise or assessment for learning;
- how pupils respond to your challenge to solve problems;
- how effectively pupils use ICT to promote learning;
- whether your teaching encourages progression in pupil mastery of a skill.

Table 15.2 Example of completed observation schedule used in a gymnastics lesson

Intended learning outcomes			
By the end of this lesson pupils will be able to: • perform a variety of rolling movements from work cards demonstrating body tension and clarity of body shape (*develop technique*); • plan and perform a sequence on apparatus to include a jump, roll and weight on hands movement, making the end of one movement the beginning of the next (*improve performance*); • use criteria provided by the teacher to give verbal feedback to a partner on their rolling sequence using appropriate terminology, e.g. tension, tucked, stretched (*analyse performance*).			
Part of lesson	*Developing technique*	*Improving performance*	*Analysing performance*
Introduction and warm-up	Teacher reinforces quality in running actions		Pupils identify improvements that would benefit others as well as themselves
Development of skill or topic *Floor work*	Pupils all perform same rolling movements – they work towards goals, showing initiative, commitment and perseverance		Pupils set personal goals with success criteria for their development and work
	Pupils choose starting and finishing positions from work cards	Pupils select and apply three rolls to a small sequence – they connect their own and others' ideas and experiences in inventive ways	Pupils are asked to observe each other's sequence and provide constructive support and feedback using specific criteria – they also learn to deal positively with praise and criticism

Table 15.2 (continued)

Apparatus	Pupils practise transition from jump on bench to roll on floor		
	Pupils plan sequence to include jump, roll and weight on hands movement – they try out alternative possibilities and follow ideas through	Pupils evaluate experiences and learning to inform future progress	
			Questions/answers on quality in jumping, rolling and taking weight on their hands – pupils analyse and evaluate information, judging its relevance and value
Conclusion	Pupils put away apparatus and then practise weight on hands movements		Pupils identify improvements that would benefit others as well as themselves

Task 15.2 requires you to select a focus for observation and to devise an instrument to be used in observing your teaching.

Task 15.2 Developing an observation schedule

Select a teaching skill you need to work on to develop your teaching ability. Devise an observation schedule to focus on your use of this teaching skill (using the information in this chapter, in Chapter 1 and examples on the companion website: www.routledge.com/cw/capel). Activity 20.d in Capel and Breckon (2014) includes two simple and useful observation instruments.

Ask your tutor to use the observation schedule to observe your use of this teaching skill in a lesson. Explain how the observation schedule should be used. Discuss the effectiveness of the observation schedule after the lesson and adapt if necessary. Also discuss the outcomes of the observation with the observer. Work to develop your ability in using the teaching skill, then repeat the observation using the same (or revised) observation schedule. Put the completed observation in your PDP.

An essential follow-up to this observation is time to discuss the teaching with the observer. In some cases you may realise what you did or did not do, but in other cases you may not be aware of events. Listen carefully to all the advice given and learn as much as you can from this feedback. When your teaching is observed by another teacher and in the subsequent discussion after the lesson, your ability to reflect critically is enhanced through your observer engaging in a debate with you. You are likely to be asked to evaluate the lesson as a whole and conduct a constructive self-criticism of your teaching, identifying your strengths and areas for improvement. Significant here are the ways in which your teaching is related to pupil learning. You may be asked to explain and justify aspects of your teaching and to ponder if, with the benefit of hindsight, you might have adopted a different approach. Together with the observer you may identify aspects of your teaching that were effective and how you can embed these into your teaching and in addition reflect on and think about how a problem might be avoided in the future. More broadly, you may debate the relationship between learning and teaching and together weigh the potential value of implementing different approaches to promote learning. You may be challenged to be imaginative and innovative in respect of future planning. In short, in situations where you are observed, there is the opportunity for you to develop the valuable reflective skills of honest self-appraisal, indepth analysis of the events of the lesson, identification of your strengths, intelligent conjecture of the causes of problems and flexibility in devising solutions.

Learning through self-reflection on your own teaching

As your ITE progresses you are expected to take more and more responsibility for your own development as a teacher. Your tutor's feedback is likely to be prefaced by questions such as 'How far did the pupils achieve the ILOs?', 'Which aspects of your teaching were most effective in promoting learning?', 'Where do you think you could make improvements in your teaching?' and 'What issues should you take into account as you plan the next lesson?' You are expected to be alert to all aspects of your teaching, particularly its effect on learning, and be able to reflect on these after the lesson. In other words, you are expected to be beginning to become a reflective professional. Indeed, your progress in the latter part of your ITE may well be judged very much on your ability to take ownership of your development as a teacher and the ways that your teaching promotes pupil learning.

The lesson evaluations that you have been completing throughout your ITE are, of course, the forerunner of documenting your reflection on your teaching. As indicated above, the key questions to be asked and answered in lesson evaluation are:

- *What* did the pupils achieve/learn or not achieve/learn?
- *Why* did they achieve/learn or not achieve/learn? In other words, why did this learning take place/not take place? What aspects of my planning/teaching were effective/less effective, e.g. was it too difficult, was there not enough time?
- *How* should I plan/teach in the next lesson to accommodate these findings? What do I continue to do next time or what do I need to do differently to promote learning, e.g. differentiate more/better, provide more specific feedback?

These questions can lead to different patterns of thinking. For example, the question 'What did the pupils learn?' requires you to conduct a form of evaluative thinking. Here you need to compare the progress pupils made with the ILOs of the lesson. On the other hand, when you ask the question 'Why did learning take place/not take place?' you are involved in a more analytical consideration. This might focus on your planning or your teaching. Both types of thinking are important when you begin to conduct research into teaching. In fact, in asking yourself these questions you are carrying out *reflection on action* – a key characteristic of a reflective professional and of carrying out research into your teaching.

Reflection on action enables you to reconsider what is worth doing and alternative approaches to what you are doing in your lessons, thus developing sensitivity to what you are doing and how. The basis for reflecting on what happens in your lessons is your knowledge about, and understanding of, for example, whether outcomes for pupils' learning were met, the appropriateness of content you planned or the effectiveness of the teaching approaches you used. Spending a few minutes at the end of a lesson reflecting on what you did, what worked, what did not work, what might have worked better and what you might do differently next time enables you to gain insight and learn from your mistakes. This relies on your observation in the lesson and your powers of recall of the lesson. To enhance the effectiveness of reflecting on your lessons you need to develop techniques to help you recall events. As soon as possible after the lesson, 'relive' the events which took place, before you forget what you saw. Jot down the main events of the lesson, particularly if there was any deviation from the lesson plan or if there were any 'critical' incidents which occurred, or take more extensive notes. You should draw on your experience of similar situations in the past and observation and feedback by your tutor. See Activity 19.2c in Capel and Breckon (2014) for an example of reflection on action.

Using video can be a valuable way to record your teaching and pupil learning, to allow you to reflect on the lesson more fully. It can also be used to assist observation of pupils (see Chapter 4). It has the advantage of allowing you to focus on any number of aspects of the learning and teaching process. The main problem with using this technique is the disruptive influence it may have on the pupils. For this reason it is better to video over a period of time to allow pupils to become accustomed to the process. It is also difficult to record dialogue, particularly outside on a windy day. Wet weather can also cause problems. Task 15.3 is an example of how video may be used. The purpose of this task is for you to compare your perspectives of a lesson with those of another student teacher.

You must note that the videoing of pupils is a sensitive issue and you should not video pupils without permission. Your placement school should have a policy on this and therefore you need to discuss it fully with your tutor before commencing.

Task 15.3 Analysing a teaching episode using video

Arrange through your tutor permission for one of your lessons to be video-taped (discuss with your tutor first). After the lesson watch the video and record what was happening during the lesson. Ask another student teacher to do the same. Compare the similarities and differences between your two records. Try to find out why the differences have occurred. Do the same task for a video-taped lesson taught by the other student teacher.

(continued)

Task 15.3 *(continued)*

    This task should make you aware that different people see the same lesson differ-
ently, depending on the perspective being taken. If you leave the observation open (as
above), the differences may be more marked than if you focus the observation in the
lesson. You may want to observe the two video tapes again with a specific observation focus in mind, for example, where was the student teacher positioned during the
lesson? Did the pupils achieve the ILOs? What time did pupils spend on task? In so
doing, you may want to use a focused observation schedule. Put your observations
and discussions into your PDP.

By regularly engaging in constructive self-criticism through systematic reflection on your own
teaching you gain valuable experience of asking yourself searching questions as to why learning
did or did not occur in your lesson. You are challenged to recall how the pupils responded
to your teaching and to make an honest appraisal of your planning and how you conducted
the lesson. Your awareness of the effect of different teaching approaches on learning is
heightened and you become more perceptive of the many variables to be found in the teaching
situation. In the interests of maximising pupil learning you are drawn into interrogating your
practice and to hypothesising a range of ways you could develop your teaching. This involves
a creative and imaginative approach as well as a willingness to refer to theory to inform and
support your decisions. You learn to stand back from your teaching and be an honest judge
of your practice. As you become more experienced you observe the different responses from
individual pupils and begin to appreciate that you need to make a range of subtle modifications
to your teaching to cater for all pupils. You become ever more alert to all aspects of pupil
learning and your teaching, and persistently search for better ways to promote learning. In
all these ways you are developing the essential dispositions in becoming a reflective teacher.

    The practices discussed above that have been part of your ITE, that is, observing other
teachers, learning from the observation of your teaching by others and the expectation
that through critical self-reflection you take responsibility for your own progress, all lay the
ground for you to become a reflective teacher. This is an attitude of mind that is expected
as part of your professional responsibility. It is an attitude that should permeate all your
work. With this approach to your teaching you are likely to continue to grow and develop as a
teacher and become more effective in promoting pupil learning. This analytical and evaluative
attitude and approach forms the basis of any research into teaching. You are encouraged to
build on these dispositions and to become involved in research into teaching. This research
can be a small-scale exercise you conduct on your own, part of a school initiative or part of an
assessed course or qualification. The process of Action Research is the classic procedure for
research into teaching and the next section explains this procedure in some detail.

Action Research

The commitment to learn from practice and to improve practice are characteristic principles
of Action Research, as is the concern to generate and produce new knowledge. Reflecting

on practice is a core component of Action Research and an important vehicle through which you can gain greater insight, understanding and awareness of your professional growth and development as a teacher, identify possible avenues for alternative practice, gain a greater sense of autonomy over your own work and begin to internalise the processes associated with the art of self-study.

Action Research is the most commonly used and most highly developed approach to interrogating and improving your own teaching. You may be involved in a small-scale Action Research project as part of your ITE; however, it is more likely that you will be involved in this form of research after you have qualified as part of continuing professional development (CPD) that is organised by your school or in relation to a CPD course you attend. (See Unit 5.4 (Leask and Liversidge) in Capel *et al.* 2013 for further detail of research as part of CPD.) Action Research is now widely used as an element of 'Learning at Work', which is an option in much study at Masters level. While this is a highly structured exercise, many of the processes you have experienced during your ITE, as outlined above, have prepared you to undertake this work.

The term Action Research refers to a process that teachers use to investigate their own practice and answer questions about the quality of learning and teaching. This process incorporates analysing and evaluating information about a particular experience, occurrence or situation after the event. This form of critical self-reflection involves systematically and deliberately thinking back over your actions. It has been described by Carr and Kemmis (1986: 162) as a 'self-reflective spiral of cycles of planning, acting, observing, reflecting then re-planning, further action, further observation and further reflection'. A simplified version of McKernan's (1996: 29) model of Action Research, as shown in Figure 15.2, exemplifies the various stages of this process.

This model illustrates an important feature of Action Research, notably, the cyclical nature of an ongoing process to improve the quality and effectiveness of practice. The first stage is shown in the wide vertical arrows in the diagram, headed with 'Identify research

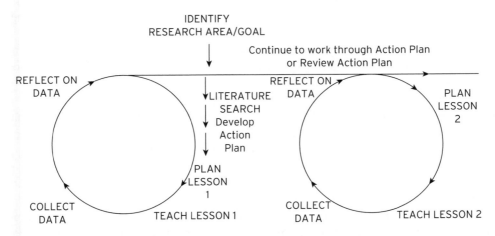

Figure 15.2 Action Research model (adapted from McKernan 1996, 29).

area/goal'. Once this has been identified, the next step is to conduct a literature search into the area. This search establishes current theories related to the area and any research that has been carried out into the area. As a result of this literature search you develop an action plan, which outlines the different teaching approaches that you anticipate you will use, the data you will collect and the instruments you will use to gather this data. In the light of the class you will be teaching you plan the first lesson, drawing from the cluster of approaches you have already identified. You teach the lesson and you or an observer gather data, as you teach and possibly after the lesson, through a way of capturing pupil response to the teaching. You then interrogate the data in much the same way as you analyse a lesson evaluation and reflect on and decide how you will teach the following lesson. According to the nature of the data you may stay within your original Action Plan or you may decide to modify this. As Figure 15.2 shows, you then plan and teach the next lesson, collect and reflect on data, and so the cycle continues.

Cohen *et al.* (2011) suggest that ideally, this step-by-step process should be monitored over varying periods of time simply because you will not solve a problem or unpack all aspects of an issue in one lesson. Rather in each lesson you try a particular combination of elements of teaching. Successful elements should be retained and built upon whereas less successful elements should be modified or discarded in the light of your reflection. This relies on your skills of observation, reflection and evaluation. Systematically reflecting on data gathered, lesson by lesson, to consider why particular outcomes were realised in the light of a particular strategy is the hallmark of Action Research.

The focus of your Action Research

Action Research characteristically starts by identifying a perceived issue or problem in a lesson. This may be identified through your lesson observations, information gathering, reflections and evaluations. Common foci for Action Research in PE include:

- solving a particular issue or problem related to promoting pupil learning, for example, raising pupils' self-esteem, improving social cohesion in a class, improving your mixed-ability teaching, finding different ways of achieving differentiation in your lessons;
- monitoring your own performance in an area that needs developing, for example, not praising pupils enough, not using demonstrations effectively, having a monotonous voice;
- enabling pupils to achieve a particular ILO, such as using ICT to effect;
- achieving a particular goal, for example, promoting creativity, getting boys and girls to work together more effectively, using particular learning resources (for example, teaching cards for use in reciprocal teaching) or teaching strategies.

Further information and details of how to engage in Action Research can be found in Chapter 20 in Capel and Breckon (2014).

Before undertaking Action Research you need to understand fully the ethical implications and implement these throughout. For example, if you are on your ITE, you should tell your tutor what you intend to do and the sort of information you are going to collect and check that your tutor is in full agreement with all aspects of your investigation. Once you are qualified you will need the approval of your head of department and possibly other senior members of staff. If you are collecting information from other people you must be sure they know why you are collecting it and that you have their full agreement and permission to collect the information. You must also maintain confidentiality. For further details about these and other ethical considerations, refer to the guidelines in Unit 5.4 (Leask and Liversidge) in Capel *et al.* (2013) and those prepared by the British Educational Research Association (BERA 2011).

Information-gathering techniques

As Cohen *et al.* (2011) note, a central feature of Action Research is the gathering of data that provides a record of the outcomes of your teaching in relation to pupils' learning. This data needs to be analysed in detail to decide on your next steps in the process. The gathering of data is therefore an important aspect of this research. The information you gather by observation or using other information-gathering techniques is of two types:

1   *quantitative* techniques: any method which produces data that can be reduced to a numerical form and can be analysed statistically (for example, a record of the number of times an event occurs). Quantitative data is normally collected in a structured format using some type of rating scale, for example, those recording: duration (a record of when an event starts and when it finishes, e.g. by using a stop watch, e.g. pupils' time on task); interval (a record of what event occurs in a set period of time, e.g. non-verbal behaviour); or an event (a record of the number of times an event occurs in a lesson, e.g. a demonstration). 'Closed' questions on questionnaires can also be quantitative;

2   *qualitative* techniques: any method used to gain insight rather than statistical analysis, for example, unstructured observations, personal perceptions about what is observed, reflective journals/diaries, some rating scales, documents, interviews, and 'open-ended' questions on questionnaires.

Quantitative and qualitative data can be gathered through observation as well as other data collection techniques such as keeping field notes/diaries, using questionnaires and conducting interviews. See Activity 20.3a in Capel and Breckon (2014), which asks you to consider the strengths and weaknesses of different data collection techniques.

Observation instruments

These are useful, structured frameworks for recording lesson observations. The advantage is that they can be constructed to focus the observation on a particular issue and can be used to provide either quantitative or qualitative information. Samples of observation schedules available include those on the companion website (www.routledge.com/cw/capel) and within Activities 20.3d and 9.2 in Capel and Breckon (2014). Hopkins (2008) and Wilson (2013) also provide examples of observation schedules and checklists developed by teachers who were concerned with gathering information on a variety of issues. Alternatively you can develop your own schedule for a specific purpose.

Field notes and diaries

Very often field notes are used as a first step prior to narrowing down the focus of an investigation. They are particularly relevant for observations designed to allow you to describe events in a lesson, either considering the whole range of events that occur (for example, recording your general impressions of a teaching environment) or describing all events in a broadly defined area of concern (for example, pupil behaviour). Such observations are designed to enable you to identify any issues or problems and to determine what you want to look at in more detail. You can then collect information systematically to focus further investigation on the issue or problem. McKernan (1996) distinguishes between three types of field notes/diary you can maintain in educational research:

1   intimate journal – a personal diary to record events on a day-to-day basis;
2   log book – used regularly to summarise key happenings and events;
3   memoir – entries made infrequently, which allows time to reflect on events and interpret them more objectively.

In a sense the PDP you are keeping throughout your ITE can be seen as the forerunner to more focused research-based field notes and diaries. Your lesson evaluations are an example of a form of diary or log book. Field notes are particularly useful if you wish to undertake a case study of an individual pupil or group of pupils; for example, if you are involved in a 'shadowing' exercise. In such instances observations and field notes are made over a period of time and can then be collated in a diary. This can then be used to reflect on and analyse patterns over a period of time. It is always important to maintain confidentiality and avoid direct reference to individuals and specific schools within your field notes.

Questionnaires

These can be a useful means of acquiring information about learning and teaching from the perspective of the teacher and/or the pupils. By asking pupils specific questions about the lesson, for example, you can gather valuable information about the impact of your teaching on the pupils. The way your questions are constructed and sequenced is of considerable importance to the effectiveness of your questionnaire. To ensure that your questionnaire is fit for purpose questions should be:

•   *accessible* – use appropriate language and incorporate types of questions and scoring systems within the developmental capabilities of your participants; be mindful of the style and size of font you use as well as how you lay out and present the questions;
•   *clear and concise* – use simple, well-focused questions and appropriate user-friendly option choices so that participants can relate to them and their responses yield meaningful data suitable for analysis;
•   *logically sequenced* – consider the order in which you ask questions so that responses are not influenced by preceding questions and that both repetition and confusion can be avoided;
•   *unambiguous* – avoid using double questions and double negatives as well as those which could lead to partial biased responses.

Several types of question can be incorporated into your questionnaire, providing varying degrees of quantitative and/or qualitative data. Closed questions, for example, give your pupils definitive choices and limit their responses to a 'yes' or 'no' type of format, whereas open-ended questions can elicit a phrase or comment and may be more illuminating, but rely on the language ability of the pupil. It is good practice to pilot your questionnaire with a representative sample of pupils (e.g. those similar in age yet not participating in your research) to establish whether it is a valid research instrument.

The questionnaire in Table 15.3 would be quick to administer and provide you with quantitative and qualitative data about a lesson. It includes both closed and open-ended questions.

If care is taken in their construction, questionnaires can be easy to administer and provide a large amount of information. One problem is that in a normal teaching situation questionnaires take time to give out, complete and return. Another problem is that they depend on whether or not the pupils have the ability to understand the questions. When constructing a questionnaire or selecting one that has already been developed, ensure that the language is at the right level for the pupils and is jargon-free so that they understand exactly what you are asking. There is also a danger that pupils may not be truthful, but may try to please the teacher by writing the type of answer they think the teacher wishes to hear. Bell (2010) provides detailed guidance on designing and administering questionnaires.

Interviews

There are three main types of interview: structured, semi-structured and unstructured.

1   *Structured* interviews allow you to work through an interview schedule and are usually composed of closed questions, which direct the response options of those you interview. With such limited flexibility, however, your data may lack evidence that is pivotal to your

Table 15.3 An example of a simple questionnaire on pupils' perceptions of learning

Question	Circle the answer that best matches your view
Do you enjoy PE lessons?	Always/mostly/sometimes/never
How much of this lesson did you enjoy?	All of it/most of it/some of it/none of it
How successful do you think you were in what you were asked to do?	Very successful/quite successful/not at all successful
How much did you learn in this lesson?	Very much/something/not much
How active do you feel you were in this lesson?	Very active/quite active/not active enough
How much equipment did you have?	A lot of equipment/some equipment/not enough equipment
How much help did you get from the teacher?	A lot of help/some help/not enough help
	Answer the question in your own words
Write down anything you particularly enjoyed about this lesson	
Write down anything you feel could improve this lesson	

research, as the questions you ask might not offer a sufficient range of responses to gain a fully comprehensive overview of the topic.

2   *Semi-structured* interviews offer a more flexible style, which can be used to collect information equivalent to that of structured interviews. You begin by identifying a number of key questions that not only elicit specific types of response, but also act as prompts. Further probing can be used to ensure that those interviewed understand the question. A technique described by Oppenheim (1992) as 'funnelling questions' helps you to gain more information about an area of interest by pursuing further questions around the same subject area or theme.

3   *Unstructured* interviews are the most flexible style and can allow you to gather complementary evidence. This approach is generally used to explore an area in preliminary research, for people with access to specialised information. However, the success of such interviews relies heavily upon the dexterity and expertise of the interviewer; for example, when the interviewer poses informed questions and adapts to the situation by reacting perceptively to new leads as they arise during the interview.

Although interviews are usually undertaken on a one-to-one basis, you can interview your research participants in groups. The main advantage of group interviews is that they can elicit rich data as your participants listen to one another. Further benefits identified by Cohen *et al.* (2011) include: people are often less intimidated, feel more at ease and can freely engage in discussion; they are less time-consuming than individual interviews; and subsequent individual interviews can explore issues which arose from the group interview. Major disadvantages of group interviews are that 'results cannot be generalised, the emerging group culture may interfere with individual expression . . . the group may be dominated by one person and "groupthink" is a possible outcome' (Fontana and Frey 2000: 652).

Using information gathered

An important point to note is that the information you collect is only the starting point for your investigations. It should be used to inform your reflections, evaluation, discussions with your tutor or other teachers, and to determine any action to be taken, for example, developing, implementing, monitoring and evaluating a solution. Perceptive reflection on the data is essential to understand reasons for the effectiveness or otherwise of particular teaching and to plan for the next lesson in the Action Research cycle.

Task 15.4 gives you guidance in conducting a mini Action Research project of your own.

Task 15.4 An Action Research project

An Action Research project may be part of assessed work during your ITE. If not, undertake this task.

Identify an issue you want to address, a problem you want to solve, for example, an aspect of your performance you want to monitor or a specific aspect of pupil learning you want to improve, with a view to improving your own practice or pupil learning.

(continued)

Task 15.4 *(continued)*

Through conducting a literature search identify what other writing/research has been carried out into the issue in question. Decide the best methods of collecting information and design your research instruments (if necessary, enlist the support of your tutor or another student teacher; it is often helpful to undertake Action Research in pairs). Arrange appropriate lesson(s) for the information to be collected. Analyse the information and try to come to some conclusions. In the light of your results consider how you might modify your practice. Try to change your practice as appropriate and monitor the changes made. Repeat the information collecting at a later date to determine how successfully you have modified your practice. Put the outcome of this investigation in your PDP.

There are two more Masters level tasks on the companion website: www.routledge.com/cw/capel.

The value of research into your teaching

By conducting research in this way you are investigating aspects of educational theory. You are coming to appreciate the complex ways in which theory and practice are related and to realise that, while there is much common ground in teaching, every situation creates a specific context for using theory to inform practice. As you work in this way you come to understand the range of elements that influence 'good practice', for example, the school context, the social dynamic in a class and the way pupils perceive the activity/subject you are teaching. You apply the outcomes to your own teaching and/or pupil learning in order to address an issue, solve a problem or achieve a particular goal. You may then look at the same issue, problem or goal in more depth or from a different perspective, or move on to another focus. You can also share your findings with others; you could for example write an article for a professional journal or present a paper at a conference to disseminate your findings.

A number of opportunities currently exist for teachers to undertake research and you are encouraged to consider engaging in this work once you are established in your first teaching post. Your professional association, the Association for Physical Education (afPE), is also active in encouraging research. Its Research and Development Working Group identifies areas of research which are currently of particular relevance to PE in the United Kingdom. It can provide guidance and some relevant initial readings, and suggestions for possible research questions to be explored in the area. The afPE website provides links to some other websites that may help you in relation to research (http://www.afpe.org.uk).

Summary and key points

This chapter has tried to help you to 'see' what is happening in order to 'read' the complex situations you encounter in the learning and teaching environment, both in practical activity settings and in the classroom. It is widely acknowledged that observing experienced teachers teach is one of the best methods of gaining insights into the learning and teaching process. The problem is that time spent in school, and in lesson observation, can be wasted if there is not a clear focus. In this chapter some techniques for focusing your observations and obtaining relevant information have been identified. The chapter has also introduced you to the need to reflect on your observations and critically analyse *what* you are doing and importantly, to be able to justify *why* you are doing it. Only by adopting a critical stance are you able to respond in a rational, reflective and professional way to the many factors which no doubt impinge upon pupil learning and your teaching of PE throughout your professional life. Undertaking Action Research should help you to identify issues and address problems identified through observation, reflection and evaluation. This means thinking critically about what you are doing, finding ways of systematically investigating it and making sense of your investigations. As you gain experience, confidence and learn to challenge, communicate and explore ideas, you become a better teacher and match up to Stenhouse's (1975) description of an extended professional.

Check which requirements of your ITE you have addressed through this chapter.

Further reading

Bell, J. (2010) *Doing your Research Project: A Guide for First-time Researchers in Education, Health and Social Science*, 5th edn, Maidenhead: Open University Press.

This book is designed for people undertaking small-scale research projects and is usefully organised into three sections: Part I – Preparing the ground; Part II – Selecting methods of data collection; and Part III – Interpreting the evidence and reporting the findings.

BERA (British Educational Research Association) (2011) *Ethical Guidelines for Educational Research*, Southwell: BERA. Available online at: http://www.bera.ac.uk.

This publication is essential reading for helping you to consider the ethical implications of research you might undertake.

Capel, S. and Breckon, P. (eds) (2014) *A Practical Guide to Teaching Physical Education in the Secondary School*, 2nd edn, Abingdon, Oxon: Routledge.

Chapter 19 provides a range of practical activities to help develop your capacity and understanding of how to engage in reflective practice. Chapter 20 is designed to develop your understanding of the principles and procedures of Action Research and recognise its potential within the context of teaching and learning.

Capel, S., Leask, M. and Turner, T. (eds) (2013) *Learning to Teach in the Secondary School: A Companion to School Experience*, 6th edn, Abingdon, Oxon: Routledge.

Unit 5.4 offers further advice on practitioner research, reflective practice and evidence-informed practice.

Hopkins, D. (2008) *A Teacher's Guide to Classroom Research*, 4th edn, Milton Keynes: Open University Press.

This book is a good starting point for anyone wishing to research their own practice. It contains practical ideas and examples of a variety of information collection techniques in addition to guidance on each aspect of the research process.

Koshy, V. (2010) *Action Research for Improving Educational Practice: A Step-by-Step Guide*, 2nd edn, London: Sage.

This book provides step-by-step advice on how to undertake Action Research from choosing a topic, devising your plan of action, gathering and analysing data to writing up your project or dissertation. It also offers advice on how to set up small-scale research projects in schools for improving practice.

Wilson, E. (ed.) (2013) *School-based Research: A Guide for Education Students,* **2nd edn, London: Sage.**

This highly accessible and comprehensive text is divided into four sections which feature: using existing research to understand and plan school-based research; carrying out and reporting on classroom-based research; methodologies; and paradigms. Chapters 14 and 15 focus on the origins of educational Action Research and how to do Action Research, respectively: Table 15.3 (p. 253) presents criteria identified by Elliott (2006) for assessing the validity of Action Research.

Zwozdiak-Myers, P. (2012) *The Teacher's Reflective Practice Handbook: Becoming an Extended Professional Through Capturing Evidence-Informed Practice,* **Abingdon, Oxon: Routledge.**

Grounded in the work of eminent scholars and practitioners within the field, this book offers an innovative framework that captures reflective practice within nine discrete, yet interrelated, dimensions to guide the study of your own teaching for professional development. It also considers qualitative distinctions in reflective practice through descriptive, comparative and critical types of discourse practitioners can engage in as they increasingly come to ask searching questions of their own teaching.

Additional resources for this chapter are available on the companion website: www.routledge.com/cw/capel.

16 Teacher beliefs

Suzie Everley and Michelle Flemons

Introduction

An initial question to ask is: what do we mean by 'beliefs'? Beliefs are propositions, ideas or views that individuals hold to be true (Matanin and Collier 2003). According to Pajares (1992), they can be learned implicitly or taught explicitly at any time during your life. Beliefs relate to very many aspects of life. For example, you may have a belief about the fundamental goal of PE or about the purpose of education. You might have a belief about, for example, the desirability or otherwise of a democratic form of government or the responsibility of the developed world to support third-world countries or streaming learners according to ability throughout schooling. Beliefs are important because they provide a reference point against which to make judgements. They guide your actions and serve to justify your attitudes. Beliefs give your decisions and responses coherence and consistency.

Beliefs generate much of your behaviour: they define you as an individual and play a significant part in how you view and interact with the world. They frame what you notice about a situation (perception), how you interpret these perceptions and give them meaning (perspective) and subsequently how you implement actions as a teacher (pedagogy) (Figure 16.1). For example, if you believe that PE is as important to those pupils who find movement tasks challenging as it is to the very promising athlete, you may notice that these former pupils are showing some disaffection towards PE, diagnose that your lesson has not catered for them sufficiently and subsequently ensure planning includes tasks that are within their reach. Throughout the chapter there are examples of the ways in which beliefs influence perceptions, perspectives and pedagogies.

This chapter considers how you formulate and act on your beliefs as a physical educationalist. Crucial to this process and your continuing development as a practising teacher is the need to reflect critically and effectively both on why you have particular beliefs and what this actually means for the pupils with whom you work. Much research has explored the concept of teacher beliefs (Ennis *et al.* 1997). Our beliefs inevitably inform action in our professional lives. However, understanding the relationship between beliefs and practice is complex and cannot be described in terms of a simple interaction that can be applied to all teachers. The relationship can best be understood through the use of reflection and reflexion. As a student teacher, your initial teacher education (ITE) will no doubt require you to develop the capacity to be both reflective and reflexive. Reflection challenges you to be aware of your beliefs and the effect of these on your practice, while reflexion is far more challenging, as it involves new understanding, a change in your beliefs and therefore a change in your practice.

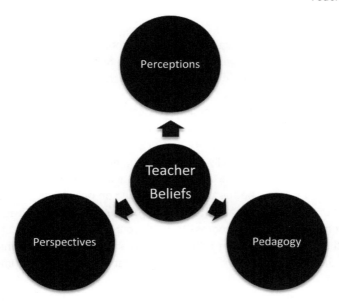

Figure 16.1 Teacher beliefs and their relationship to perceptions, perspectives and pedagogy.

The aim of this chapter is to support you in the process of understanding how beliefs affect teaching behaviours and sets you specific tasks you can utilise on your journey towards qualified teacher status (QTS) and beyond. Early in the chapter we set some simple reflective tasks that work on a descriptive level before moving towards more complex considerations that exist within reflective practice. You may find it appropriate to address some of the tasks more than once as you progress through your ITE and beyond.

Objectives

At the end of this chapter you should be able to:

- identify and understand what your beliefs actually are and how they impact on your learning in ITE;
- understand what impact beliefs have on how you teach and behave in the classroom;
- explain the relationship between the evolution of beliefs and socialisation;
- utilise reflective and reflexive processes to locate your own beliefs effectively within the structure of your ITE and beyond;
- adopt a strategic approach to adhering to beliefs when integrating into a new department.

Check the requirements of your ITE to see which relate to this chapter.

Teacher beliefs

Your beliefs have a significant impact on how you respond to your ITE. They act as filters that can be used either to validate what you are learning or alternatively dismiss new ideas as they do not clearly match your current beliefs and perceptions of how teaching is best conducted.

PE teachers usually enter the profession because they have been successful in PE, physical activity and/or sport, they love working with young people and they want to continue having an association with physical activity and/or sport. Very often they have developed their sense of self as being a physically active person, maybe a sportsperson, a dancer or an athlete. Their biographies have been woven from their sporting identities (Harvey and O'Donovan 2013). You want to be the best teacher you can be; in light of this, you will no doubt endeavour to improve your understanding of your subject, pedagogic approaches and the nature of young people as you progress through your ITE.

Beliefs should be subject to regular critical analysis and thus are evolutionary in nature. Therefore it will not be surprising if your views constantly change over time (Pilitis and Duncan 2012).

Teaching is more than knowing the tools of the trade. It is about being able to inspire and work with others, sharing your ideas in a productive and positive way. PE teachers have individual beliefs as well as beliefs which they share with others. The latter are the outcome of a process called socialisation, which is central to the development of our beliefs and ultimately our practices. Socialisation can be understood to mean those processes through which individuals acquire the knowledge, understanding and social skills that enable them to integrate with a group or community. Some beliefs are very difficult to challenge. Understanding the significance of teacher beliefs and how to challenge and embrace them should promote more effective teaching and learning.

For some in the profession, an essential belief may be that PE should be an inclusive activity with a focus on participation. This could subsequently mean that you may place an emphasis on group work and learning arising from interaction with others, where there is no single target outcome but rather a range of possible responses. In such contexts, interaction and creativity are rewarded. Here teaching would be very concerned with the process of learning rather than the product and would encourage a range of outcomes. Potentially, and in contrast, for others in the profession an essential belief may be that the purpose of PE should be to develop highly refined skills and focus on performance outcomes; therefore they may have an approach to their teaching that focuses pupils on modelling sporting behaviours and honing performance to a particular ideal. In these contexts, accuracy and progression in skill execution would be rewarded. In this case teaching would be principally concerned with the product of learning rather than the process and would work towards very specific outcomes.

Crucial here is the fact that beliefs are not static but shaped over time, as not only your knowledge develops, but your experiences broaden and deepen within a professional context. As a student teacher, you hold beliefs about desirable curricular outcomes, pedagogic processes and worthwhile knowledge. You can come to understand the beliefs you hold and how these might impact on your approach to teaching through critical consideration.

Moon (2004) suggests that you can understand your own experiences and their implications through this process of reflection.

In order to ensure you can make an impact on pupils' lives and inspire all pupils to participate in physical activity in the long term, your beliefs need to be articulated and defended. Essentially, your beliefs should determine the pedagogic approaches you take in your teaching.

Thinking about beliefs

Prior to considering what beliefs you hold yourself, it is of value for you to look at what beliefs others have and consider how these are 'played out' in practice. You can do this by observing practising teachers and talking to them about the relationship between what they believe and how this affects their teaching. Complete Task 16.1 to start thinking about the relationship between beliefs and pedagogy.

Task 16.1 The relationship between beliefs and pedagogy

Observe a practising teacher in your placement school, making notes on the following questions:

- What are the intended learning outcomes of the lesson?
- How is the lesson organised?
- How is the lesson differentiated?
- How much, and what kind of, input does the teacher make?
- How is the teacher evaluating, guiding and rewarding learning?
- What are the actual expectations of participants?

As you watch, make a record of what you have observed and think about what beliefs you think underpin what actually happened in the lesson. Speak to the teacher to ask him/her what his/her beliefs are. Talk to the teacher about the relationship between what s/he did and what you saw in the lesson.

Now consider:

- What is the relationship (if any) between what the teacher says and what s/he does?
- How are the teacher's beliefs affecting his/her actions?
- What are the learning consequences of this for the pupils?

Discuss your notes with your tutor and put these in your professional development portfolio (PDP).

By completing Task 16.1 you should begin to gain some understanding of how beliefs affect action and learning. The challenge now is to think about your own beliefs and why you hold them; to consider how they have emerged and how they are likely to affect what you do as you learn to teach.

Occupational socialisation

The beliefs you hold are inevitably shaped by your own experiences. When you first applied to enter ITE, you were no doubt required to present a synopsis of your own qualifications and experience that made you a strong candidate to enter the profession. This will have involved thinking about the influences on your own engagement with PE, physical activity, sport and coaching. The experiences you identified provide a clue as to what your beliefs as a teacher are likely to be. However, whilst you are learning to teach and later as you practice as a qualified teacher your beliefs are likely to evolve as you continue to develop your understanding of PE. Thinking of your time prior to ITE, your ITE and your subsequent time in school as a practising teacher as distinct phases in your development can assist us in identifying the nature of beliefs. More formally, these stages are identified as: the anticipatory phase (prior to you entering ITE), the professional phase (during your ITE) and the organisational phase as a qualified practising teacher. This process is called occupational socialisation (Lortie 1975). It is during this process as you move through the different phases that your beliefs are influenced, challenged and fostered (Hutchinson 1993; Hushman and Napper-Owens 2012). Figure 16.2 illustrates the processes of occupational socialisation.

The following sections consider each of these three phases and support you in identifying the relationship between the phases, your beliefs and professional development.

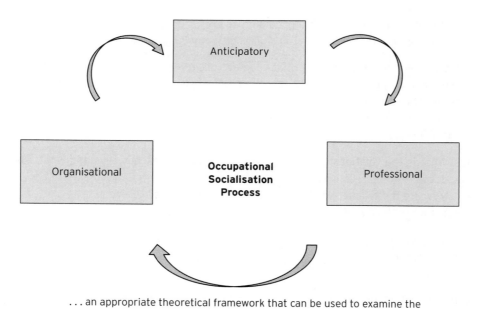

. . . an appropriate theoretical framework that can be used to examine the
socialisation of teachers in physical education
(Stroot and Williamson 1993)

Figure 16.2 The occupational socialisation process.

The acculturation/anticipatory phase

The period preceding entering ITE, described by Lawson (1986) as the 'acculturation phase', is seen as the most influential. Earlier Lortie (1975) noted that what you experience in this phase has a significant influence on your beliefs; for example, what it takes to be an effective teacher, how pupils should behave, what knowledge should be transmitted and how pupils' learning should be assessed. The approximately 15,000 hours you have spent in the classroom before entering ITE has been referred to by Lortie (2002) and Schempp (1989) as an apprenticeship of observation. You therefore arrive in ITE with deeply embedded beliefs about what PE and PE teaching are or should be. This can ultimately act as a facilitator or barrier to accessing and utilising learning opportunities within your ITE given that what teachers believe affects their practice (Stran and Curtner-Smith 2009). For example, if your beliefs endorse the view that the aim of PE is to enable pupils to carry out skills and procedures as directed by the teacher, you will be resistant to the proposal that espouses pupils should learn by discovery methods and be encouraged to create their own solutions to open-ended tasks.

Your initial perceptions regarding the requirements for teaching PE are conceived during this phase. These are largely determined by personal, situational and societal factors, otherwise known as your Subjective Warrant (Dewar and Lawson 1984: 23). See Table 16.1 for further information about the Subjective Warrant.

As can be seen from Table 16.1, the factors influencing the development of the Subjective Warrant are personal, situational and societal.

Personal factors relate to gender, ethnicity, self-concept, aspirations and the influence of significant others. Most commonly, an individual entering ITE has an interest in and is good at PE, physical activity and/or sport, enjoys working with young people and is influenced by significant others, namely teachers, parents and friends. The influence of significant others acts as a catalyst for entering ITE. Parents influence the association with physical activity and sport. Teachers, through an 'apprenticeship of observation' and the delivery of a curriculum (traditional or otherwise), have an influence, as do friends, through their degree of support and acceptance of your interests.

Table 16.1 The factors influencing an individual's subjective warrant for PE in the acculturation/ anticipatory phase that is carried forward into the professional phase

Personal factors	Situational factors	Societal factors
Significant others, gender, ethnicity, self-concept and aspirations	Socioeconomic status, academic achievement, primary and secondary school involvement and achievements in PE, interschool competition and taking part in club sports outside of school Other related work experience	Cultural stereotypes for PE and sport Perceptions of: 1 Status and economic rewards of the PE profession 2 Working conditions (job security, hours of working, holidays) of the profession 3 Requirements for entering ITE and the profession and the impact of professional recruitment processes

Adapted from Dewar and Lawson (1984: 23).

Situational factors are associated with socioeconomic status and academic achievement, affecting access to physical activity and sporting opportunities and academic progression. For example, primary school involvement in physical activity and sport such as playing for school and club teams and secondary school involvement, including coaching and leadership, can have a profound impact on beliefs. For example, the longer you have spent in coaching, the more likely you are to espouse teacher-centred approaches in school, thus creating role conflict for yourself between coaching and pupil-centred teaching expectations (Curtner-Smith *et al.* 2008; Lee and Curtner-Smith 2011; Richards and Templin 2012; Deenihan and MacPhail 2013).

Societal factors include cultural stereotypes within PE, physical activity and sport. The perceptions of status and economic reward also affect decisions concerning whether individuals seek to enter the PE profession as well as the processes through which you have to go in applying for an ITE place.

In Task 16.2 you are asked to consider your own Subjective Warrant.

Task 16.2 Personal, situational and societal factors influencing your decision to enter ITE

List the personal, situational and societal factors that have influenced you in deciding to enter ITE. Discuss your work with your tutor and keep it in your PDP.

Your reflections on your Subjective Warrant inevitably inform your perceptions of and responses to the ITE in which you are now engaging and it is to this context, the professional phase, that we now turn.

Your Subjective Warrant has a direct relationship with the conception of your beliefs with regard to what you perceive the value of PE to be and how it should be delivered, before you have even entered ITE. This period is considered particularly significant therefore, because it forms the foundation on which all future beliefs are constructed.

Professional phase

The professional phase is the period during which you are engaging in formal preparation to enter the teaching profession, your ITE. This is a significant period during which you are likely to be challenged to reflect on your beliefs and to consider how feasible they are in the light of the realities of the school contexts in which you are working. In some instances, new information given to student teachers challenges their original beliefs (Timken and McNamee 2012) and you need to be prepared to engage with the prospect of re-evaluating your beliefs and modifying these. In this case you are involved in critical self-reflection and reconsideration of your beliefs; in other words, you will have been undertaking reflexion.

According to Matanin and Collier (2003), Piaget's concepts of assimilation and accommodation were used by Posner *et al.* (1982) to describe how your beliefs change. Assimilation is the process through which new information is incorporated into pre-existing beliefs. Accommodation is where the new belief replaces or modifies an existing belief.

Ideally, you will be given opportunities either to assimilate or accommodate new ideas from your ITE contexts within your current beliefs.

Your current beliefs are very important in relation to how you interpret information given to you during your ITE (Siedentop and Tannehill 2000). For the majority of you, if your beliefs match or complement what you are being taught, you will assimilate these ideas. If you are introduced to something that does not match or complement your beliefs, you may well cast this aside and reject these ideas. It is wise to reflect on your ideas and beliefs regularly and challenge them with new information you are receiving throughout your ITE. Learning new ideas is one thing; acting on them, however, is another (Matanin and Collier 2003).

In Task 16.3 you are asked to examine how your existing beliefs have affected your acceptance of the subject content knowledge you have been presented with in your ITE and challenged your beliefs. Where your belief has shifted, you will have used reflexion, in that you have examined your beliefs and decided to modify them. Use this information to set yourself targets to effect change in your teaching to match your modified beliefs. This is likely to involve exploring new priorities and teaching approaches on your next school placement.

> **Task 16.3 Reflecting on your beliefs alongside ITE subject content knowledge**
>
> Think critically about your reaction to the subject content knowledge to which you have been introduced in your ITE to date. List subject content knowledge and ideas to which you have been introduced that challenge your beliefs. Consider if you have accommodated or assimilated these new views into your existing belief system. Highlight any obvious shifts in your current belief system. Discuss your notes with your tutor. Put your notes in your PDP as evidence of Masters level work.

The next consideration is how beliefs developed during initial ITE affect your integration into the workplace and the potential opportunities, challenges and conflicts this might represent. The next section therefore focuses on the organisational phase of your professional development.

Organisational phase

Occupational socialisation is an appropriate framework that can be used to interpret and analyse your Subjective Warrant (your beliefs/perceptions towards PE and PE teaching and teaching/coaching orientation) (Stran and Curtner-Smith 2009; Richards and Templin 2012; Deenihan and MacPhail 2013). Your Subjective Warrant is evolutionary and potentially incorporates career development on account of: a joy of working with and helping children, enjoyment of PE and physical activity and continued association with physical activity and sport (Woods and Roades 2010). The occupational socialisation process encompasses how you transition from one role (e.g. pupil, student teacher, teacher) to another throughout life (Hushman and Napper-Owens 2012), i.e. the way in which you progress through the phases described above.

The organisational phase starts when you enter the profession as a newly qualified teacher (NQT). There is, in fact, an overlap between the organisational phase and the professional phase given that your socialisation into the organisational phase starts when you go on your school placement, so giving you an insight into institutional contexts.

In practice, the expression of your beliefs, when in a formal professional setting, is negotiated with respect to a number of factors. These include not only the ethos of the department and school but also responses to government policy initiatives and other practical demands placed on institutions and individuals (Figure 16.3). For example, teachers may well find that an emphasis on pupil assessment and the time constraints associated with PE lessons compel them to use strategies which conflict with their beliefs about the most appropriate ways to motivate pupils (Taylor *et al.* 2009; Stylianou *et al.* 2013). In a situation such as that described above you may be unhappy that, on account of set criteria against which the pupils are assessed, the tasks you have to set are very specific and leave no opportunity for pupils to create and explore material. Figure 16.3 depicts how government policy affects school ethos, which in turn impacts on the ethos of the department you may work in, which ultimately influences your teaching practices.

As the newest and most inexperienced member within the department, your voice may not always be heard, or your ideas facilitated (Aldous and Brown 2010). In order to survive within your workplace, you may need to adopt a 'pedagogy of necessity' (Tinning 1988). This means that you will do whatever is necessary to fit in and be accepted by the school and by your colleagues. Zeichner and Tabacknick (1981) describe this as 'wash out'. In other words, there is a possibility that your beliefs and new found skills are literally washed out and there are limited opportunities for these to be pursued or developed. This is not to say that you will necessarily be unable to actualise the teaching approaches you wish to, but more that you will need to consider how to integrate these into your teaching and thus be true to your beliefs. Hushman and Napper-Owens (2012) suggest that NQTs actively seek ways of addressing challenges they may face in this regard and often have to compromise, adapting their pedagogy to align with aspects of the school or departmental philosophy. Hushman and Napper-Owens (2012) made the following suggestions in order to help reduce the negative effects of socialisation: use staff workshops, meetings and peer-to-peer teaching to suggest alternative approaches; encourage professional development and reflection on current

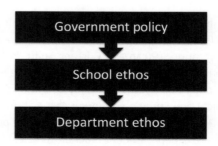

Figure 16.3 Professional settings in which your beliefs may be challenged or endorsed.

practices; and lead thinking on ways of bringing together old and new practices within the department.

Task 16.4 encourages you to examine your current beliefs and practices in a professional setting. Consider this when reflecting on and evaluating your school placement as a whole. Task 16.4 can be used to identify how your own beliefs relate to those of your department; it can also be used as part of your discussion at NQT meetings with your tutor.

Task 16.4 Integrating beliefs into professional settings

Working with your tutor in school placement, consider:

- how your beliefs interact with those of others in the department;
- strategies for adapting your teaching practices to support the department;
- strategies through which your beliefs can be positively exploited by the department.

Put these notes in your PDP.

In order to have a strategic approach to developing your teaching in the organisational phase, it is important to work closely with your ITE or NQT tutor in order to share your perspectives and understand those of the department. Establishing a strategy involves:

- identifying and justifying what you want to achieve;
- understanding how you can approach this, e.g. via curriculum change or use of different teaching approaches;
- identifying the barriers to realising change;
- identifying the resources available to you;
- creating an overall plan linking the above to benefit your teaching, the department and, ultimately, your pupils.

Pajares (1992) analysed beliefs in relation to four fundamental assumptions. Firstly, as mentioned above, beliefs are formed early in life and then driven by you, continually fighting against contradictions that stem from life and school experiences. Secondly, your beliefs act as continuous filters to how you interpret new information during your ITE. The third assumption is that the earlier the belief is incorporated into the belief system, the more resistant it is to change. Finally, beliefs are very rarely changed during adulthood. The issue with this last point is that, even if beliefs are based on incorrect or incomplete knowledge, they tend to persist.

As can be seen from the above, changing beliefs is very challenging. Of great importance is the way in which you make sense of your experience and elicit meaning from your past, present and anticipated future. One means of developing such understanding is through the use of autobiographical reflection. Such an approach forms a key element of much ITE, particularly at postgraduate level, and it is to this that we now turn.

Autobiographies

The importance of autobiographies

In light of the discussion thus far, it is clear that your biography significantly affects your beliefs and thus orientation towards teaching, response to your ITE and identity as a teacher. It is the case, therefore, that reflecting on your own life events can facilitate your understanding of your beliefs and 'who you are' as a teacher.

Considering your own biography is one way of identifying those cultural frameworks that have influenced your identity (Fivush *et al.* 2011). Evaluating the narrative through which you construct your autobiography, or 'tell your story', is one way of understanding those significant events that have informed your beliefs and views and the conceptualisation of who you are as a developing teacher.

Reflection and autobiographies

Part of the process of identifying how you have come to hold your current beliefs is to go through the process of understanding what you consider as key events or interactions that have affected you on your journey to develop as a teacher thus far. It is important to understand what it is that you consider to be significant and then to understand the nature of the impact this has had on you. This is much more than simple reflection on particular episodes, as is suggested by much literature on the reflective process (Everley 2011). Consideration of how events 'knit' together to create a wider, progressive journey is both complex and critical.

What you actually remember is significant in itself, as your 'autobiographical memory' is both socially and culturally mediated (Fivush *et al.* 2011). Going through the process of telling your life story can highlight those key aspects of your own history that have shaped your beliefs and determine how you are developing as a student teacher.

Whilst autobiographies are largely presented as chronological accounts of a single journey, Grant *et al.* (2013) highlight that the iterative processes in which you might engage in the process of explaining life events is very likely to be far more complex and lack such linearity. Once you reflect on your own biography, you may well find that it is more a 'patchworked' account of key encounters that have shaped your beliefs.

In either instance, what you need to do is to try to understand the path you have taken and consider how the episodes in this path have worked together to formulate your current beliefs. Even 'patchworked' accounts relate thematically in terms of cultural and social context. Now complete Task 16.5.

Task 16.5 Reflective autobiographies

Identify significant 'events' that informed your journey into entering ITE. These may be personal interactions or relationships, experiences or transitional occurrences.

(continued)

Task 16.5 *(continued)*

Consider the personal, situational and societal factors affecting these 'events'. What underpins their significance for you? What would your orientation to education and teaching have been at the time? What beliefs can be inferred from this analysis?

Discuss your autobiography with your tutor. Add your written reflections to your PDP and refer back to this when working on Task 16.6, below, where you are asked to think more critically about the impact these factors have had upon the way you think and act as a student teacher.

Reflexivity and autobiography – 'autobiographical reasoning'

Reflective accounts enable us to understand the influences you have experienced and how these have affected your actions. In order for such a process to become deeply meaningful and form part of a genuine developmental process, it is necessary to engage in reflexive action in relation to examining and maybe modifying beliefs. At the level of ITE, turning reflections into meaningful action requires some degree of reflexivity, of attending to the way in which you might understand your responses to those key events that have shaped your journey to become a student teacher. Such 'autobiographical reasoning' (Habermas and Bluck 2000) means that you can link both actions and rationalisations and understand why you do what you do. As Fivush *et al.* (2011) identify, when autobiographical information is explored, the result is much more than simple episodic recall; in fact, a complex picture of experiential relationships emerges. Task 16.6 supports your engagement in a reflexive approach to learning as a student teacher. This is an exercise that can be repeated throughout your development as both student and practising teacher.

Task 16.6 Reflexive autobiographies: reflecting on Task 16.5

Beginning with your notes from Task 16.5, and working with another student teacher in order to facilitate the development of a more critical perspective, think about the impact your reflections have actually had on your practice. Ask yourself the following questions:

- Did you create a 'timeline' of events or a more 'patchworked' account?
- Is a causal relationship evident between different events and the beliefs you hold?

Then with another student teacher, construct your 'story' around the key events that you identified by explaining the relationship between these situations. Ask the other student teacher to pose critical questions of you, requiring you to explain how you feel these have affected your beliefs as a prospective teacher. Together discuss how events in your story have affected what you actually do in school. Put a record of this discussion into your PDP as evidence of Masters level work.

Herein, reflexive practice results in what you may term authentic development in teaching; going through a process of autobiographical reasoning facilitates developing an understanding of who you are and, in this particular context, what your identity as a teacher actually is. It is how you see yourself as a teacher that we now consider.

Identity

Developing understanding of reflexivity informs your conceptualisation of 'self' and the identities you develop as a PE teacher. Although identity is a concept in its own right and is different from your Subjective Warrant, the two are related and your personal, situational and societal interactions affect how you perceive yourself and create an identity (Figure 16.4).

Going through the process of describing your journey in respect of your beliefs is a way of making sense of yourself as a teacher and is crucial to establishing your identity (Fivush *et al.* 2011). The process should not only facilitate your understanding of who you are as a teacher and the beliefs that underpin this, but also create an awareness of how your own professional identity is developing.

The process of understanding who you are through autobiographical reflection is the point at which 'experience' ultimately becomes meaningful – arguably the point at which the experience really happens (Grant *et al.* 2013). In other words, it is the way you remember experiences that is important. Crucially, your beliefs and concept of 'self' affect the way in which you teach. The personal and the pedagogical cannot be separated (Fernandez-Balboa 1997).

However, the identity you hold for yourself may not always be consistent with that perceived by others. A question you may wish to ask yourself can relate to how you present yourself to others. Essentially, it is important to consider what you believe you do in relation to what you actually do and ensure your beliefs are evident in your pedagogical practice. Furthermore, you also need to consider how you can sustain your identity in the varying contexts within which you will ultimately be working. Task 16.7 is the type of task that many of you will be required to complete as part of your ITE as you embark on your journey into teaching.

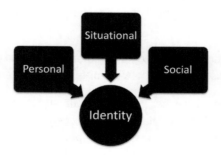

Figure 16.4 Interactions leading to our concept of identity.

> **Task 16.7 Identifying the relationship between teacher beliefs and teaching practices**
>
> In dialogue with two teachers, identify their underlying beliefs in respect of PE and how they think this informs their work with pupils. Observe each teacher teaching two classes, noting both teacher behaviour and pupil response. Using the notes from both the discussions and the observations, write an essay of 2,000 words with the title:
>
> 'Using your own informed reflections on teacher beliefs, examine the relationship between these and teachers' pedagogical approaches. Importantly, consider the impact that teacher beliefs have on pupil learning.'
>
> Store this in your PDP as evidence of Masters level work.

Summary and key points

If, as we identified at the beginning of this chapter, beliefs are propositions that individuals hold to be true (Matanin and Collier 2003), then your beliefs form a crucial part of your initial and continuing development as a PE teacher. PE is built on teacher beliefs. Your belief system impacts on the way in which you teach and ultimately influences what the pupils then experience in their PE lessons in school. Your beliefs are shaped by socialisation into and within teaching and education contexts, particularly in the anticipatory/acculturation phase. This informs the anticipatory phase of the next generation of PE teachers. These beliefs develop as individuals within the profession interact. Beliefs may remain in situ or may be reviewed and modified, resulting in an evolution of your views of the nature and aspirations of PE.

Processes of reflection (identifying what has occurred) and reflexion (re-evaluating your beliefs and reconsidering how modified views need to impact on your thinking, rationalisation and action as a teacher) enable you to understand your identity as a teacher and establish pedagogic approaches that are consistent with the beliefs you hold. Following a continuing process of evaluating practice that includes a focus on pupil response and learning enables you to evolve into a highly effective teacher.

Your ITE experience should create a climate that encourages you, as Pajares (1992) suggests, to accommodate new information and evolve as a PE teacher. In order for you to create change and move forward in PE, you will need to be articulate and challenge existing beliefs. Weaknesses in current beliefs that do not promote positive change need to be exposed as unsatisfactory through thoughtful and well-researched arguments. It is salutary to realise that, in general, while PE teachers reflect on their teaching, they seldom engage in reflexion. As a result, long-established beliefs are continually being recycled and reused, therefore reducing the capacity to promote positive change.

This chapter considered how you formulate and act out your beliefs as a PE teacher. Crucial to this process and your continuing development as a teacher is the need to reflect critically and effectively both on why you have particular beliefs and what this actually means for your pedagogical practice and ultimately the pupils with whom you work.

Using autobiographical reflections helps you to understand how you arrived where you are in your professional choices and development. Continuing to engage critically in considering the nature of your pedagogic choices ensures a conscious, deliberate and purposeful engagement in actualising your beliefs in practice. Thus you work towards ensuring that what you claim to be achieving in your teaching is consistent with what you actually do.

Check which requirements of your ITE you have addressed through this chapter.

Further reading

Lortie, D. (2002) *Schoolteacher: A Sociological Study*, 2nd edn, Chicago: University of Chicago Press.

Upon its initial publication in 1975, many reviewers dubbed this the best social portrait of the profession since Willard Waller's classic *The Sociology of Teaching*. This new printing of Lortie's classic, including a new preface bringing the author's observations up to date, is an essential view into the world and culture of the profession you are entering.

Matanin, M. and Collier, C. (2003) 'Longitudinal analysis of pre service teacher's beliefs about teaching physical education', *Journal of Teaching in Physical Education*, 22: 153–168.

This paper explores the evolution of three preservice physical educators' beliefs throughout a four-year ITE programme. Data from interviews, surveys and document analysis indicated that participants assimilated programme messages into their beliefs about teaching relative to elementary content, teaching effectiveness and the importance of planning. They were less likely to assimilate messages about classroom management and the purpose of PE due to the impact of their own biographies.

Moon, J.A. (2004) *Reflection in Learning and Professional Development: Theory and Practice*, Abingdon, Oxon: RoutledgeFalmer.

This text provides a framework for reflection in professional contexts; it provides a series of tools for experiential and reflective learning with examples as to how to present these in academic contexts. It facilitates the establishment of theoretical links with practice and is of particular value to those entering the teaching profession.

17 Beyond your teacher education

Gill Golder and Julie Stevens

Introduction

As you move from student to qualified teacher it is essential to recognise that gaining qualified teacher status (QTS) at the end of your initial teacher education (ITE) is not the end of your learning to become a teacher or about teaching – rather, it is the end of the beginning phase. The changing nature of teaching and learning in schools means that when you embark on a career teaching PE you will face challenges with, among other things, changes in government policy, emphasis on new national priority areas, changes to curriculum content and changes in perceptions about the most suitable ways of teaching to ensure pupil progress.

Your ongoing professional development as a teacher is a learning journey that enables you to stick with familiar highways or to take uncharted routes and explore different ways of working. Most commonly known as continuing professional development (CPD), the learning journey provides you with opportunities to develop aspects of your teaching, such as your pedagogic practices, subject content and curriculum knowledge, critical thinking and reflective practice, leadership and management skills.

This chapter considers life beyond your ITE experiences. It starts by looking at the steps you take as you apply for and gain your first teaching post and start your induction period as a newly qualified teacher (NQT). It then considers the process of structuring your CPD to inform your career progression after the initial transition from student to qualified teacher.

The experiences you have as you develop your career will be influenced by a number of factors, not least: changes to the teaching profession; different school structures; and focus on accountability and inspection. As you develop professionally you will also develop personally and schools will be very keen to support teachers who show a commitment to their own CPD, which helps them to improve the quality of teaching and learning and to raise pupils' attainment. Teachers are the greatest and most valuable asset a school has and if you are proactive and structured in your approach to CPD you will make yourself indispensable. Continuing to keep the professional development portfolio (PDP) you start during your ITE enables you to evidence your career progression (see Introduction in this book and also Capel *et al.* (2013) for more information about a PDP).

Most of the content of the chapter is relevant wherever you teach. However, where a specific example is given, it is clear whether it refers to England; to England and Wales; to England, Wales and Northern Ireland; or to the United Kingdom (UK). Wherever you apply for jobs or end up teaching, research and apply the information in this chapter to the specific requirements and/or organisations relevant to your situation, as appropriate.

Objectives

At the end of this chapter you should be able to:

- apply for and prepare for an interview for your first teaching position;
- make the transition from student teacher to NQT;
- understand the importance of CPD as your career progresses;
- understand the importance of maintaining a PDP from which you can generate a five-year plan.

Check the requirements of your ITE to see which relate to this chapter.

Applying for teaching positions

Applying for teaching posts is an important and time-consuming process. The posts you select to apply for will depend on a number of factors, such as the area in which you want to work, the type of school in which you want to teach and the age range of pupils you want to teach. You should start to get an idea of the kind of school or educational establishment you would like to work in through the experience you already have and the advertisements for posts, which are advertised widely. Your ITE will have provided you with experience in at least two schools. No doubt you will have been surprised at the differences in the schools and their systems, regardless of the fact that they may be working to the same National Curriculum (NC) and may all be quality-assured using the same inspection criteria (e.g. by the Office for Standards in Education (Ofsted) (England); Estyn (Wales); Education and Training Inspectorate (ETNI; Northern Ireland); Education Scotland Inspection and Review (Scotland)).

Applying for teaching posts is time-consuming and invariably each school requests something slightly different (in, for example, information/formatting). However, you must comply with their requests in order to be successful in a competitive job market. To prepare for the job application process, draw up a grid to enable you to gather data about the school and the post you want to apply for. This may include:

- the type of school it is, number on roll and the age range. Does it have post-16 students and teach accredited PE courses?
- the 'essential' and 'desirable' skills and characteristics within the job description;
- the key strengths and recommendations from the school's most recent inspection report from the relevant inspection body;
- key Reporting and Analysis for Improvement through school Self-Evaluation (RAISE) online information and school performance tables (see websites for Department for Education (DfE) (England); Welsh Government Education and Skills (Wales); Department of Education Northern Ireland (DENI); Education Scotland (Scotland));
- the school mission statement and philosophy;

- the quality of and information available on the school website. Does PE feature anywhere?
- information about the PE department, staffing and timetable.

Your letter of application should be written succinctly and be grammatically correct, with accurate spelling. It should explain your beliefs about PE and highlight the value of the subject in the curriculum for all pupils. Keep information about yourself professional and ensure the application refers specifically to the school you are applying to. Keep your curriculum vitae up to date and ready to send if required.

Interviews can often be arranged at short notice and you need to be fully prepared and 'ready to go'. You should 'look the part' in both formal clothes and your teaching kit. Ensure you leave enough time to get to the school on time on the day of the interview and re-read your grid of information about the school. Be prepared to answer questions based on the school's mission statement and philosophy. Interviews are usually a full-day event at the school and often include a number of activities with staff and pupils in order to assess your suitability for the post. The day may include:

- a tour of the school and facilities;
- scenario tasks;
- a teaching episode;
- informal discussions with the department;
- a pupil panel (beware of being overly familiar or unprofessional!);
- a formal interview, usually with the headteacher, head of PE and at least one governor.

By preparing adequately, you will have some relevant questions to ask at the end of your formal interview to make sure that the school is right for you. Asking what support is available for an NQT during the induction year is a highly relevant question and the answer will give you a feel for whether there is an established programme available for NQTs. If you are offered the post you will have to decide whether you want to work there and perhaps negotiate a starting salary. If you are unsuccessful you can often receive some useful feedback about your strengths and any weaknesses you need to work on for your next interview. If you do not secure a job immediately, other options include working for a supply agency or regular supply work within a particular area or school. Unit 8.1 (Lawrence and Capel) in Capel *et al.* (2013) provides further detail on applying for your first post.

Now complete Task 17.1.

Task 17.1 Applying for jobs

Complete an application form and write an accompanying letter for a hypothetical post at your placement school. Request a mock interview with a member of the school's management team. Prepare for and engage in the mock interview process and afterwards get feedback from the interviewer/interview panel. Write notes on the feedback given and store in your PDP to enable you to take it on board and respond to it prior to attending an interview for an actual post.

Bridging the gap between ITE and NQT

Having accepted a teaching post, making the transition from being a student teacher to an NQT is not as easy as it seems. However, there are steps you can take to alleviate the common causes of concern for many NQTs and support the transition process. As you move towards the end of your ITE period, formal summative reports of your progress against the standards you are required to meet to gain QTS (in England called Teachers' Standards) are made, usually through discussions between yourself and those responsible for your development, using the evidence generated about your development throughout your ITE. The feedback you receive on your teaching and the impact it has on pupil progress provides a very useful starting point for you to set personalised targets to help you bridge the gap between ITE and NQT and to support your professional development.

Some form of career entry profile is commonly used in ITE to enable you to reflect upon your main successes, key aspects of your work in schools that have been particularly rewarding, specific elements with which you currently feel less confident or have had less exposure to and aspirations for your career progression in the future. This form of reflection is critical for you to maintain the confidence and competence you have developed over the course of your ITE.

Throughout your ITE you will have kept some form of PDP in which you have tracked your progress against the standards you are required to meet to gain QTS. As you gain more information about the school you are joining as an NQT you can start to develop this to form a training plan to provide a structure to your CPD. Task 17.2 focuses on identifying your immediate professional development needs.

Task 17.2 Identifying your immediate professional development needs

Gather the information below about your placement school (or the school you will be teaching in as an NQT):

- school policies and procedures, to get a feel for how the school operates;
- how the school organises the pastoral curriculum and the knowledge you need to deliver this.
- And, in England, Wales and Northern Ireland:
  o the Key Stage 3 and 4 core curriculum content and knowledge to teach them (see Chapter 18);
  o the Key Stage 4 and 5 examination syllabi and subject knowledge requirements to teach them.

Use this information to identify areas for development and identify means of addressing these areas for development. Store the information in your PDP.

It is important to realise that you are not alone when making the transition from student teacher to NQT. The school you are joining will want you to feel part of the team as quickly as possible because if you are feeling safe and secure in your new teaching environment your impact on pupils will be more positive. In addition, your ITE provider will have a vested interest in your continued success as an NQT and be keen to work in partnership with your school to provide continued support or CPD opportunities. Developing effective liaison between your ITE provider and the school might be something you can promote by sharing your targets for development and updating your contact details. Finally, if your school is affiliated to a Local Authority they will want to ensure that NQTs are supported, to which end they offer opportunities for you to learn alongside other NQTs in the authority and to network beyond the school in which you are teaching.

Simple steps you can take as you prepare for your first term of employment are:

- Research the school further – find out what the policies and practices are in the school that you will have to follow and which will help you settle in quickly to the professional expectations you will have to demonstrate. These include, for example, behaviour policies, child protection, health and safety.
- Revisit the school – once the nerves and excitement of an interview day have subsided it is good to return to find out more about the day-to-day life of the school, get to know your way around and ask all those questions you did not ask at interview. Most schools will have an induction day; use this to get to know staff and some pupils.
- Find out the curriculum content – where possible, get copies of schemes of work and units of work, examination specifications and subject assessment materials to familiarise yourself with the way the department structures learning.
- Get a draft timetable that you are likely to be teaching so that you can pre-plan and ensure that your subject content and curriculum knowledge are current and relevant before you start; developing your knowledge if you need to.

Throughout your ITE you have not only benefited from support from tutors (often both in school and a higher education institution), but also from other student teachers who have been experiencing their own learning journey through their ITE. One way to bridge the gap between ITE and NQT is to continue this network of people and share experiences and learning. This idea is based around Wenger's (1998) theory of Communities of Practice (CoP):

> Communities of practice are groups of people who share a concern or a passion for something they do and learn how to do it better as they interact regularly.
>
> (Wenger-Trayner date unknown)

MacPhail *et al.* (2014) suggest a CoP is sustained over time, involves shared member goals, involves frequent discourse, is active and social and is characterised by problems being solved by the members. There are many ways that you, as a student teacher and NQT, can be involved in this type of community. With ever-increasing opportunities via social media and other digital technologies, keeping in contact and sharing ideas have never been so easy. Now undertake Task 17.3.

Task 17.3 Starting your own Community of Practice

Communities develop their practice through a variety of activities. Try and set up your own CoP with other student teachers on your ITE.

Use one or more of these starter threads to share information and solve problems:

- Problem solving – 'I'm stuck; can we brainstorm ideas on . . . .?'
- Requests for information – 'Does anyone know where can I find . . . ?'
- Seeking experience – 'Has anyone dealt with this situation . . . ?'
- Mapping knowledge and identifying gaps – 'Who knows what and what gaps are there . . . ?'
- Sharing resources –'I used this resource with my year 8s, feel free to adapt and use . . . '

Record in your PDP what works effectively and what does not and why, so that you can use this information to develop a CoP in future.

Inevitably, as you move into your induction period and take on a 90 per cent timetable as well as the other responsibilities expected of a qualified rather than a student teacher (e.g. as a form teacher, attending parent consultation events, being part of a duty team), you will feel more pressure on your time. The time you had to plan, create resources, mark pupils' work and assess their progress will reduce. If it does not reduce, the time you have for other elements of your life will. It is therefore essential that as you come to the end of your ITE you become more autonomous and self-directed and develop practices, for planning in particular, that are sustainable during your NQT induction period and beyond. By having discussions with current NQTs and experienced teachers about planning and preparation you can start to develop your own unique way of planning efficiently and effectively but still maintain high-quality learning opportunities for all pupils. Try out different forms of planning in your final school placement while you still have the benefit of a critical friend in the form of your subject tutor. This will help with the shock of taking on a greater teaching load in your induction period.

The induction process

Having completed your ITE and gained QTS you will be ready to begin your career in the teaching profession. Every school (and other educational establishment) is different, with different pressures, and you will need to think about how your school placements and the theoretical aspects from your ITE relate to your new situation. However, in the UK, there is statutory induction to support the process; it is important that you research the specific induction requirements as the way that induction works in Northern Ireland and Scotland is significantly different to that in England and Wales.

In the UK your NQT induction is a three-term period of assessment, usually completed within one academic year. In the unlikely event that you fail your induction you need to make sure you are clear about the implications; for example, in England and Wales you can only complete your induction once; there is no opportunity to take it again and you cannot work as a teacher in England or Wales. You are encouraged to complete your induction as soon as possible after qualifying as a teacher but there is no set time limit. QTS qualifies you to teach all over the world but if you wish to teach abroad before completing your induction and then return to teach in the UK you will need to complete the induction period satisfactorily. (For further guidance, see statutory guidance on induction for NQTs from: the DfE (2013c) (England); the Welsh Government; DENI (Northern Ireland) and General Teaching Council (GTC, Scotland).)

Statutory induction is not a legal requirement to teach in academies, free schools, British Schools Overseas, the independent sector or in further education establishments in the UK. However, these establishments may implement the requirements if they choose to – in which case, if your first teaching post is in one of these types of establishments, you are able to complete your NQT year in full. However, you need to be aware that if you work in one of these establishments that does not implement the requirements in your first few years of teaching, you will not complete your induction period and this would need to be completed in another school or establishment at a later date.

Assessment of your induction year is based on you meeting the minimum requirements for teachers' practice and conduct set out in the relevant teachers' standards and what can reasonably be expected of you in your work context by the end of the induction.

> Judgements should reflect the expectation that NQTs have effectively consolidated their initial teacher training (ITT) and demonstrated their ability to meet the relevant standards consistently over a sustained period in their practice.
>
> (DfE 2013c: 7)

All NQTs have a range of support and development available to help them pass the induction year, as shown in Figure 17.1.

It will be important to use the reduced teaching timetable in your NQT year effectively as, once you have a 100 per cent timetable after your NQT year, you will rarely have the opportunity to observe other teachers, visit other schools or benefit from the knowledge and experience of other colleagues. There is usually a wealth of teaching experience within every school and it will be valuable to observe outstanding teachers in a variety of subject areas, focusing your observations on specific aspects of your practice you would like to improve, e.g. organisation of groups, behaviour management of specific pupils, successful integration of pupils for whom English is an additional language. Ensure you build these opportunities into your development plan.

You will have an induction tutor with whom you will have a review meeting each term. The meeting will focus on areas of the standards you are required to meet that have gone well and those that you need to improve. You will be observed teaching within the first four weeks at the school and then each half-term during your NQT year, with a follow-up meeting after each observation to review and revise your objectives. Professional development is an ongoing activity throughout your career, so be patient and understand that you will develop over time and there will be some 'light bulb' moments when you realise you have made significant progress. Just as you did during school placement, you will need to reflect on your

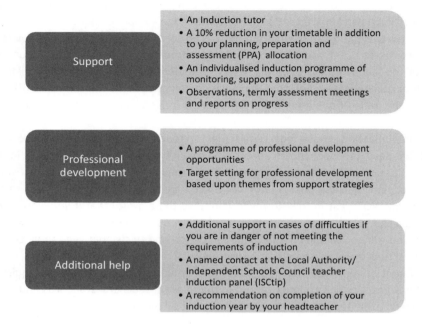

Figure 17.1 Support and development available in your induction year (adapted from Training and Development Agency (TDA) online induction guidance).

progress and set short- and medium-term targets to help you become a more independent teacher. Now complete Task 17.4.

Task 17.4 How to make the most of your reduced teaching timetable during your NQT year

Discuss with NQTs in your placement school how they have prioritised their time, what activities they have undertaken, what they have learned and what impact it had on their teaching. Also, find out from them what you should expect during your induction year. Find out from senior staff which members of staff would be best to observe for different expertise in specific areas.

Record the information in your PDP for reference when you start your first teaching post.

Your professional, academic and personal development

Whether you plan to be an outstanding subject teacher for your whole career or a headteacher within ten years, it is essential that you have a development plan. Having experienced the target-setting process as a student teacher and then as an NQT, with systematic, rigorous self-reflection it will be vital to continue the process as your career develops. At the final assessment meeting in your induction year, you will identify target areas for development over the next two or three years and devise a structured development plan to achieve your goals. Opportunities will arise within your school (or other schools) for you to apply for a different role, for example as an assistant head of year, but it will be important to position yourself by gaining experience to be able to apply for the post. You may be able to gain temporary experience of the role if it is vacant or you could achieve this by, for example, shadowing the head of year, studying the job description and finding out how the pastoral care system works in other schools. Recording in your PDP your progress in your professional, academic and personal development will enable you to plot your route to your next role or position. Now complete Task 17.5.

Task 17.5 Setting yourself targets

Setting yourself short-, medium- and longer-term targets over one, three and ten years will help you focus on where you are now and how you are going to achieve your career aspirations. There are a variety of ways of doing this; the template below provides one example. Try setting yourself targets over time which build on your strengths and address areas for development by planning how you are going to make progress towards them. Store this in your PDP.

Short- (current year)/medium- (up to 3 years)/long-term target setting (more than three years)			
Objective: (*What specifically do you want to achieve?*)			
Rationale: (*Why have you decided to make this an objective – what is the outcome?*)			
Evidence: (*On what basis are you making this decision?*)			
Key actions	**Resources**	**Outcome**	**Completion**

Continuing professional development

Your engagement with CPD is your responsibility. All CPD should ultimately impact on pupil learning, progress and development. 'The quality of teachers and leaders is the most important factor in improving educational standards for children' (National College for Teaching and Leadership (NCTL) 2013). Your progress as a teacher will be monitored through the school's appraisal/performance management process (these are part of national schemes in England, Wales and Northern Ireland. In Scotland individual schools and authorities have their own agreed monitoring process). Using your own development plan you can engage in CPD that will enable you to progress; this can take a range of forms:

- Within school: whole-school training linked to school improvement plans and national initiatives, departmental or pastoral training, individual coaching and mentoring with a 'critical friend' to develop individual practice, collaborative work and the sharing of good practice.

- School networks: the NCTL is a government agency in England set up in 2013 to enable and support the development of a self-improving school-led system. One of the NCTL's key aims is to help schools help each other to improve.
- Other external expertise can be offered by a range of providers locally, regionally or nationally which schools can buy into depending on the needs of their staff. Some of this may be PE-specific, e.g. through the Association for Physical Education (afPE).

Your professional development needs will be influenced by national agenda, the government in power and educational reports. National agendas are decided by the government and vary according to national statistics and political pressures. Schools are required to respond to these agendas and often further training is required to help teachers and school staff understand and implement the new measures, e.g. closing the attainment gap for different groups of pupils.

Higher qualifications

Masters qualifications

ITE starts you on a journey of discovery; it enables you to develop your knowledge and understanding and to build a set of skills that will be evident in your progress against the standards you are required to meet to gain QTS. Once you have gained QTS, your journey of discovery is just beginning. Undertaking a Masters degree or gaining Masters credits could be one way to accelerate your journey or even change the pathway your take through your career. A Masters degree will enable you to question educational practice and theory and identify and reflect upon key concepts in education. It is possible to complete a Masters degree in a variety of ways: there are full-time taught programmes, part-time programmes or flexible online programmes to choose from. Gaining Masters credits is a good way of gaining career credentials that help to establish you as a leader in your field.

The current standards for teachers vary in England, Wales, Northern Ireland and Scotland, but they all have a requirement relating to knowledge and understanding; for example, the Teachers' Standards in England state teachers 'keep their knowledge and skills as teachers up-to-date and are self-critical' (DfE 2011: 10). As a teacher it is therefore essential that you become a reflective practitioner, reviewing your teaching and pupils' learning regularly to check the quality and impact of what you do. Chapter 15 and Unit 5.4 (Leask and Liversidge) in Capel *et al.* (2013) both look at reflective practice in more detail. The Quality Assurance Agency (QAA) Framework for Higher Education Qualifications for the UK states that Masters students should demonstrate:

> a systematic understanding of knowledge, and a critical awareness of current problems and/or new insights, much of which is at, or informed by, the forefront of their academic discipline, field of study or area of professional practice.

> (QAA 2008: 20)

From these two statements there is clear synergy between an effective teacher and a student working at Masters level.

Academic writing at Masters level requires you to engage in relevant academic reading to develop a coherent and critical argument or debate about your topic. Varley and Green (2011) put forward a simple model to support the writing process for Masters level work that involves *pre-writing*, including note making, reading and planning; *writing*, which involves drafting, editing, revising and proof reading; and *post-writing*, which involves discussing, evaluation and expanding ideas.

QAA subject benchmarking statements in the UK define what can be expected of a postgraduate in terms of the abilities and skills needed to develop understanding or competence in the subject and describe what gives a subject its coherence and identity. Common characteristics that are evident in high-quality Masters work are identified below.

- research and investigation – identify, select, critically analyse and evaluate educational ideas, perspectives and theories;
- organisation and preparation – formulate a coherent set of aims;
- practical competence – if collecting data, select and apply appropriate methodologies to carry out the study;
- coherence – show clarity and coherence in structure and writing;
- creativity and innovation of ideas – the ability to generate new ideas and connections, apply existing material to new contexts;
- understanding of relevant contexts – locate work in the bigger picture;
- critical evaluation;
- applying theory to practice.

Alternative higher qualifications

The NCTL has devised higher qualifications and study modules for middle leaders, senior leaders and those aspiring to headship in England comprised of three modules. The aims of these qualifications are to focus on supporting improvements in the leadership of schools and children's centres; these are outlined in Table 17.1.

- Teaching Leaders is designed to raise levels of pupil achievement in challenging schools through outstanding middle leadership.
- National Professional Qualification for Senior Leadership is designed for those with a leadership role with cross-school responsibilities, e.g. Special Educational Needs Co-Ordinator, Deputy Head.
- National Professional Qualification for Headship is designed for aspiring or practising headteachers.

Now complete Task 17.6.

Task 17.6 Higher qualifications/level training of teachers

Discuss with staff in your placement school the additional higher level training, including Masters level or leadership qualifications, they have undertaken and how they have used research to impact upon practice.

Record the information in your PDP for future reference.

Table 17.1 The current Framework for leadership qualifications in England (NCTL 2013: 9)

Level	Qualification	Modules*		
		Theme: Educational excellence	Theme: Operational management	Theme: Strategic leadership
Level 1 Leading a team	National Professional Qualification for Middle Leadership • Two essential and • One elective module	• Leading teaching • Leading inclusion	• Managing systems and processes • Leading an effective team • Leading and developing staff	• Succeeding in middle leadership • Leading change for improvement • Leading in a diverse system
Level 2 Leading across an organisation	National Professional Qualification for Senior Leadership • Two essential and • Two elective modules	• Closing the gap • Improving the quality of teaching • Research and development in teaching	• Effective whole-school management • School self-evaluation • Leading professional development	• Succeeding in senior leadership • Leading change for improvement • Leading in a diverse system • Effective partnership working

Level 3
Aspiring to lead an organisation
	National Professional Qualification for Headship
	• Three essential and
	• Two elective modules
		• Leading and improving teaching
		• Curriculum development
		• Leading inclusion: achievement for all
		• Closing the gap
			• Leading an effective school
			• Using data and evidence to improve performance
			• Leading staff and effective teams
				• Succeeding in headship
				• Leading change for improvement
				• School improvement through effective partnerships
				• Leading in diverse contexts
				• Free school leadership:
				  o Relationships and reputation
				  o Freedoms and constraints

*Each bullet point is a different module title.

The teaching profession

Being aware of current issues within teaching and educational policy is one of your professional responsibilities. This section outlines a number of elements and issues which are impacting upon teachers and teaching today. With each change of government, there are policy changes. For example, in England in 2010 the newly elected government proposed and followed through with changes to the NC, school inspection and accountability, teachers' pay and conditions, school structures and ITE.

All teachers in the UK, whether a student teacher working towards QTS, an NQT or a teacher of many years' experience, are expected to achieve the minimum level of practice as set out by the relevant standards (for example, in England the Teachers' Standards (DfE 2011) or in Scotland the GTC Scotland Professional Standards (GTCS 2012)). The performance of all teachers is assessed/reviewed against these standards as part of the school's appraisal/performance management systems on an ongoing basis; the professional expectation is that you will continue making progress in each of the relevant standards over the course of your teaching career. A good way to help you decide on how you would like to develop as a teacher is to recognise the difference between a teacher who has 30 years of progressive experience and a teacher who has taught the same year 30 times over. It is important, therefore, that you continually strive to improve your teaching and meet the needs of individual pupils you teach, rather than teaching the same topic in the same way to all pupils, year after year. Understanding how to progress and improve the quality of your teaching will impact on pupils, helping them to become more confident and competent individuals. The expectations of teachers are summed up by the following:

> As their careers progress, teachers will be expected to extend the depth and breadth of knowledge, skill and understanding that they demonstrate in meeting the standards, as is judged to be appropriate to the role they are fulfilling and the context in which they are working.
>
> (DfE 2011: 7)

Following recommendations from the School Teachers Review Body, from September 2013, schools in England and Wales are able to link teachers' pay to performance, enabling the school to pay good teachers more. The move away from a national pay structure for teachers to a performance-related pay system has been implemented in a bid to drive up results, reward good performance and attract and retain good teachers who make a positive difference to their pupils' learning and achievements. During your annual appraisal/performance management review after your induction year your line manager will discuss your progress against your targets set for the year and decide whether to recommend a pay award. Current pay and conditions documents provide guidance of how this decision is made.

> continued good performance as defined by an individual school's pay policy should give a classroom or unqualified teacher an expectation of progression to the top of their respective pay range.
>
> (DfE 2013b: 25)

When you have gained more experience and undertaken CPD you may be ready to apply for a position of responsibility within your current school or a new school. In England and Wales, the Teaching and Learning Responsibility (TLR) allowances are broken down into TLR1, TLR2 and TLR3. Additional pay allowances for TLR1 or TLR2 can be awarded to a classroom teacher for undertaking a sustained additional responsibility to ensure the continued delivery of high-quality teaching and learning and for which the teacher is made accountable. TLR3 is a fixed-term award to a classroom teacher for a clearly time-limited school improvement project or one-off externally driven responsibilities. Accepting a TLR means that you accept a significant responsibility that:

a   is focused on teaching and learning;
b   requires the exercise of a teacher's professional skills and judgement;
c   requires the teacher to lead, manage and develop a subject or curriculum area or to lead and manage pupil development across the curriculum;
d   has an impact on the educational progress of pupils other than the teacher's assigned classes or groups of pupils; and
e   involves leading, developing and enhancing the teaching practice of other staff.

(DfE 2013b: 27–28)

A TLR1 post is where, in addition to the above criteria, the teacher will also carry out line management responsibility for a significant number of people. The definition of significant has to be determined at school level.

Being part of a professional association, whether a professional body or teaching union, is crucial, particularly for a PE teacher, due to the higher risk element of certain activities and environments in which you teach (Chapter 12 focuses on safety). For your own peace of mind, it is important to know you have legal representation, support and advice if an incident occurs whilst pupils are in your care. There are a number of different teaching unions and you should take time to understand what each union provides to help you decide which one is right for you. The afPE is the only PE subject association in the UK. It aims to promote and maintain high standards and safe practice at all levels of PE. It also provides additional public liability insurance for PE teachers. afPE also represents its members' views regarding national and local developments within the subject and provides a range of resources, professional development opportunities, regular updates, member journals and health and safety advice.

Accountability and NQTs

The current climate in education in the UK has resulted in an increasing focus on accountability in education. The standards for teachers across the UK refer to the professional duty of a teacher, for example, teachers are 'accountable for achieving the highest possible standards in work and conduct' (DfE 2011: 10). School inspection frameworks in the UK also aim to drive improvement for pupils of all ages. For example, in England, the Ofsted inspection framework for schools is the statutory basis for inspection and summarises the main features of school inspections carried out under section 5 of the Education Act 2005. It focuses on underperformance and promotes equality of opportunity for all groups of learners.

Inspectors are required to report on[1] the quality of education provided in the school and must, in particular, cover:

- the achievement of pupils at the school
- the quality of teaching in the school
- the behaviour and safety of pupils at the school
- the quality of leadership in, and management of, the school.

When reporting, inspectors must also consider:

- the spiritual, moral, social and cultural development of pupils at the school;
- the extent to which the education provided by the school meets the needs.

(Ofsted 2014: 5)

As a student teacher and an NQT you are subject to inspection, the same as any other member of staff in the school. For each of the judgements made, criteria and grade descriptors are applied, adopting a 'best-fit' approach which relies on the professional judgement of the Ofsted inspectors. In addition to the generic grade descriptors for school inspection there is a series of subject-specific grade criteria. It is essential that you become familiar with both of these as judgements of your teaching ability will be made using them. Now complete Task 17.7.

Task 17.7 Pupil progress in your subject
In your final placement as a student teacher (or later as an NQT), ask a colleague to observe one of your lessons using the relevant subject-specific inspection criteria (Ofsted criteria in England). At the end of the lesson discuss with the observer how you enabled all pupils to make progress in the lesson. Store this information in your PDP and use it to improve your ability to enable all pupils to make progress.

Summary and key points

This chapter has explored the transition between your ITE, the next stages in your journey as an NQT and your first steps on the career development ladder. The steps to help you overcome the initial 'reality shock' in relation to your new responsibilities as a qualified teacher were explored; in particular, the importance of developing your PDP to enable you to set targets that meet your own individual development needs and how this helps with the process of applying for your first teaching post and later to inform your CPD.

Jones (2010) explored the period of transition for pupils as they move from primary to secondary school (from Key Stage 2 to 3 in England). She suggested that, for pupils and teachers alike, this crucial period in a pupil's education is a journey with orientations, stops and reorientations, checking and refining skills. Much the same can be said for you as you embark on your career in teaching. This chapter has outlined how the induction period of support is an important phase which, when strategically planned and drawing on your previous experiences, has the potential to deepen learning that has already taken place in

ITE as well as preparing you for future learning as an NQT and beyond. In their research Haggarty and Postlethwaite (2012) suggested that, as beginning teachers move from the role of student teachers in ITE to NQTs in schools, the role of induction tutor is very important in how they begin to formulate their own teaching style and beliefs about teaching. This chapter reinforces the significance of how you prepare for and engage with the process of induction as being equally important.

In order to continue your development as a teacher and improve the effectiveness of your teaching, CPD needs to be ongoing throughout your career. It should ensure that you remain up to date with regard to curriculum knowledge, content, pedagogy and developments in your subject, explore innovation and creativity in learning and teaching strategies, and remain mindful and aware of changes in education and the impact of government policy and agendas on your professional roles and responsibilities. To do this you should seek to:

- implement a continuous and cyclical process of planning, teaching and critical reflection/ review;
- engage in substantial and sustained CPD activities over time, making connections between new learning and existing practice and engaging in active learning;
- use CPD and professional communities of practice to retain a desire to learn, love of your subject and passion for teaching.

A career in teaching will give you a different challenge every day of your working life. There will be highs and lows, most memorable moments and moments you would prefer to forget. But from every aspect you will learn alongside your pupils – to teach is to learn.

Good luck in your career as a teacher, the development of your teaching and enhancement of pupil learning; by taking control of your career development you will enjoy the journey, wherever that journey may take you.

Check which requirements of your ITE you have addressed through this chapter.

Further reading

Arends, D. and Kilcher, A. (2010) *Teaching for Student Learning: Becoming an Accomplished Teacher*, Abingdon, Oxon: Routledge.

This book shows teachers how to move from novice to expert status by integrating both research and the wisdom of practice into their teaching. It emphasises how accomplished teachers gradually acquire and apply a broad repertoire of evidence-based teaching practices in the support of pupil learning. Sections 1 and 5 are of particular relevance to this chapter.

Capel, S. and Whitehead, M. (2013) *Debates in Physical Education*, Abingdon, Oxon: Routledge.

This book explores major issues PE teachers encounter in their daily professional lives. It engages with established and contemporary debates, promotes and supports critical reflection and aims to stimulate both novice and experienced teachers to reach informed judgements and argue their own point of view with deeper theoretical knowledge and understanding. In addition, concerns for the short-, medium- and long-term future of the subject are voiced, with a variety of new approaches proposed. Part V, 'Looking ahead', is of particular relevance to this chapter.

Capel, S., Leask, M. and Turner, T. (eds) (2010) *Readings for Learning to Teach in the Secondary School: A Companion to M Level Study*, Abingdon, Oxon: Routledge.

This book brings together key articles to develop and support student teachers' understanding of the theory, research and evidence base that underpins effective practice. Designed for all students engaging with M Level study, each reading is contextualised and includes questions to encourage reflection and help you engage with material critically. Annotated further reading for every section supports your own research and writing.

Capel, S., Leask, M. and Turner, T. (eds) (2013) *Learning to Teach in the Secondary School: A Companion to School Experience*, 6th edn, Abingdon, Oxon: Routledge.

This book offers a comprehensive, indepth and practical introduction to the skills needed to qualify as a teacher, and is designed to help you to develop those qualities that lead to good practice and a successful future in education. Unit 8, 'Your professional development', in particular is of great relevance.

Note

1   Under sections 5(5), (5A) and (5B) of the Education Act 2005 (as amended).

18 Developing your knowledge, skills and understanding for teaching PE

Susan Capel and Margaret Whitehead

Introduction

The quality of PE teaching, and hence of pupils' learning, is down to every single PE teacher; to each and every one of you. Throughout, this book has emphasised that your work in PE should have the learner as your focus; the needs of the pupils you are teaching are most important in all aspects of your work and they must have first consideration. The activity or material is simply the vehicle through which learning takes place.

Throughout this book you have been introduced to some of the knowledge, skills and understanding you need to teach PE effectively. Although a number of different aspects of knowledge, skills and understanding have been introduced – some as a specific focus, others tangentially – the focus has largely been on pedagogical content knowledge. There is a range of other knowledge, skills and understanding you need to teach PE effectively, much of which has not been covered in this book. Shulman (1987) identified seven categories of knowledge. In addition, in order to be an effective PE teacher it is important that you have knowledge about yourself. The first part of this chapter looks at Shulman's knowledge bases and gives examples of how they are applicable to teaching PE. It then looks at the importance of knowledge about yourself.

Objectives

At the end of this chapter you should be able to:

- recognise the importance of having good knowledge, skills and understanding in a range of knowledge bases to teach PE effectively;
- understand the importance of having knowledge of yourself and how this impacts on your development and application of knowledge, skills and understanding to teach PE effectively;
- understand the importance of reflection in using your knowledge, skills and understanding to promote and support pupils' learning;

(continued)

(continued)

- appreciate that all elements of teaching are significant to promote learning;
- recognise that at the end of your ITE you have only developed part of the knowledge, skills and understanding you need to teach PE effectively;
- appreciate that it is important to be committed to continuing to develop your knowledge, skills and understanding across all knowledge bases to improve your teaching of PE to all pupils continually.

Check the requirements of your initial teacher education (ITE) to see which relate to this chapter.

Effective PE teaching

Before considering the knowledge, skills and understanding you need to teach PE effectively, reference is made in this chapter and elsewhere to effective PE teacher/teaching, but what does effective mean? Reference to effective teaching in general and effective PE teaching in particular generally refers to teacher behaviours and classroom processes and practices that promote better pupil outcomes. Thus, effective PE teachers focus on pupil outcomes and adopt behaviours and classroom processes and practices that enable pupils to achieve those outcomes. A review by Ho and Sammons (2013: 2) into effective teaching identified that effective teachers:

- are clear about instructional goals;
- are knowledgeable about curriculum content and the strategies for teaching this;
- communicate to their pupils what is expected of them, and why;
- make expert use of existing instructional materials in order to devote more time to practices that enrich and clarify the content;
- are knowledgeable about their pupils, adapting instruction to their needs and anticipating misconceptions in their existing knowledge;
- teach pupils metacognitive strategies and give them opportunities to master them;
- address higher- as well as lower-level cognitive objectives;
- monitor pupils' understanding by offering regular, appropriate feedback;
- integrate their instruction with that in other subject areas;
- accept responsibility for pupil outcomes.

As this list illustrates, to be an effective PE teacher you need to draw on a range of knowledge, skills and understanding and integrate this together in order for pupils to achieve intended learning outcomes. Now complete Task 18.1.

> **Task 18.1 Effective PE teaching**
>
> Critically analyse Ho and Sammons' (2013) list, paying particular attention to both any knowledge, skills and understanding listed which you think is less important in PE teaching and any that you think needs to be added to the list to describe effective PE teaching. Critically reflect on the extent of your knowledge, skills and understanding in each area on your list. Discuss with your tutor how you might develop your knowledge, skills and understanding further in areas you identify as needing further development.
>
> Using the list above and drawing on other sources, write a 2,500-word reflective essay entitled 'A critical consideration of the key aspects of effective PE teaching'.
>
> In your professional development portfolio (PDP) store your list of the knowledge, skills and understanding you need to develop and record your development in each area during the course of your ITE and beyond. Also store your essay in your PDP as evidence of Masters level work.

Knowledge, skills and understanding you need for teaching

This book is not comprehensive. Although a number of different aspects of knowledge, skills and understanding have been introduced, the focus has largely been on pedagogical content knowledge. There is, therefore, other knowledge, skills and understanding you need beyond that covered in this book. The next section of the chapter focuses on the range of knowledge, skills and understanding you need for teaching.

One frequently used categorisation of knowledge for teaching is that of Shulman (1987), who identified seven knowledge bases that student teachers need to develop:

- content knowledge (the principles of conceptual organisation and of enquiry in the subject). It includes what Schwab (1964) called substantive knowledge (knowing which are the important concepts and skills in the subject) and syntactic knowledge (knowing how the concepts and skills are structured and organised within the subject);
- curriculum knowledge (the materials and programmes that are teachers' 'tools of the trade');
- general pedagogical knowledge (the broad principles and strategies of classroom management and organisation applicable to teaching in general);
- pedagogical content knowledge (the knowledge which enables teachers to frame their content knowledge in a context-specific way, which helps them to communicate the subject matter to pupils effectively);
- knowledge of learners and their characteristics, including the empirical or social knowledge of learners in general (what pupils of a particular age range are like, how they behave in schools/classrooms, their interests and preoccupations, their social nature, how contextual factors such as weather or specific events can affect their work and

behaviour and the nature of the pupil–teacher relationship) and cognitive knowledge of learners (knowledge of child development which informs practice and knowledge about what a particular group of learners can and cannot know, do or understand that comes from regular contact with a specific group of learners);

- knowledge of educational contexts (teaching contexts, ranging from the workings of the group, classroom, school governance/financing, to the character of communities and cultures, including the type and size of school, the catchment area, the class size, the extent and quality of support for teachers, the amount of feedback teachers receive on their performance, the quality of relationships in the school, and the expectations and attitudes of the headteacher, that have a significant impact on teaching performance);

- knowledge of educational ends, purposes, values and philosophical and historical influences (the purposeful activity through short-term goals for a lesson or series of lessons and long-term goals of intrinsically valuable experience or eventual value to a society).

Each of these knowledge bases is now considered in turn.

Content knowledge

Content knowledge is the principles of conceptual organisation and of enquiry in the subject, but what is content knowledge for PE?

There are different views as to what comprises content knowledge for PE. Many would argue that content knowledge comprises those activities included in the curriculum or even just sports activities. However, if this is how content knowledge is viewed, and is all the content knowledge that PE teachers focus on developing, we would argue that this is too limiting and does not provide PE teachers with the underpinning knowledge they need to understand the subject and hence to facilitate pupils' learning.

We would suggest that content knowledge for PE is more than activities included in the curriculum or sports activities and that the substantive knowledge (i.e. the important concepts and skills in the subject) comprises an understanding of the nature of movement. There are different ways of looking at movement and the principles or constituents underpinning it. Some of these are considered in other chapters in this book, e.g. Laban's principles of movement (see Chapter 4), biomechanical, kinesiological, physiological, psychological and sociological (see Chapter 11). As examples, Laban's principles underpin the range of movement capacities pupils need to participate in all physical activity, biomechanical principles underpin learning/teaching points for mastery of a skill and aspects of physiology underpin a teacher's ability to encourage pupils to adopt healthy, active lifestyles. These basic principles combine to facilitate an understanding of the way basic skills are developed and refined in their application for use in physical activities. Without such understanding, it is argued, you cannot, for example, understand the curriculum content you are teaching, provide feedback to help each pupil improve their skills or provide pupils with the knowledge and understanding needed to take responsibility to pursue a physically active life. Now complete Task 18.2.

> ### Task 18.2 Understanding movement content knowledge
>
> List different ways of viewing movement within each of the following perspectives: Laban's principles, biomechanical, kinesiological, physiological, psychological and sociological. Identify areas in which you need to develop your knowledge and understanding and seek to improve your knowledge and understanding in these areas.
>
> Read around each of these ways of viewing movement and write a 2,500-word essay on 'How different ways of viewing movement enable you to understand the curriculum content you are teaching in your placement school'.
>
> Store your areas for development and your progress, as well as your essay, in your PDP to provide evidence of Masters level work.

Curriculum knowledge

The curriculum you are teaching in your placement school may be written by the school or it may be part of a larger curriculum framework, e.g. National Curriculum for Physical Education (NCPE). It is important to understand this curriculum as it 'comprises the materials and programmes that are teachers' "tools of the trade"'. It will have, for example, underpinning ends, purposes, aims and goals identifying what it is aiming to achieve, the range of content to be taught and how progression is nurtured/realised from the time pupils start school to the time they leave school. It may also identify other aspects relevant to the teaching of the curriculum, for example, levels of attainment pupils should achieve at particular points. Now complete Task 18.3.

> ### Task 18.3 Curriculum knowledge
>
> Read the overarching curriculum document which underpins the PE curriculum in your placement school (e.g. the NCPE). Write down what the ends, purposes, aims and goals of the curriculum are, what range of content it includes, how progression is promoted from the time pupils start in the school to the time they leave school, how what should be taught in the secondary school builds on the curriculum in the primary age phase, and any other requirements specified which you consider relevant. Discuss your understanding of the curriculum with another student teacher and write an essay on 'How the ends, purposes, aims and goals of the curriculum inform the implementation of the content in schools generally and inform your teaching in your placement school specifically'. Store this information in your PDP for future reference and to provide evidence of Masters level work.

As the PE curriculum you are teaching in your placement school is likely to be broad and balanced, it is important that you understand how the content you teach on school placement fits into the broad and balanced curriculum and that you have the knowledge, skills and understanding to teach the curriculum. The broad range of categories of activities included in the curriculum you are teaching may include, for example, athletics, dance, games, gymnastics, outdoor and adventurous activities, swimming and water activities. However, even within each category there are a range of types of activity and furthermore specific activities that can be taught. As an example, games can be classified into four different types, each comprised of specific activities – or games:

- invasion games – in which the objective is to invade another team's half of the space or playing area. Specific activities include, for example, basketball, football, hockey, netball and rugby;
- net/wall games – in which the objective is to send an object over a net or off a wall into the most open space. Specific activities include, for example, badminton, tennis, squash and volleyball;
- striking/fielding games – in which the objective is to strike a ball with a bat to open spaces. Specific activities include, for example, baseball, cricket and softball;
- target games – in which the objective is to send an object towards a target. Specific activities include, for example, archery and golf.

Now complete Task 18.4.

Task 18.4 Range of activities taught within PE

Using the example of the four different types of games, add to each of these types any other specific activities you might teach in your placement school. Then identify and list types of activity that could be included in each of the other five categories of activities (athletics, dance, gymnastics, outdoor and adventurous activities, swimming and water activities), as well as any others that are included in the PE curriculum in your placement school (e.g. health-related or fitness activities) and any 14-19 accredited qualifications which pupils can work towards. Identify how each category of activity can be classified into types of activity and the principles underlying the classification. Add examples of specific activities to each type of activity. Discuss your thoughts with another student teacher to inform both your developing understanding of the curriculum and the development of your knowledge and skills. Store the information in your PDP.

Task 18.4 raises a couple of points. First, in PE, the curriculum content is the vehicle through which learning takes place. There is a wide possible range of types of activity and activities themselves that can be included in any PE curriculum. In order for there to be breadth and balance in the PE curriculum decisions have to be made about, for example:

- how many categories, types and specific activities can be taught in the time available so that pupils move beyond an introductory level in a number of activities;
- how long should be spent on each category, type or specific activity and when, e.g. is the same activity taught in successive years or are different activities taught?;

- whether the focus should be on highlighting the principles, with specific activities used as an example of a category or type of activity or on teaching (a limited number of) specific activities;
- how much time is given to pupils developing their knowledge, skills and understanding of principles to help inform their choices of specific activities in which to participate outside and after they leave school.

The curriculum may also include accredited qualifications which pupils can work towards, e.g. the 14–19 Curriculum in England, Wales and Northern Ireland (see Chapter 14).

Second, it is unlikely that you will have good knowledge in each and every one of these categories, types and specific activities – although once you know which category, type or specific activity you are teaching, there is plenty of material to inform the development of your knowledge and understanding. In order to develop your knowledge and understanding, you may need to practise on your own, or with others, particular categories of activity, types of activity or a specific activity you are likely to teach. This is the equivalent of developing curriculum knowledge in, say English, where you would perhaps need to read and analyse particular books.

General pedagogical knowledge

You are a teacher first and a PE teacher second; therefore it is important to understand the broad principles and strategies of classroom management and organisation applicable to teaching in general. It is also important because there may be school-specific policies which you are required to follow, e.g. on behaviour management. General pedagogical knowledge is the focus of *Learning to Teach in the Secondary School* (Capel *et al.* 2013). You may find it useful to use units from that book in conjunction with the subject-specific chapter in this book which focuses on pedagogical content knowledge (see below).

Pedagogical content knowledge

Pedagogical content knowledge is the subject-specific application of general pedagogical knowledge. Pedagogical content knowledge enables you to frame your content knowledge in a context-specific way, which helps you to communicate the subject matter to pupils effectively.

Not all pupils are as keen on PE or physical activity as perhaps you were or are not keen on PE at all and hence do not participate in any physical activity outside of PE lessons. Assuming one of the aims of the PE curriculum in which you are working is for pupils to develop confidence, physical competence, motivation, knowledge and understanding to take responsibility to participate in physical activity outside and after they leave school, how you teach is as important as, if not more important than, what you teach: the curriculum content. It is therefore important that you have a good understanding of pedagogical content knowledge that can support pupils in working towards achieving the ends, purposes, aims and goals of the curriculum to which you are working and also that you develop your knowledge, skills and understanding in each of these aspects. In Chapter 11 the importance of developing your knowledge, skills and understanding in the largely pedagogical content knowledge covered in Chapters 2–10 was emphasised, as well as the importance of looking at that in an integrated way. You may want to return to that chapter now to refresh your memory.

Knowledge of learners and their characteristics

As has been stressed throughout this book, your work in PE should have the learner as your focus to promote the learning of each individual pupil. In order to achieve this, you need to understand pupils at a particular age in general, what a particular group of learners can and cannot know, do or understand that comes from regular contact with a specific group of learners, and more specifically, you need to know each individual pupil.

For example, as a PE teacher it is important to understand child development – in particular, puberty and its impact on the pupils you are teaching. It is important to understand, for example, that there is no set age when puberty starts: the age at which puberty begins and the rate of development differ between individuals. Generally, girls develop quicker than boys. Most girls begin puberty at 8–14 years of age, with the average age being 11 years. Most boys begin puberty at 9–14 years of age, with the average age being 12 years. Most girls and boys reach maturity within four years of starting puberty. However, some of the pupils you teach might have experienced puberty earlier than normal or puberty might occur later than normal. This variation impacts on pupils you teach in a number of ways.

Puberty causes a number of changes to occur which can be categorised as:

- *physical changes* – including rapid growth spurts;
- *psychological changes* – which can cause teenagers to become moody, self-conscious and aggressive;
- *behavioural changes* – which can cause some teenagers to experiment with new and potentially risky activities, such as smoking, drinking alcohol and sex.

You may want to read further about child development, as well as other knowledge you need of learners, if you identify a need to develop your knowledge about learners and their characteristics. Identifying other knowledge is a focus of Task 18.5 (see below).

Knowledge of educational contexts

Your teaching does not occur in a vacuum; it is important to understand the context in which you are teaching. As an example, the expectations and attitudes of the headteacher have a significant impact on teaching performance. In PE, the headteacher may, for example, be more interested in having winning school teams than on all pupils developing the confidence, physical competence, motivation, knowledge and understanding to take responsibility to participate in physical activity throughout life. Unless PE teachers make a strong case to the head as to the value of PE for all pupils in its own right, the expectations of the head may impact on the teaching in PE. As another example, pupils in a particular year group in your placement school may be taught in mixed-ability, streamed or setted (or banded) groups for different subjects. Further, what happens in PE might be different to what happens in 'academic' subjects. For example, pupils may be streamed or setted for 'academic' subjects and be in mixed-ability groups for PE. Each of these different means of grouping pupils sends a message to pupils which in turn can impact on their motivation in PE. Identifying other knowledge is a focus of Task 18.5 (below).

Your development as a teacher does not stop at the end of your ITE. Chapter 17 looked at your development beyond your ITE. Another aspect of your knowledge of educational contexts – the extent and quality of support for teachers and the amount of feedback teachers receive on their performance – will be important in your early professional development after you qualify as a teacher.

Knowledge of educational ends, purposes, values and philosophical and historical influences

The PE curriculum you are teaching in your placement school has a history and has been developed to achieve broad ends, purposes, aims and goals. However, it also fits into a broader school curriculum (for example, an NCPE will fit into a broader National Curriculum (NC)). It is important that you are aware of the history of the subject and also the wider context in which it is operating, so that you can see how (and why) what is being taught today has developed over time. It is also important that the units of work and lesson plans you develop are working towards achieving the ends, purposes, aims and goals of the PE curriculum and schemes of work towards which you are working in your placement school. It is also important that you understand how the PE curriculum articulates with the overall curriculum in your placement school and any wider NC. Now complete Task 18.5.

Task 18.5 Developing your knowledge in three of Shulman's (1987) knowledge bases
Working with another student teacher, list the knowledge, skill and understanding you need to develop in each of the last three of Shulman's (1987) knowledge bases, above: 'knowledge of learners and their characteristics'; 'knowledge of educational contexts'; and 'knowledge of educational ends, purposes, values and philosophical and historical influences'. Then, identify your level of knowledge in each of these (1 = good knowledge; 3 = average knowledge; 5 = little/no knowledge). Where you identify areas for development, discuss with your tutor how you can develop this knowledge.
Write a short reflection on why this knowledge is important and how it informs your teaching.
In your PDP, store your list and the areas you identify for development and record your progress in developing this knowledge. Also store your reflection in your PDP as evidence of Masters level work.

Although Shulman (1987) identified seven knowledge bases, it is generally recognised that, in addition, as teachers, you need knowledge of yourself.

Knowledge of yourself

It is important to remember that teaching is not value-neutral. For example, what content you choose to teach and how you choose to teach it, what you choose (maybe subconsciously) to learn/take in during your ITE or later as a teacher and apply in your (placement) school, what knowledge (and aspects of knowledge) you choose to prioritise and what you choose to ignore are all related to your background and to your beliefs.

One example of how beliefs influence your teaching is seen through looking at aims. The aims to which you should be working might be stated in the curriculum. For example, the NCPE in England aims to ensure that all pupils:

- develop competence to excel in a broad range of physical activities;
- are physically active for sustained periods of time;
- engage in competitive sports and activities;
- lead healthy, active lives.

As another example, the Singapore teaching and learning syllabus (Ministry of Education (MOE) 2014: 3) states: 'the purpose of physical education is to enable students to demonstrate individually and with others the physical skills, practices, and values to enjoy a lifetime of active, healthy living'. The goals are stated as:

1   Acquire a range of movement skills to participate in a variety of physical activities.
2   Understand and apply movement concepts, principles and strategies in a range of physical activities.
3   Demonstrate safe practices during physical and daily activities with respect to themselves, others and the environment.
4   Display positive personal and social behaviour across different experiences.
5   Acquire and maintain health-enhancing fitness through regular participation in physical activities.
6   Enjoy and value the benefits of living a physically active and healthy life (MOE 2014: 8).

Each of these two lists of aims will generate a particular curriculum and particular pedagogy. However, although ends, purposes, aims and goals are identified in a curriculum, they are still open to interpretation. How you interpret these ends, purposes, aims and goals and therefore what, and particularly, how you teach is mediated by your beliefs. It is salutary to realise that it is possible that you may encounter situations where you know what the ends, purposes, aims and goals of the curriculum are, but believe that other ends are more important. Similarly, you may find yourself working in a department with colleagues who hold very different views from yours. Either of these situations could put you in a challenging position. For example, if you believe that it is important for all pupils to develop confidence, physical competence, motivation, knowledge and understanding to take responsibility to participate in physical activity throughout life but the others in the school or department believe that selecting the most able pupils to compete in the inter-school competitions is the most important aspect of work in PE, there is the likelihood of conflict. You will need to negotiate with colleagues to find common ground so that your teaching can be true to your beliefs but at the same time satisfy aspects of the school or department aspirations. It is as well to remember that, in taking up a job, you need to ensure that your beliefs are broadly in line with those of the school or department. Chapter 16 looked at your beliefs, an important aspect of knowing yourself as a teacher.

The importance of reflection

To understand your beliefs and how these impact on your teaching of PE, as well as to evaluate the impact of your teaching on pupils' learning, you need to reflect on all aspects of your teaching. Chapter 15 focused on reflective practice.

It is important that you do not just copy how you were taught; it is also important that you are teaching, not just organising and instructing. Therefore your reflection needs to focus on executing your lessons skilfully and appropriately so that all your work focuses on the pupils and their learning. However, it also needs to go beyond that. Teaching is more than a science – there is also an art to teaching (see introduction).

Summary and key points

As stated at the start of the chapter, the quality of PE teaching, and hence of pupils' learning, is down to every single PE teacher; to each and every one of you. Although what you teach is very important and developing good content knowledge in the range of types of activity, category of activity and individual activities you are going to teach is likely to be one of your priorities, especially as you are starting out in your ITE, it is important to remember that your knowledge of types of activity and specific activities needs to be underpinned by a good knowledge of movement. It is also important to remember that the activity or material is simply the vehicle through which learning takes place and that your primary focus should be on the learner. The needs of the pupils you are teaching are most important in all aspects of your work and what and how you teach should be selected for a particular group and particular individuals at a particular time. In order to be able to do this effectively, you need to work towards developing your knowledge, skills and understanding in Shulman's seven knowledge bases to enable you to give them serious consideration in all aspects of your teaching. It also requires you to integrate your knowledge from the different knowledge bases.

In Chapter 11 the focus was on learner-centred teaching using a physical literacy perspective. Emphasis was placed on the need to see teaching not as comprising a cluster of knowledge and skills that you learn and use, but rather to view all that you are learning as providing a rich source of information and practices which you can draw on to cater for whichever class or individual with whom you are working. We reiterate that here: as a teacher, you need to bring together knowledge from a range of different knowledge bases.

It is also important to recognise that you do not just develop knowledge, skills and understanding in a vacuum and then deliver, i.e. you are not trained. Teaching is not value-neutral and you need to be educated through your ITE and beyond in respect of the nature of what you are doing, why and how. This requires you to have knowledge of yourself and particularly your beliefs. It also requires that you are reflective and reflexive.

Your ITE is only the beginning of your learning. Your learning and development will continue throughout your career as a teacher. As a start, your ability to apply some of the knowledge, skills and understanding covered in your ITE may not happen until you start out as a new teacher. Thus, you may want to revisit aspects of this book in general and this chapter in particular when you start teaching.

Check which requirements of your ITE you have addressed through this chapter.

Further reading

Capel, S., Leask, M. and Turner, T. (eds) (2013) *Learning to Teach in the Secondary School: A Companion to School Experience*, 6th edn, Abingdon, Oxon: Routledge.

This book considers a range of knowledge, skills and understanding needed for teaching generally. It largely focuses on general pedagogical knowledge. It should be read alongside this book which translates content from the generic into PE-specific application.

Ho, J. and Sammons, P. with Bakkum, L. (2013) *Effective Teaching: A Review of Research and Evidence*, Reading: CfBT Educational Trust.

This review of research is concerned with how to define a teacher's effectiveness and what makes an effective teacher. It draws out implications for improving classroom practice.

Kirk, D. (2010) *Physical Education Futures*, Abingdon, Oxon: Routledge.

In this book Kirk looks first at the dominant form of PE in schools today and some reasons for this. He then looks at possible futures and argues that for PE to remain in the school curriculum radical reform is needed in the longer term. If there is more of the same in PE he argues that the subject could face extinction from the curriculum. Reading this book will be useful to help you consider what you are doing, why and how in the name of PE.

References

afPE (Association for Physical Education) (2012) *Safe Practice in Physical Education and Sport*, 8th edn, Leeds: afPE/Coachwise.

Alderson, P. (2008) Children as researchers: participation rights and research methods, in P. Christensen and A. James (eds) *Research with Children: Perspectives and Practices*, 2nd edn, Abingdon, Oxon: Routledge, pp. 276-290.

Aldous, D. and Brown, D. (2010) 'Framing bodies of knowledge within the acoustics of the school: exploring pedagogical transition through newly qualified physical education teacher experiences', *Sport, Education and Society*, 15, 4: 411-429.

Allen, M. and Toplis, R. (2013) Student teacher's role and responsibilities, in S. Capel, M. Leask and T. Turner (eds) *Learning to Teach in the Secondary School: A Companion to School Experience*, 6th edn, Abingdon, Oxon: Routledge, pp. 25-41.

Allen, T. (2013) Drivers and barriers to raising achievement – research paper for Ofsted's 'Access and achievement in education 2013 review'. Online, available at: http://www.ofsted.gov.uk/accessandachievement (accessed 8 December 2014).

Almond, L. and Whitehead, M.E. (2012a) 'Physical literacy: Clarifying the nature of the concept', *Physical Education Matters*, 7, 1, Spring: 68-71.

Almond, L. and Whitehead, M.E. (2012b) 'The value of physical literacy', *Physical Education Matters*, 7, 2, Summer: 61-63.

Almond, L. and Whitehead, M. (2012c) 'Translating physical literacy into practice for all teachers', *Physical Education Matters*, 7, 3, Autumn: 67-70.

Ames, C. (1992) Achievement goals, motivational climate and motivational processes, in G. C. Roberts (ed.) *Motivation in Sport and Exercise*, Champaign, IL: Human Kinetics, pp. 161-176.

Anderson, L.W., Krathwohl, D.R., Airasain, P.W., Cruikshank, K.A., Mayer, R.R., Pintrich, P.R., Raths, J. and Wittrock, M.C. (eds) (2001) *A Taxonomy for Learning, Teaching and Assessing – A Revision of Bloom's Taxonomy of Educational Objectives*, complete edition, New York: Addison Wesley Longman.

Arends, D. and Kilcher, A. (2010) *Teaching for Student Learning: Becoming an Accomplished Teacher*, Abingdon, Oxon: Routledge.

ARG (Assessment Reform Group) (1999) *Assessment for Learning: Beyond the Black Box*, Cambridge: University of Cambridge School of Education.

ARG (Assessment Reform Group) (2002) *Assessment for Learning: 10 Principles*, Cambridge: University of Cambridge, Assessment Reform Group.

Argyris, C. and Schon, D. (1974) *Theory into Practice: Increasing Professional Effectiveness*, San Francisco, CA: Jossey-Bass.

Bailey, K. and Nunan, D. (eds) (1996) *Voices from the Language Classroom*, Cambridge: Cambridge University Press.

Bailey, R. (2002) 'Questioning as a teaching strategy in physical education', *The Bulletin of Physical Education*, 38, 2: 119-126.

Bailey, R. (2006) 'Physical education and sport in schools: a review of benefits and outcomes', *Journal of School Health*, 76, 8: 397-401.

Bailey, R., Morley, D. and Dismore, H. (2009) 'Talent development in physical education: a national survey of policy and practice in England', *Physical Education and Sport Pedagogy*, 14, 1: 59-72.

Bartlett, R. (2014) *Introduction to Sports Biomechanics: Analysing Human Movement Patterns*, Abingdon, Oxon: Routledge.

Beaumont, G. (2007) 'Health and safety', *Physical Education Matters*, 2, 1: 31.

Beaumont, G. (2008) 'Cotton wool kids: risk and children', *Physical Education Matters*, 2, 1: 31.

Bell, J. (2010) *Doing your Research Project: A Guide for First-time Researchers in Education, Health and Social Science*, 5th edn, Maidenhead, Berks: Open University Press.

Benn, T., Pfister, G. and Jawad, H. (eds) (2011) *Muslim Women and Sport (Routledge Studies in Physical Education and Youth Sport)*, Abingdon, Oxon: Routledge.

Bennett, N. (1976) *Teaching Styles and Pupil Progress*, London: Open Books.

BERA (British Educational Research Association) (2011) *Ethical Guidelines for Educational Research*, Southwell: BERA. Online, available at: http://www.bera.ac.uk (accessed 8 December 2014).

Berstein, E., Phillips, S.R. and Silverman, S. (2011) 'Attitudes and perceptions of middle school students toward competitive activities in physical education', *Journal of Teaching in Physical Education*, 30: 69-83.

Best, D. (1985) *Feeling and Reason in the Arts*, London: Allen & Unwin.

Bhopal, K. (2004) 'Gypsy travellers and education: changing needs and changing perceptions', *British Journal of Educational Studies*, 52, 1: 47-64.

Biddle, S.J.H. (2001) Enhancing motivation in physical education, in G.C. Roberts (ed.) *Advances in Motivation in Sport and Exercise*, Champaign, IL: Human Kinetics, pp. 101-128.

Biggs, J. and Tang, C. (2007) *Teaching for Quality Learning at University*, 3rd edn, Buckingham: SRHE (Society for Research in Higher Education) and Open University Press.

Black, P. and Wiliam, D. (1998) *Inside the Black Box: Raising Standards through Classroom Assessment*, London: Kings College.

Black, P. and Wiliam, D. (2002) *Working Inside the Black Box: Assessment for Learning in the Classroom*, London: Kings College.

Black, P., Harrison, C., Lee, C., Marshall, B. and William, D. (2003) *Assessment for Learning: Putting it into Practice*, Maidenhead, Berks: Open University Press.

Blair, R. (2013) An evaluation of a continuing professional development programme for community football coaches delivering physical education lessons in primary schools. Unpublished PhD thesis, Brunel University.

Bloom, B., Englehart, M.D., Furst, E.J., Hill, W.H. and Krathwohl, D.R. (eds) (1956) *Taxonomy of Educational Objectives: The Classification of Educational Goals, Handbook I: Cognitive Domain*. New York: D. McKay.

Bowler, M., Bassett, S. and Newton, A. (2013) Assessing pupils' learning, in S. Capel and P. Breckon (eds) *A Practical Guide to Teaching Physical Education in the Secondary School*, 2nd edn, Abingdon, Oxon: Routledge, pp. 197-210.

Branden, N. (1995) *The Six Pillars of Self-Esteem*, New York: Bantam.

Brown, G.A. and Edmondson, R. (1984) Asking questions, in E. C. Wragg (ed.) *Classroom Teaching Skills*, London: Croom Helm, pp. 97-120.

Bruner, J. (1966) *Towards a Theory of Instruction*, New York: WW Norton.

Burton, D. (2013) Ways pupils learn, in S. Capel, M. Leask and T. Turner (eds) *Learning to Teach in the Secondary School: A Companion to School Experience*, 6th edn, Abingdon, Oxon: Routledge, pp. 307-324.

Capel, S. and Blair, R. (2013) Why do physical education teachers adopt a particular way of teaching? in S. Capel and M. Whitehead (eds) *Debates in Physical Education*, Abingdon, Oxon: Routledge.

Capel, S. and Blair, R. (2014) Understanding your views about physical education and how this impacts on your teaching and pupils' learning, in S. Capel and P. Breckon (eds) *A Practical Guide to Teaching Physical Education in the Secondary School*, 2nd edn, Abingdon, Oxon: Routledge, pp. 20-29.

Capel, S. and Breckon, P. (2014) *A Practical Guide to Teaching Physical Education in the Secondary School*, 2nd edn, Abingdon, Oxon: Routledge.

Capel, S. and Piotrowski, S. (eds) (2000) *Issues in Physical Education*, London: RoutledgeFalmer.

Capel, S. and Whitehead, M. (eds) (2013) *Debates in Physical Education*, Abingdon, Oxon: Routledge.

Capel, S., Blair, R. and Longville, J. (2014) Teaching to enable intended learning outcomes to be achieved, in S. Capel and P. Breckon (eds) *A Practical Guide to Teaching Physical Education in the Secondary School*, 2nd edn, Abingdon, Oxon: Routledge, pp. 158-165.

Capel, S., Breckon, P. and O'Neil, J. (2006) *A Practical Guide to Teaching Physical Education in the Secondary School*, Abingdon, Oxon: Routledge.

Capel, S., Leask, M. and Turner, T. (eds) (2010) *Readings for Learning to Teach in the Secondary School: A Companion to M Level Study*, Abingdon, Oxon: Routledge.

Capel, S., Leask, M. and Turner, T. (eds) (2013) *Learning to Teach in the Secondary School: A Companion to School Experience*, 6th edn, Abingdon, Oxon: Routledge.

Carr, W. and Kemmis, S. (1986) *Becoming Critical: Education, Knowledge and Action Research*, Lewes: Falmer Press.

Casbon, C. and Spackman, L. (2005) *Assessment for Learning in Physical Education*, Leeds: British Association of Advisers and Lecturers in Physical Education/Coachwise Business Solutions.

Central Advisory Council for Education (1967) *Children and their Primary Schools: A report of the Central Advisory Council for Education (England) (the Plowden Report)*, London: Her Majesty's Stationery Office.

Chappell, A. (2014) Safe practice, risk assessment and risk management, in S. Capel and P. Breckon (eds) *A Practical Guide to Teaching Physical Education in the Secondary School*, 2nd edn, Abingdon, Oxon: Routledge.

Child, D. (2007) *Psychology and the Teacher*, London: Continuum.

Christensen, P. and James, A. (2008) *Research with Children: Perspectives and Practices*, 2nd edn, Abingdon, Oxon: Routledge.

Coates, J. and Vickerman, P. (2008) 'Let the children have their say: children with special educational needs experiences of physical education – a review', *Support for Learning*, 23, 4: 168–175.

Coates, J. and Vickerman, P. (2013) 'A review of methodological strategies for consulting children with special educational needs in physical education', *European Journal of Special Needs Education*, 28, 3: 333–347.

Cohen, L., Manion, L. and Morrison, K. (2004) *A Guide to Teaching Practice*, 5th edn, London: RoutledgeFalmer.

Cohen, L., Manion, L. and Morrison, K. (2011) *Research Methods in Education*, 7th edn, Abingdon, Oxon: Routledge.

Cole, P.G. and Chan, L.K.S. (1994) *Teaching Principles and Practice*, 2nd edn, New York: Prentice Hall.

Cole, R. (2008) *Educating Everybody's Children: Diverse Teaching Strategies for Diverse Learners*, revised and expanded 2nd edn, Alexandria, VA: Association for Supervision and Curriculum Development. Online, available at: http://www.ascd.org/publications/books/107003.aspx (accessed 3 October 2014).

Cox, C.B. and Dyson, R.E. (eds) (1975) *Black Paper 1975 – The Fight for Education*, London: Dent.

Crouch, H. (1984) *Netball Coaching Manual*, Kingston-upon-Thames: Croner Publications.

Curtner-Smith, M., Hastie, P. and Kinchin, G. (2008) 'Influence of occupational socialization on beginning teachers' interpretation and delivery of sport education', *Sport, Education and Society*, 13, 1: 97–117.

Daniels, S. (2008) 'Physical education, school sport and traveller children', *PEM*, 13, 3: 32–37.

Davies, J. (2013) Young people's voices in PE, Guest lecture: Cardiff Metropolitan University.

Davies, P. (1990) *Differentiation Strategies, Based on an Internal Working Paper*, Cardiff: WJEC.

Davis, B. (2009) *Tools for Teaching: Learning Styles and Preferences*, 2nd edn, San Francisco: Jossey Bass.

Davis, R.J., Bull, C.R., Roscoe, J.V. and Roscoe, D.A. (2000) *Physical Education and the Study of Sport*, 4th edn, London: Mosby.

DCSF (Department for Children, Schools and Families) (2009) http://www.standards.dfes.gov.uk/schemes2/Secondary_PE/ (accessed 20 May 2014).

Deci, E.L. and Ryan, R.M. (1985) *Intrinsic Motivation and Self Determination in Human Behaviour*, New York: Plenum Press.

Deenihan, J. and MacPhail, A. (2013) 'A preservice teacher's delivery of sport education: influences, difficulties and continued use', *Journal of Teaching in Physical Education*, 32, 2: 166–185.

Delaney, T. (2009) *The Sociology of Sports: An Introduction*, Jefferson, NC: McFarland and Co.

DENI (Department of Education Northern Ireland) http://www.deni.gov.uk/ (accessed 8 December 2014).

Derri, V., Emmanoullidou, K., Vassilladou, O., Kioumourtzoglus, E. and Loza Olave, E. (2007) 'Academic learning time in physical education (ALT-PE): is it related to fundamental movement skill acquisition and learning?' *International Journal of Sport Science*, 3, 3: 12–23.

DES (Department of Education and Science) (1990) *Starting with Quality: Report of the Committee of Enquiry into the Quality of Educational Experiences Offered to 3–4 Year Olds*, London: HMSO.

DES/WO (Department of Education and Science and the Welsh Office) (1992) *Physical Education in the National Curriculum*, London: HMSO.

Dewar, A.M. and Lawson, H.A. (1984) 'The subjective warrant and recruitment into physical education', *Quest*, 36, 1: 15–25.

Dewey, J. (1933) *How We Think: A Restatement of the Relation of Reflective Thinking to the Educative Process*, Boston, MA: DC Heath.

DfE (Department for Education) (2011) *Teachers' Standards: Guidance for School Leaders, School Staff and Governing Bodies*, London: Crown.

DfE (Department for Education) (2013a) *The National Curriculum in England: Framework Document*, London: Crown. Ref: DFE-00183-2013. Online, available at: http://www.gov.uk/dfe/nationalcurriculum (accessed 8 December 2014).

DfE (Department for Education) (2013b) *School Teachers' Pay and Conditions Document 2013 and Guidance on School Teachers Pay and Conditions*, London: DfE.

DfE (Department for Education) (2013c) *Statutory Guidance on Induction for Newly Qualified Teachers (England)*, London: DfE.

DfE (Department for Education) (2013d) *Special Educational Needs Statistics*. Online, available at: https://www.gov.uk/government/statistics/special-educational-needs-in-england-january-2013 (accessed 24 December 2014).

DfE (Department for Education) (2014a) *The National Curriculum for England*, London: DfE. Online, available at: https://www.gov.uk/government/collections/national-curriculum (accessed 8 December 2014).

DfE (Department for Education) (2014b) *The National Curriculum for Physical Education*, London: HMSO. Online, available at: https://www.gov.uk/government/uploads/system/uploads/attachment_data/file/239086/SECONDARY_national_curriculum_-_Physical_education.pdf (accessed 12 August 2014).

DfE (Department for Education) (2014c) *Behaviour and Discipline in Schools. Advice for Head Teachers and Staff*, London: DfE. Ref: DFE-00023-2014. Online, available at: www.gov.uk/government/publications (accessed 8 December 2014).

DfE (Department for Education) (2014d) *SEND Code of Practice 0-25 Years*, London: HMSO.

DfE (Department for Education) (2014e) *Statutory Policies for Schools: Advice on the Policies and Documents that Governing Bodies and Proprietors of Schools are Required to Have by Law*, London: Crown.

DfE (Department for Education) (2014f) *Keeping Children Safe in Education: Statutory Guidance for Schools and Colleges*, London: Crown.

DfE (Department for Education) (2014g) Health and Safety: Advice on Legal Duties and Powers. For Local Authorities, School Leaders, School Staff and Governing Bodies, London: Crown.

DfE (Department for Education) (d.u) *School Performance Tables*, London: DfE. Online, available at: http://www.education.gov.uk/schools/performance/.

DfEE (Department for Education and Employment) (1998) *Health and Safety of Pupils on Educational Visits*, London: DfEE.

DfES (Department for Education and Skills) (2001) *The Special Educational Needs and Disability Act*, London: HMSO.

DfES (Department for Education and Skills) (2002) *Key Stage 3 National Strategy: Access and Engagement in Physical Education. Teaching Pupils for whom English is an Additional Language*, London: DfES: 0659/2002.

DfES (Department for Education and Skills) (2004a) *Key Stage 3 National Strategy: Pedagogy and Practice: Teaching and Learning in the Secondary School, Unit 7: Questioning*, London: DfES.

DfES (Department for Education and Skills) (2004b) *Key Stage 3 National Strategy: Pedagogy and Practice: Teaching and Learning in the Secondary School, Unit 12: Assessment for Learning*, London: DfES.

DfES (Department for Education and Skills) (2004c) *Key Stage 3 National Strategy: Pedagogy and Practice: Teaching and Learning in Secondary Schools, Unit 11: Active Engagement Techniques*, London: DfES.

Disability Rights Commission (2006) *The Disability Equality Duty*, London: Disability Rights Commission.

Dorobantu, M. and Biddle, S. (1997) 'The influence of situational and individual goals on intrinsic motivation of Romanian adolescents towards physical education', *European Yearbook of Sport Psychology*, 1: 148-165.

Dunn, R. and Griggs, S. (eds) (2000) *Practical Approaches to Using Learning Styles in Higher Education*, Wesport, CT: Bergin and Garvey.

Durrant, A. (2009) *An Introduction to Exercise and Sport for People who have Autism*, Amanda Durrant Publishers, available via Amazon.

Education Scotland Inspection and Review http://www.educationscotland.gov.uk/inspectionand review/.

Elbourn, J. (1999) *How to Develop and Monitor a Safe, Effective and Appropriate Physical Education Programme at Key Stages 3 and 4*, Bristol: Standards for Education.

Elliott, A.J. and Church, M.A. (1997) 'A hierarchical model of approach and avoidance achievement motivation', *Journal of Personality and Social Psychology*, 72: 218-232.

Elliott, J. (1991) *Action Research for Educational Change*, Milton Keynes: Open University Press.

Elliott, J. (2006) *Reflecting Where the Action is*, Abingdon, Oxon: Routledge.

Ennis C.D, Cothran, D.J. and Loftus, S.J (1997) 'The influence of teachers' educational beliefs on their knowledge organization', *Journal of Research and Development in Education*, 30, 2: 73-86.

Entwistle, N. (1992) *The Impact of Teaching on Learning Outcomes in Higher Education: A Literature Review*, Sheffield: USDU.

Epstein, J. (1989) Family structures and student motivation: A developmental perspective, in C. Ames and R. Ames (eds) *Research on Motivation in Education: Vol. 3*, New York: Academic Press, pp. 259–295.

Evans, J. (2014) 'Equity and inclusion in physical education PLC', *European Physical Education Review*, 20, 3: 319–334.

Evans, J. and Williams, T. (1989) Moving up and getting out: the classed and gendered career opportunities of physical education teachers, in T.J. Templin and P.G. Schempp (eds) *Socialization into Physical Education: Learning to Teach*, Indianapolis, Ind: Benchmark Press, pp. 235–248.

Everley, S. (2011) Evaluating adventure education experiences – the inside view, in M. Berry and C. Hodgson (eds) *Adventure Education: An Introduction*, Abingdon, Oxon: Routledge, pp. 126–145.

Fernandez-Balboa, J.M. (1997) 'Knowledge base in physical education teacher education: A proposal for a new era', *Quest*, 49: 161–181.

Fisher, R. (2009) *Creative Dialogue: Talk for thinking in the Classroom*, Abingdon, Oxon: Routledge.

Fitts, P.M. and Posner, M.I. (1967) *Human Performance*, Belmont, CA: Brooks Cole.

Fitzgerald, H. (2005) 'Still feeling like a spare piece of luggage? Embodied experiences of (dis)ability physical education and school sport', *Physical Education and Sport Pedagogy*, 10, 1: 41–59.

Fivush, R., Habermas, T., Waters, T. and Zaman, W. (2011) 'The making of autobiographical memory: Intersections of culture, narratives and identity', *International Journal of Psychology*, 46, 5: 321–345.

Floyd, R. (2007) *Manual of Structural Kinesiology*, 16th edn, New York: McGraw-Hill.

Fontana, A. and Frey, J. (2000) *The Interview: From Structured Questions to Negotiated Text*, 2nd edn, Thousand Oaks, CA: Sage.

Gallahue, D. L. and Donnelly, F. C. (2003) *Developmental Physical Education for All Children*, 4th edn, Champaign, IL: Human Kinetics.

Galton, M. and Croll, P. (1980) *Onside the Primary Classroom*, London: Routledge and Kegan Paul.

Gano-Overway, L. and Guivernau, M. (2014) 'Caring in the gym: reflections from middle school physical education teachers', *European Physical Education Review*, 20: 264–281.

Gardner, J. (ed.) (2012) *Assessment and Learning*, 2nd edn, London: Sage Publications Ltd.

Gervis, M. and Capel, S. (2013) Motivating pupils, in S. Capel, M. Leask and T. Turner (eds) *Learning to Teach in the Secondary School: A Companion to School Experience*, 6th edn, Abingdon, Oxon: Routledge, pp. 147–165.

Gibbs, G. (1988) *Learning by Doing: A Guide to Teaching and Learning Methods*, Oxford: Oxford Polytechnic Further Education Unit.

Goldman, E. (2004) *As Others See Us: Body Movement and the Art of Successful Communication*, Abingdon, Oxon: Routledge.

Goodley, D. (2014) *Dis/ability Studies: Theorising Disablism and Ableism*, Abingdon, Oxon: Routledge.

Government Equalities Office (2008) *The Equality Bill*, London: HMSO.

Graham, G. (1995) 'Physical education through students' eyes and in students' voice: implications for teachers and researchers', *Journal of Teaching in Physical Education*, 14: 478–482.

Grant, A., Short, N.P., Turner, L. and Turner, L. (2013) Storying life and lives, in N.P. Short, L. Turner and A. Grant (eds) *Contemporary British Autoethnography*, Rotterdam: Sense Publishers.

Grasha, A. (1996) *Teaching with Style*, Pittsburgh PA: Alliance Publishers.

Green, A. and Leask, M. (2013) What do teachers do? in S. Capel, M. Leask and T. Turner (eds) *Learning to Teach in the Secondary School: A Companion to School Experience*, 6th edn, Abingdon, Oxon: Routledge, pp. 9–24.

Green, K. (2000) 'Exploring the everyday 'philosophies' of physical education teachers from a sociological perspective', *Sport, Education and Society*, 5, 2: 109–129.

Green, K. and Hardman, K. (eds) (2005) *Physical Education Essential Issues*, London: Sage.

Griffin, L.L. and Butler, J.L. (2005) *Teaching Games for Understanding: Theory, Research and Practice*, Champaign, IL: Human Kinetics.

Grout, H. and Long, G. (2009) *Improving Teaching and Learning in Physical Education*, Maidenhead, Berks: Open University Press/McGraw Hill.

Grout, H., Long, G. and Taylor, S. (2011) *101 Classroom Games, Energise Learning in any Subject*, Champaign, IL: HumanKinetics.

GTCS (General Teaching Council Scotland) (2012) Information on induction and early professional development for teachers. Online, available at: http://www.in2teaching.org.uk/teacher-induction-scheme/teacher-induction-scheme.aspx (accessed 7 October 2014).

Guillaume, A.M. and Rudney, G.C. (1993) 'Student teachers' growth towards independence: An analysis of their changing concerns', *Teaching and Teacher Education*, 9, 1: 65-80.

Habermas, T. and Bluck, S. (2000) 'Getting a life: The emergence of the life story in adolescence', *Psychological Bulletin*, 126, 5: 248-269.

Haggarty, L. and Postlethwaite, K. (2010) 'An exploration of changes in thinking in the transition from student teacher to newly qualified teacher', *Research Papers in Education*, 27, 2: 241-262.

Hardy, C. and Mawer, M. (eds) (1999) *Learning and Teaching in Physical Education*, London: Falmer Press.

Harvey, S. and O'Donovan, T. (2013) 'Pre service physical education teachers' beliefs about competition in physical education', *Sport, Education and Society*, 18, 6: 767-787.

Hastings, S. (2006) 'Body language', *Times Educational Supplement*, 3 February: 17-18.

Haydn, T. (2013) 'First do no harm': assessment, pupil motivation and learning, in S. Capel, M. Leask and T. Turner (eds) *Learning to Teach in the Secondary School: A Companion to School Experience*, 6th edn, Abingdon, Oxon: Routledge, pp. 417-438.

Haydon, G. (2013) Aims of education, in S. Capel, M. Leask and T. Turner (eds) *Learning to Teach in the Secondary School: A Companion to School Experience*, 6th edn, Abingdon, Oxon: Routledge, pp. 457-467.

Hayes, S. and Stidder, G. (2013) *Equity and Inclusion in Physical Education*, 2nd edn, Abingdon, Oxon: Routledge.

Heath, S., Brooks, R., Cleaver, E. and Ireland, E. (2009) *Researching Young Peoples' Lives*, London: Sage.

Ho, J. and Sammons, P. with Bakkum, L. (2013) *Effective Teaching: A Review of Research and Evidence*, Reading: CfBT Educational Trust.

Hopkins, D. (2008) *A Teacher's Guide to Classroom Research*, 4th edn, Milton Keynes: Open University Press.

Hopple, C. and Graham, G. (1995) 'What children think, feel and know about physical fitness testing', *Journal of Teaching in Physical Education*, 14: 408-417.

Hoyle, E. (1975) Professionality, professionalism and control in teaching, in V. Houghton, R. McHugh and C. Morgan (eds) *Management in Education: The Management of Organisations and Individuals*, London: Ward Lock Educational in association with the Open University Press.

HSE (Health and Safety Executive) (2011) *Five Steps to Risk Assessment*, London: Crown.

HSE (Health and Safety Executive) (2013a) *Incident Reporting in Schools (Accidents, Diseases and Dangerous Occurrences): Guidance for Employers*, London: Crown.

HSE (Health and Safety Executive) (2013b) *Reporting Accidents and Incidents at Work: A Brief Guide to the Reporting of Injuries, Diseases and Dangerous Occurrences Regulations 2013 (RIDDOR)*, London: Crown.

Hughes, H. and Fleming, S. (2013) 'Play to learn: a case-study of parent/carer and child engagement with a physical activity website resource', *Education 3-13*: 1-13.

Hushman, G. and Napper-Owens, G. (2012) 'Strategies to reduce negative socialisation in the first years of teaching', *Strategies: A Journal for Physical and Sport Educators*, 25, 7: 8-10.

Hutchinson, C. (1993) 'Prospective teachers' perspectives on teaching physical education: an interview study on the recruitment phase of teacher socialization', *Journal of Teaching in Physical Education*, 12: 344-354.

Hutzler, Y. and Levi, I. (2008) 'Including children with a disability in physical education: general and specific attitudes of high-school students', *European Journal of Adapted Physical Activity*, 1, 2: 21-30.

Jarvis, M. (2014) *Brilliant Ideas for Using ICT in the Classroom: A Very Practical Guide for Teachers and Lecturers*, Abingdon, Oxon: Routledge.

Jensen, E. (2009) *Super Teaching: Learner Differences*, 4th edn, London: Corwin Press.

Jepson, M. and Walsh, B. (2013) Adolescence, health and well-being, in S. Capel, M. Leask and T. Turner (eds) *Learning to Teach in the Secondary School: A Companion to School Experience*, 6th edn, Abingdon, Oxon: Routledge, pp. 219-233.

John, P. (2010) Lesson planning and the student teacher: rethinking the dominant model, in S. Capel, M. Leask and T. Turner (eds) *Readings for Learning to Teach in the Secondary School*, Abingdon, Oxon: Routledge, pp. 64-78.

Jones, J. (2010) 'The role of assessment for learning in the management of primary to secondary transition: implications for language teachers', *The Language Learning Journal*, 38, 2: 175-191.

Jones, R., Potrac, P., Cushion, C. and Ronglan, L.T. (2011) *The Sociology of Sports Coaching*, Abingdon, Oxon: Routledge.

Jones, V. and Barber, L. (2014) Applying theories of learning to your practice, in S. Capel and P. Breckon (eds) *A Practical Guide to Teaching Physical Education in the Secondary School*, 2nd edn, Abingdon, Oxon: Routledge, pp. 129-144.

Joyce, B. and Weil, M. (1996) *Models of Teaching*, 5th edn, Boston, MA: Allyn and Bacon.

Joyce, B., Calhoun, E. and Hopkins, D. (2002) *Models of Learning Tools for Teaching*, 2nd edn, Buckingham: Open University Press.

Keay, J. (2013) Developing further as a teacher, in S. Capel, M. Leask and T. Turner (eds) *Learning to Teach in the Secondary School: A Companion to School Experience*, 6th edn, Abingdon, Oxon: Routledge, pp. 529–540.

Kelly, A., Devitt, C., O'Keefe, D. and Donovan, A.M. (2014) 'Challenges in implementing inclusive education in Ireland: principal's views of the reasons students aged 12+ are seeking enrollment to special schools', *Journal of Policy and Practice in Intellectual Disabilities*, 11, 1: 68–81.

Kelly, L. (1997) Safety in PE, in S. Capel (ed.) *Learning to Teach Physical Education in the Secondary School: A Companion to School Experience*, London: Routledge, pp. 115–129.

Killingbeck, M. (2012) Movement analysis in dance, in L. Sanders (ed.) *Dance Teaching and Learning: Shaping Practice*, London: Youth Dance England.

Kirk, D. (2010) *Physical Education Futures*, Abingdon, Oxon: Routledge.

Kirk, D., Nauright, J., Hanrahan, S., Macdonald, D. and Jobling, I. (1996) *The Sociocultural Foundations of Human Movement*, Melbourne: Macmillian.

Koshy, V. (2010) *Action Research for Improving Educational Practice: A Step-by-Step Guide*, 2nd edn, London: Sage Publications Ltd.

Kratzig, G. and Arbuthnott, K. (2006) 'Perceptual learning style and learning proficiency: a test of the hypothesis', *Journal of Education Psychology*, 98, 1: 238–246.

Kyriacou, C. (2009) *Effective Teaching in Schools: Theory and Practice*, 3rd edn, Cheltenham: Nelson Thornes.

Lambe, J. and Bones, R. (2006) 'Student teacher's perceptions about inclusive classroom teaching in Northern Ireland prior to teacher practice experience', *European Journal of Special Needs Education*, 21, 2: 167–186.

Lawrence, J. (2014) Creating an effective learning environment, in S. Capel and P. Breckon (eds) *A Practical Guide to Teaching Physical Education in the Secondary School*, 2nd edn, Abingdon, Oxon: Routledge, pp. 145–157.

Lawrence, J. and Capel, S. (2013) Getting your first post, in S. Capel, M. Leask and T. Turner (eds) *Learning to Teach in the Secondary School: A Companion to School Experience*, 6th edn, Abingdon, Oxon: Routledge, pp. 509–528.

Lawson, H. (1986) 'Occupational socialization and the design of teacher education programs', *Journal of Teaching in Physical Education*, 5, 2: 107–116.

Leach, J. and Moon, B. (1999) *Learners and Pedagogy*, London: Paul Chapman.

Leamnson, R. (1999) *Thinking about Teaching and Learning: Developing Habits with First Year College University Students*, Sterling, VA: Stylus.

Leask, M. (2013) Teaching styles, in S. Capel, M. Leask and T. Turner (eds) *Learning to Teach in the Secondary School: A Companion to School Experience*, 6th edn, Abingdon, Oxon: Routledge, pp. 345–359.

Leask, M. and Liversidge, T. (2013) Improving your teaching: an introduction to practitioner research, reflective practice and evidence-informed practice, in S. Capel, M. Leask and T. Turner (eds) *Learning to Teach in the Secondary School: A Companion to School Experience*, 6th edn, Abingdon, Oxon: Routledge, pp. 360–371.

Lee, H. and Curtner-Smith, M. (2011) 'Impact of occupational socialization on the perspectives and practices of sport pedagogy doctoral students', *Journal of Teaching in Physical Education*, 30, 3: 296–313.

Leslie, D. and Collins, S. (2013) Accountability, contractual and statutory duties, in S. Capel, M. Leask and T. Turner (eds) *Learning to Teach in the Secondary School: A Companion to School Experience*, 6th edn, Abingdon, Oxon: Routledge, pp. 541–550.

Lewin, C. and Solomon, Y. (2013) 'Silencing the school bell? Reflecting on one school's transformational journey', *International Review of Qualitative Research*, 6, 3: 376–394.

Lortie, D. (1975) *Schoolteacher: A Sociological Study*, Chicago: University of Chicago Press.

Lortie, D. (2002) *Schoolteacher: A Sociological Study*, 2nd edn, Chicago: University of Chicago Press.

Lowe, M. (2013) Active learning, in S. Capel, M. Leask and T. Turner (eds) *Learning to Teach in the Secondary School: A Companion to School Experience*, 6th edn, Abingdon, Oxon: Routledge, pp. 325–344.

McCullick, B.A., Lux, K.M., Belcher, D.G. and Davies, N. (2012) 'A portrait of the PETE major: re-touched for the early twenty-first century, *Physical Education and Sport Pedagogy*, 17, 2, April: 177–193.

Macfadyen, T. and Bailey, R. (2002) *Teaching Physical Education*, London: Continuum.

McKeough, A., Lupart, J. and Marini, A. (eds) (1995) *Teaching for Transfer: Fostering Generalization in Learning*, Mahwah NJ: Lawrence Erlbaum.

McKernan, J. (1996) *Curriculum Action Research: A Handbook of Methods and Resources for the Reflective Practitioner*, 2nd edn, London: Kogan Page.

MacPhail, A., Patton, K., Parker, M. and Tannehill, D. (2014) 'Leading by example: teacher educators' professional learning through communities of practice', *Quest*, 66, 1: 39–56.

Maher, A. and Macbeth, J. (2013) 'Physical education, resources and training: the perspective of special educational needs coordinators working in secondary schools in North-West England', *European Physical Education*, 19: 76–90.

Marland, M. (2002) *The Craft of the Classroom*, 3rd edn, London: Heinemann Educational.

Matanin, M. and Collier, C. (2003) 'Longitudinal analysis of pre service teacher's beliefs about teaching physical education', *Journal of Teaching in Physical Education*, 22: 153–168.

Mawer, M. (1995) *The Effective Teaching of Physical Education*, Harlow: Pearson Education.

Maynard, T. and Furlong, G.J. (1993) Learning to teach and models of mentoring, in D. McIntyre, H. Hagger and M. Wilkin (eds) *Mentoring: Perspectives on School-Based Teacher Education*, London: Kogan Page, pp. 69–85.

Metzler, M.W. (1989) 'A review of research on time in sport pedagogy', *Journal of Teaching in Physical Education*, 8, 2: 87–103.

Metzler, M.W. (1990) *Instructional Supervision for Physical Education*, Champaign, Ill.: Human Kinetics.

MOE (Ministry of Education) (2014) *Physical Education Teaching and Learning Syllabus*, Singapore: Ministry of Education.

Moon, J.A. (2004) *Reflection in Learning and Professional Development: Theory and Practice*, Abingdon, Oxon: RoutledgeFalmer.

Morgan, K. (2011) *Athletics Challenges*, 2nd edn, Abingdon, Oxon: Routledge.

Morgan, K. and Carpenter, P.J. (2002) 'Effects of manipulating the motivational climate in physical education lessons', *European Journal of Physical Education*, 8: 209–232.

Morgan, K., Kingston, K. and Sproule, J. (2005) 'Effects of different teaching styles, on the teacher behaviours that influence motivational climate in physical education', *European Physical Education Review*, 11, 3: 257–286.

Morley, D. and Bailey, R. (2006) *Meeting the Needs of Your Most Able Pupils: Physical Education and Sport* [with CD-ROM] Gifted and Talented Series, London: David Fulton.

Morley, D., Bailey, R., Tan, J. and Cooke, B. (2005) 'Inclusive physical education: teachers' views of teaching children with special educational needs and disabilities in physical education', *European Physical Education Review*, 11, 1: 84–107.

Mosston, M. and Ashworth, S. (2002) *Teaching Physical Education*, 5th edn, San Francisco, CA: Benjamin Cummings.

Mouratidis, A., Vansteenkiste, M., Lens, W. and Sideris, G. (2008) 'The motivating role of positive feedback in sport and physical education: evidence for a motivational model', *Journal of Sport and Exercise Psychology*, 30: 240–268.

Muijs, D. and Reynolds, D. (2011) *Effective Teaching: Evidence and Practice*, 3rd edn, London: Sage.

NCF (National Coaching Foundation) (1994) *Planning and Practice: Study Pack 6*, Leeds: NCF.

NCTL (National College of Teaching and Leadership) (2013) Online, available at: http://www.education.gov.uk/aboutdfe/executiveagencies/a00223538/nat-college-teach-leader (accessed 8 December 2014).

Nicholls, J.G. (1989) *The Competitive Ethos and Democratic Education*, Cambridge, MA: Harvard University Press.

Ntoumanis, N. (2001) 'A self-determination approach to the understanding of motivation in physical education', *British Journal of Educational Psychology*, 71: 225–242.

Ntoumanis, N. (2012) A self-determination theory perspective on motivation in sport and physical education: current trends and possible future research directions, in G.C. Roberts and D.C. Treasure (eds) *Motivation in Sport and Exercise*, Volume 3, Champaign, IL: Human Kinetics, pp. 91–128.

O'Bryant, C.P., O'Sullivan, M. and Raudensky, J. (2000) 'Socialization of prospective physical education teachers: the story of new blood', *Sport, Education and Society*, 5, 2: 177–193.

Observing and Analysing Pupils' Movement (OALM) CDRom. See The Movement Observation Series OCM and OALM at http://www.tacklesport.com/s/movement-observation/ (accessed 15 September 2014).

Observing Children Moving (OCM) CDRom. See The Movement Observation Series OCM and OALM at http://www.tacklesport.com/s/movement-observation/ (accessed 15 September 2014).

Oeser, O.A. (ed.) (1955) *Teacher, Pupil and Task*, New York: Harper and Row.

Ofqual (Office of Qualifications and Examinations Regulation) (2013) *Corporate Plan 2013-16*. Ref. Ofqual/13/5310. Online, available at: http://ofqual.gov.uk/documents/corporate-plan/ (accessed 4th May 2014).

Ofsted (Office for Standards in Education) (2003) *Quality and Standards in Secondary Initial Teacher Training*, London: GreenShires Print Group. Online, available at: http://www.ofsted.gov.uk/resources/ quality-and-standards-secondary-initial-teacher-training (accessed 19 March 2014).

Ofsted (Office for Standards in Education) (2008) *Assessment for Learning: The Impact of the National Strategy Support*. Online, available at: http://www.ofsted.gov.uk/resources/assessment-for-learning-impact-of-national-strategy-support (accessed 19 March 2014).

Ofsted (Office for Standards in Education) (2013a) *Beyond 2012 – Outstanding Physical Education for All. Physical Education in Schools 2008-12*. Online, available at: http://www.ofsted.gov.uk/resources/ beyond-2012-outstanding-physical-education-for-all (accessed 3 October 2014).

Ofsted (Office for Standards in Education) (2013b) *Initial Teacher Education Inspection Handbook*, Manchester: Ofsted.

Ofsted (Office for Standards in Education) (2014a) *The Framework for School Inspection*, Manchester: Ofsted.

Ofsted (Office for Standards in Education) (2014b) *School Inspection Handbook*, Manchester: Crown.

Ofsted (Office for Standards in Education) (2014c) *Inspecting Safeguarding in Maintained Schools and Academies*, Manchester: Crown.

Oppenheim, A. (1992) *Questionnaire Design, Interviews and Attitude Measurement*, London: Cassell.

O'Sullivan, M. and MacPhail, A. (eds) (2010) *Young People's Voices in Physical Education and Youth Sport*, Abingdon, Oxon: Routledge.

Oxford English Dictionary on-line version http://www.oxforddictionaries.com/definition/english/ (accessed 13 September 2014).

Pajares, M.F. (1992) 'Teachers' beliefs and educational research: cleaning up a messy construct', *Review of Educational Research*, 62: 307-332.

Pask, G. (1976) 'Styles and strategies of learning', *British Journal of Educational Psychology*, 46: 4-11.

Penney, D. and Evans, J. (1994) 'It's just not (and not just) cricket', *British Journal of Physical Education*, 25, 3: 9-12.

Perrott, E. (1982) *Effective Teaching: A Practical Guide to Improving Your Teaching*, London: Longman.

Piaget, J. (1960) *The Psychology of Intelligence*, Totowa, NJ: Littlefield Adams.

Piaget, J. (1972) *Psychology and Epistemology*, Harmondsworth: Penguin Books.

Pilitis, G. and Duncan, R. (2012) 'Changes in belief orientations of preservice teachers and their relation to inquiry activities', *Journal of Science Teacher Education*, 23, 8: 909-936.

Placek, J. (1983) Conceptions of success in teaching: busy, happy and good? in T. Templin and J. Olsen (eds) *Teaching Physical Education*, Champaign IL: Human Kinetics, pp. 45-56.

Posner, G., Strike, K., Hewson, P. and Gertzog, W. (1982) 'Accommodation of a scientific conception: toward a theory of conceptual change', *Scientific Education*, 66: 211-227.

Prusak, K.A., Treasure, D.C., Darst, P.W. and Pangrazi, R.P. (2004) 'The effects of choice on the motivation of adolescent girls in physical education', *Journal of Teaching in Physical Education*, 23: 19-29.

QAA (Quality Assurance Agency for Higher Education) (2008) *Framework for Higher Education Qualifications*, Mansfield: QAA.

Raymond, C. (ed.) (1999) *Safety Across the Curriculum*, London: RoutledgeFalmer.

Reeve, J. (2009) 'Why teachers adopt a controlling motivating style toward students and how they can become more autonomy supportive', *Educational Psychologist*, 44: 159-175.

Richards, K. and Templin, T. (2012) 'Toward a multidimensional perspective on teacher-coach role conflict', *Quest*, 64, 3: 164-176.

Richardson, V. and Fallona, C. (2001) 'Classroom management as method and manner', *Journal of Curriculum Studies*, 33, 6: 705-728.

Rink, J. (2013) *Teaching Physical Education for Learning*, 7th edn, New York: McGraw Hill Education.

Rink, J. and Hall, T. (2008) 'Research on effective teaching in elementary school physical education', *Elementary School Journal*, 108, 3: 207-218.

Robertson, J. (1996) *Effective Classroom Control: Understanding Teacher-Student Relationships*, 3rd edn, London: Hodder and Stoughton.

Roffey, S. (2011) *Changing Behaviour in Schools: Promoting Positive Relationships and Well Being*, London: Sage Publications.

Rogers, B. (2000) *Behaviour Management - A Whole School Approach*, London: Sage Publications.

Rogers, B. (2011) *Classroom Behaviour: A Practical Guide to Effective Teaching, Behaviour Management and Colleague Support*, 3rd edn, London: Sage.

Rogers, C. (1975) Freedom to learn, in N. Entwistle and D. Hounsell (eds) *How Students Learn*, Lancaster: University of Lancaster.

Rogers, C. (2007) 'Experiencing an inclusive education: parents and their children with special educational needs', *British Journal of Sociology of Education*, 28, 1: 55–68.

Runswick-Cole, K. (2011) 'Time to end the bias towards inclusive education?' *British Journal of Special Education*, 38, 3: 112–120.

Sallis, J.F., Prochaska, J.J. and Taylor, W.C. (2000) 'A review of correlates of physical activity of children and adolescents', *Medicine and Science in Sports and Exercise*, 3: 963–975.

Sanders, L. (ed.) (2012) *Dance Teaching and Learning: Shaping Practice Youth Dance*, London: Youth Dance England.

Sandford, R., Armour, K. and Duncombe, R. (2010) Finding their voice: disaffected youth insights on sport/ physical activity interventions, in M. O'Sullivan and A. MacPhail (eds) *Young People's Voices in Physical Education and Youth Sport*, Abingdon, Oxon: Routledge, pp. 65–87.

Sawyer, K.R. (2006) Analysing collaborative discourse, in K. Sawyer (ed.) *The Cambridge Handbook of Learning Sciences*, Cambridge: Cambridge University Press.

Schempp, P. (1989) Apprenticeship of observation and the development of physical education teachers, in T. Templin and P. Schempp (eds) *Socialization into Physical Education: Learning to Teach*, Indianapolis: Benchmark Press, pp. 13–38.

Schempp, P. (2003) *Teaching Sport and Physical Activity: Insights on the Road to Excellence*, Champaign, IL: Human Kinetics.

Schmidt, R.A. and Wrisberg, C.A. (2008) *Motor Learning and Performance: A Situation-Based Learning Approach*, 4th edn, Leeds: Human Kinetics.

Schön, D.A. (1983) *The Reflective Practitioner: How Professionals Think in Action*, London: Temple.

Schön, D.A. (1987) *Educating the Reflective Practitioner*, San Francisco, CA: Jossey Bass.

Schunk, D. (2000) *Learning Theories*, 3rd edn, Upper Saddle River, NJ: Merrill/Prentice Hall.

Schwab, J.J. (1964) The structure of the disciplines: meanings and significance, in G. Ford and L. Purgo (eds) *The Structure of Knowledge and the Curriculum*, Chicago: Rand McNally.

Severs, J. (2003) *Safety and Risk in Primary School Physical Education*, London: Routledge.

Shulman, L.S. (1987) 'Knowledge and teaching: foundations of the new reform', *Harvard Educational Review*, 57: 1–22.

Shulman, L.S. (1999) Knowledge and teaching: foundation of the new reform, in J. Leach and B. Moon (eds) *Learners and Pedagogy*, London: Paul Chapman, pp. 61–77.

Siedentop, D. (1991) *Developing Teaching Skills in Physical Education*, 3rd edn, Mountain View, CA: Mayfield.

Siedentop, D. (1994) *Sport Education*, Champaign, IL: Human Kinetics.

Siedentop, D. and Tannehill, D. (2000) *Developing Teaching Skills in Physical Education*, 4th edn, New York: McGraw Hill Higher Education.

Siedentop, D., Tousigant, M. and Parker, M. (1982) *Academic Learning Time – Physical Education Coaching Manual*, Columbus, OH: The Ohio State University, School of Health, Physical Education and Recreation.

Slavin, R. (2003) *Educational Psychology: Theory and Practice*, 7th edn, Boston: Allyn and Bacon.

Smith, A. and Thomas, N. (2006) 'Including pupils with special educational needs and disabilities in National Curriculum Physical Education: a brief review', *European Journal of Special Needs Education*, 21, 1: 69–83.

Spackman, L. (2002) 'Assessment for learning: the lessons for physical education', *The Bulletin of Physical Education*, 38, 3: 179–195.

Spendlove, D. (2009) *Putting Assessment for Learning into Practice*, London: Continuum.

Stenhouse, L. (1975) *An Introduction to Curriculum Research and Development*, London: Heinemann Educational.

Stran, M. and Curtner-Smith, M. (2009) 'Influence of occupational socialization on two preservice teachers' interpretation and delivery of the sport education model', *Journal of Teaching in Physical Education*, 28, 1: 38–53.

Stroot, S. and Williamson, K. (1993) 'Issues and themes of socialization into physical education', *Journal of Teaching in Physical Education*, 12: 337–343.

Stylianou, M., Hodges Kulinna, P., Cothran, D. and Kwon, J.Y. (2013) 'Physical education teachers' metaphors of teaching and learning', *Journal of Teaching in Physical Education*, 32: 22–45.

Swansea Civil Justice Centre (2002) *Rhian Elizabeth Ashton (Claimant) and Neath Port Talbot County Borough Council (Defendant) Approved Judgment*, Swansea: Swansea Civil Justice Centre.

Taylor, I., Ntoumanis, N. and Smith, B. (2009) 'The social context as a determinant of teacher motivational strategies in physical education', *Psychology of Sport and Exercise*, 10, 2: 235–243.

TDA (Training and Development Agency for Schools) (2007) *Professional Standards for Teachers*, London: TDA.

Teixeira, P., Carraca, E., Markland, D., Silva, N. and Ryan R. (2012) 'Exercise, physical activity and self-determination theory: a systematic review', *International Journal of Behavioral Nutrition and Physical Activity*, 9: 78–84.

The Education Endowment Foundation (2014) *Sutton Trust – EEF Teaching and Learning Toolkit*. Online, available at: http://educationendowmentfoundation.org.uk/toolkit/.

The Free Dictionary (2014) on-line version http://www.thefreedictionary.com/safe (accessed 8 December 2014).

Thomas, S.M. (1994) 'Adventure education: risk and safety at school', *Perspectives 50*, Exeter: University of Exeter Press.

Timken, G. and McNamee, J. (2012) 'New perspectives for teaching physical education: preservice teachers' reflections on outdoor and adventure education', *Journal of Teaching in Physical Education*, 31: 21–38.

Tinning, R.I. (1988) 'Student teaching and the pedagogy of necessity', *Journal of Teaching in Physical Education*, 7: 82–89.

Tod, D. (2014) *Sport Psychology: The Basics*, Abingdon, Oxon: Routledge.

Treasure, D. (2001) Enhancing young people's motivation in youth sport: an achievement goal approach, in G.C. Roberts (ed.) *Advances in Motivation in Sport and Exercise*, Champaign, IL: Human Kinetics, pp. 79–100.

UK Legislation (2010) *The Equality Act*, London: HMSO.

UK Legislation (2014) *The Children and Families Act*, London: HMSO.

UK Legislation (Health and Safety)/UK Parliament Statutes/Health and Safety at Work etc Act 1974 (1974 c 37). Online, available at: http://www.legislation.gov.uk/ukpga/1974/37 (accessed 3 October 2014).

Vallerand, R.J. and Losier, G.F. (1999) 'An integrative analysis of intrinsic and extrinsic motivation in sport', *Journal of Applied Sport Psychology*, 11: 142–169.

Van Den Berghe, L., Vansteenkiste, M., Cardon, G., Kirk, D. and Haerens, L. (2012) 'Research on self-determination in physical education: key findings and proposals for future research', *Physical Education and Sport Pedagogy*, 19: 97–121.

Varley, L. and Green, A. (2011) Academic writing at M level, in A. Green (ed.) *Becoming a Reflective English Teacher*, Maidenhead, Berks: Open University Press.

Vermette, P.J., Jones, K.A., Jones, J. L., Werner, T., Kline, C. and D'Angelo, J. (2010) 'A model for planning learning experiences to promote achievement in diverse secondary classrooms', *SRATE Journal* (the Journal of the Southeastern Regional Association of Teacher Educators), 19, 2: 70–83.

Vickerman, P. (2007) *Teaching Physical Education to Children with Special Educational Needs*, Abingdon, Oxon: Routledge.

Vickerman, P. and Blundell, M. (2012) 'English learning support assistants experiences of including children with special educational needs in physical education', *European Journal of Special Needs Education*, 27, 2: 143–156.

Vickerman, P. and Coates, J. (2009) 'Trainee and recently qualified physical education teachers' perspectives on including children with special educational needs', *Physical Education and Sport Pedagogy*, 14, 2: 137–153.

Vygotsky, L.S. (1962) *Thought and Language*, Cambridge, MA: MIT Press.

Watermeyer, B. (2012) *Towards a Contextual Psychology of Disablism (Routledge Advances in Disability Studies)*, Abingdon, Oxon: Routledge.

Watkins, J. (2014) *Fundamental Biomechanics of Sport and Exercise*, Abingdon, Oxon: Routledge.

Webster, C., Connolly, G. and Schempp, P. (2009) 'The finishing touch: anatomy of expert lesson closures', *Physical Education and Sport Pedagogy*, 14, 1: 73–87.

Welsh Government (date unknown) Information on induction and early professional development for teachers. Online, available at: http://wales.gov.uk/topics/educationandskills/schoolshome/schoolfundingandplanning/trainingdevelopment/iepd/?lang=en (accessed 7 October 2014).

Wenger, E (1998) *Communities of Practice: Learning, Meaning and Identity*, Cambridge: Cambridge University Press.

Wenger-Trayner, E. (date unknown) *Communities of Practice: A Brief Introduction*. Online, available at: http://wenger-trayner.com/theory/ (accessed 2 April 2014).

Whitehead, M. (2000) Aims as an issue in physical education, in S. Capel and S. Piotrowski (eds) *Issues in Physical Education*, London: RoutledgeFalmer, pp. 7–21.

Whitehead, M.E. (ed.) (2010) *Physical Literacy Throughout the Lifecourse*, Abingdon, Oxon: Routledge.

Whitehead, M.E. (2013a) 'The history and development of physical literacy', *ICSSPE Bulletin – Journal of Sport Science and Physical Education*, 65. Online, available at: https://www.icsspe.org/content/no-65-cd-rom (accessed 1 September 2014).

Whitehead, M.E. (2013b) 'Definition of physical literacy and clarification of related issues', *ICSSPE Bulletin – Journal of Sport Science and Physical Education*, 65. Online, available at: https://www.icsspe.org/content/no-65-cd-rom (accessed 1 September 2014).

Whitehead, M.E. (2013c) 'The value of physical literacy', *ICSSPE Bulletin – Journal of Sport Science and Physical Education*, 65. Online, available at: https://www.icsspe.org/content/no-65-cd-rom (accessed 1 September 2014).

Whitehead, M.E. (2013d) 'Stages in a physical literacy journey', *ICSSPE Bulletin – Journal of Sport Science and Physical Education*, 65. Online, available at: https://www.icsspe.org/content/no-65-cd-rom (accessed 1 September 2014).

Whitehead, M.E. (2013e) 'Creating learning experiences to foster physical literacy', *ICSSPE Bulletin – Journal of Sport Science and Physical Education*, 65. Online, available at: https://www.icsspe.org/content/no-65-cd-rom (accessed 1 September 2014).

Whitehead, M.E. (2013f) 'Content implications of working to promote physical literacy', *ICSSPE Bulletin – Journal of Sport Science and Physical Education*, 65. Online, available at: https://www.icsspe.org/content/no-65-cd-rom (accessed 1 September 2014).

Whitehead, M.E. (2013g) What is the education in physical education? in S. Capel and M. Whitehead (eds) *Debates in Physical Education*, Abingdon, Oxon: Routledge, pp. 22–36.

Whitehead, M.E. (2013h) What is physical literacy and how does it impact on physical education? in S. Capel and M. Whitehead (eds) *Debates in Physical Education*, Abingdon, Oxon: Routledge, pp. 37–52.

Whitehead, M.E. (2014a) Definition on the International Physical Literacy Association website: www.physical-literacy.org.uk (accessed 4 October 2014).

Whitehead, M.E. (2014b) How aims and objectives influence teaching, in S. Capel and P. Breckon (eds) *A Practical Guide to Teaching Physical Education in the Secondary School*, 2nd edn, Abingdon, Oxon: Routledge, pp. 15–19.

Whitehouse, K. (2014) Teaching to promote positive behaviour, in S. Capel and P. Breckon (eds) *A Practical Guide to Teaching Physical Education in the Secondary School*, 2nd edn, Abingdon, Oxon: Routledge, pp. 166–179.

Whitlam, P. (2003) Risk management principles, in J. Severs (2003) *Safety and Risk in Primary School Physical Education*, London: Routledge.

Whitlam, P. (2005) *Case Law in Physical Education and School Sport: A Guide to Good Practice*, Leeds: Coachwise/BAALPE.

Williams, G., Pinder, S., Thomson, A. and Williams, D. (2010) *Dictionary of Physical Education and School Sport*, London: A&C Black.

Wilson, E. (ed.) (2013) *School-based Research: A Guide for Education Students*, 2nd edn, London: Sage.

Winnick, J. (2011) *Adapted Physical Education and Sport*, 5th edn, Champaign, IL: Human Kinetics.

Woods, A. and Roades, J. (2010) 'National Board Certified physical educators: background characteristics, subjective warrants and motivations', *Journal of Teaching in Physical Education*, 29, 3: 312–331.

Wragg, E.C. (2001) *Assessment and Learning in the Secondary School*, London: RoutledgeFlamer.

Wragg, E.C. and Brown, G. (2001) *Questioning in the Secondary School*, London: RoutledgeFalmer.

Xiang, P., McBride, R., Guan, J. and Solmon, M. (2003) 'Children's motivation in elementary physical education: a longitudinal study', *Research Quarterly for Exercise and Sport*, 75: 71–80.

Youens, B. (2013) External assessment and examinations, in S. Capel, M. Leask and T. Turner (eds) *Learning to Teach in the Secondary School: A Companion to School Experience*, 6th edn, Abingdon, Oxon: Routledge, pp. 439–453.

YST (Youth Sport Trust) (2008) *High Quality Physical Education for Pupils with Autism*, Loughborough: Youth Sport Trust.

Zeichner, K.M. and Tabacknick, B.R. (1981) 'Are the effects of university teacher education "washed out" by school experience?' *Journal of Teacher Education*, XXXII, 3: 7–11.

Zounhia, K., Chatoupis, C., Amoutzas, K. and Hatziharistos, D. (2006) Greek physical education student teachers' reasons for choosing teaching as a career, *Studies in Physical Culture and Tourism*, 13, 2: 99–108.

Zwozdiak-Myers, P. (2012) *The Teacher's Reflective Practice Handbook: Becoming an Extended Professional through Capturing Evidence-informed Practice*, Abingdon, Oxon: Routledge.

Zwozdiak-Myers, P. (2014) Action research, in S. Capel and P. Breckon (eds) *A Practical Guide to Teaching Physical Education in the Secondary School*, 2nd edn, Abingdon, Oxon: Routledge, pp. 253–266.

Zwozdiak-Myers, P. and Capel, S. (2013) Communicating with pupils, in S. Capel, M. Leask and T. Turner (eds) *Learning to Teach in the Secondary School: A Companion to School Experience*, 6th edn, Abingdon, Oxon: Routledge, pp. 129–146.

Author index

Subject index

Learning to Teach Physical Education in the Secondary School Companion Texts

A Practical Guide to Teaching Physical Education in the Secondary School, Second Edition
Edited by Susan Capel and Peter Breckon
ISBN: 978-0-415-81482-9

A Practical Guide to Teaching Physical Education in the Secondary School is written for all student teachers on university and school-based initial teacher education courses. It offers a wealth of tried and tested strategies together with practical activities and materials to support both your teaching and your pupils' learning. It is designed for you to dip in and out of, to enable you to focus on specific areas of teaching or foci on your course.

This second edition is fully updated with the most recent research and developments in the field and includes brand new chapters.

Debates in Physical Education
Edited by Susan Capel and Margaret Whitehead
ISBN: 978-0-415-67625-0

Debates in Physical Education explores major issues all PE teachers encounter in their daily professional lives. It engages with established and contemporary debates, promotes and supports critical reflection and aims to stimulate both novice and experienced teachers to reach informed judgements and argue their point of view with deeper theoretical knowledge and understanding.